AND YOU ARE...? AND YOU ARE...?
AND YOU'RE WHO, AGAIN?!
CUT IT OUT, YOU GUYS
IT'S ME! WATSUKI! REALLY...

和月伸宏

NOBUHIRO WATSUKI

PACKING IT ON.

HAVING HAD NO TIME FOR EXERCISE, IT'S TO BE EXPECTED ...REALLY, CAN'T BE HELPED, BUT.... WHAT'S WORSE IS, BECAUSE I'VE BEEN SO BUSY THERE'S BEEN NO TIME EVEN TO SHAVE, EVERYONE I KNOW IS TREATING ME LIKE YOU SEE ABOVE.

THE GOAL FOR THIS YEAR, THEN, IS TO DIET, AND TO REMEMBER TO SHAVE. THAT, AND GIVING *RUROUNI KENSHIN* MY ALL, OF COURSE! I SO-O-O WANNA PLAY *SHIN (NEW) SAMURAI SPIRITS*, BUT... (SHAPE-UP! PUNISHMENT!! *KRACK!!*)

Rurouni Kenshin, which has found fans not only in Japan but around the world, first made its appearance in 1992, as an original short story in Japan's **Weekly Shonen Jump Special**. Later rewritten and published as a regular, continuing **Jump** series in 1994, **Rurouni Kenshin** ended serialization in 1999 but continued in popularity, as evidenced by the 2000 publication of **Yahiko no Sakabatô** ("Yahiko's Reversed-Edge Sword") in Japan's **Weekly Shonen Jump**. His most current work, **Busô Renkin** ("Armored Alchemist"), began publication this June, also in Japan's **Jump**.

RUROUNI KENSHIN VOL. 3
The SHONEN JUMP Graphic Novel Edition

STORY AND ART BY
NOBUHIRO WATSUKI

English Adaptation/Gerard Jones
Translation/Kenichiro Yagi
Touch-Up Art & Lettering/Steve Dutro
Cover, Graphics & Layout Design/Sean Lee
Editor/Avery Gotoh

Managing Editor/Frances E. Wall
Editorial Director/Elizabeth Kawasaki
VP & Editor in Chief/Yumi Hoashi
Sr. Director of Acquisitions/Rika Inouye
Sr. VP of Marketing/Liza Coppola
Exec. VP of Sales & Marketing/John Easum
Publisher/Hyoe Narita

Printed in the U.S.A.

Published by VIZ Media, LLC
P.O. Box 77010 • San Francisco, CA 94107

SHONEN JUMP Graphic Novel Edition
10 9 8 7 6 5
First printing, January 2004
Fifth printing, September 2006

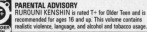

www.viz.com

PARENTAL ADVISORY
RUROUNI KENSHIN is rated T+ for Older Teen and is recommended for ages 16 and up. This volume contains realistic violence, language, and alcohol and tobacco usage.

SHONEN JUMP GRAPHIC NOVEL

Rurouni Kenshin™

MEIJI SWORDSMAN ROMANTIC STORY

Vol. 3: A REASON TO ACT

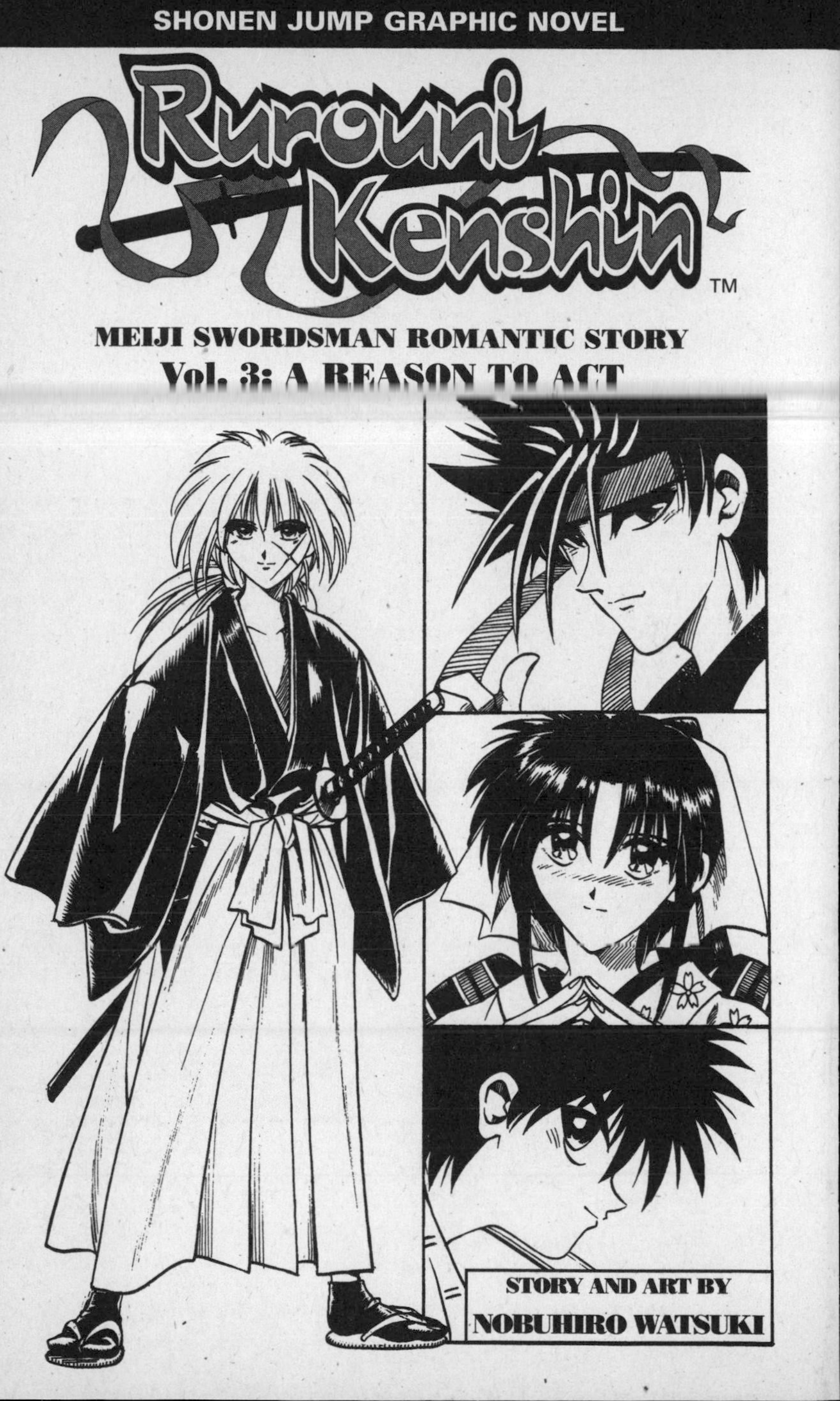

STORY AND ART BY

NOBUHIRO WATSUKI

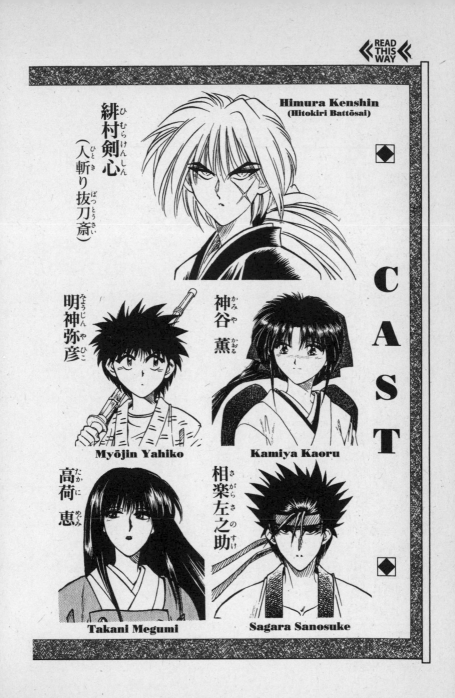

READ THIS WAY

CAST

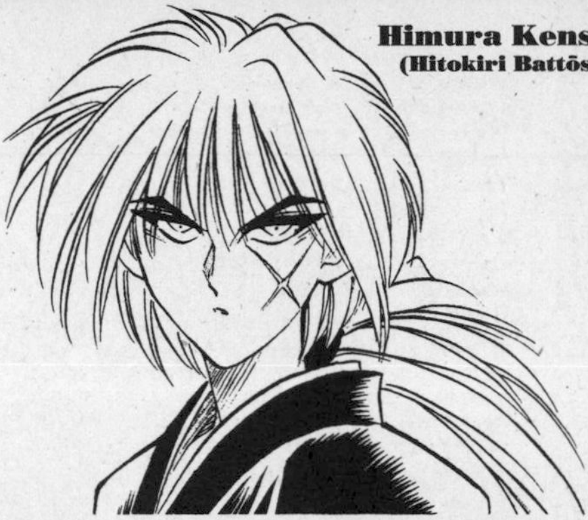

緋村剣心（人斬り抜刀斎）

Himura Kenshin (Hitokiri Battōsai)

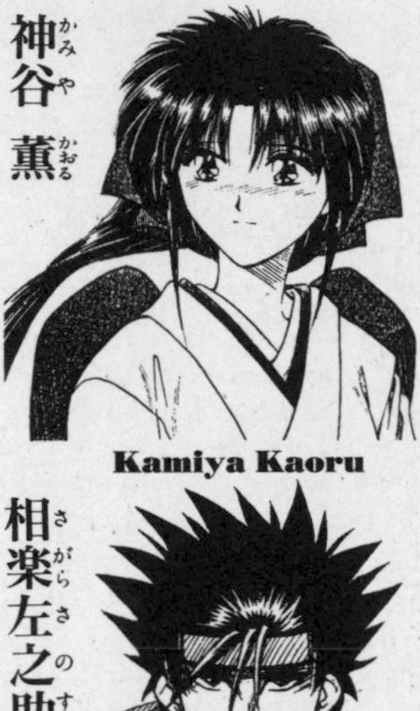

神谷薫

Kamiya Kaoru

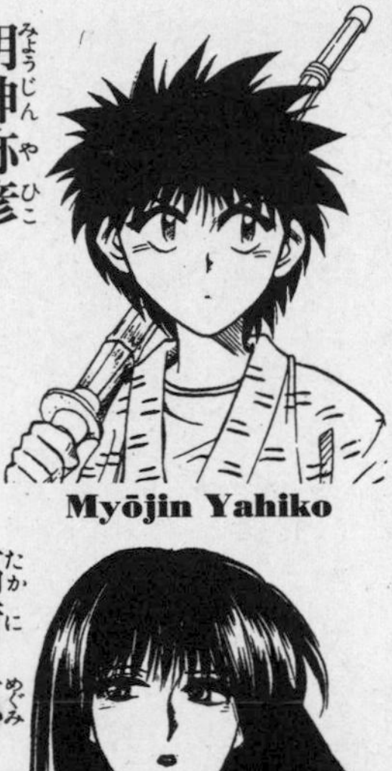

明神弥彦

Myōjin Yahiko

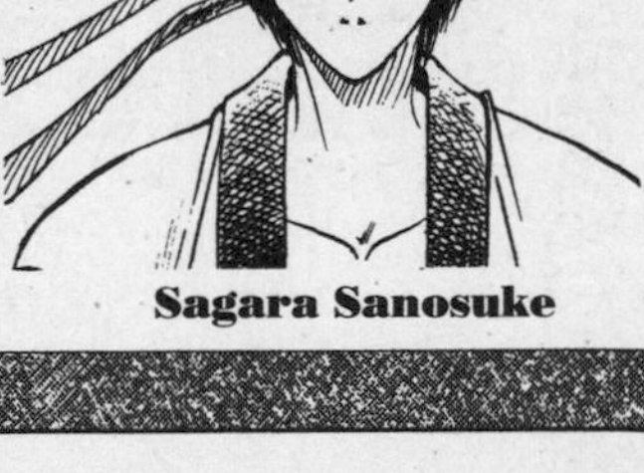

相楽左之助

Sagara Sanosuke

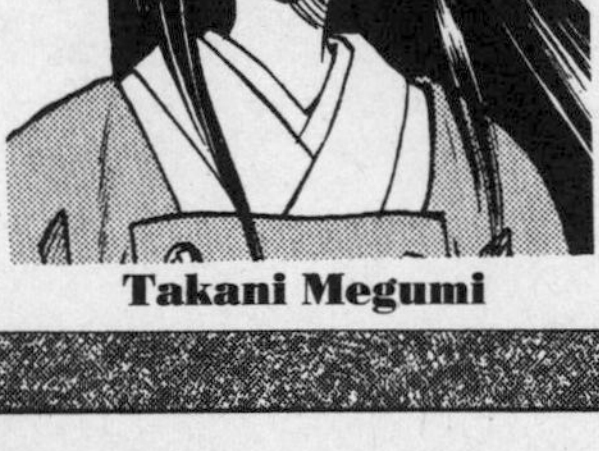

高荷恵

Takani Megumi

るろうに剣心

和月伸宏

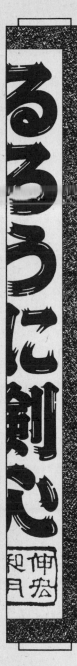

Takeda Kanryū

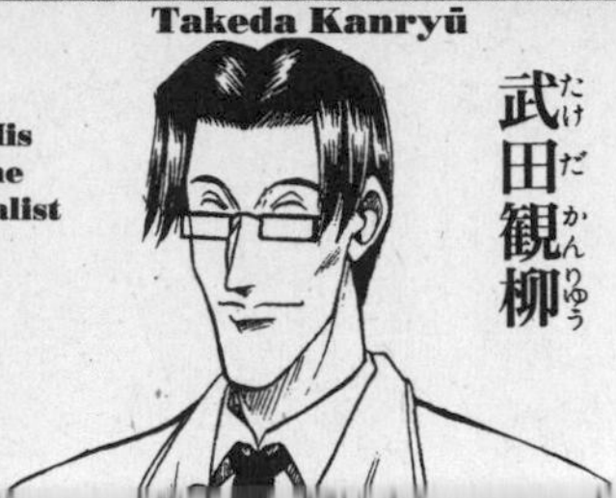

武田観柳（たけだかんりゅう）

四乃森蒼紫（しのもりあおし）

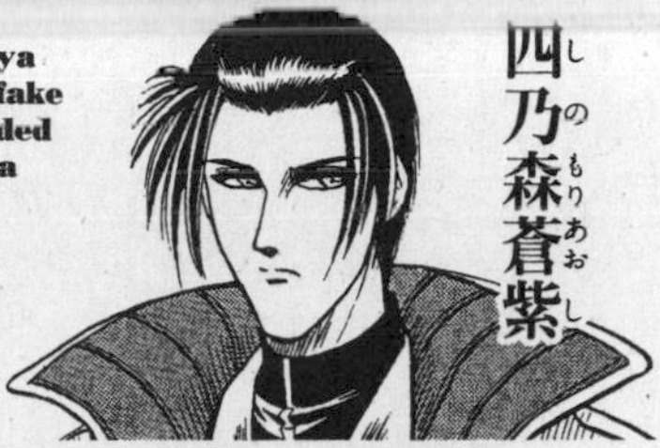

Shinomori Aoshi

Once he was a *hitokiri*, an assassin, called *Battōsai*. His name was legend among the *Ishin Shishi* or pro-imperialist "patriot" warriors who launched the Meiji era.

Now Himura Kenshin is a *rurouni*, a wanderer, who carries a reversed-edge *sakabatō* blade to prohibit himself from killing.

Having rescued the Kamiya dojo from the hoax of a "fake Battōsai," Kenshin's decided to stay on at the dojo for a while.

THUS FAR

After losing all its students, the Kamiya dojo and its *"Kasshin-ryū"* sword style is taking its first steps toward revival. Kenshin brings in Myōjin Yahiko, son of an ex-samurai rescued from the yakuza, and also Sagara Sanosuke, who gave up a life as a fighter-for-hire due to Kenshin's example.

Earlier tonight, Kenshin is dragged to a gambling den by Sanosuke. There they learn that one of Sanosuke's gambling buddies is dead because of opium use. Suddenly, Takani Megumi bursts in, asking for Kenshin's protection from the private army of Takeda Kanryū...for reasons apparently having something to do with the drug....

CONTENTS

Rurouni Kenshin

Meiji Swordsman Romantic Story

BOOK THREE: A REASON TO ACT

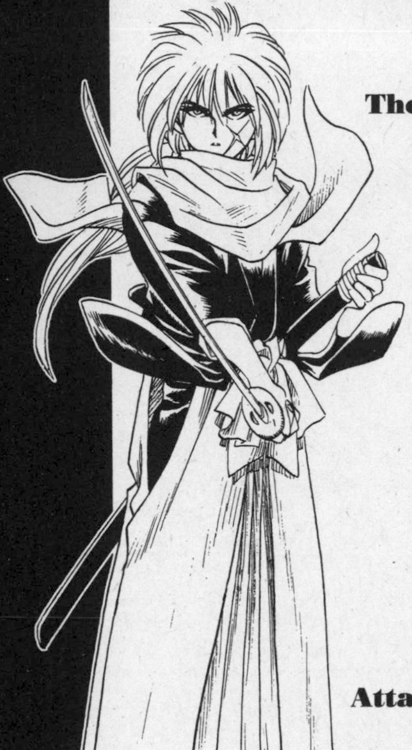

READ THIS WAY

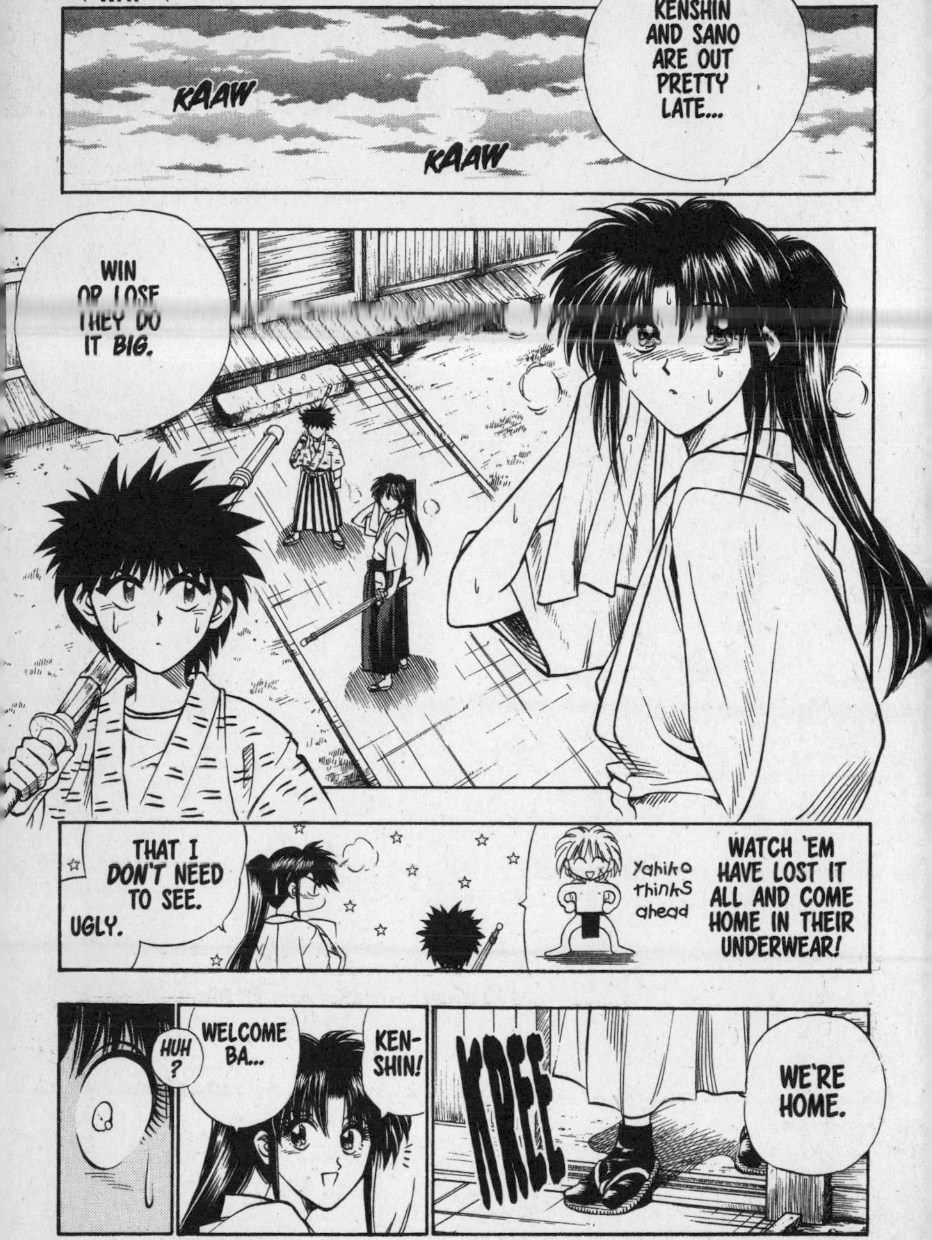
KENSHIN AND SANO ARE OUT PRETTY LATE...
KAAW
KAAW
WIN OR LOSE THEY DO IT BIG.
WATCH 'EM HAVE LOST IT ALL AND COME HOME IN THEIR UNDERWEAR!
Yahiko thinks ahead
THAT I DON'T NEED TO SEE.
UGLY.
WE'RE HOME.
KREE
KEN-SHIN!
WELCOME BA...
HUH ?

Act 16 - Megumi, Kanryū, and...

Act 16
Megumi, Kanryū, and...

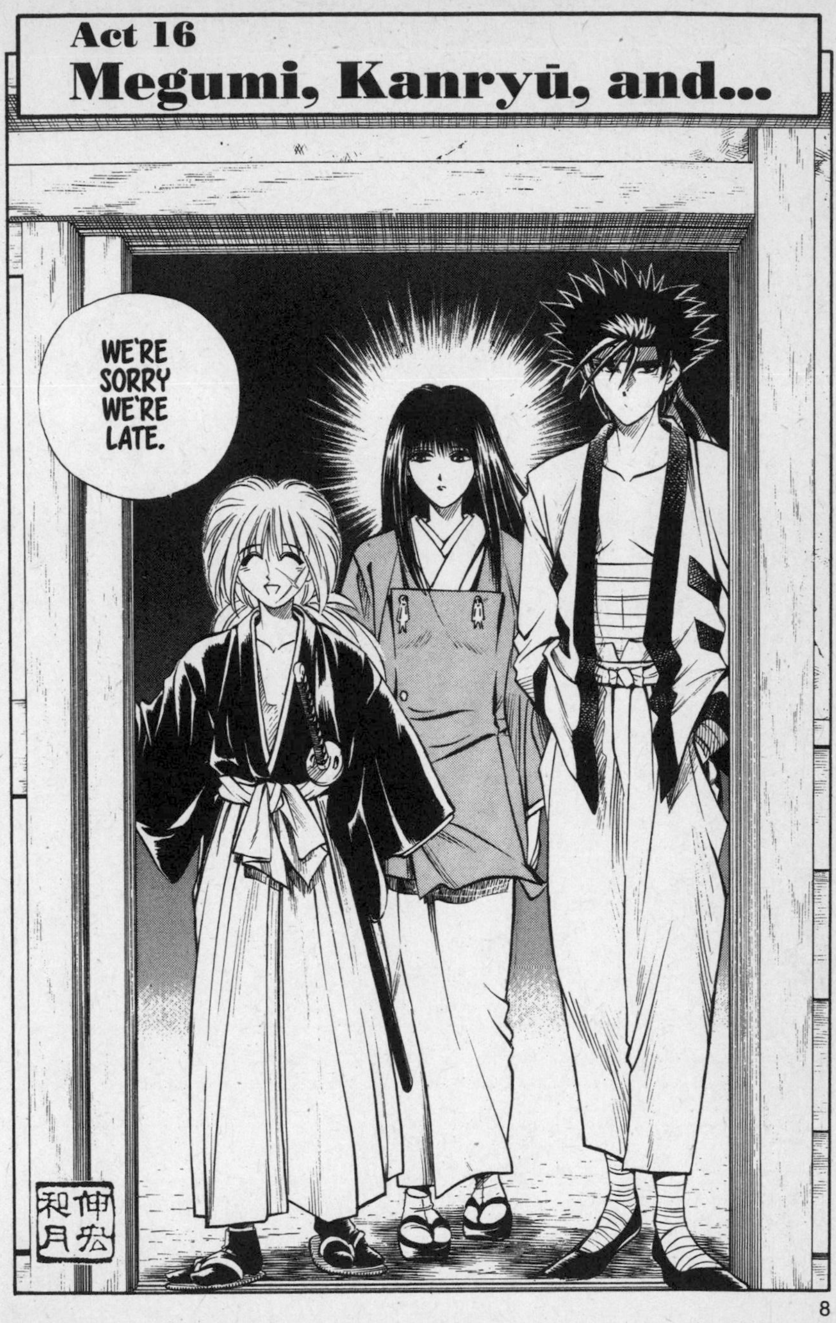
WE'RE SORRY WE'RE LATE.

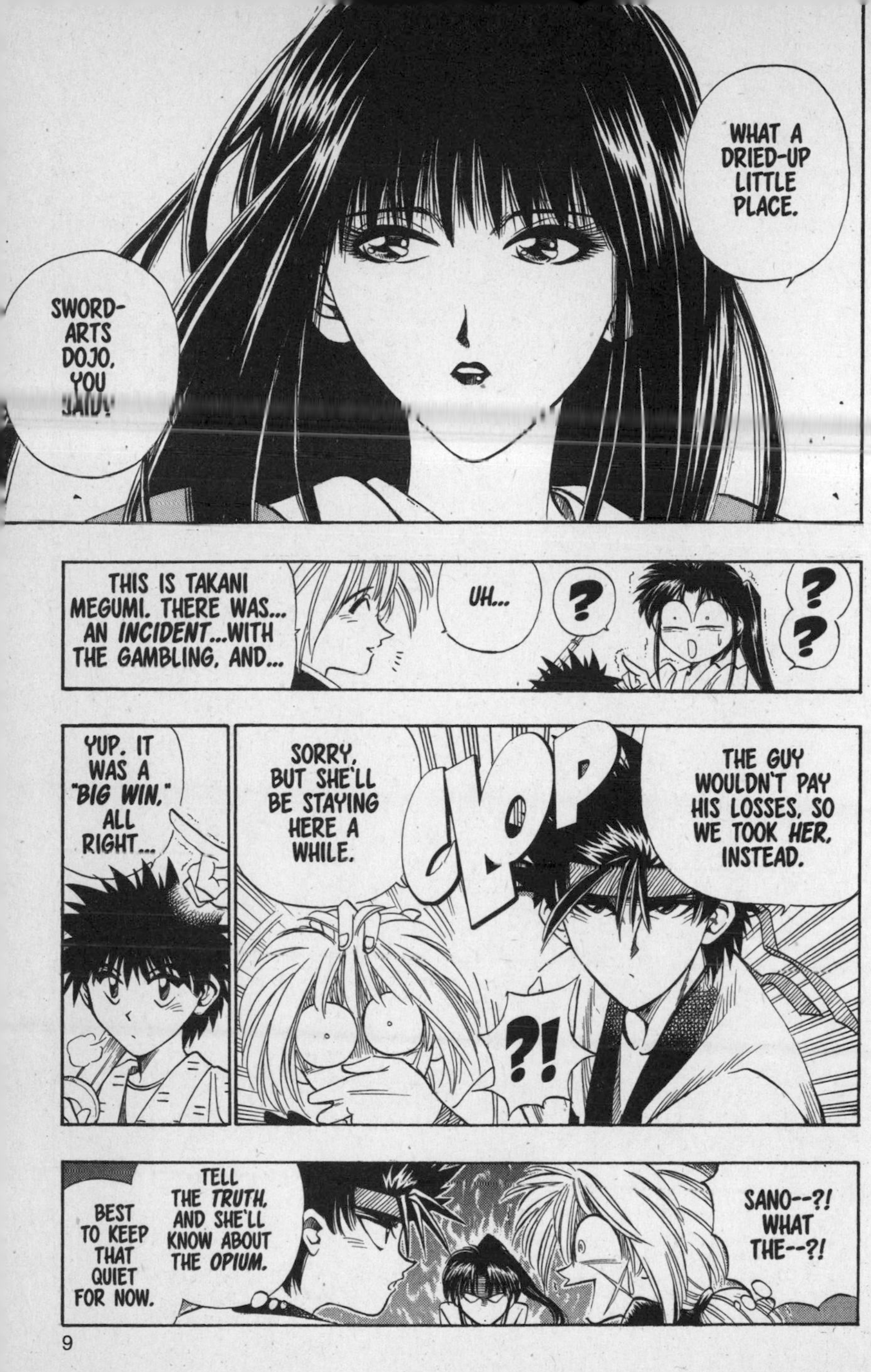
WHAT A DRIED-UP LITTLE PLACE.
SWORD-ARTS DOJO, YOU SAID!
? ?
?
UH...
THIS IS TAKANI MEGUMI. THERE WAS... AN *INCIDENT*...WITH THE GAMBLING, AND...
THE GUY WOULDN'T PAY HIS LOSSES, SO WE TOOK *HER*, INSTEAD.
CHOP
?!
SORRY, BUT SHE'LL BE STAYING HERE A WHILE.
YUP. IT WAS A "*BIG WIN*," ALL RIGHT...
SANO--?! WHAT THE--?!
TELL THE *TRUTH*, AND SHE'LL KNOW ABOUT THE *OPIUM*.
BEST TO KEEP THAT QUIET FOR NOW.

READ THIS WAY

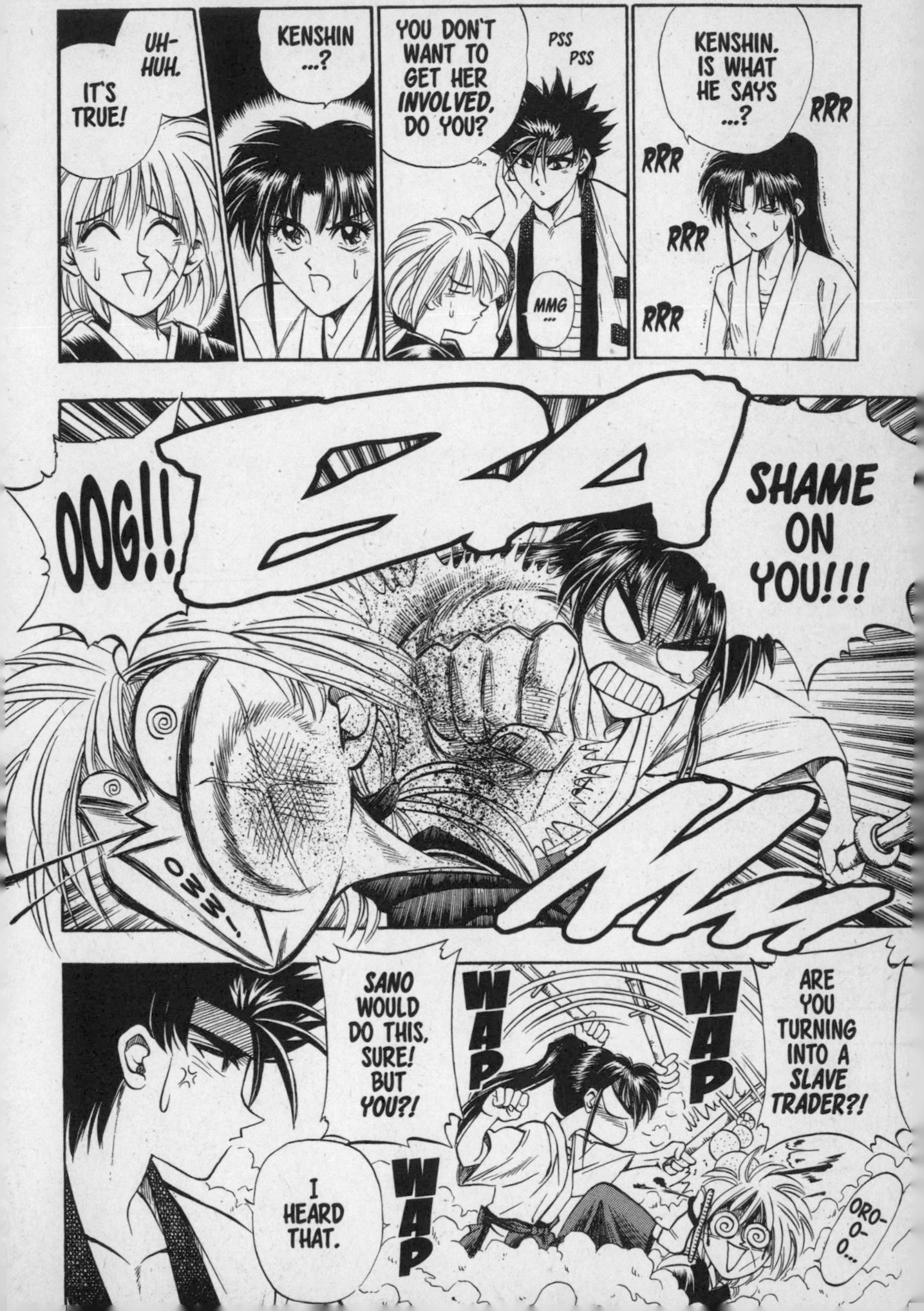
KENSHIN. IS WHAT HE SAYS ...?
RRR
RRR
RRR
RRR
PSS PSS
YOU DON'T WANT TO GET HER INVOLVED, DO YOU?
MMG ...
KENSHIN ...?
UH-HUH.
IT'S TRUE!
SHAME ON YOU!!!
OOG!!
OWW!
ARE YOU TURNING INTO A SLAVE TRADER?!
WAP
WAP
WAP
WAP
ORO-O-O...
SANO WOULD DO THIS, SURE! BUT YOU?!
I HEARD THAT.

READ THIS WAY

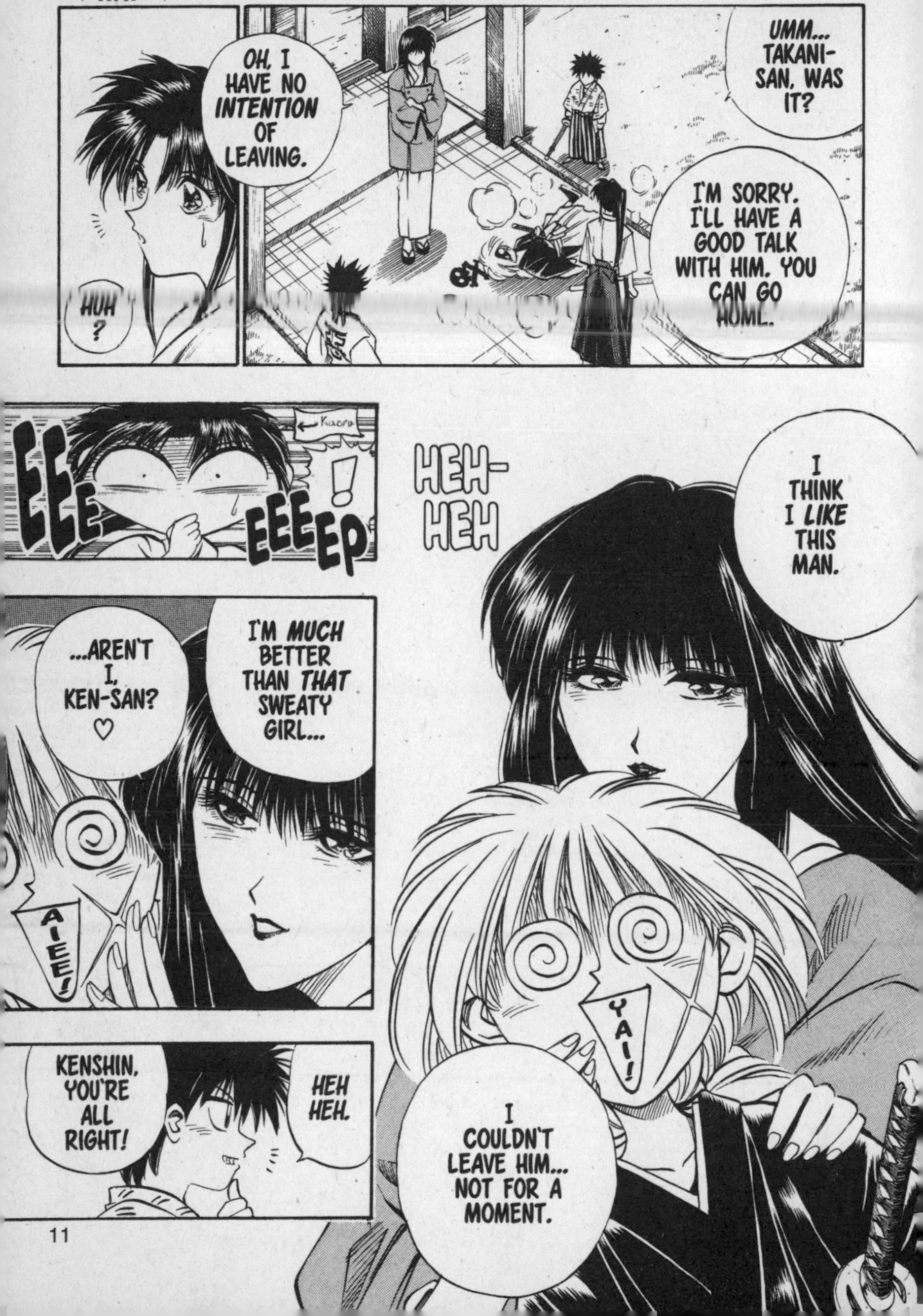
UMM... TAKANI-SAN, WAS IT?
I'M SORRY. I'LL HAVE A GOOD TALK WITH HIM. YOU CAN GO HOME.
OH, I HAVE NO INTENTION OF LEAVING.
HUH?
HEH-HEH
I THINK I LIKE THIS MAN.
YAI!
I COULDN'T LEAVE HIM... NOT FOR A MOMENT.
← Kaoru
EEEEEEEP
!
I'M MUCH BETTER THAN THAT SWEATY GIRL...
...AREN'T I, KEN-SAN? ♡
AIEE!
HEH HEH.
KENSHIN, YOU'RE ALL RIGHT!

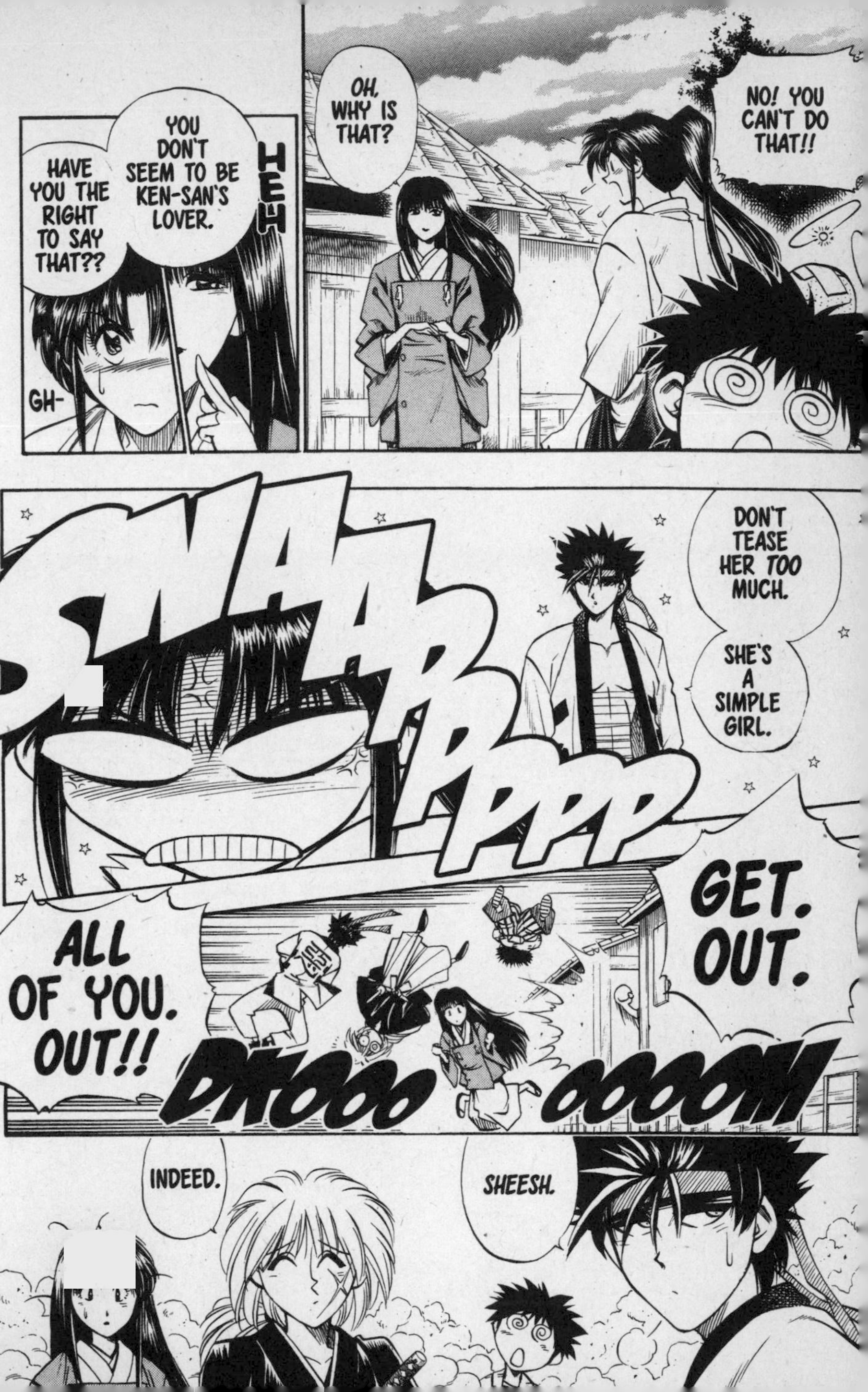
NO! YOU CAN'T DO THAT!!
OH, WHY IS THAT?
YOU DON'T SEEM TO BE KEN-SAN'S LOVER.
HEH
HAVE YOU THE RIGHT TO SAY THAT??
GH-
DON'T TEASE HER TOO MUCH.
SHE'S A SIMPLE GIRL.
SMAPPPP
GET. OUT.
ALL OF YOU. OUT!!
DHOOOOOOOOM
SHEESH.
INDEED.

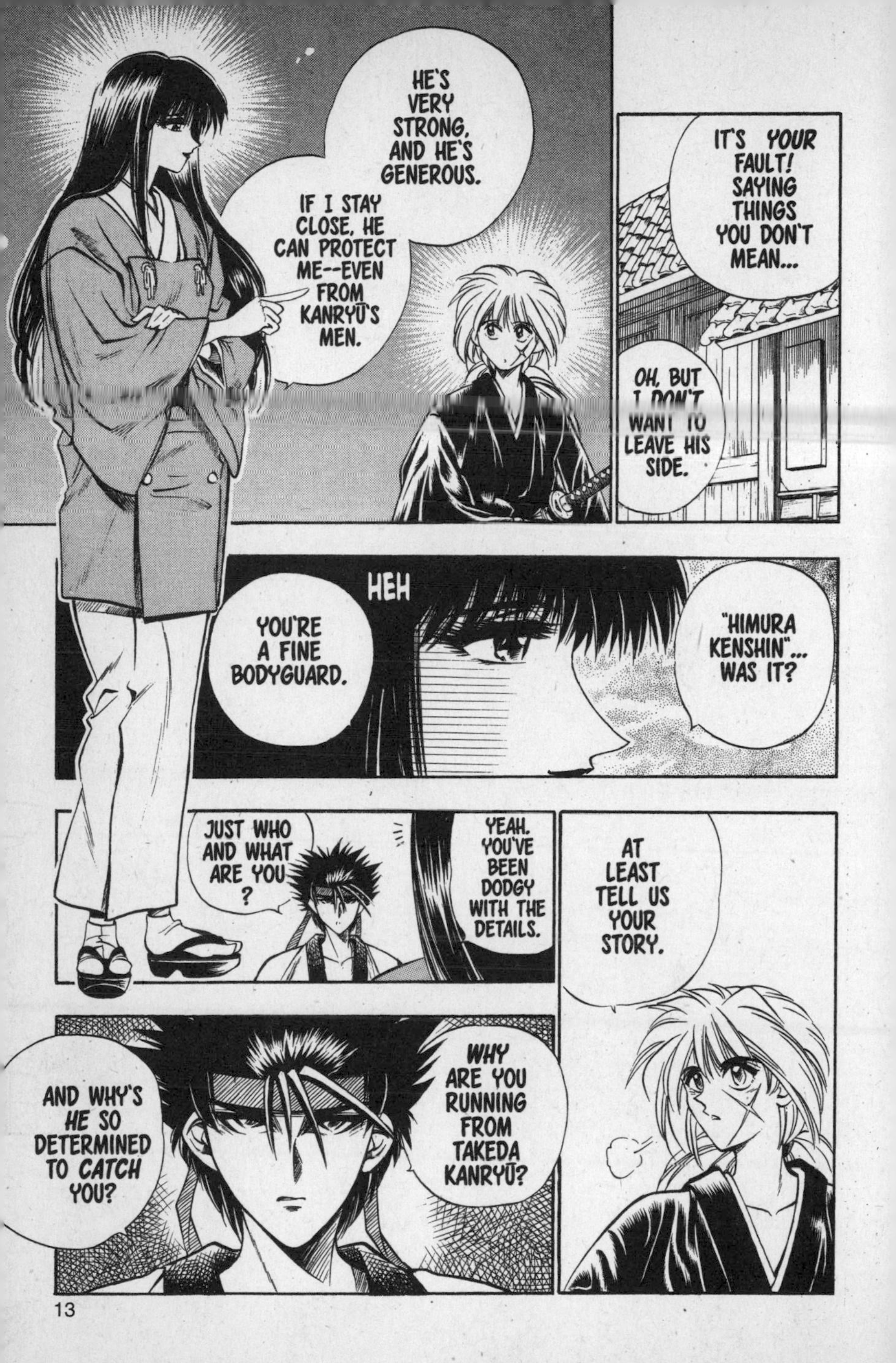
IT'S YOUR FAULT! SAYING THINGS YOU DON'T MEAN...
OH, BUT I DON'T WANT TO LEAVE HIS SIDE.
HE'S VERY STRONG, AND HE'S GENEROUS.
IF I STAY CLOSE, HE CAN PROTECT ME--EVEN FROM KANRYŪ'S MEN.
"HIMURA KENSHIN"... WAS IT?
HEH
YOU'RE A FINE BODYGUARD.
AT LEAST TELL US YOUR STORY.
YEAH. YOU'VE BEEN DODGY WITH THE DETAILS.
JUST WHO AND WHAT ARE YOU?
WHY ARE YOU RUNNING FROM TAKEDA KANRYŪ?
AND WHY'S HE SO DETERMINED TO CATCH YOU?

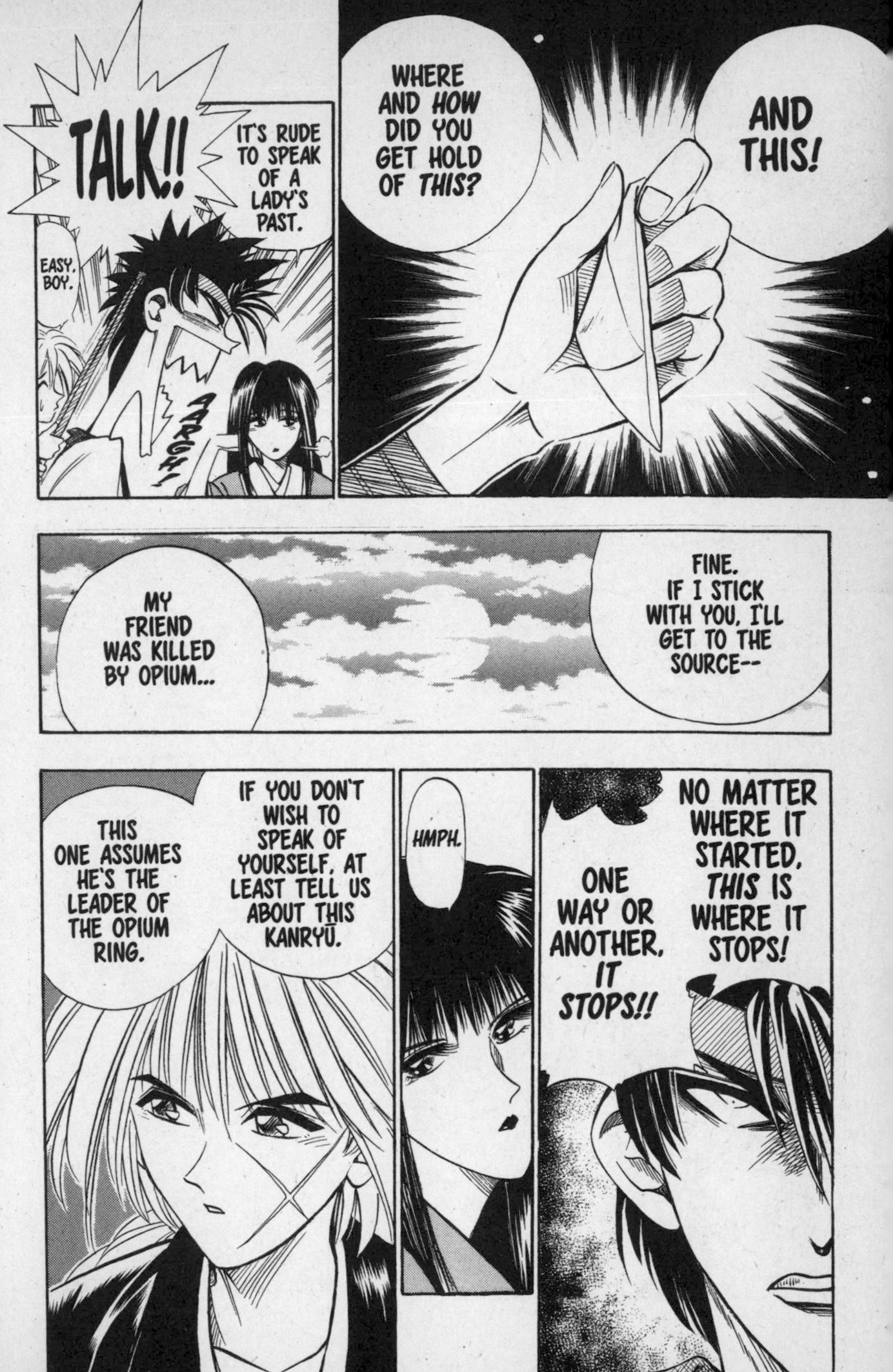
WHERE AND HOW DID YOU GET HOLD OF THIS?
AND THIS!
IT'S RUDE TO SPEAK OF A LADY'S PAST.
TALK!!
AARGH!
EASY, BOY.
FINE. IF I STICK WITH YOU, I'LL GET TO THE SOURCE--
MY FRIEND WAS KILLED BY OPIUM...
NO MATTER WHERE IT STARTED, THIS IS WHERE IT STOPS!
ONE WAY OR ANOTHER, IT STOPS!!
HMPH.
IF YOU DON'T WISH TO SPEAK OF YOURSELF, AT LEAST TELL US ABOUT THIS KANRYŪ.
THIS ONE ASSUMES HE'S THE LEADER OF THE OPIUM RING.

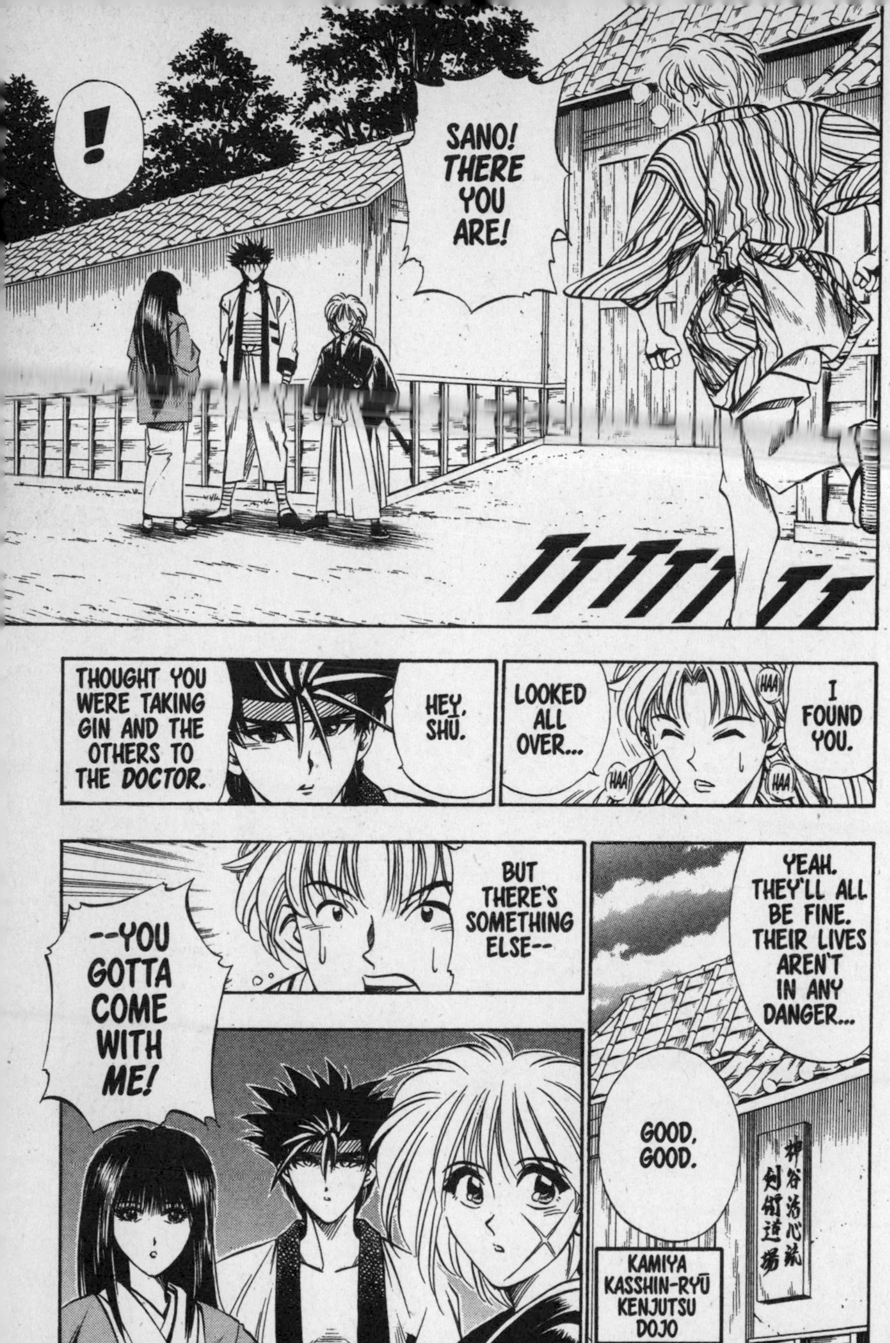
SANO! THERE YOU ARE!
!
TTTTTTT
I FOUND YOU.
HAA
HAA
HAA
LOOKED ALL OVER...
HEY, SHU.
THOUGHT YOU WERE TAKING GIN AND THE OTHERS TO THE *DOCTOR*.
YEAH. THEY'LL ALL BE FINE. THEIR LIVES AREN'T IN ANY DANGER...
GOOD, GOOD.
神谷活心流剣術道場
KAMIYA KASSHIN-RYŪ KENJUTSU DOJO
BUT THERE'S SOMETHING ELSE--
--YOU GOTTA COME WITH *ME!*

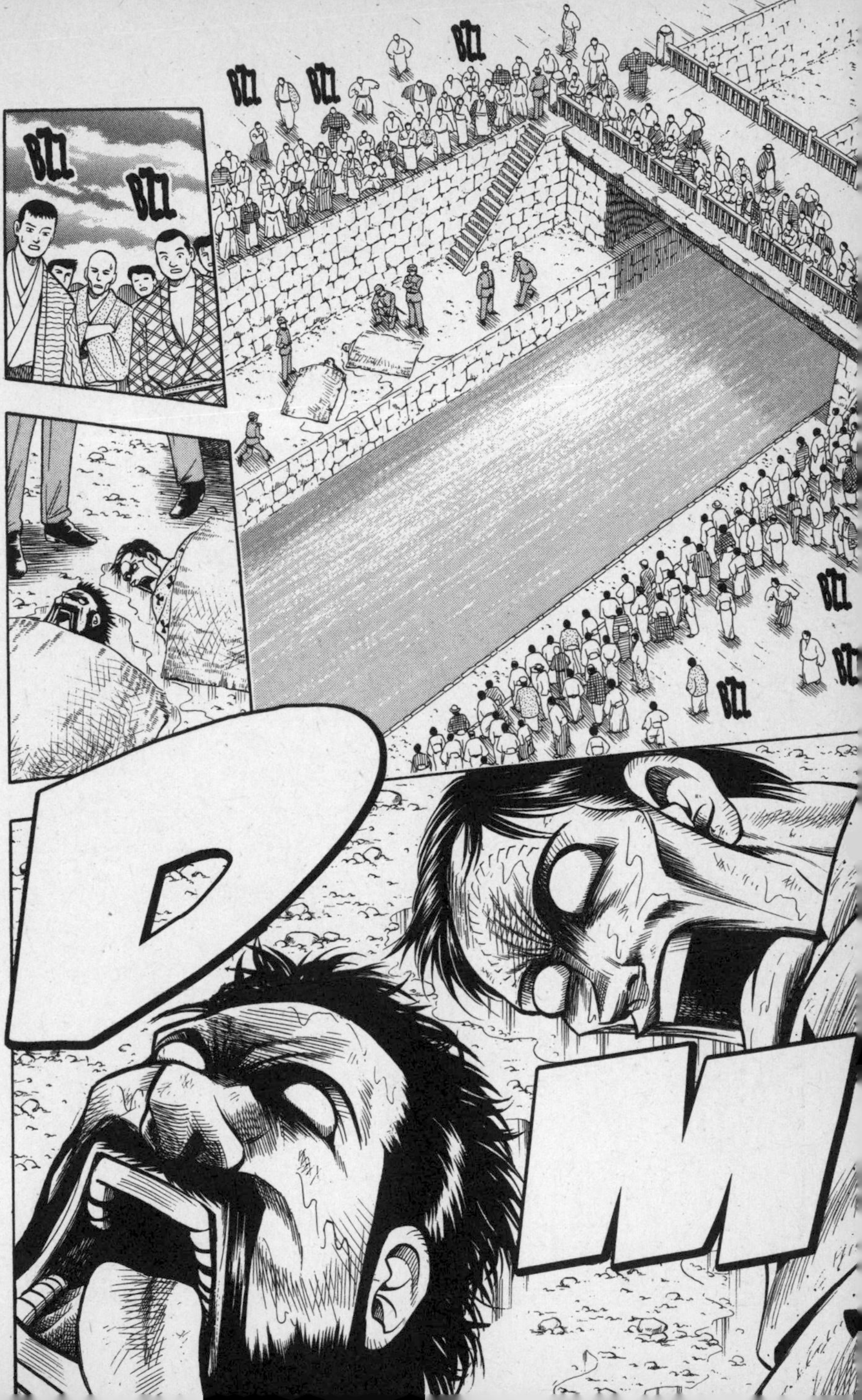
BZZ
BZZ
BZZ
BZZ
BZZ
BZZ
BZZ
BZZ
D
M

READ THIS WAY

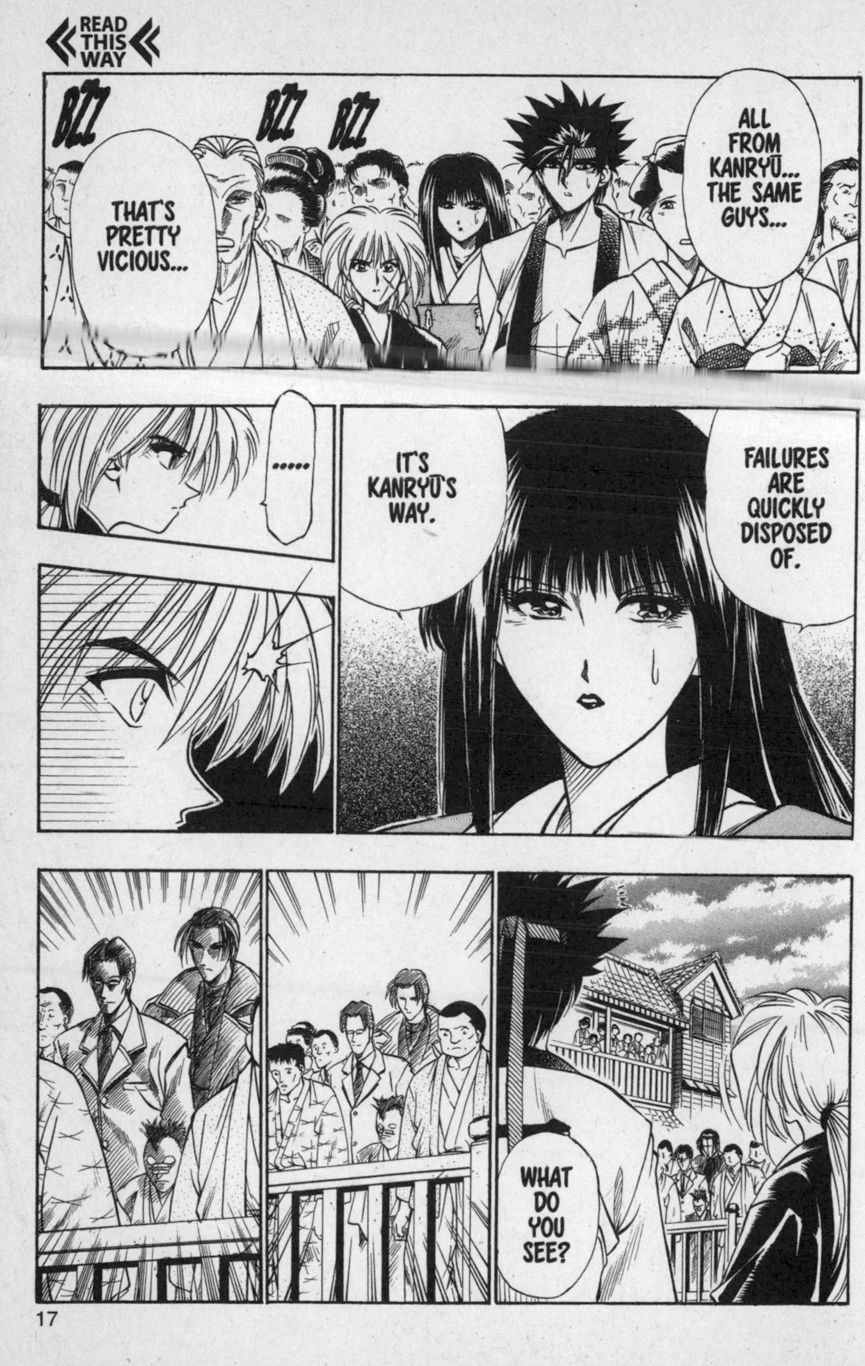

ALL FROM KANRYŪ... THE SAME GUYS...
BZZ
BZZ
BZZ
THAT'S PRETTY VICIOUS...
FAILURES ARE QUICKLY DISPOSED OF.
IT'S KANRYŪ'S WAY.
.....
WHAT DO YOU SEE?

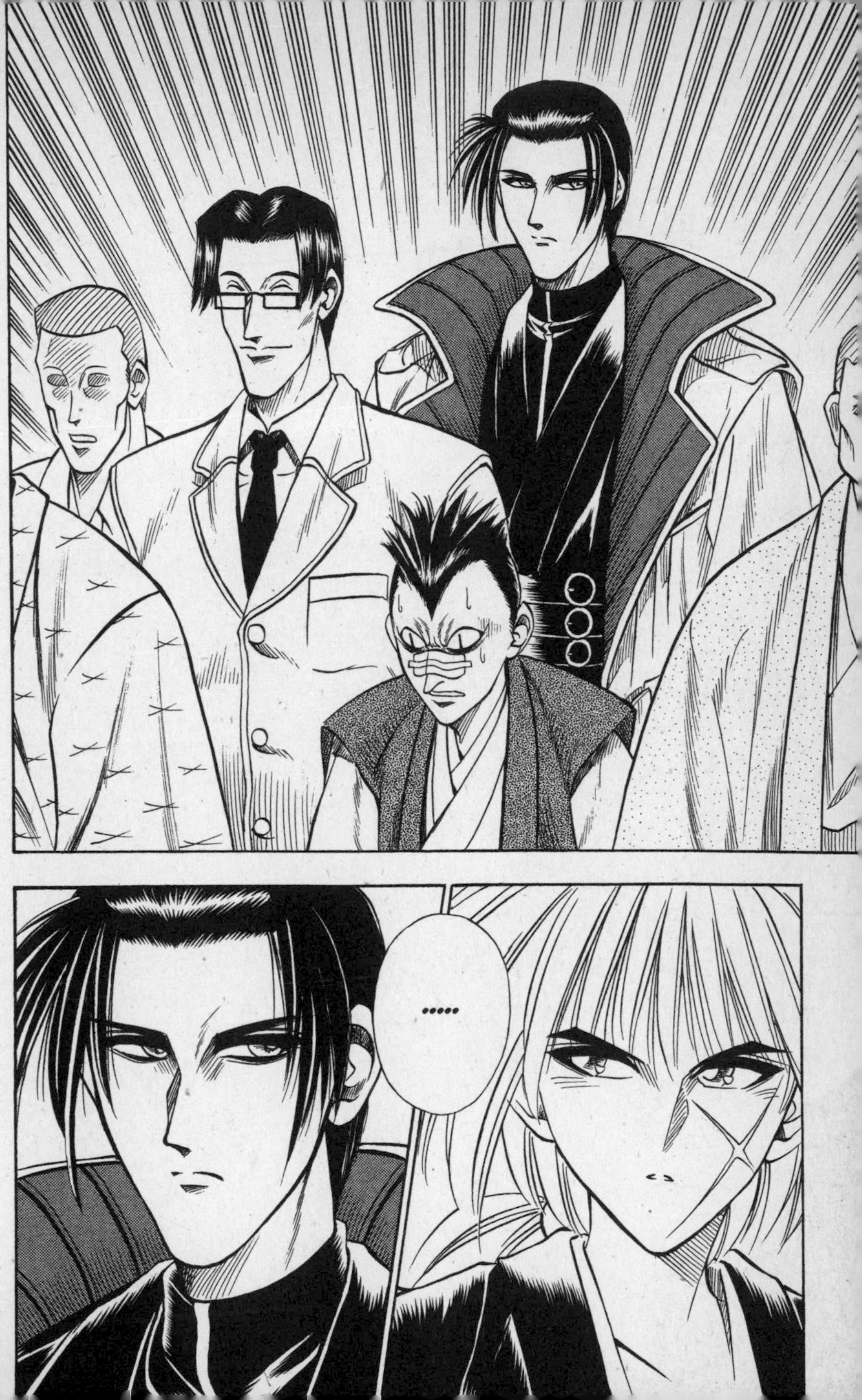
.....

READ THIS WAY

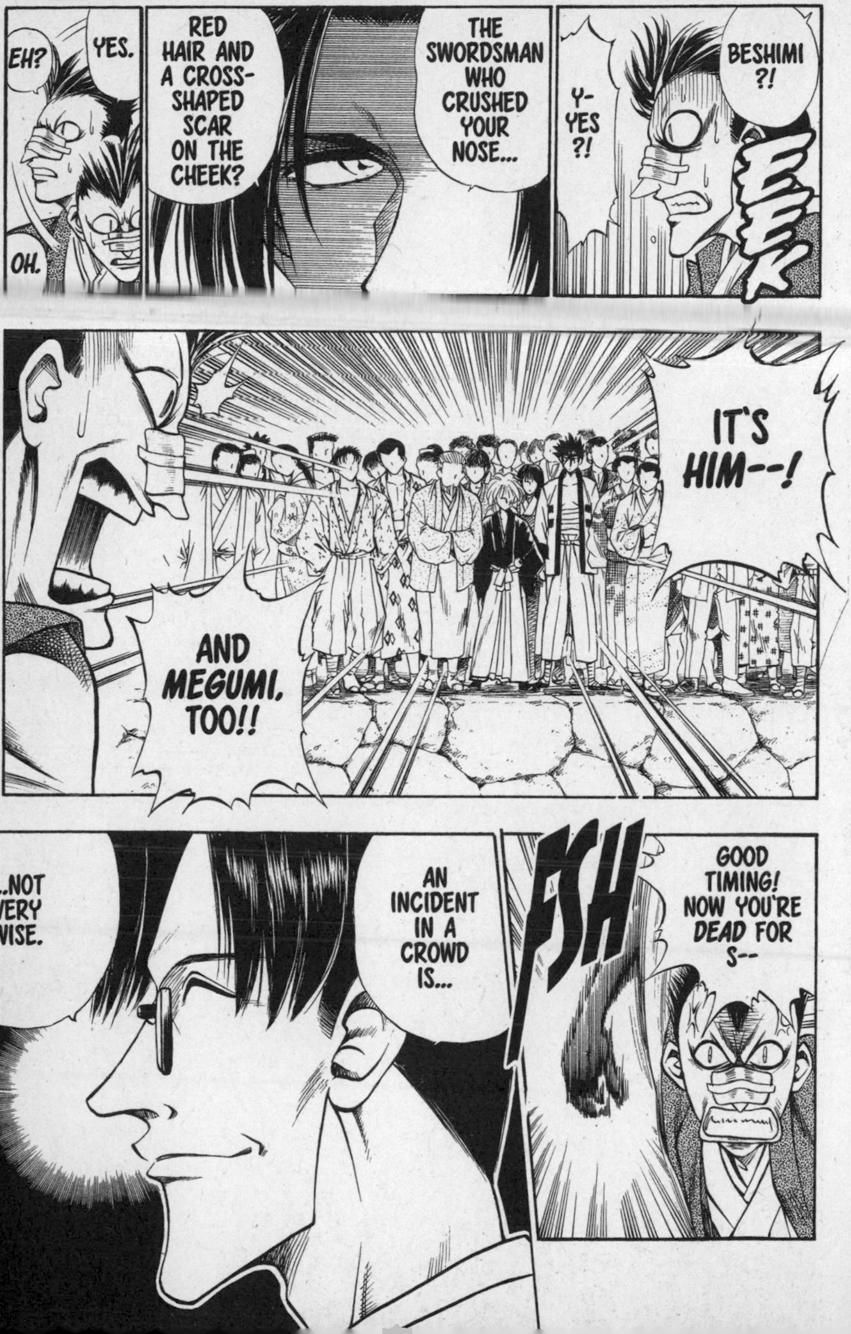
BESHIMI ?!
Y-YES ?!
THE SWORDSMAN WHO CRUSHED YOUR NOSE...
RED HAIR AND A CROSS-SHAPED SCAR ON THE CHEEK?
YES.
EH?
OH.
IT'S HIM--!
AND MEGUMI, TOO!!
GOOD TIMING! NOW YOU'RE DEAD FOR S--
FSH
AN INCIDENT IN A CROWD IS...
...NOT VERY WISE.

READ THIS WAY

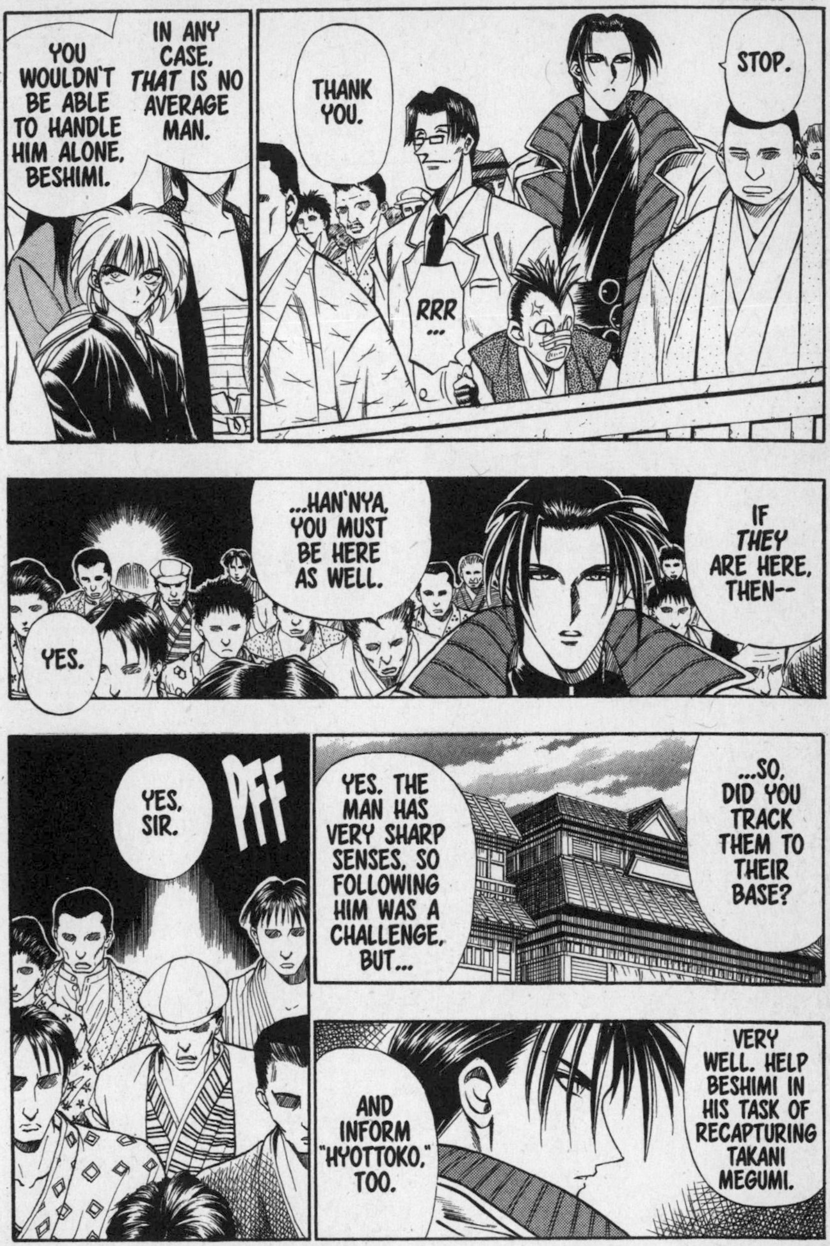
STOP.
THANK YOU.
RRR...
IN ANY CASE, *THAT* IS NO AVERAGE MAN.
YOU WOULDN'T BE ABLE TO HANDLE HIM ALONE, BESHIMI.
IF *THEY* ARE HERE, THEN--
...HAN'NYA, YOU MUST BE HERE AS WELL.
YES.
...SO, DID YOU TRACK THEM TO THEIR BASE?
YES. THE MAN HAS VERY SHARP SENSES, SO FOLLOWING HIM WAS A CHALLENGE, BUT...
VERY WELL. HELP BESHIMI IN HIS TASK OF RECAPTURING TAKANI MEGUMI.
AND INFORM "HYOTTOKO," TOO.
YES, SIR.
PFF

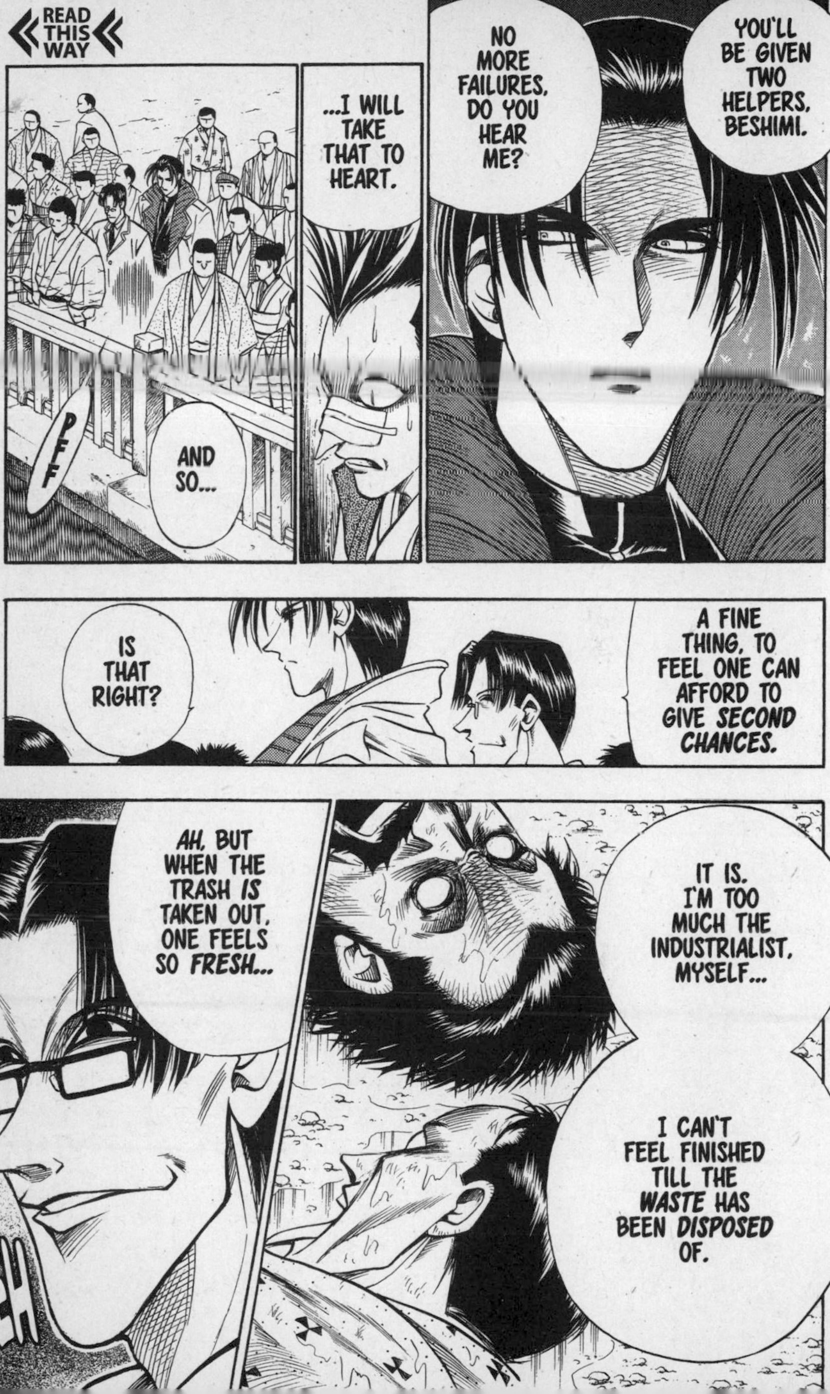
READ THIS WAY
YOU'LL BE GIVEN TWO HELPERS, BESHIMI.
NO MORE FAILURES, DO YOU HEAR ME?
...I WILL TAKE THAT TO HEART.
AND SO...
PFFF
A FINE THING, TO FEEL ONE CAN AFFORD TO GIVE *SECOND CHANCES.*
IS THAT RIGHT?
IT IS. I'M TOO MUCH THE INDUSTRIALIST, MYSELF...
I CAN'T FEEL FINISHED TILL THE *WASTE* HAS BEEN *DISPOSED* OF.
AH, BUT WHEN THE TRASH *IS* TAKEN OUT, ONE FEELS SO *FRESH*...
HEH

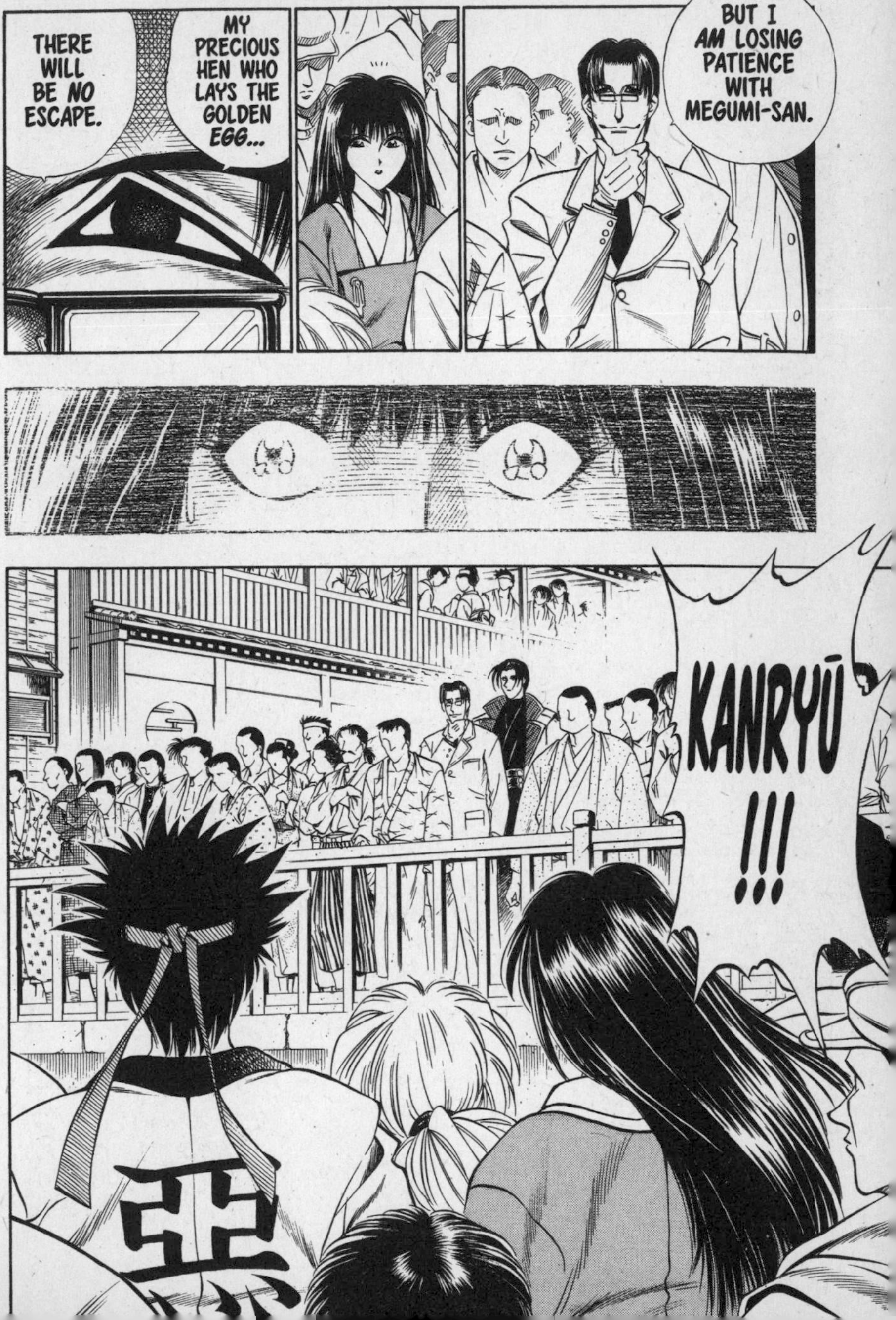
BUT I AM LOSING PATIENCE WITH MEGUMI-SAN.
MY PRECIOUS HEN WHO LAYS THE GOLDEN EGG...
THERE WILL BE NO ESCAPE.
KANRYŪ!!!

READ THIS WAY

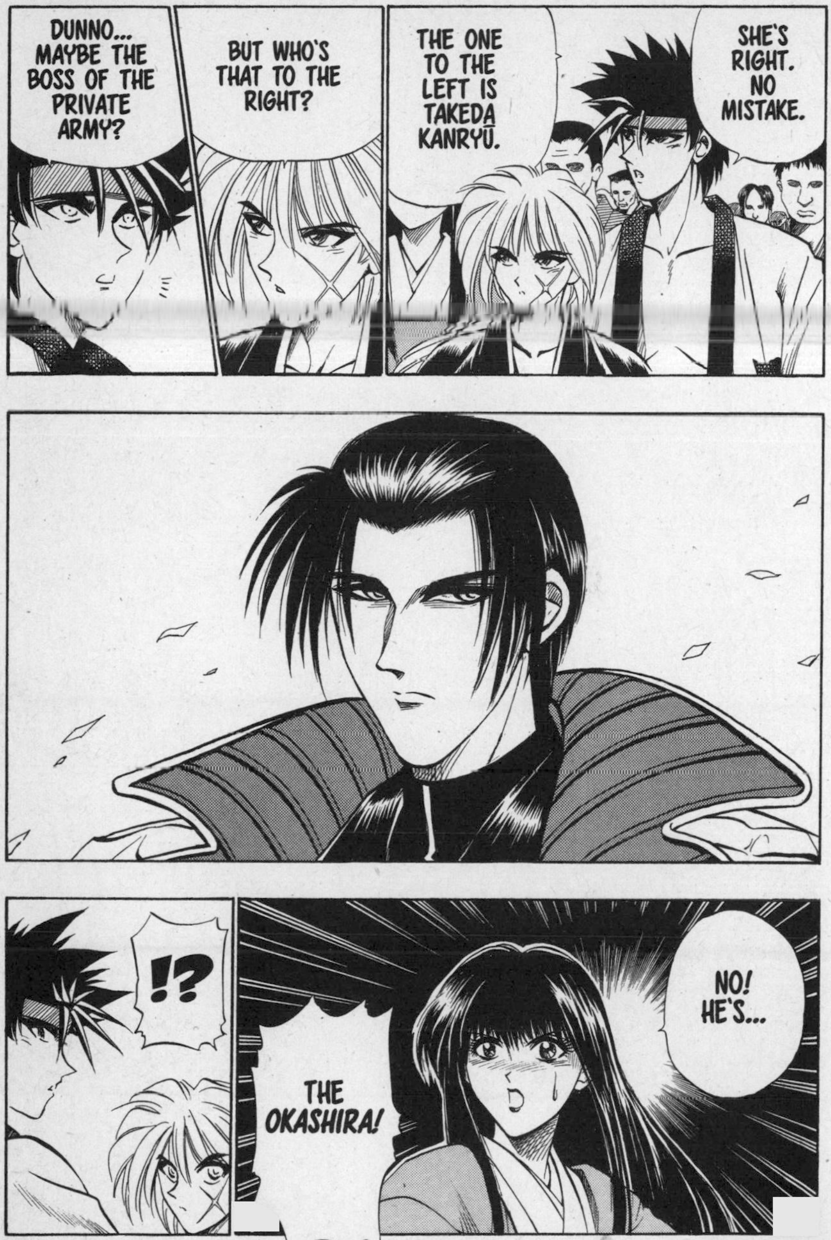
SHE'S RIGHT. NO MISTAKE.
THE ONE TO THE LEFT IS TAKEDA KANRYŪ.
BUT WHO'S THAT TO THE RIGHT?
DUNNO... MAYBE THE BOSS OF THE PRIVATE ARMY?
NO! HE'S...
THE OKASHIRA!
!?

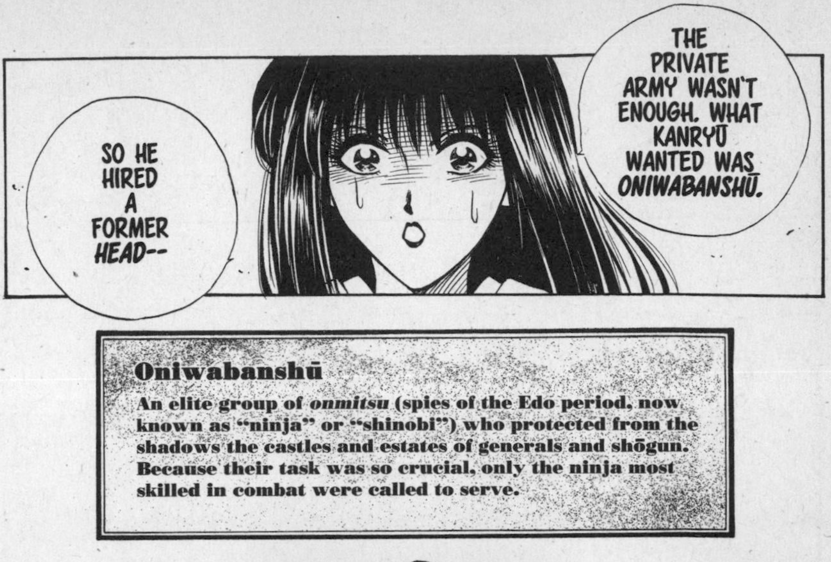
THE PRIVATE ARMY WASN'T ENOUGH. WHAT KANRYŪ WANTED WAS ONIWABANSHŪ.
SO HE HIRED A FORMER HEAD--

Oniwabanshū

An elite group of *onmitsu* (spies of the Edo period, now known as "ninja" or "shinobi") who protected from the shadows the castles and estates of generals and shōgun. Because their task was so crucial, only the ninja most skilled in combat were called to serve.

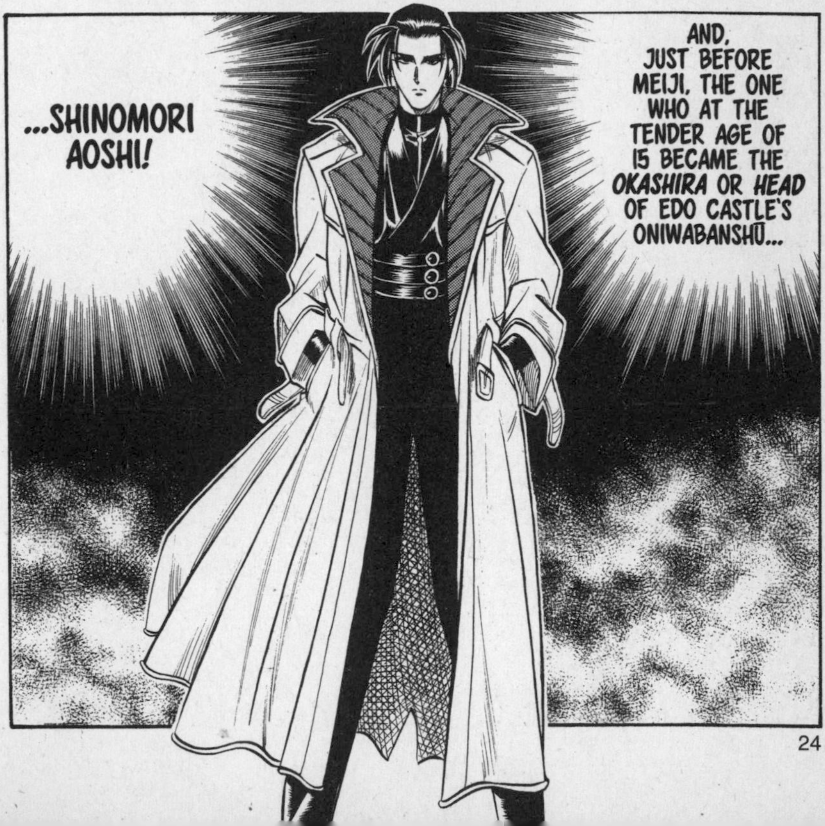
AND, JUST BEFORE MEIJI, THE ONE WHO AT THE TENDER AGE OF 15 BECAME THE OKASHIRA OR HEAD OF EDO CASTLE'S ONIWABANSHŪ...
...SHINOMORI AOSHI!

READ THIS WAY

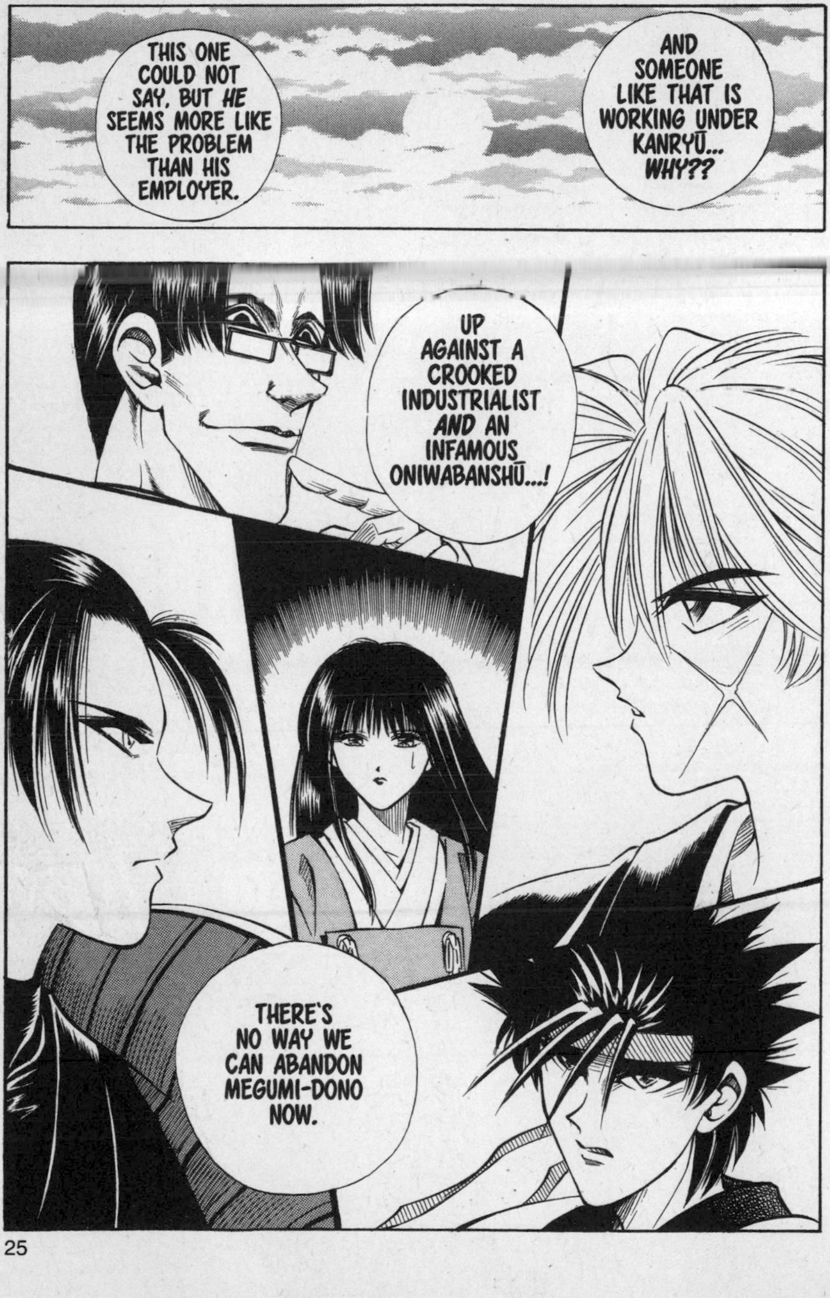
AND SOMEONE LIKE THAT IS WORKING UNDER KANRYŪ... *WHY??*
THIS ONE COULD NOT SAY, BUT *HE* SEEMS MORE LIKE THE PROBLEM THAN HIS EMPLOYER.
UP AGAINST A CROOKED INDUSTRIALIST *AND* AN INFAMOUS ONIWABANSHŪ...!
THERE'S NO WAY WE CAN ABANDON MEGUMI-DONO NOW.

READ THIS WAY

The Secret Life of Characters (8)
—Oniwabanshū • Beshimi—

As a character largely created on-the-spot, I can't say there's much here in the way of a motif. The truth is that, when Watsuki first discussed the "Megumi Arc" with his editor, the opinion was expressed that having a swordsman of Kenshin's caliber fighting a group of punk-thugs still coming into their first facial hair mi-i-ight not make for the most epic of manga. Enter the Oniwabanshū—a real, historic entity—soon made over into onmitsu or ninja, with the remaining details to be fleshed out as the story progressed.

The first of them, Beshimi, was not intended as a stand-alone character, but as a taste of things to come. Without a personality already sketched out for him, he turned out kind of timid...although, as you read further in the story, you'll begin to see another side of him (which I'm going to keep secret, for now).

As mentioned, Beshimi's kind of an "as-you-go" character and so there's no design motif. One thing, though, was that aside from Aoshi, what I wanted for the Oniwabanshū was a variety of shapes and temperaments. Thus, he ended up shorter in stature than Kenshin. It may in fact be his shortness and his timidity that's garnered him his own little group of fans, people who write me saying, "Beshimi KAWAI'I (Beshimi is cute)!!" Not too sure how to feel about that one....

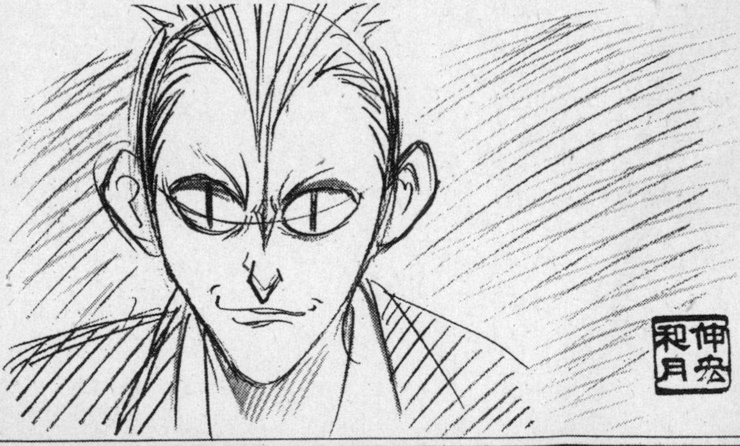
伸宏
和月

READ THIS WAY

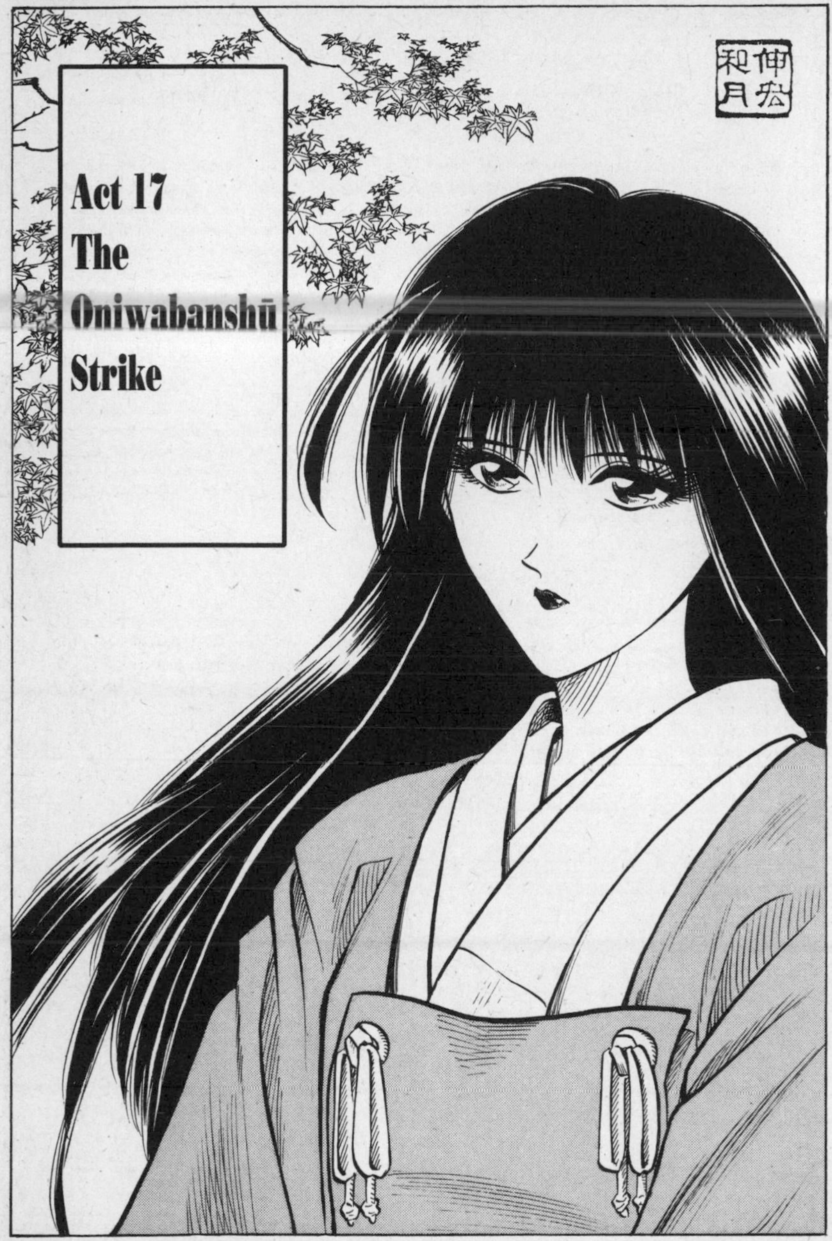
Act 17
The Oniwabanshū Strike

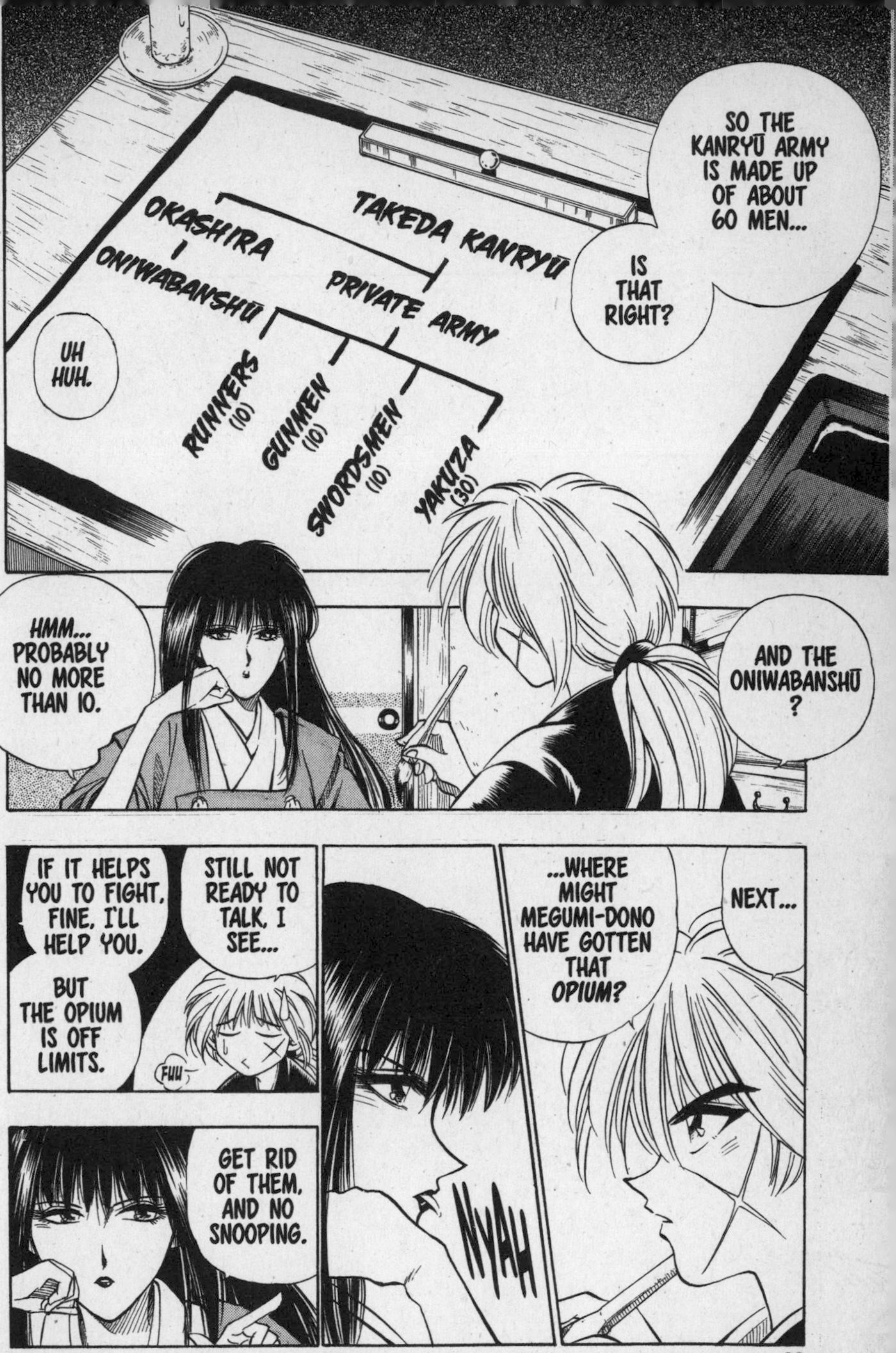
SO THE KANRYŪ ARMY IS MADE UP OF ABOUT 60 MEN...
IS THAT RIGHT?
UH HUH.
TAKEDA KANRYŪ
OKASHIRA
ONIWABANSHŪ
PRIVATE ARMY
RUNNERS (10)
GUNMEN (10)
SWORDSMEN (10)
YAKUZA (30)
AND THE ONIWABANSHŪ?
HMM... PROBABLY NO MORE THAN 10.
NEXT...
...WHERE MIGHT MEGUMI-DONO HAVE GOTTEN THAT OPIUM?
NYAH
STILL NOT READY TO TALK, I SEE...
IF IT HELPS YOU TO FIGHT, FINE, I'LL HELP YOU.
BUT THE OPIUM IS OFF LIMITS.
FUU
GET RID OF THEM, AND NO SNOOPING.

READ THIS WAY

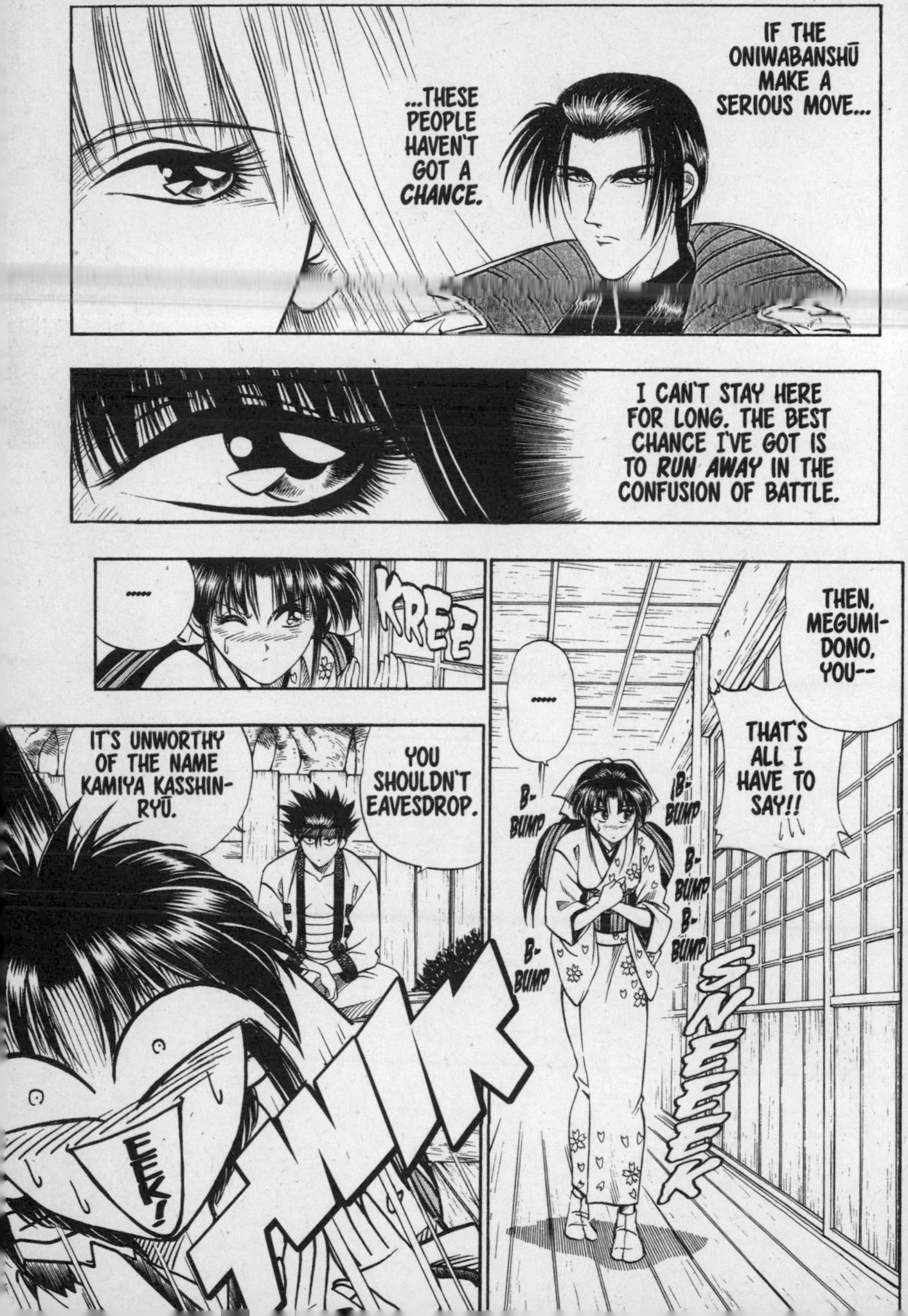
IF THE ONIWABANSHŪ MAKE A SERIOUS MOVE...
...THESE PEOPLE HAVEN'T GOT A CHANCE.
I CAN'T STAY HERE FOR LONG. THE BEST CHANCE I'VE GOT IS TO RUN AWAY IN THE CONFUSION OF BATTLE.
THEN, MEGUMI-DONO, YOU--
THAT'S ALL I HAVE TO SAY!!
......
B-BUMP
B-BUMP
B-BUMP
B-BUMP
B-BUMP
B-BUMP
SNEEEEEK
KREE
......
YOU SHOULDN'T EAVESDROP.
IT'S UNWORTHY OF THE NAME KAMIYA KASSHIN-RYŪ.
EEK!

READ THIS WAY

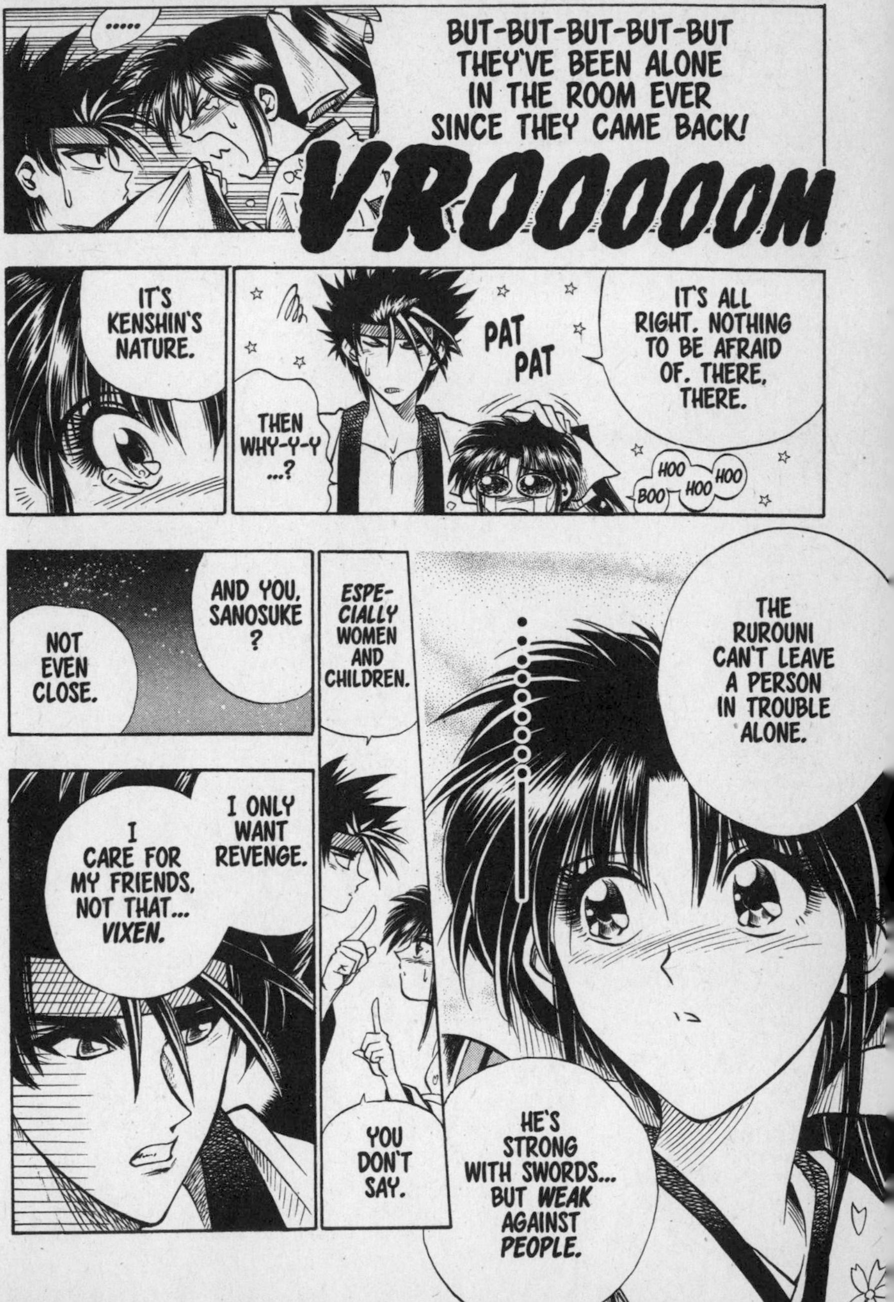
BUT-BUT-BUT-BUT-BUT THEY'VE BEEN ALONE IN THE ROOM EVER SINCE THEY CAME BACK!
VROOOOOM
......
IT'S ALL RIGHT. NOTHING TO BE AFRAID OF. THERE, THERE.
PAT PAT
HOO HOO HOO BOO
THEN WHY-Y-Y ...?
IT'S KENSHIN'S NATURE.
THE RUROUNI CAN'T LEAVE A PERSON IN TROUBLE ALONE.
HE'S STRONG WITH SWORDS... BUT WEAK AGAINST PEOPLE.
ESPE-CIALLY WOMEN AND CHILDREN.
YOU DON'T SAY.
AND YOU, SANOSUKE ?
NOT EVEN CLOSE.
I ONLY WANT REVENGE.
I CARE FOR MY FRIENDS, NOT THAT... VIXEN.

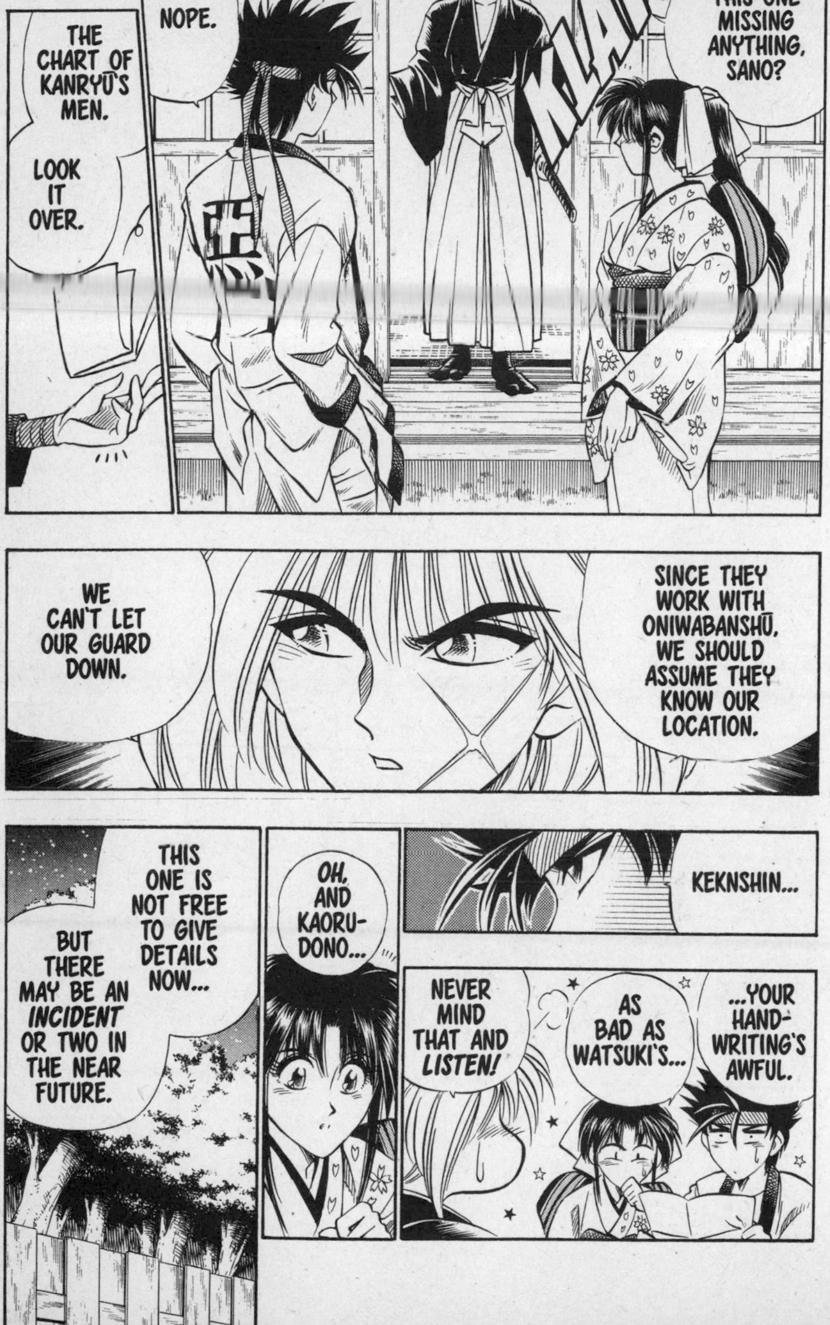
IS THIS ONE MISSING ANYTHING, SANO?
KLATTA
NOPE.
THE CHART OF KANRYŪ'S MEN.
LOOK IT OVER.
SINCE THEY WORK WITH ONIWABANSHŪ, WE SHOULD ASSUME THEY KNOW OUR LOCATION.
WE CAN'T LET OUR GUARD DOWN.
KEKNSHIN...
...YOUR HANDWRITING'S AWFUL.
AS BAD AS WATSUKI'S...
NEVER MIND THAT AND *LISTEN!*
OH, AND KAORU-DONO...
THIS ONE IS NOT FREE TO GIVE DETAILS NOW...
BUT THERE MAY BE AN *INCIDENT* OR TWO IN THE NEAR FUTURE.

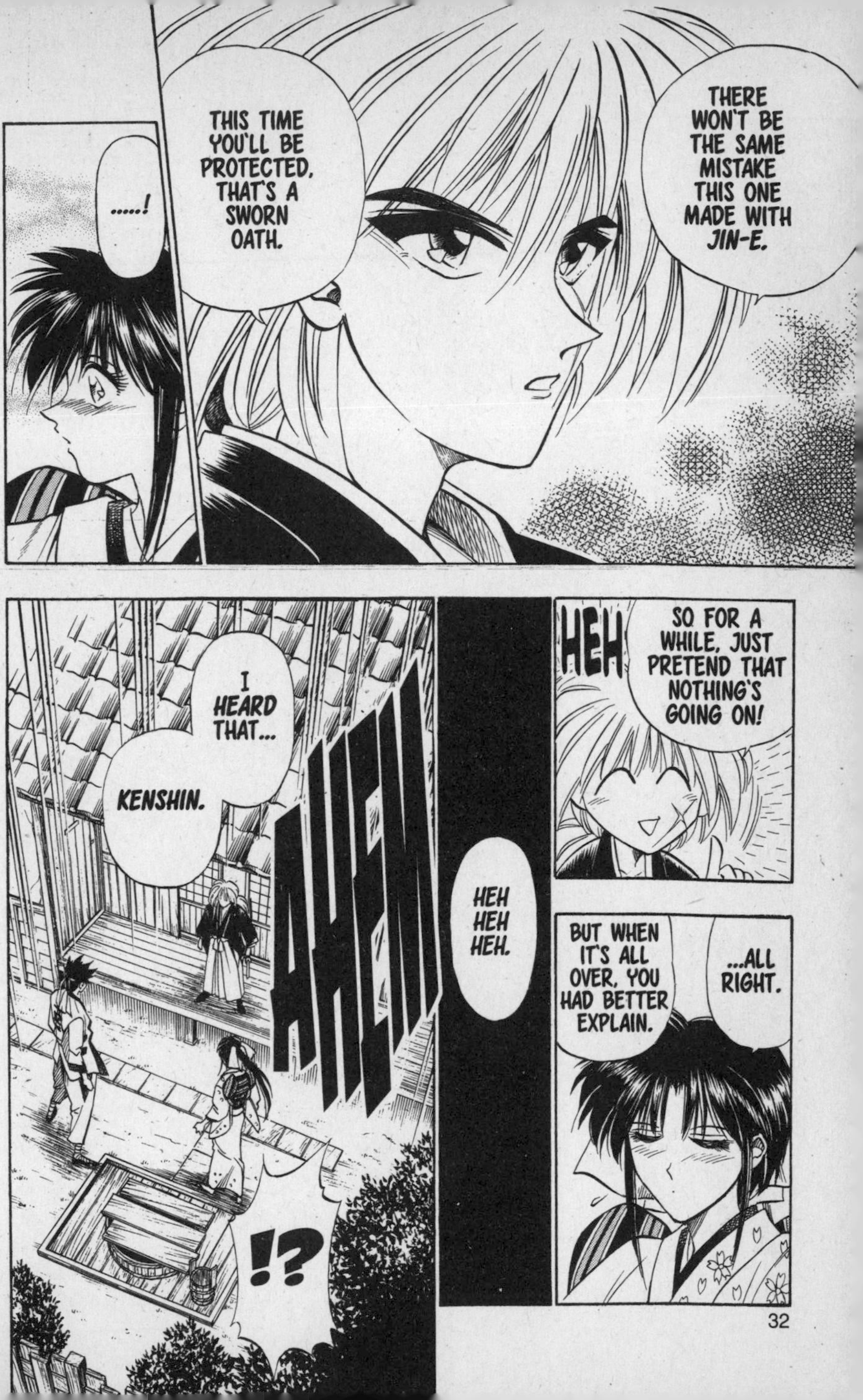
THERE WON'T BE THE SAME MISTAKE THIS ONE MADE WITH JIN-E.
THIS TIME YOU'LL BE PROTECTED, THAT'S A SWORN OATH.
......!
HEH
SO FOR A WHILE, JUST PRETEND THAT NOTHING'S GOING ON!
...ALL RIGHT.
BUT WHEN IT'S ALL OVER, YOU HAD BETTER EXPLAIN.
HEH HEH HEH.
I HEARD THAT...
KENSHIN.
AHEM
!?

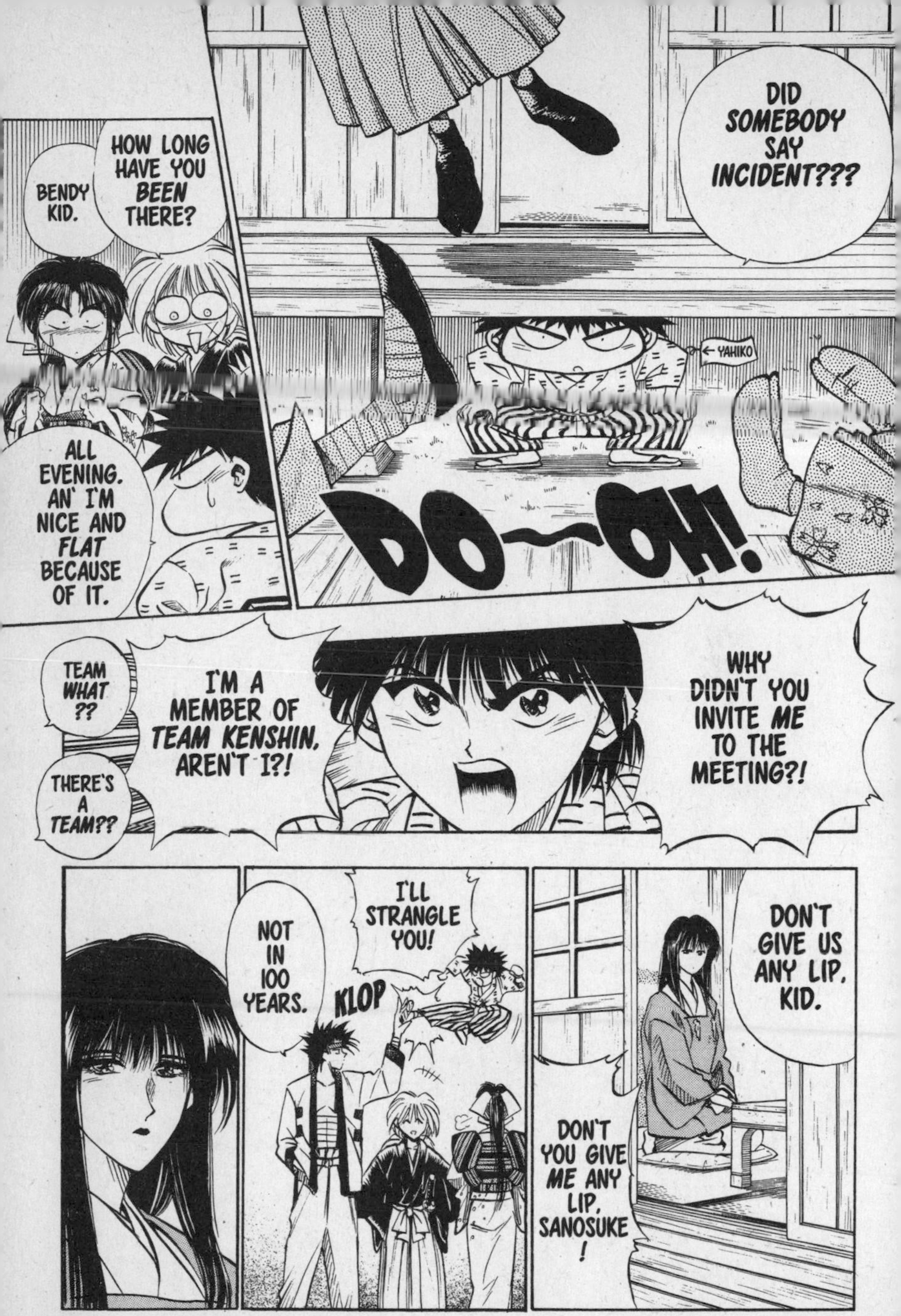
DID SOMEBODY SAY INCIDENT???
← YAHIKO
DO—OH!
HOW LONG HAVE YOU BEEN THERE?
BENDY KID.
ALL EVENING. AN' I'M NICE AND FLAT BECAUSE OF IT.
WHY DIDN'T YOU INVITE ME TO THE MEETING?!
I'M A MEMBER OF TEAM KENSHIN, AREN'T I?!
TEAM WHAT??
THERE'S A TEAM??
DON'T GIVE US ANY LIP, KID.
DON'T YOU GIVE ME ANY LIP, SANOSUKE!
I'LL STRANGLE YOU!
NOT IN 100 YEARS.
KLOP

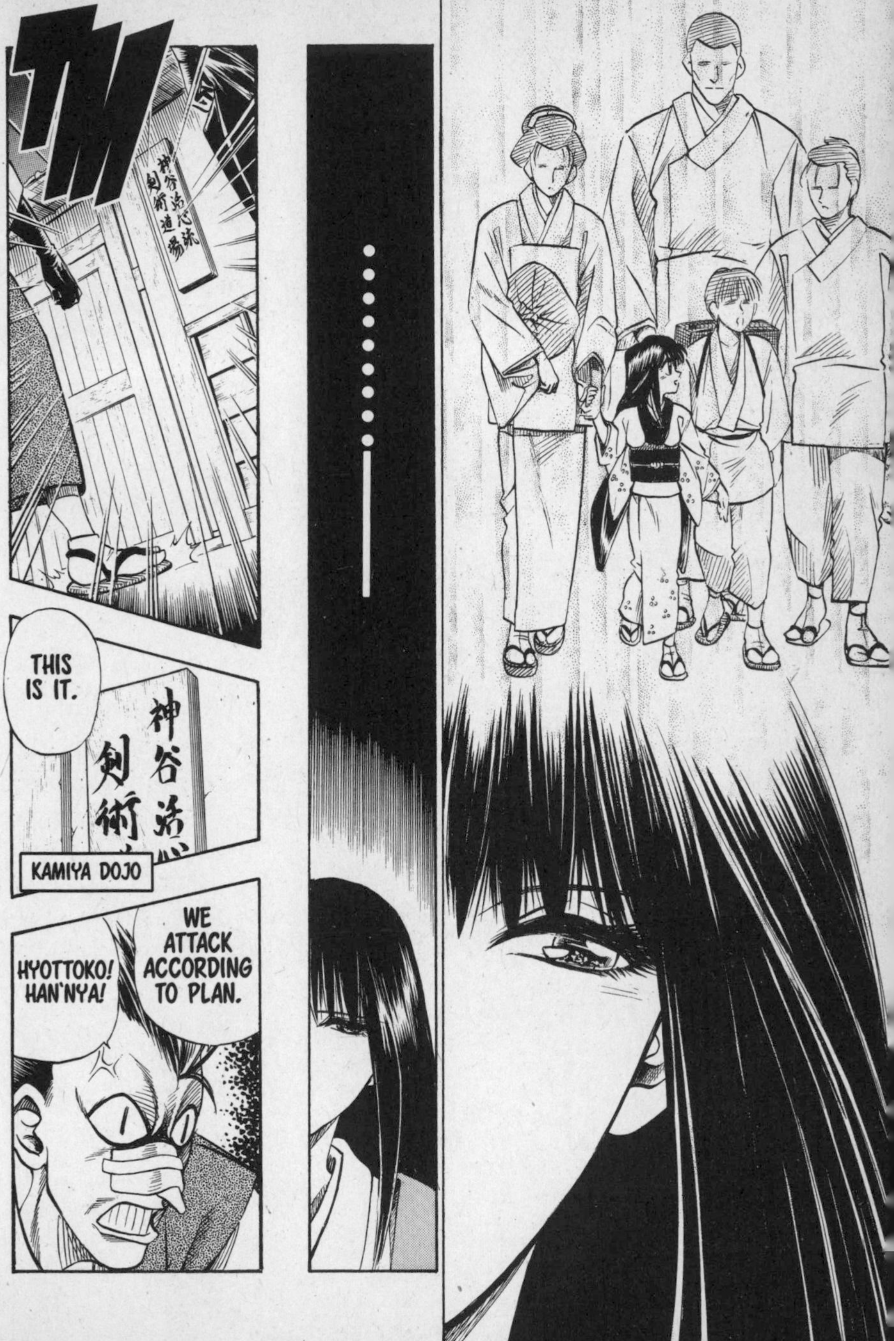

神谷活心流
剣術道場
THIS IS IT.
KAMIYA DOJO
WE ATTACK ACCORDING TO PLAN.
HYOTTOKO! HAN'NYA!

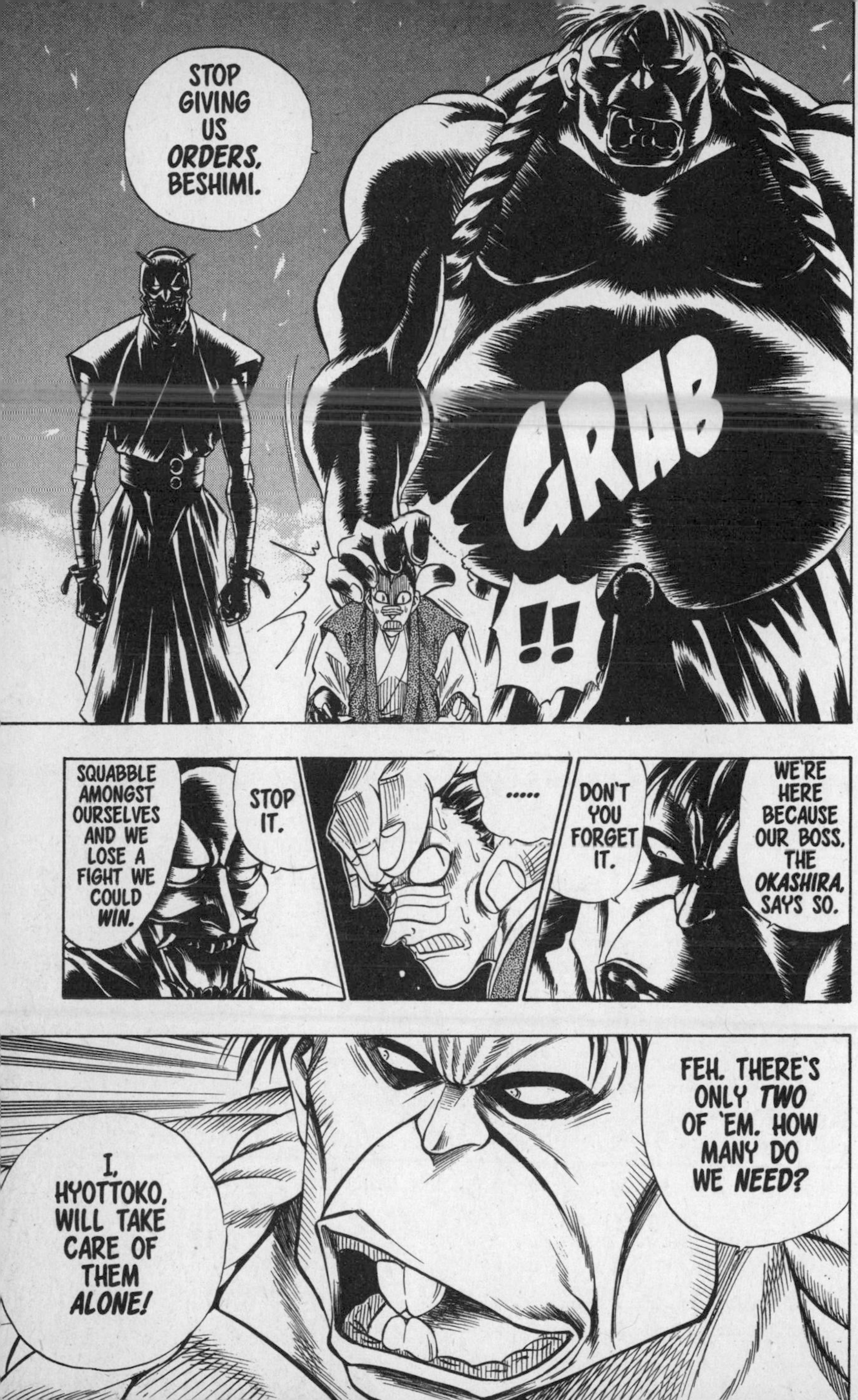
STOP GIVING US ORDERS, BESHIMI.
GRAB
!!
WE'RE HERE BECAUSE OUR BOSS, THE OKASHIRA, SAYS SO.
DON'T YOU FORGET IT.
.....
STOP IT.
SQUABBLE AMONGST OURSELVES AND WE LOSE A FIGHT WE COULD WIN.
FEH. THERE'S ONLY TWO OF 'EM. HOW MANY DO WE NEED?
I, HYOTTOKO, WILL TAKE CARE OF THEM ALONE!

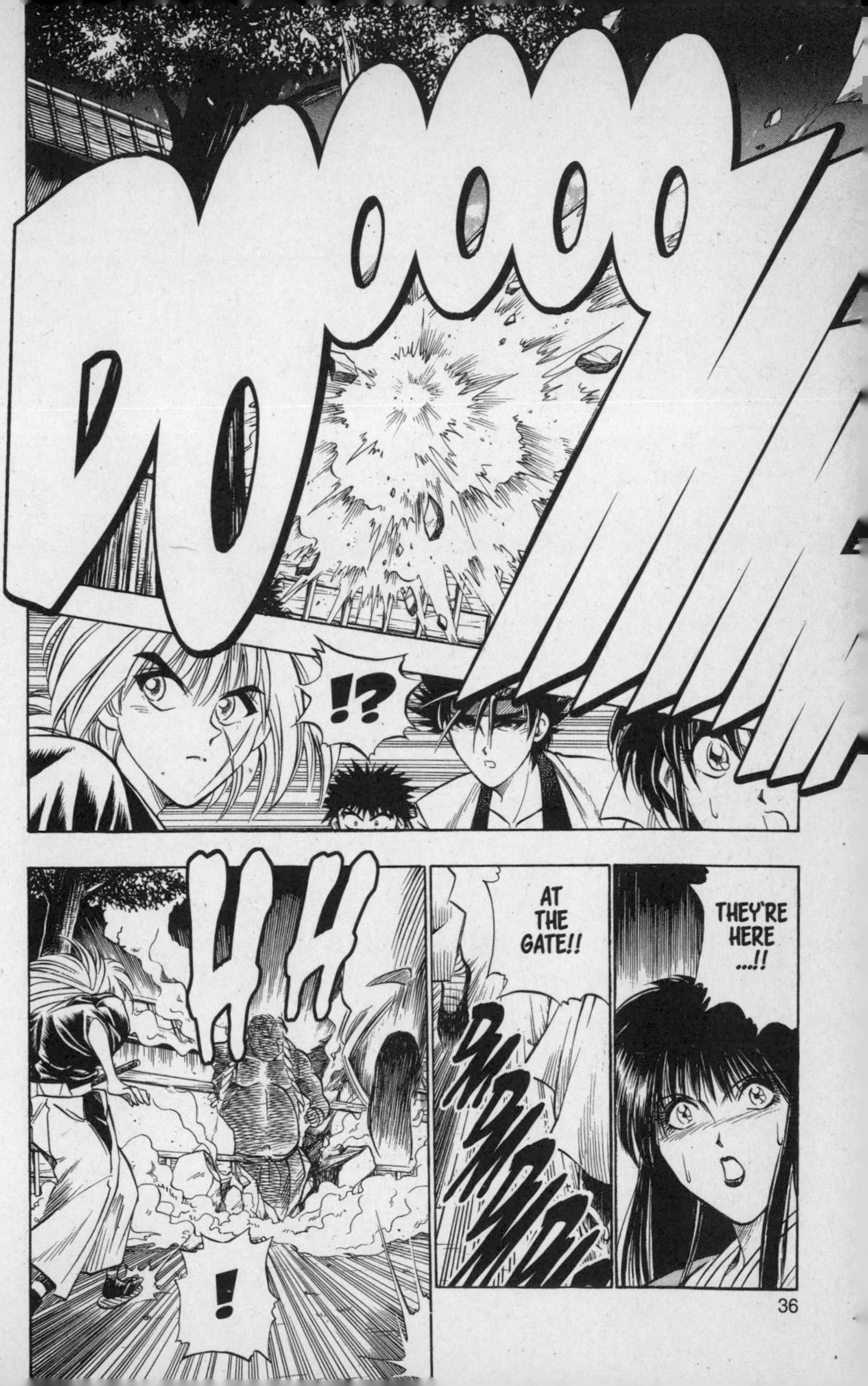
!?
THEY'RE HERE ...!!
AT THE GATE!!
!

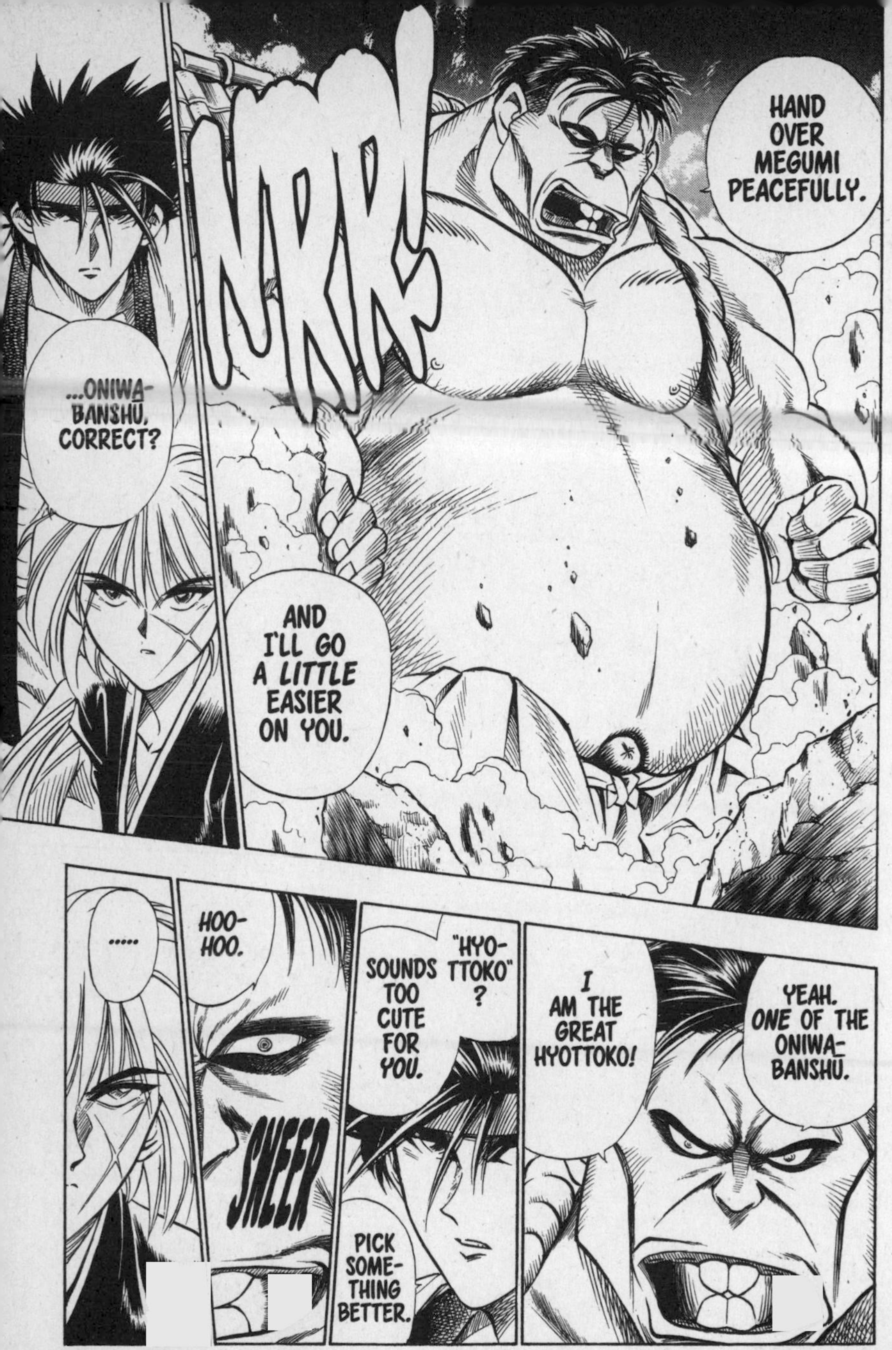
HAND OVER MEGUMI PEACEFULLY.
AND I'LL GO A *LITTLE* EASIER ON YOU.
...ONIWA-BANSHU, CORRECT?
YEAH. *ONE* OF THE ONIWA-BANSHU.
I AM THE GREAT HYOTTOKO!
"HYO-TTOKO" ?
SOUNDS TOO CUTE FOR YOU.
PICK SOME-THING BETTER.
HOO-HOO.
SNEER
......

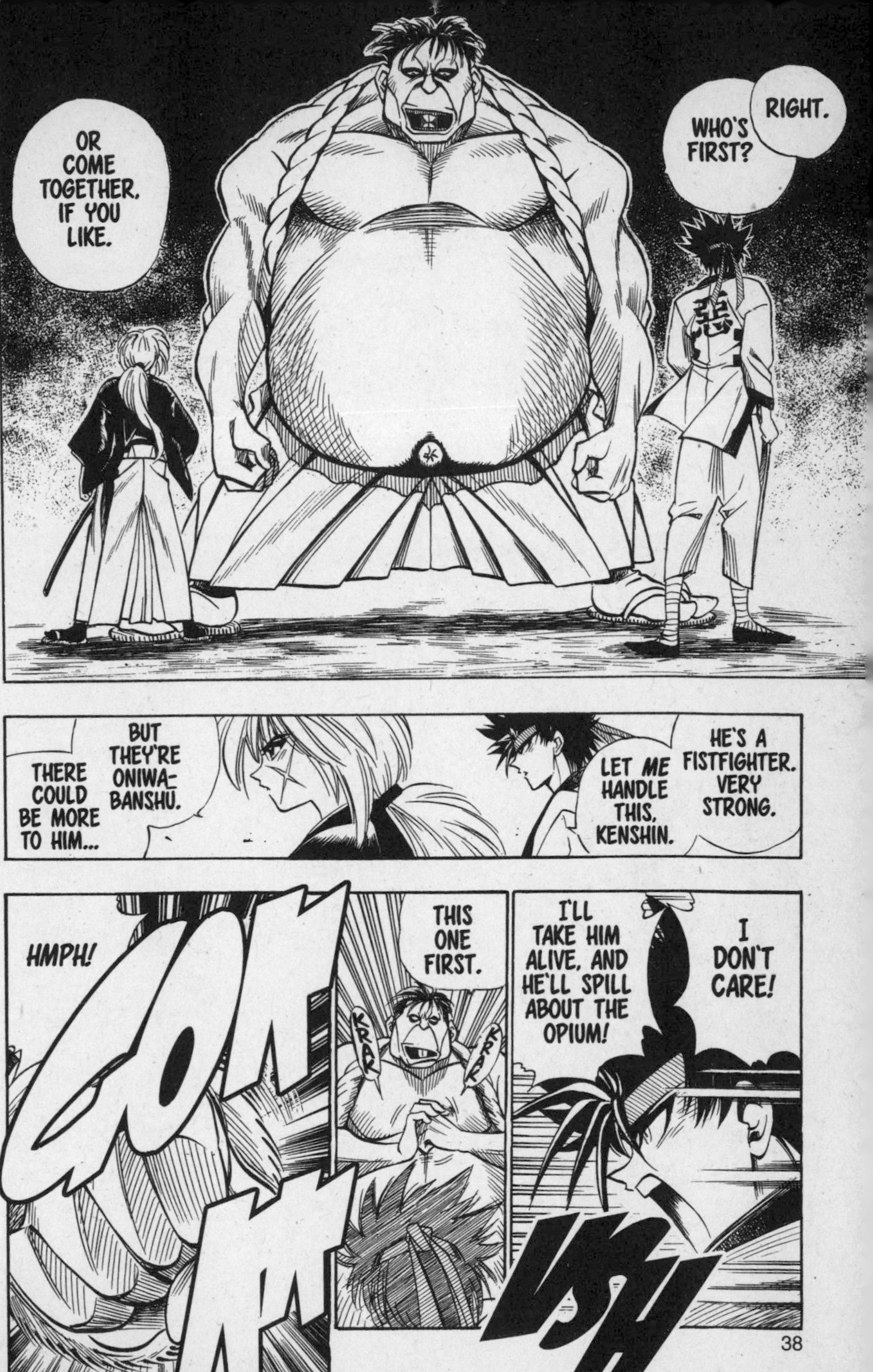
RIGHT.
WHO'S FIRST?
OR COME TOGETHER, IF YOU LIKE.
HE'S A FISTFIGHTER. VERY STRONG.
LET *ME* HANDLE THIS, KENSHIN.
BUT THEY'RE ONIWA-BANSHU.
THERE COULD BE MORE TO HIM...
I DON'T CARE!
I'LL TAKE HIM ALIVE, AND HE'LL SPILL ABOUT THE OPIUM!
VSH
THIS ONE FIRST.
KRAK
KRAK
HMPH!

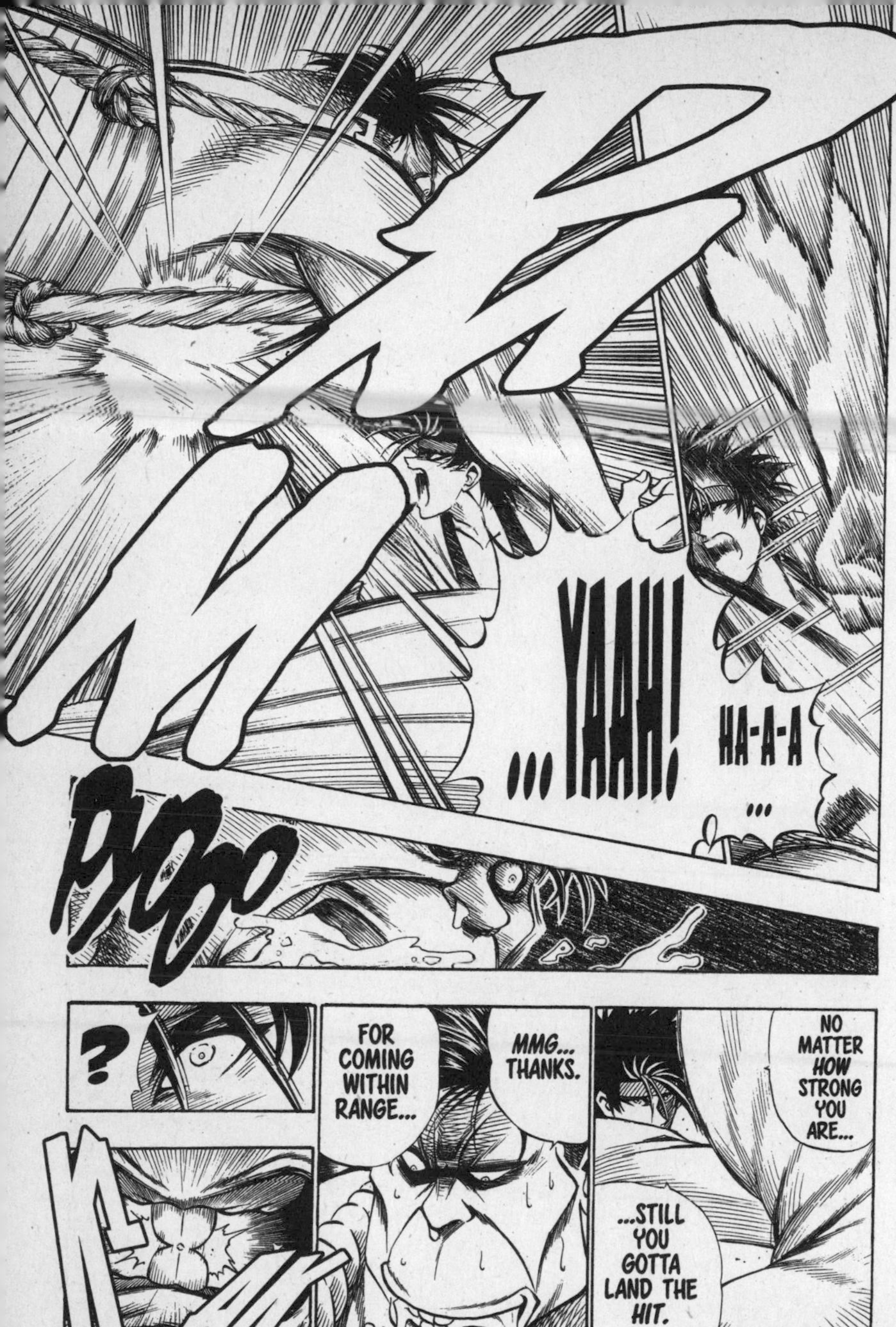
HA-A-A
...
...YAAH!
NO MATTER HOW STRONG YOU ARE...
...STILL YOU GOTTA LAND THE HIT.
MMG... THANKS.
FOR COMING WITHIN RANGE...
?

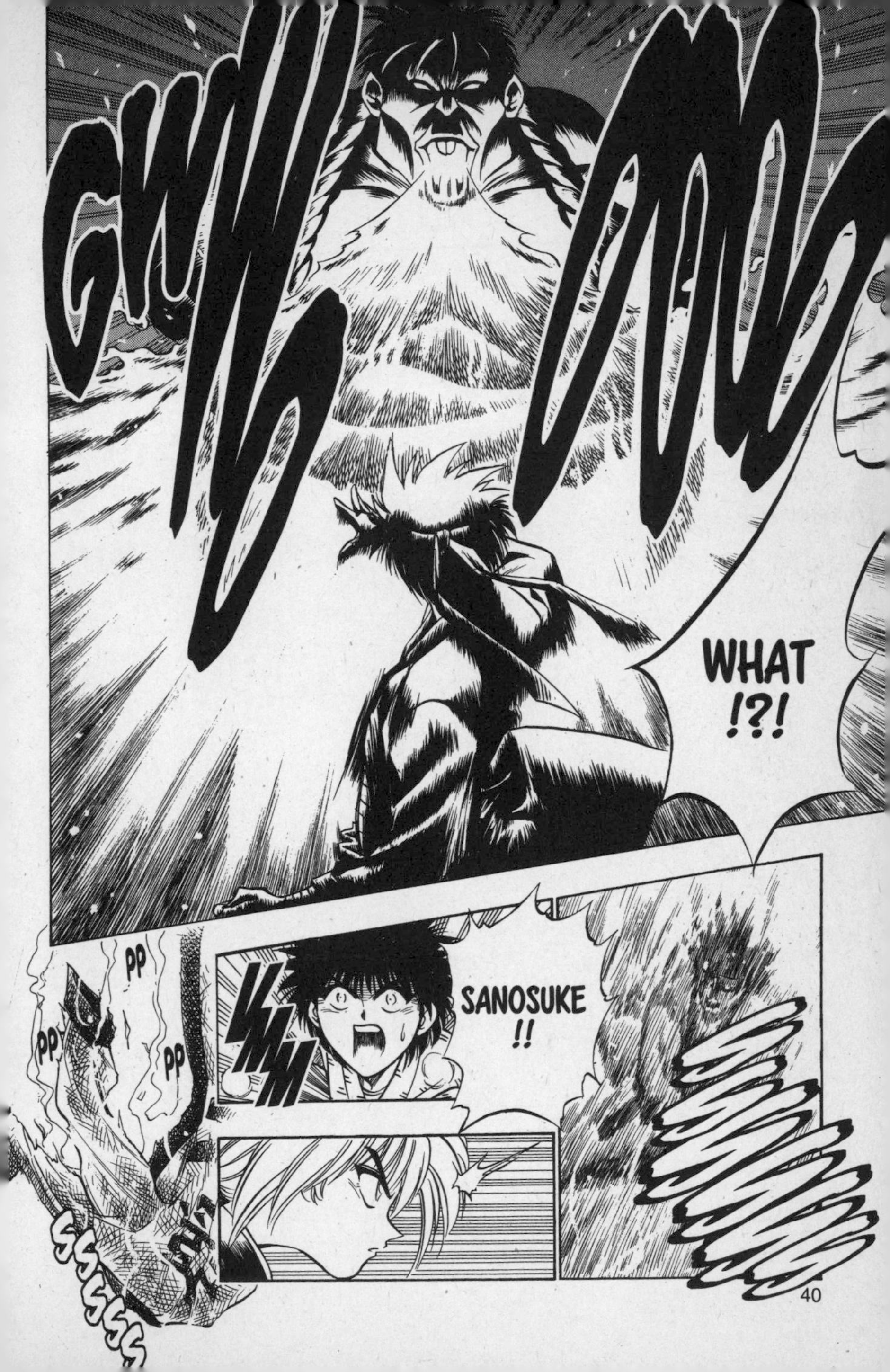
WHAT !?!
SANOSUKE !!
PP
PP
PP
SSSSSS

READ THIS WAY

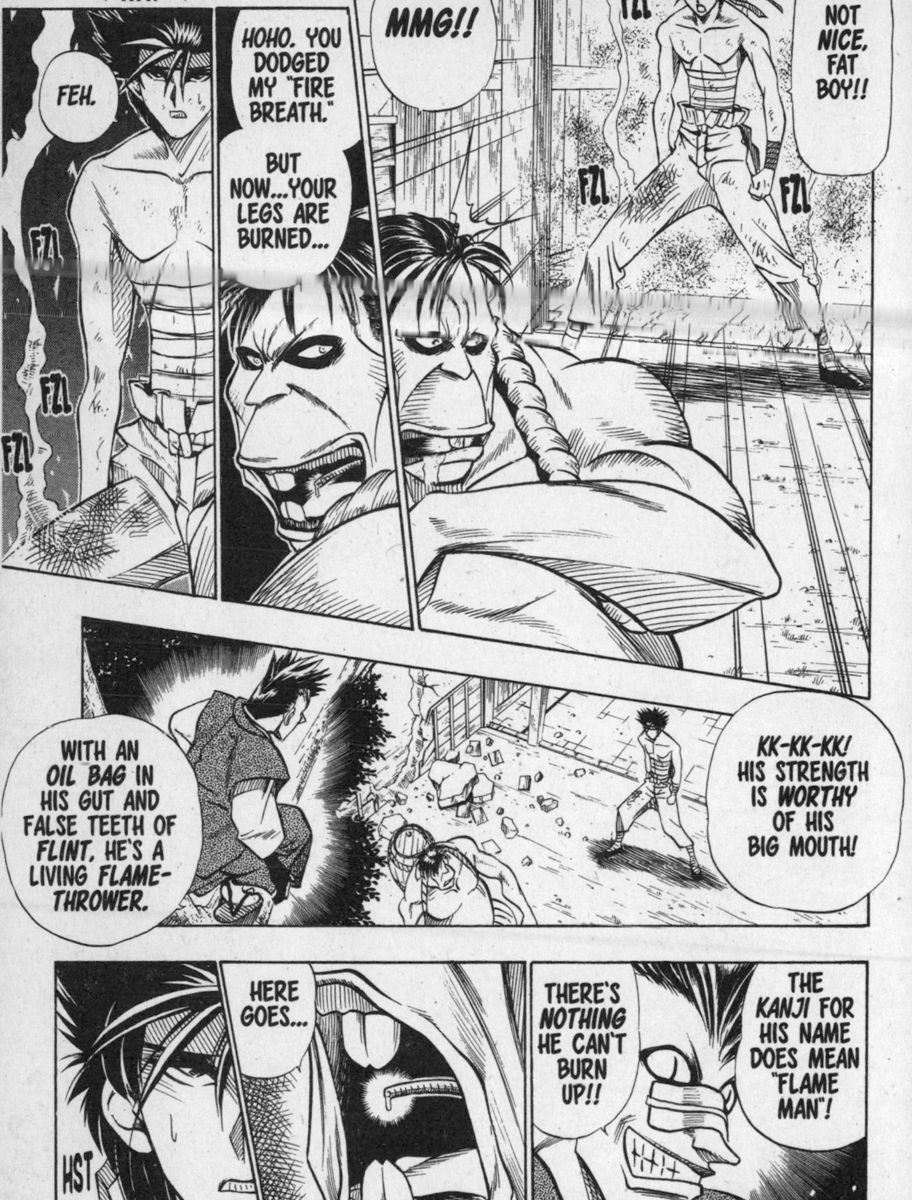
FZL
FZL
NOT NICE, FAT BOY!!
FZL
FZL
MMG!!
HOHO. YOU DODGED MY "FIRE BREATH."
BUT NOW...YOUR LEGS ARE BURNED...
FEH.
FZL
FZL
FZL
KK-KK-KK! HIS STRENGTH IS WORTHY OF HIS BIG MOUTH!
WITH AN OIL BAG IN HIS GUT AND FALSE TEETH OF FLINT, HE'S A LIVING FLAME-THROWER.
THE KANJI FOR HIS NAME DOES MEAN "FLAME MAN"!
THERE'S NOTHING HE CAN'T BURN UP!!
HERE GOES...
HST

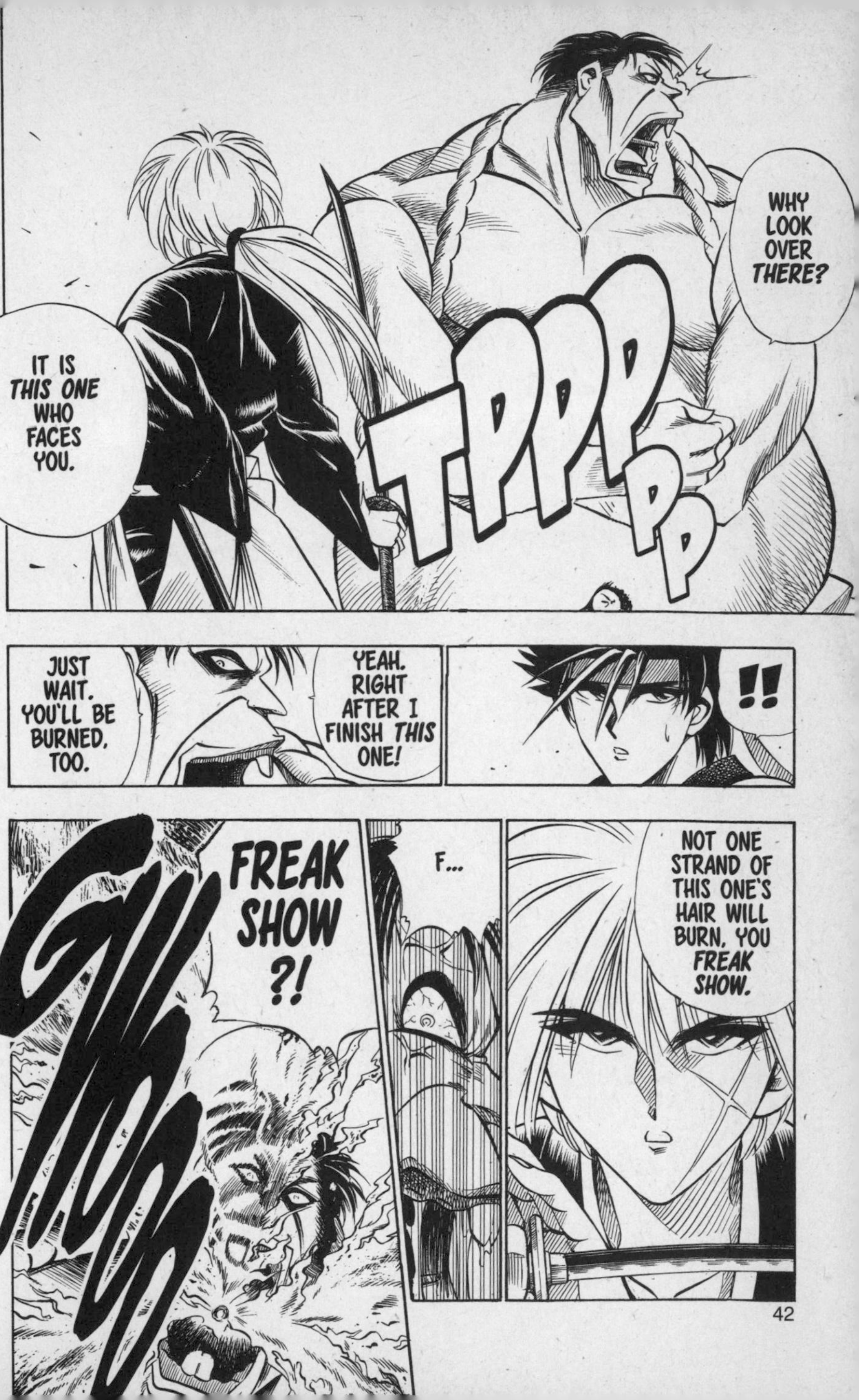
WHY LOOK OVER THERE?
IT IS THIS ONE WHO FACES YOU.
TPPP PP
!!
JUST WAIT. YOU'LL BE BURNED, TOO.
YEAH. RIGHT AFTER I FINISH THIS ONE!
NOT ONE STRAND OF THIS ONE'S HAIR WILL BURN, YOU FREAK SHOW.
F...
FREAK SHOW?!

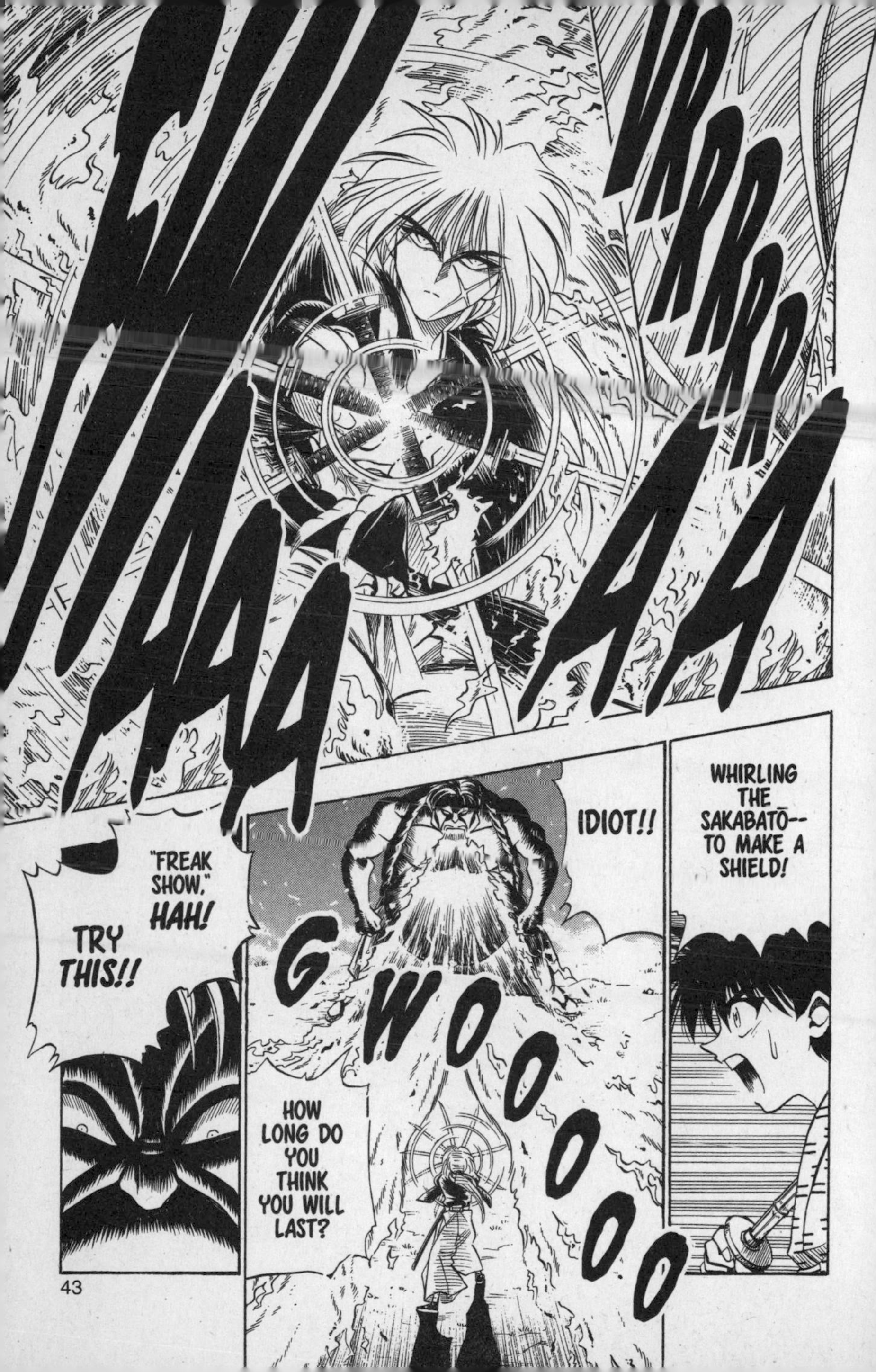
WHIRLING THE SAKABATŌ-- TO MAKE A SHIELD!
IDIOT!!
GWOOOOOOO
HOW LONG DO YOU THINK YOU WILL LAST?
"FREAK SHOW," HAH!
TRY THIS!!

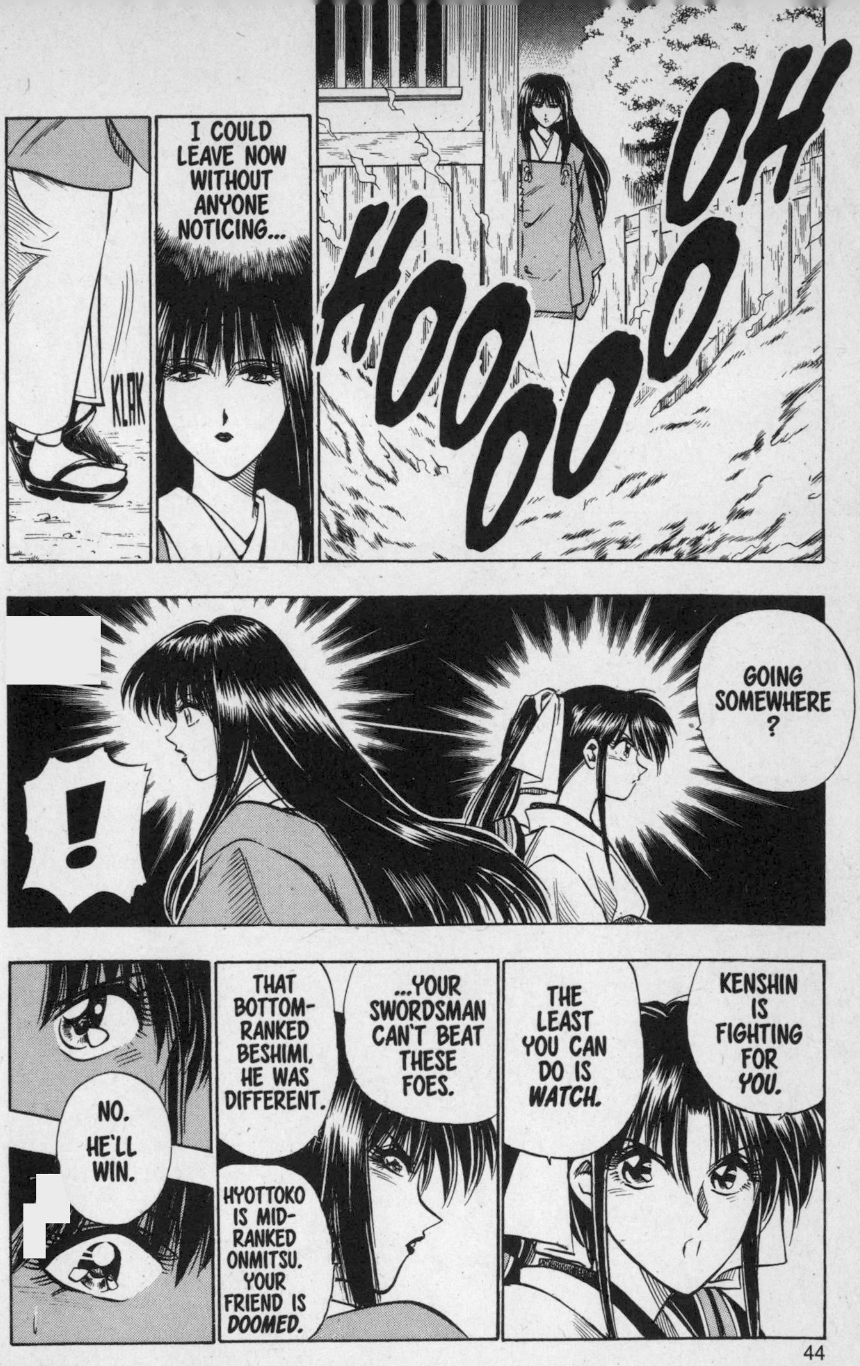
HOOOOOOOH
I COULD LEAVE NOW WITHOUT ANYONE NOTICING...
KLAK
GOING SOMEWHERE?
!
KENSHIN IS FIGHTING FOR *YOU.*
THE LEAST YOU CAN DO IS *WATCH.*
...YOUR SWORDSMAN CAN'T BEAT THESE FOES.
THAT BOTTOM-RANKED BESHIMI, HE WAS DIFFERENT.
HYOTTOKO IS MID-RANKED ONMITSU. YOUR FRIEND IS *DOOMED.*
NO. HE'LL WIN.

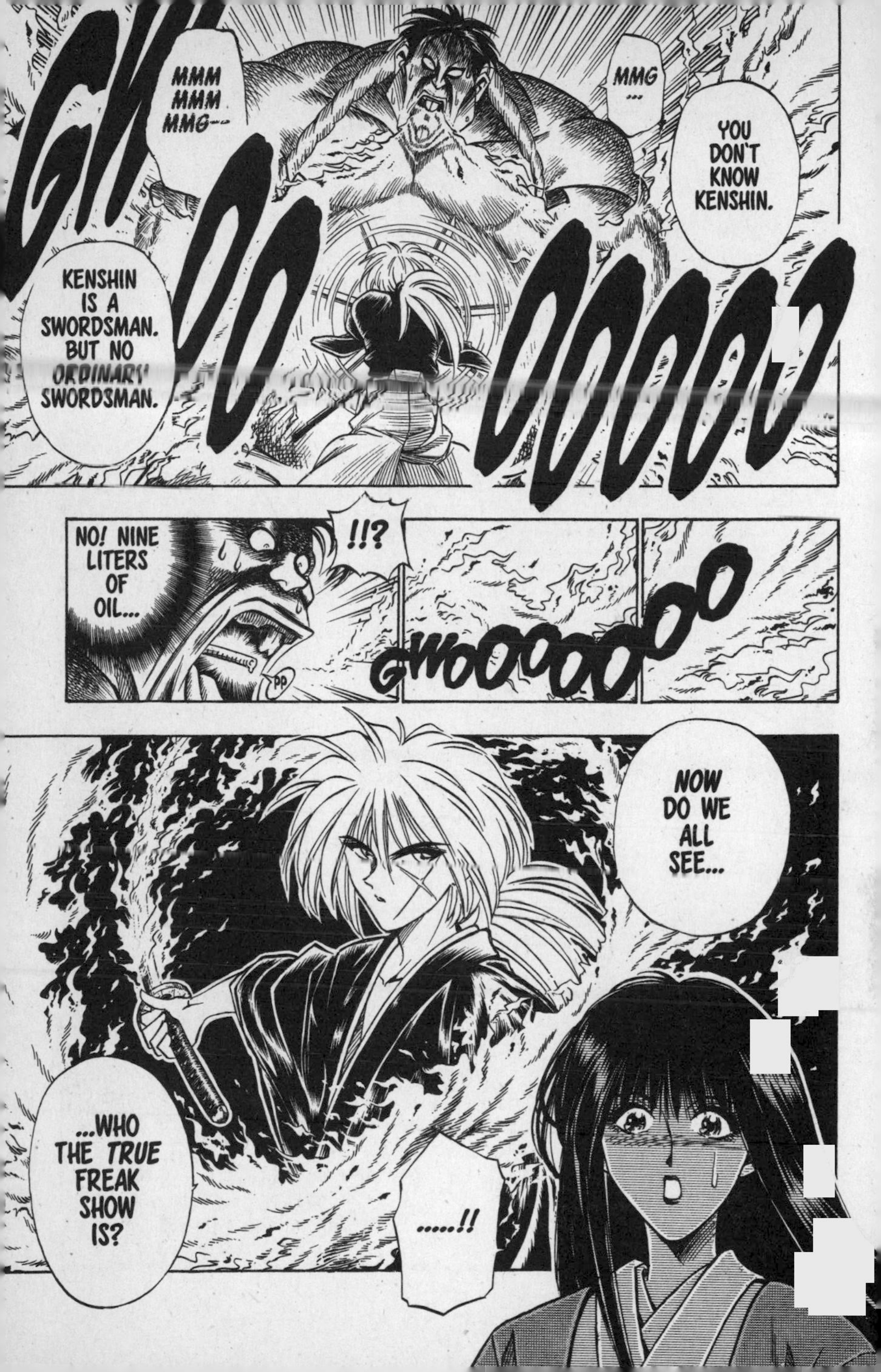
MMG ...
YOU DON'T KNOW KENSHIN.
MMM MMM MMG--
KENSHIN IS A SWORDSMAN. BUT NO ORDINARY SWORDSMAN.
!!?
NO! NINE LITERS OF OIL...
NOW DO WE ALL SEE...
...WHO THE TRUE FREAK SHOW IS?
......!!

READ THIS WAY

The Secret Life of Characters (9)
—Oniwabanshū • Hyottoko—

No motif here, either. Drawing upon my rudimentary kanji knowledge for the name (Hyottoko=fire+man), I eventually got a character who was, what do you know! A fire-breather.

Since he's an onmitsu (a ninja, in other words, although when you just write it like that, "ninja," it seems so cheesy, which is why it's onmitsu), I figured it was only natural for him to be a little flashy. In that sense, the fire-breathing didn't seem so bad. Looking back now, though, he does seem a bit out of place, not really organic to the world he's in. Personality-wise, he's the guy who makes a big entrance and then gets just as spectacularly beaten—ridiculously overconfident and a bit of an idiot. Natural evolution of the character, I guess.

As for the matter of the fire-breathing and its defeat by Kenshin with the sword-spinning technique, know that I've been roundly criticized by fans, dōjinshi "fanzine" creators, and even personal friends for it. "They're both circus-freaks!" they exclaimed, leaving me with a bit of puzzled sadness. (In my defense, I was in the grip of summer doldrums at the time—not much of an excuse, but there you go. Forgive me.)

As mentioned earlier, what I'd wanted for the Oniwabanshū was an assortment of shapes and temperaments. What with there being an oil bag in his stomach, it figured that he'd be extremely fat. Never having drawn such a figure before, though, it was only after quite a while and several versions that I came up with something I could draw not only comfortably, but repeatedly. How cool was it to know that, once I got used to it, it actually came pretty easily.

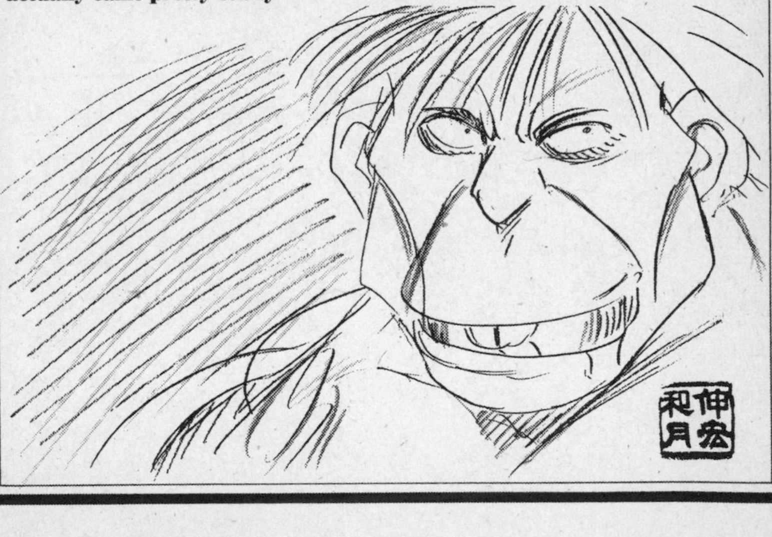
伸宏
和月

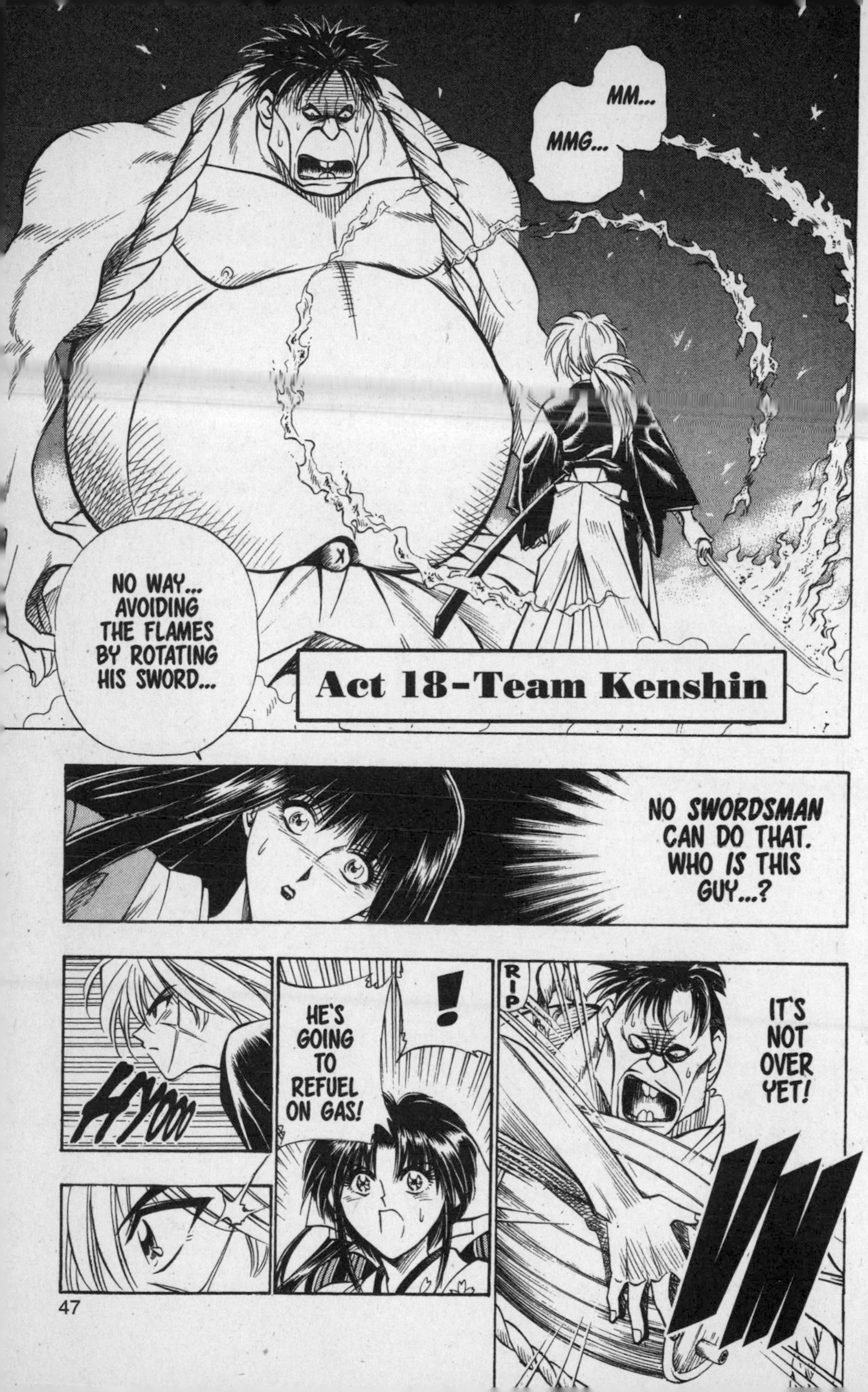
MM... MMG...
NO WAY... AVOIDING THE FLAMES BY ROTATING HIS SWORD...
Act 18-Team Kenshin
NO SWORDSMAN CAN DO THAT. WHO IS THIS GUY...?
RIP
IT'S NOT OVER YET!
!
HE'S GOING TO REFUEL ON GAS!
HYOOO

READ THIS WAY

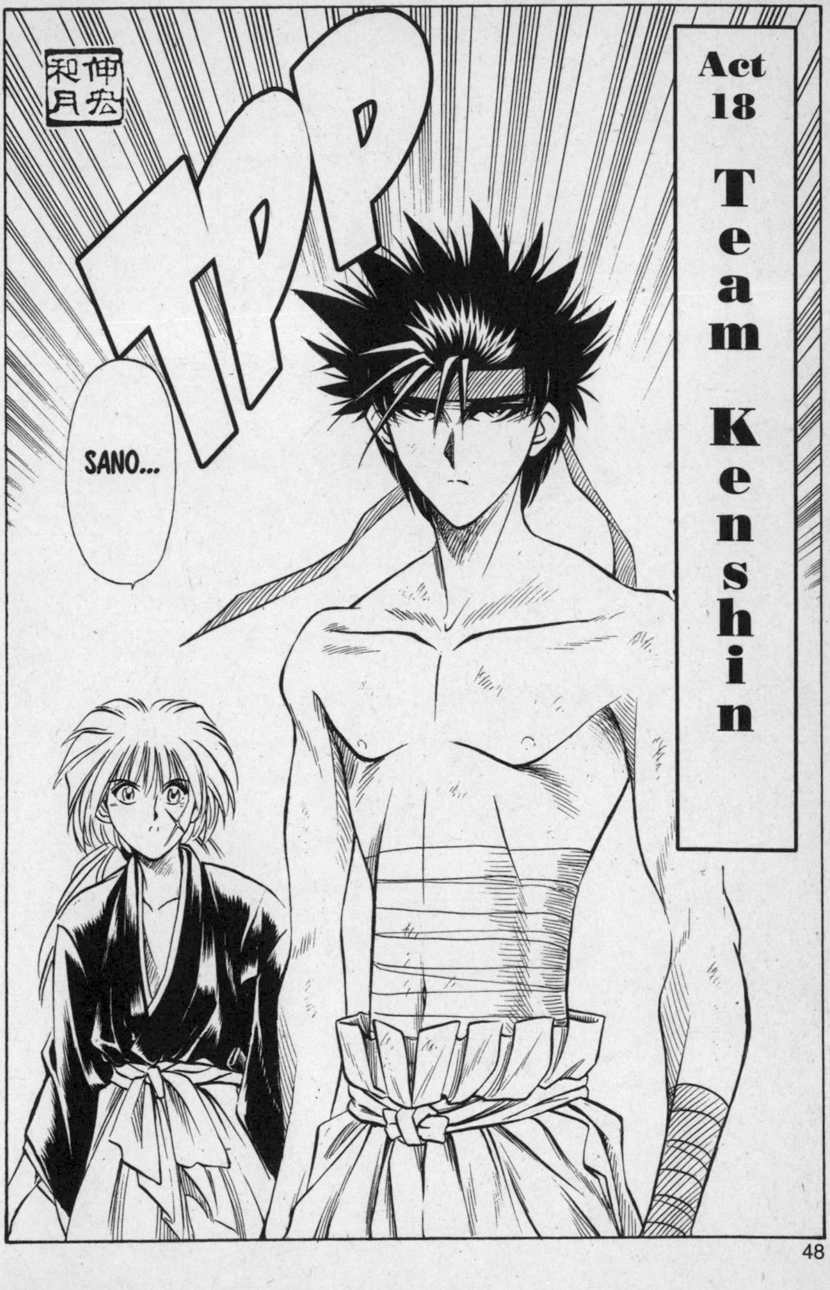
Act 18
Team Kenshin
TAP
伸宏和月
SANO...

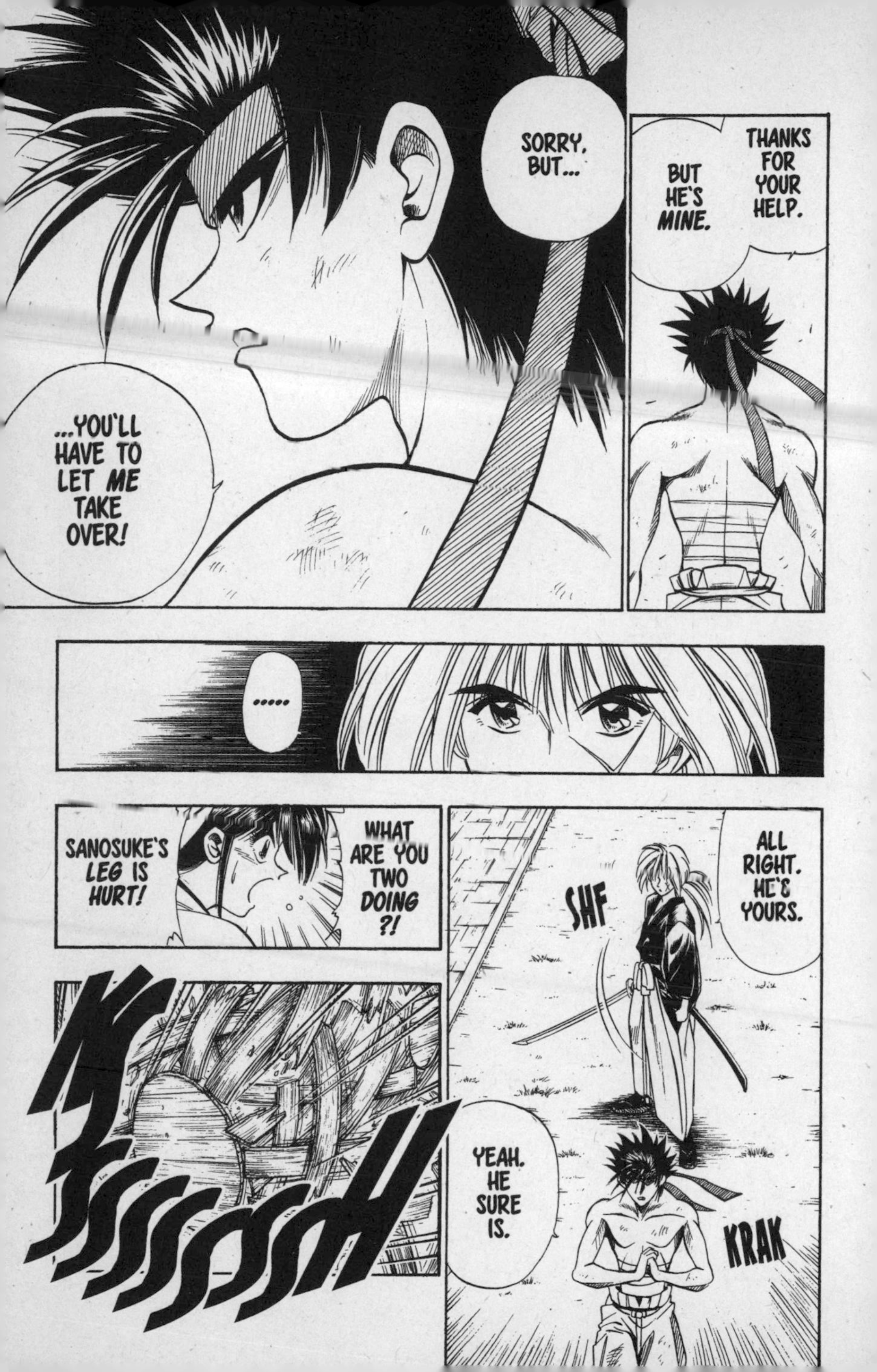
THANKS FOR YOUR HELP.
BUT HE'S *MINE.*
SORRY, BUT...
...YOU'LL HAVE TO LET *ME* TAKE OVER!
......
ALL RIGHT. HE'S YOURS.
SHF
YEAH. HE SURE IS.
KRAK
WHAT ARE YOU TWO *DOING* ?!
SANOSUKE'S *LEG* IS *HURT!*
KSSSSSH

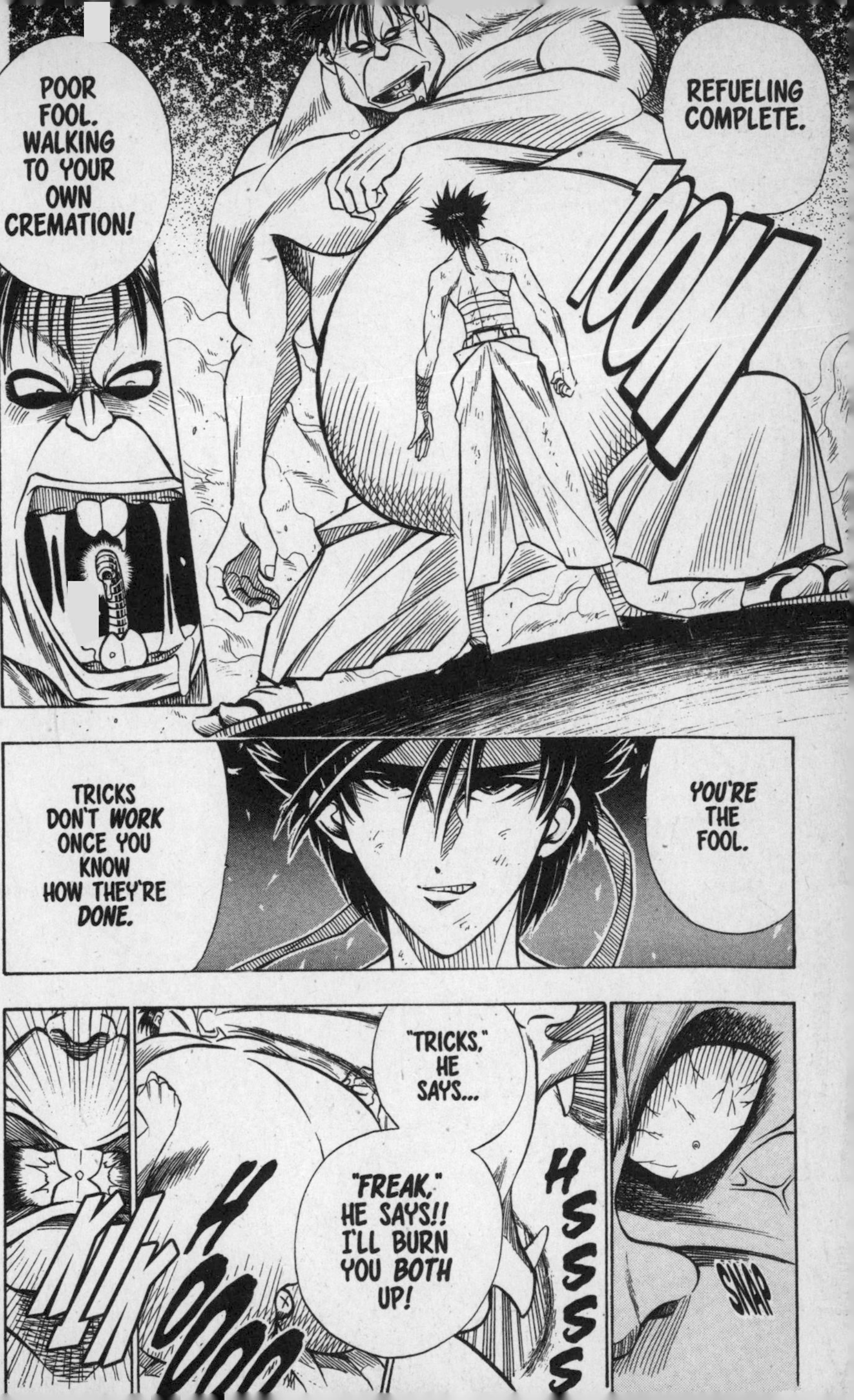
REFUELING COMPLETE.
TOOM
POOR FOOL. WALKING TO YOUR OWN CREMATION!
YOU'RE THE FOOL.
TRICKS DON'T WORK ONCE YOU KNOW HOW THEY'RE DONE.
SNAP
HSSSS
"TRICKS," HE SAYS...
"FREAK," HE SAYS!! I'LL BURN YOU BOTH UP!

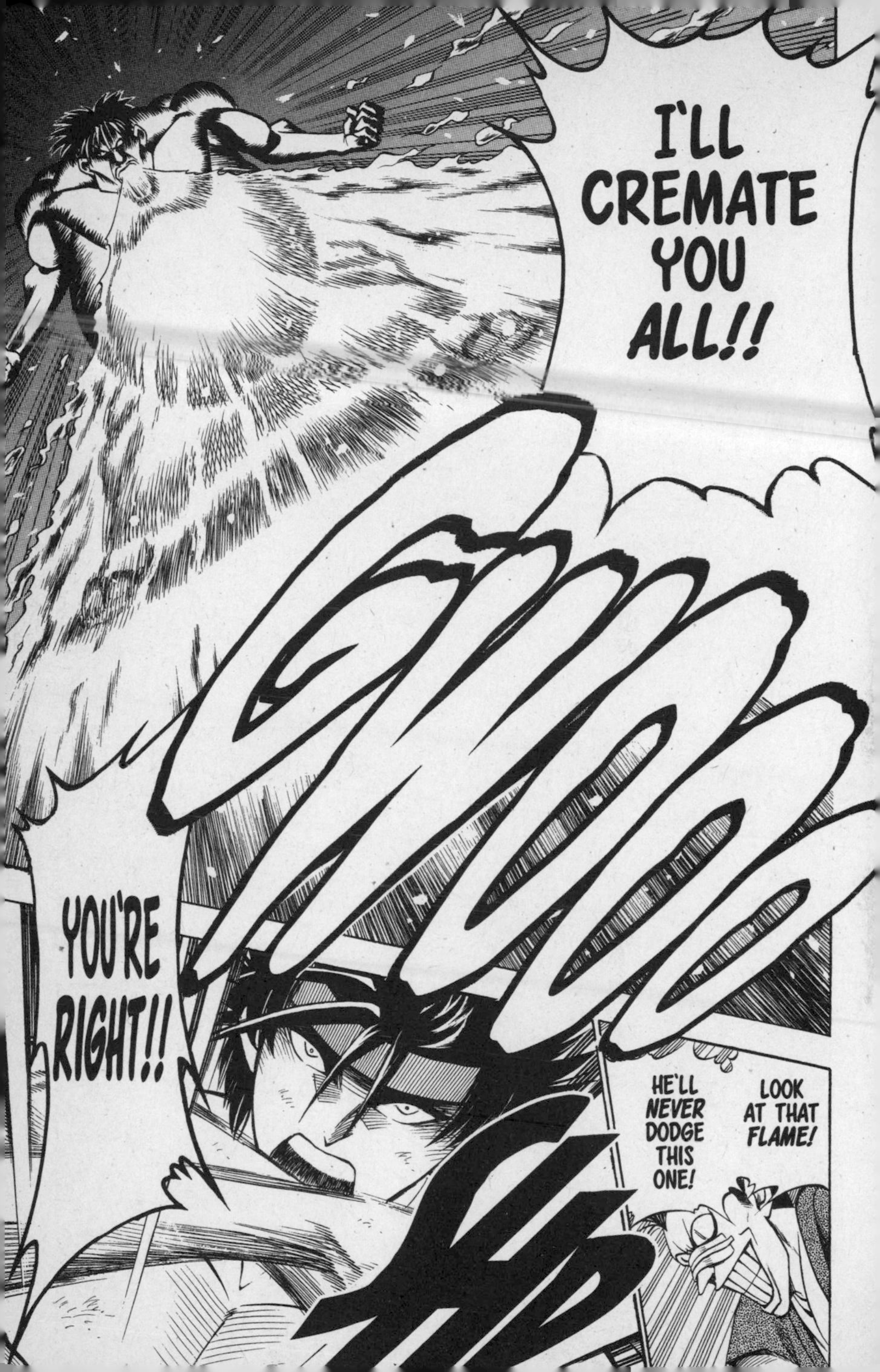
I'LL CREMATE YOU ALL!!
LOOK AT THAT FLAME!
HE'LL NEVER DODGE THIS ONE!
YOU'RE RIGHT!!

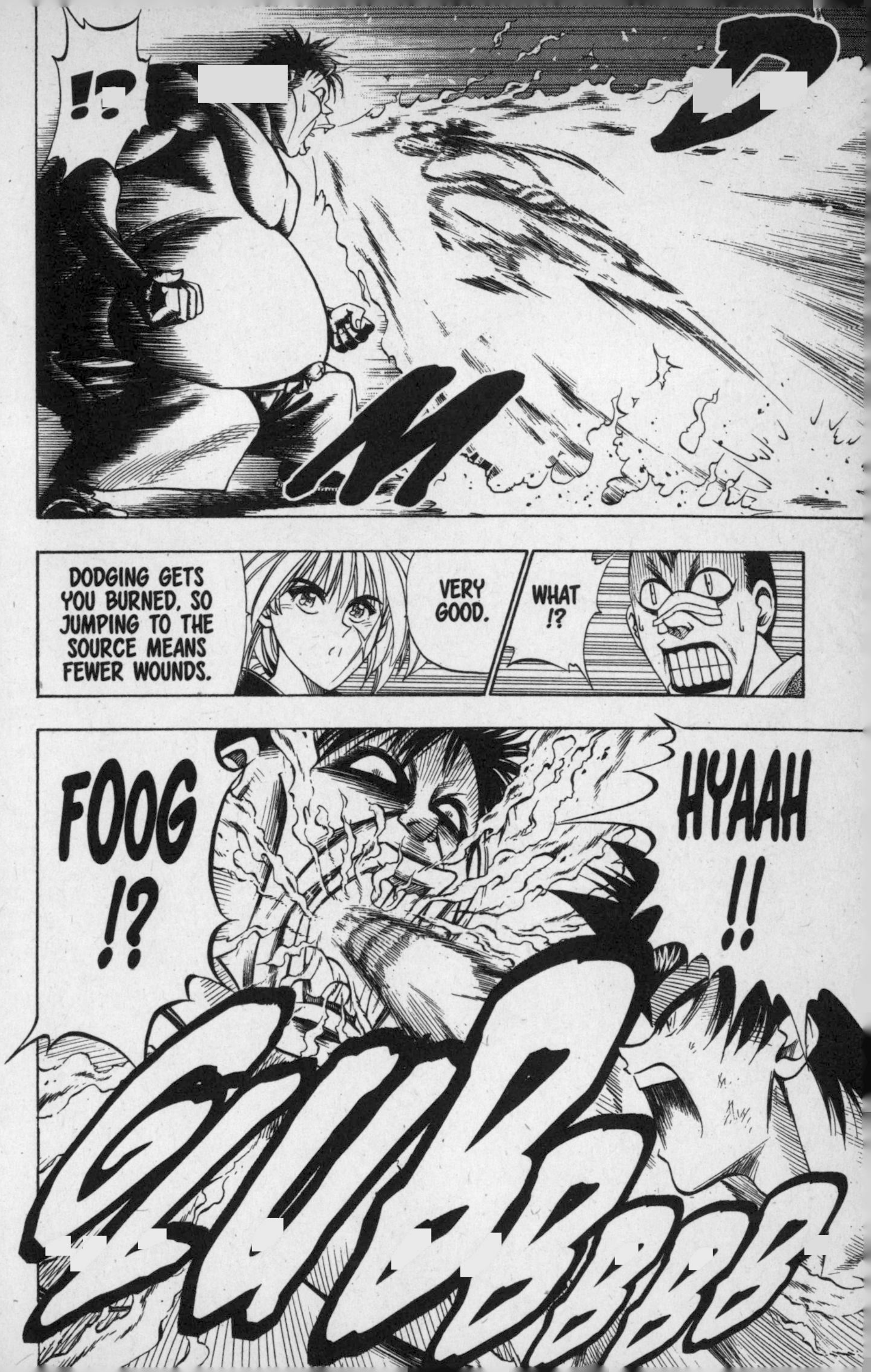
!?
WHAT !?
VERY GOOD.
DODGING GETS YOU BURNED, SO JUMPING TO THE SOURCE MEANS FEWER WOUNDS.
HYAAH !!
FOOG !?

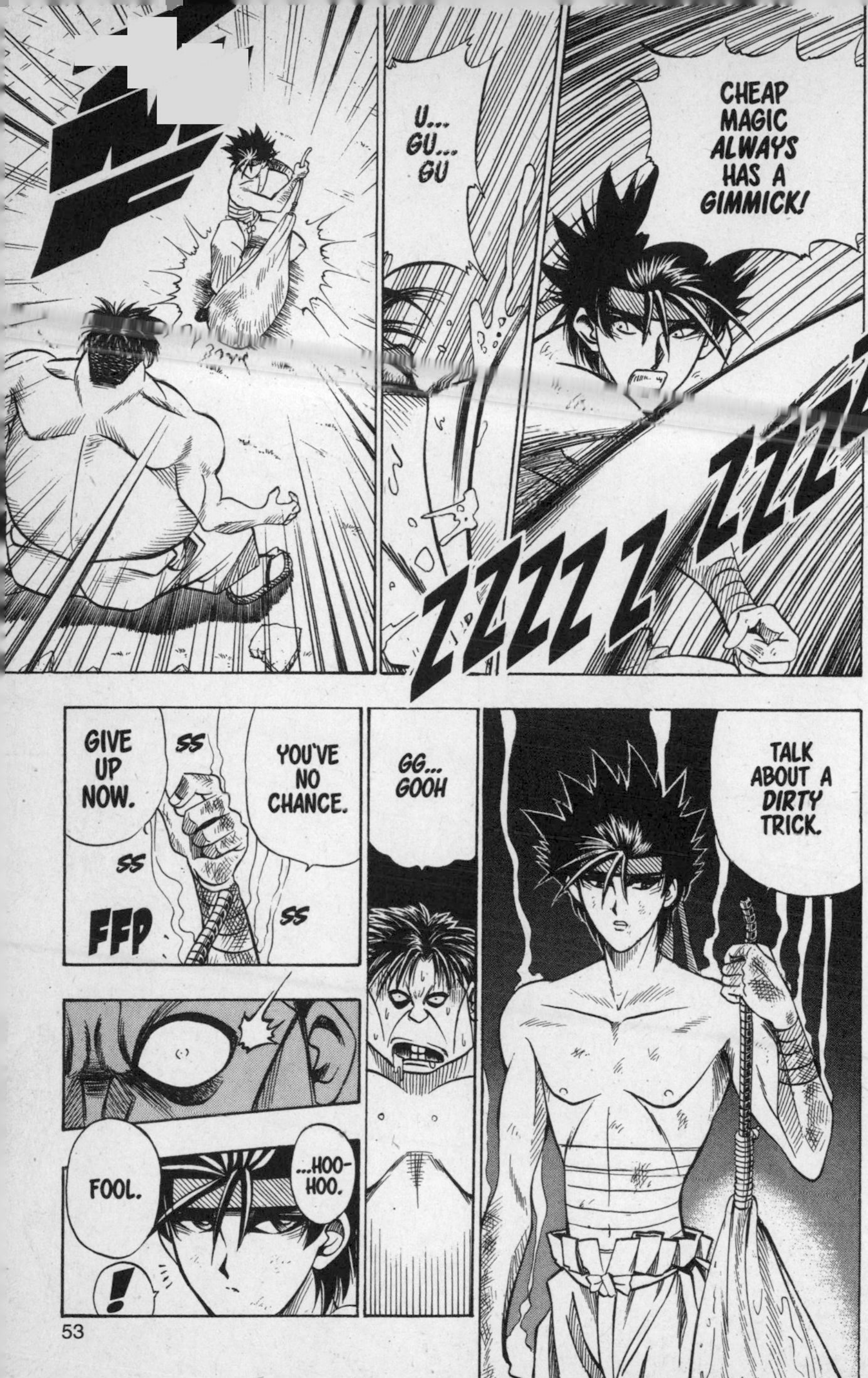
CHEAP MAGIC ALWAYS HAS A GIMMICK!
ZZZZZ ZZZZZ
U... GU... GU
TALK ABOUT A DIRTY TRICK.
GG... GOOH
YOU'VE NO CHANCE.
GIVE UP NOW.
SS
SS
SS
FFP
...HOO-HOO.
FOOL.
!

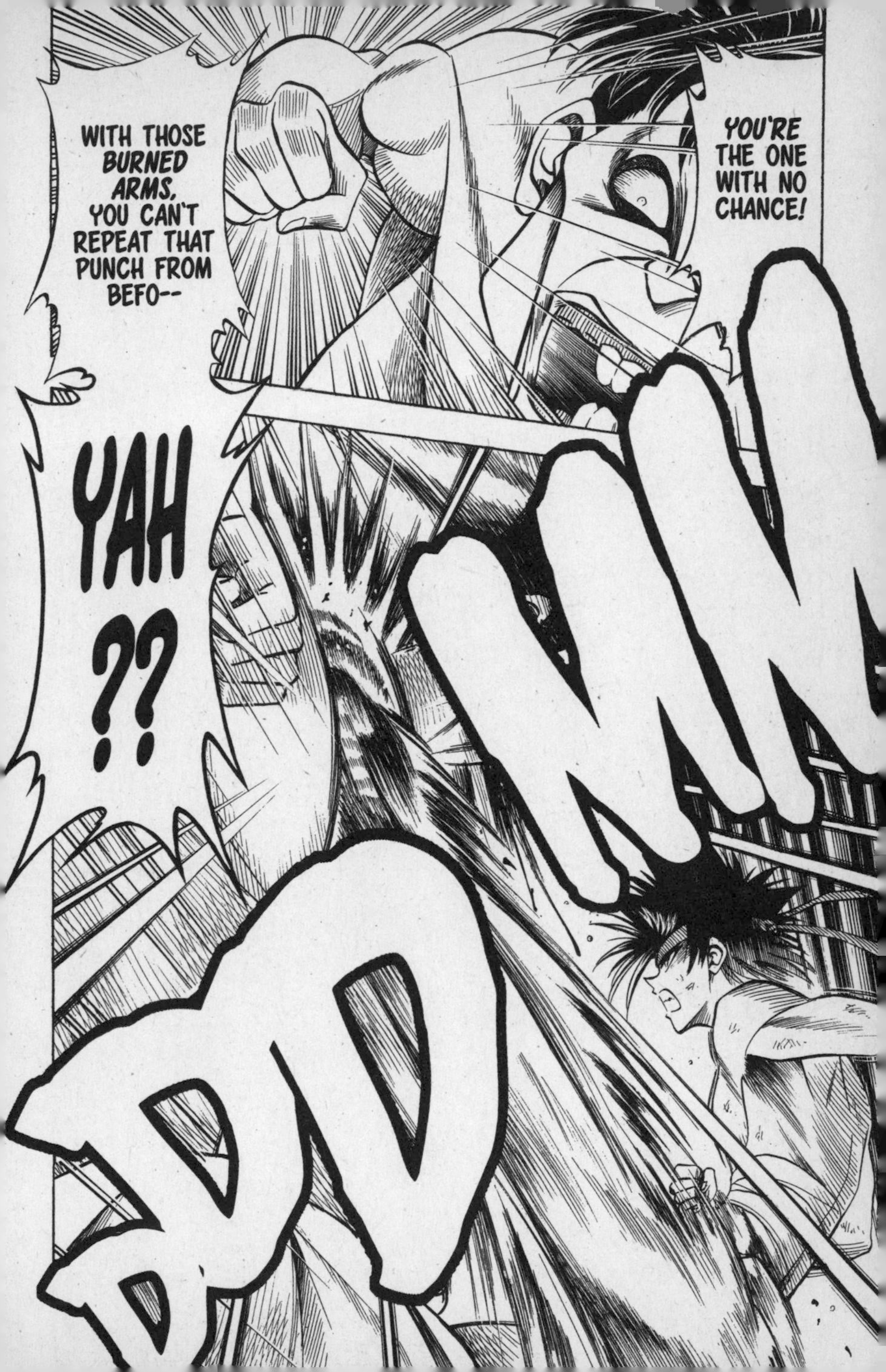
YOU'RE THE ONE WITH NO CHANCE!
WITH THOSE BURNED ARMS, YOU CAN'T REPEAT THAT PUNCH FROM BEFO--
YAH ??
BOOM

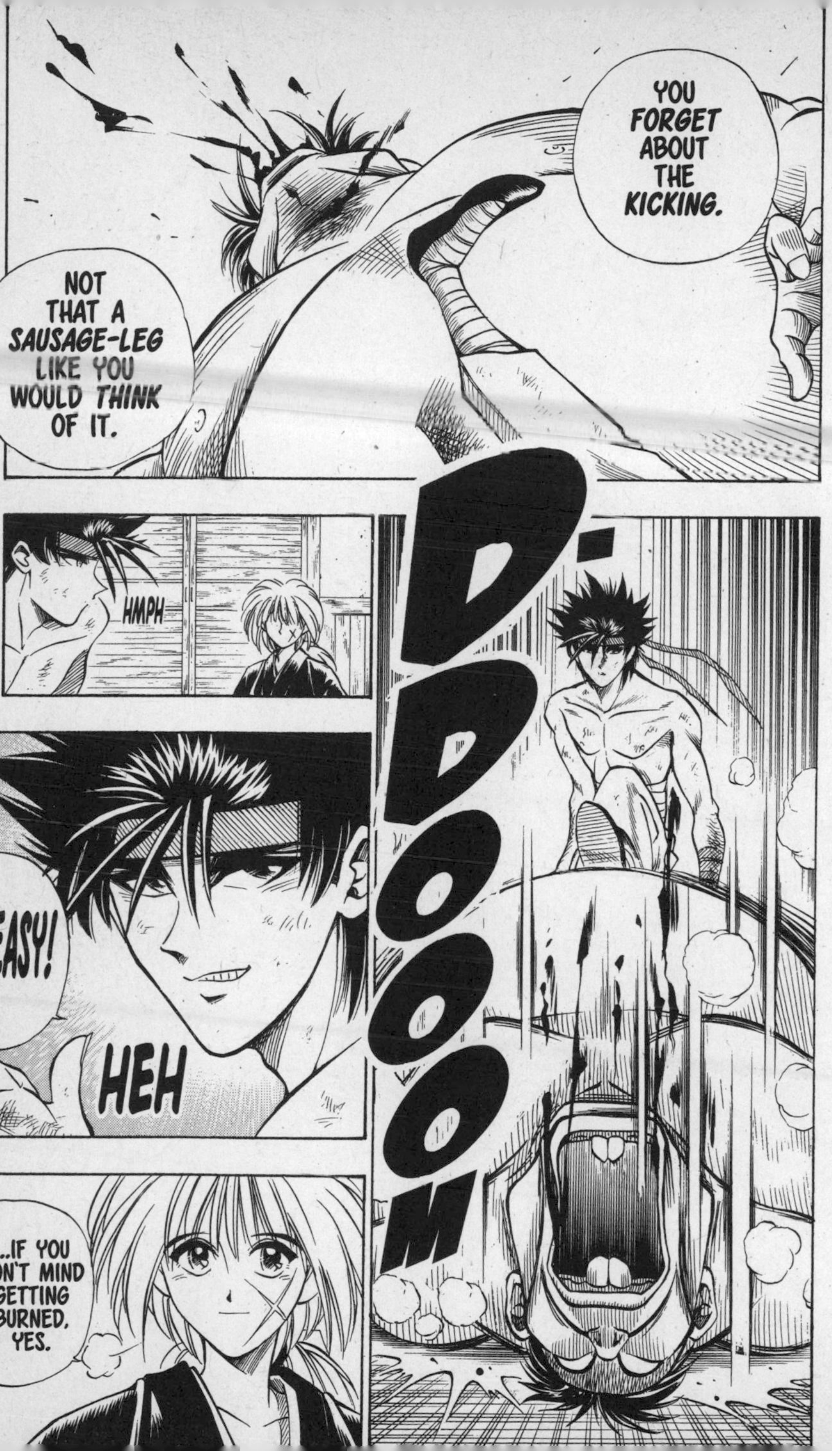
YOU FORGET ABOUT THE KICKING.
NOT THAT A SAUSAGE-LEG LIKE YOU WOULD THINK OF IT.
D-DOOOM
HMPH
EASY!
HEH
...IF YOU DON'T MIND GETTING BURNED, YES.

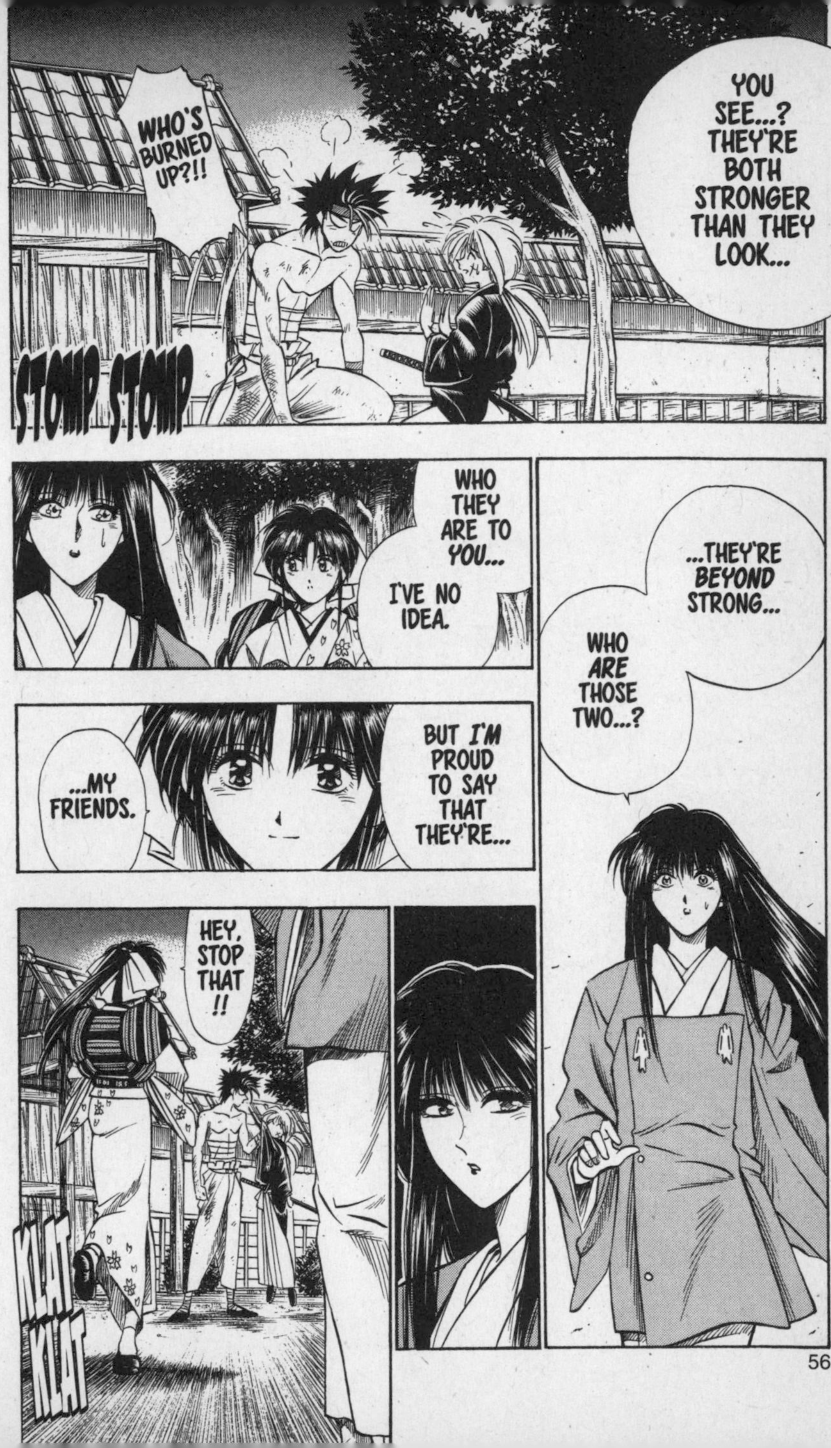
YOU SEE...? THEY'RE BOTH STRONGER THAN THEY LOOK...
WHO'S BURNED UP?!!
STOMP STOMP
...THEY'RE BEYOND STRONG...
WHO ARE THOSE TWO...?
WHO THEY ARE TO YOU...
I'VE NO IDEA.
BUT I'M PROUD TO SAY THAT THEY'RE...
...MY FRIENDS.
HEY, STOP THAT !!
KLAT KLAT

READ THIS WAY

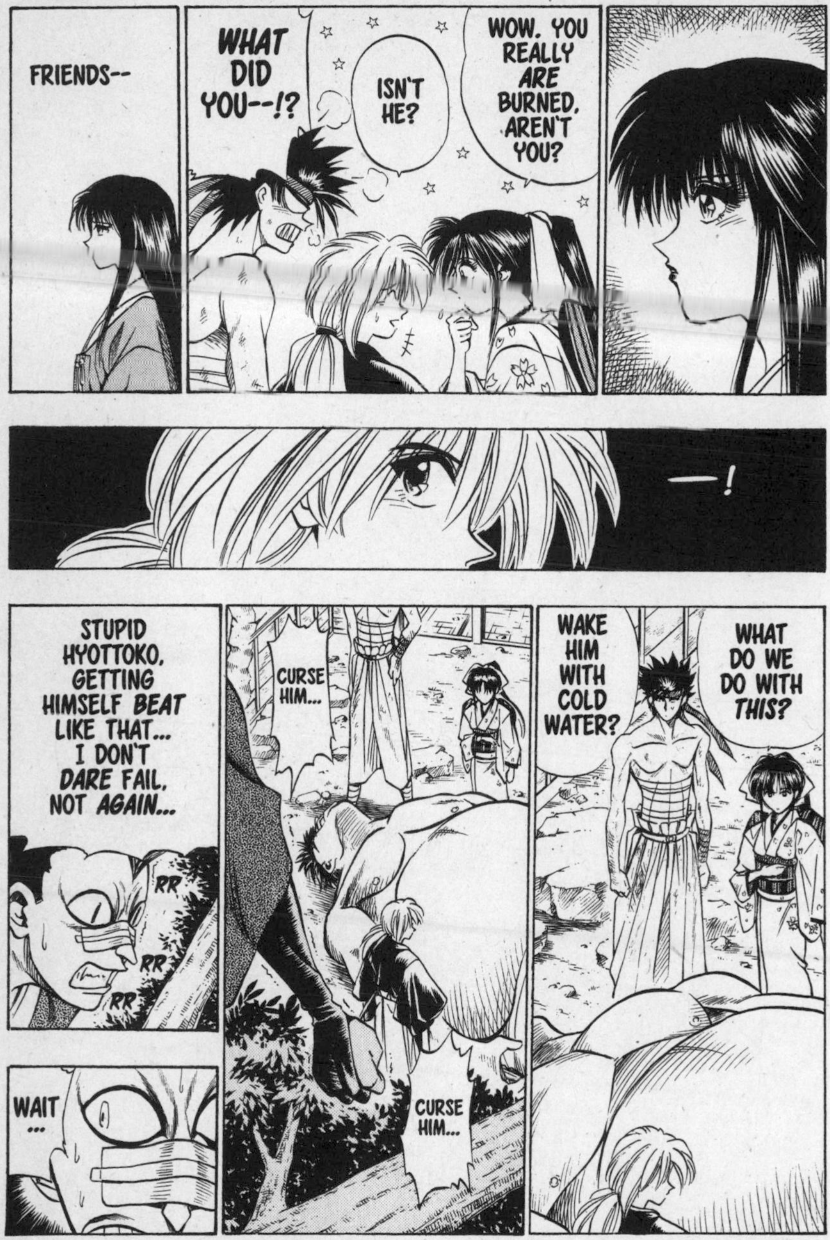
WOW. YOU REALLY ARE BURNED, AREN'T YOU?
ISN'T HE?
WHAT DID YOU--!?
FRIENDS--
—!
WHAT DO WE DO WITH THIS?
WAKE HIM WITH COLD WATER?
CURSE HIM...
CURSE HIM...
STUPID HYOTTOKO, GETTING HIMSELF BEAT LIKE THAT... I DON'T DARE FAIL, NOT AGAIN...
RR
RR
RR
WAIT...

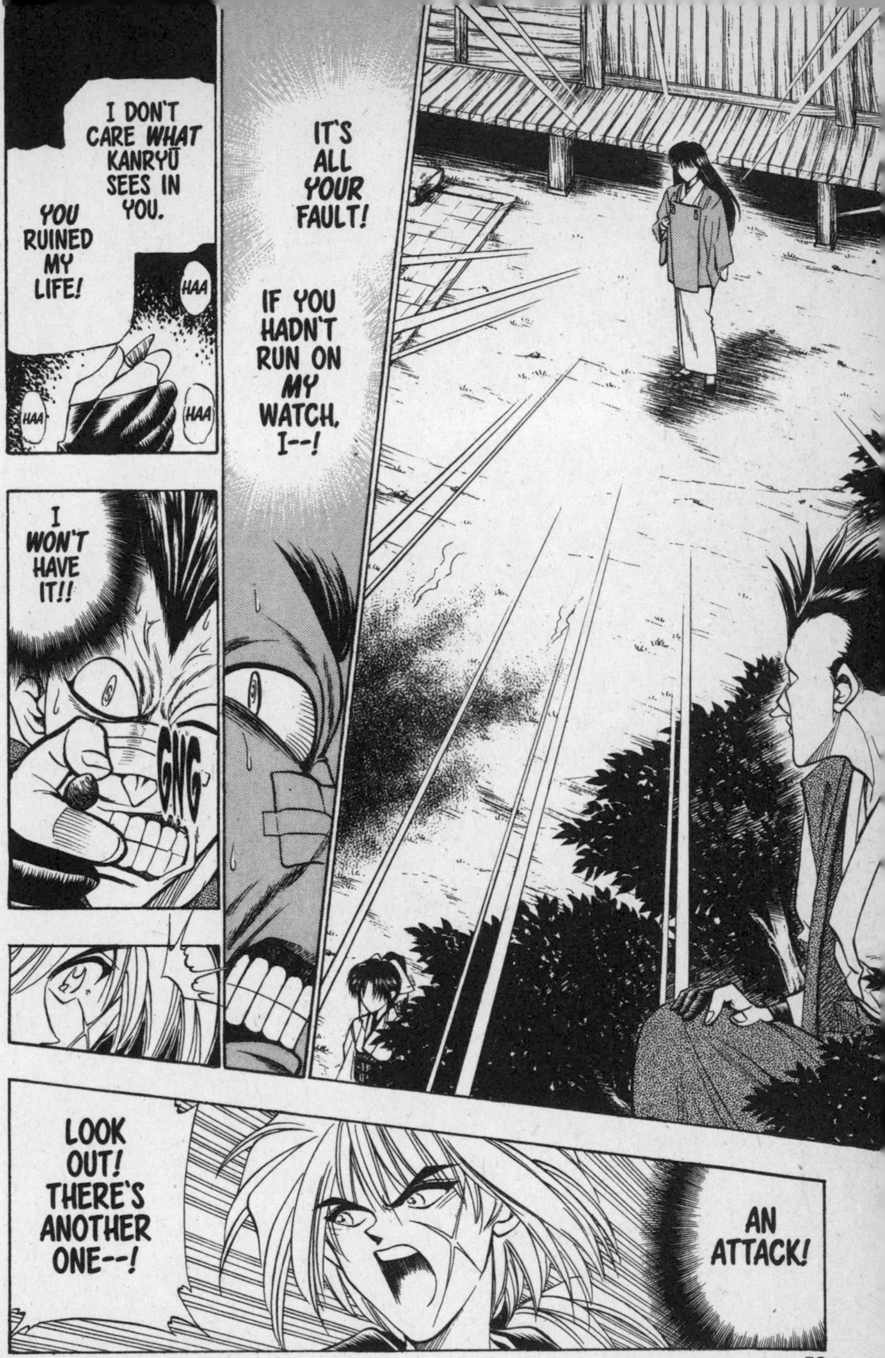
IT'S ALL *YOUR* FAULT!
IF YOU HADN'T RUN ON *MY* WATCH, I--!
I DON'T CARE *WHAT* KANRYŪ SEES IN YOU.
YOU RUINED MY LIFE!
HAA
HAA
HAA
I *WON'T* HAVE IT!!
GNG
AN ATTACK!
LOOK OUT! THERE'S ANOTHER ONE--!

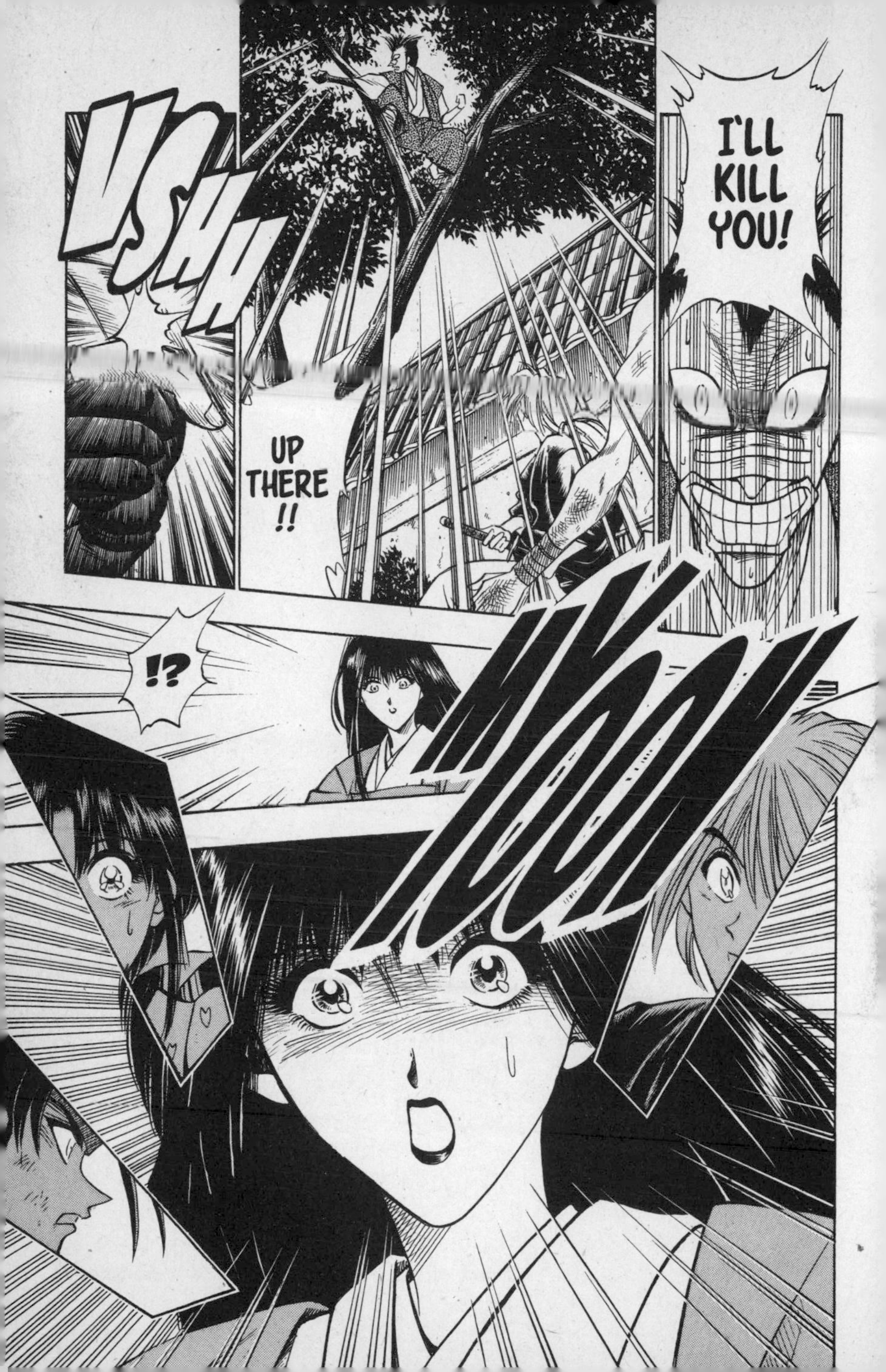
I'LL KILL YOU!
UP THERE !!
VSHH
!?

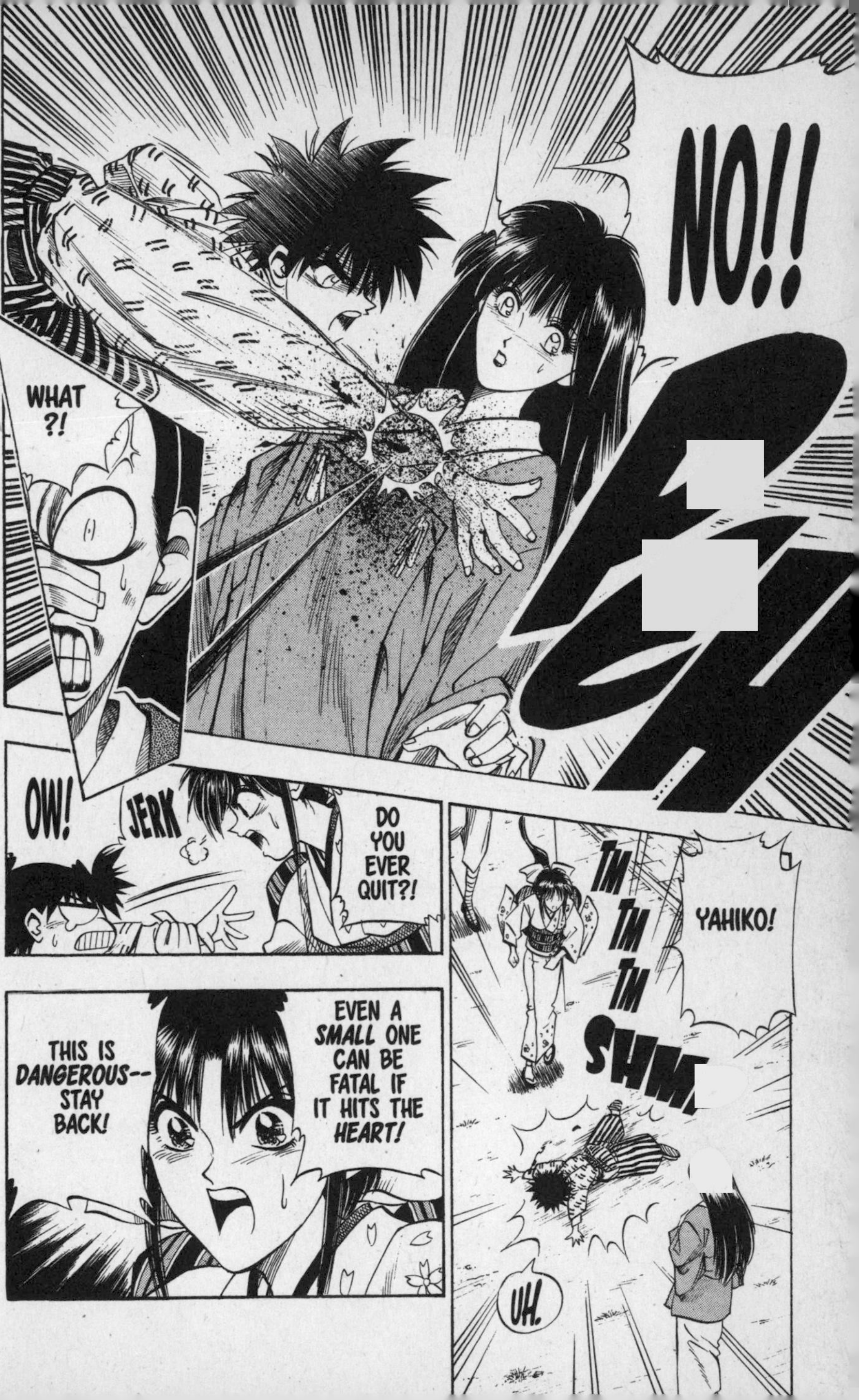
NO!!
WHAT ?!
YAHIKO!
TM TM TM
UH.
DO YOU EVER QUIT?!
JERK
OW!
EVEN A *SMALL* ONE CAN BE FATAL IF IT HITS THE *HEART*!
THIS IS DANGEROUS-- STAY BACK!

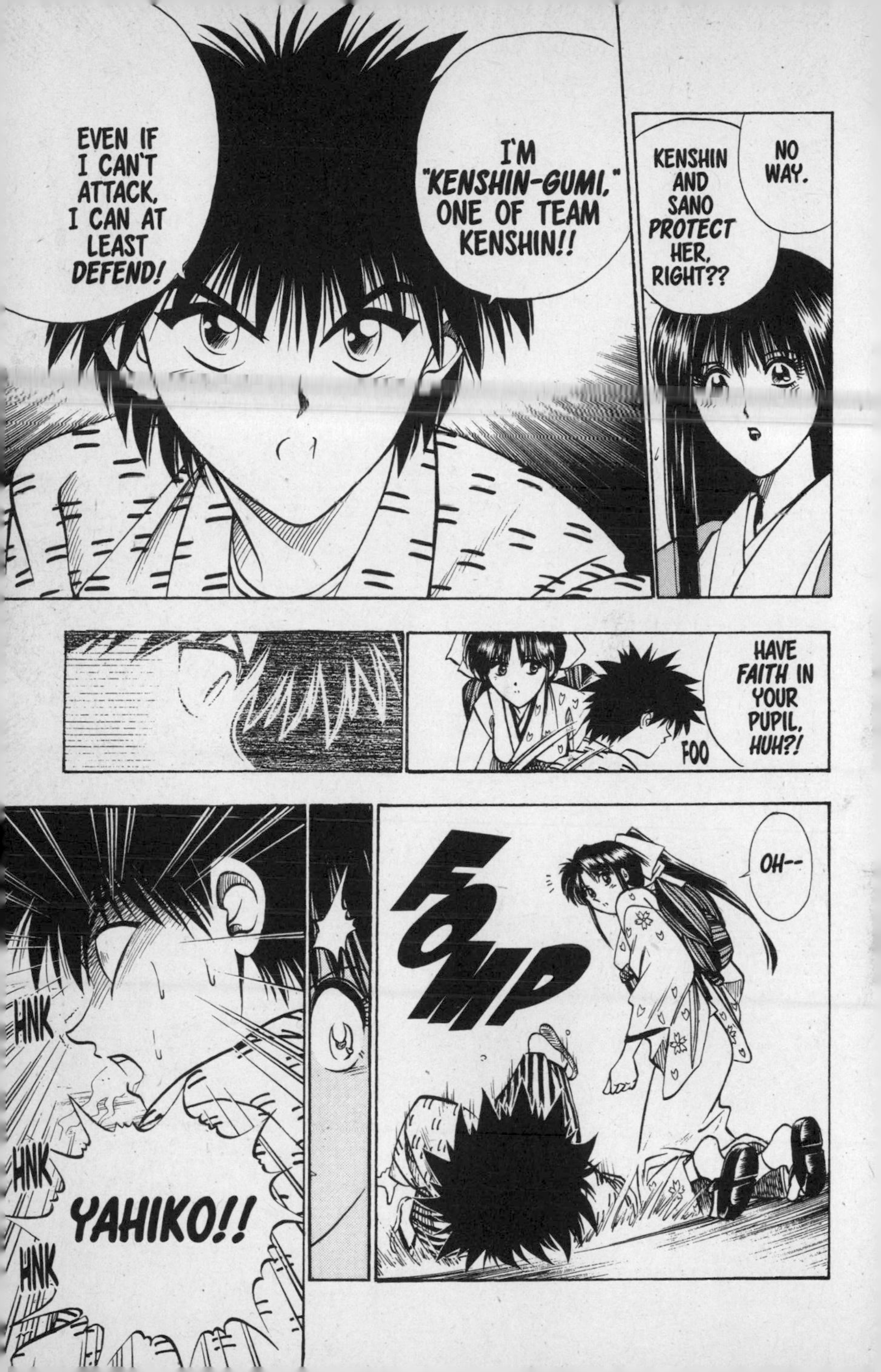
NO WAY.
KENSHIN AND SANO PROTECT HER, RIGHT??
I'M "KENSHIN-GUMI," ONE OF TEAM KENSHIN!!
EVEN IF I CAN'T ATTACK, I CAN AT LEAST DEFEND!
HAVE FAITH IN YOUR PUPIL, HUH?!
FOO
OH--
FOMP
HNK
HNK
YAHIKO!!
HNK

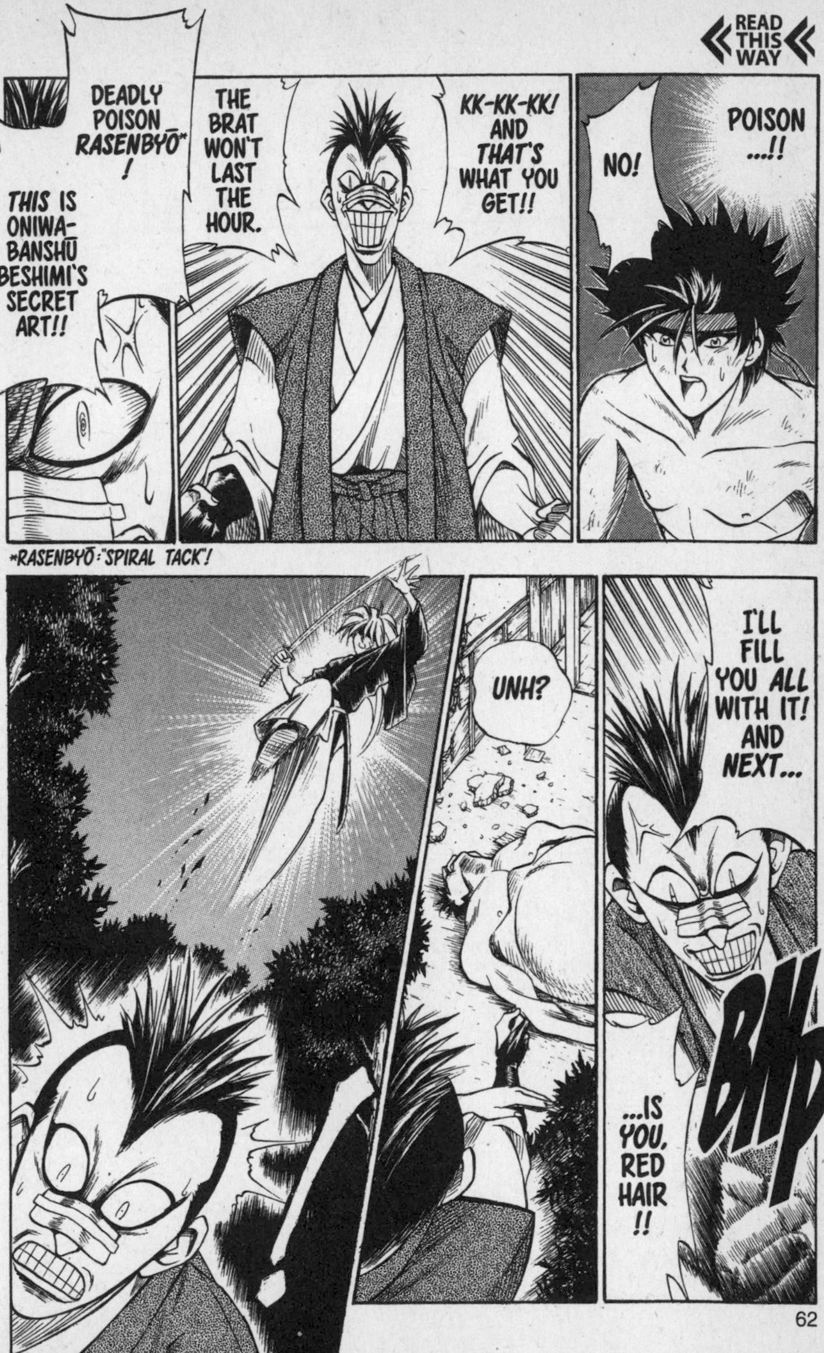
READ THIS WAY
POISON ...!!
NO!
KK-KK-KK! AND THAT'S WHAT YOU GET!!
THE BRAT WON'T LAST THE HOUR.
DEADLY POISON RASENBYŌ* !
THIS IS ONIWA-BANSHŪ BESHIMI'S SECRET ART!!
I'LL FILL YOU ALL WITH IT! AND NEXT...
...IS YOU, RED HAIR !!
BMP
UNH?

*RASENBYŌ: "SPIRAL TACK"!

READ THIS WAY

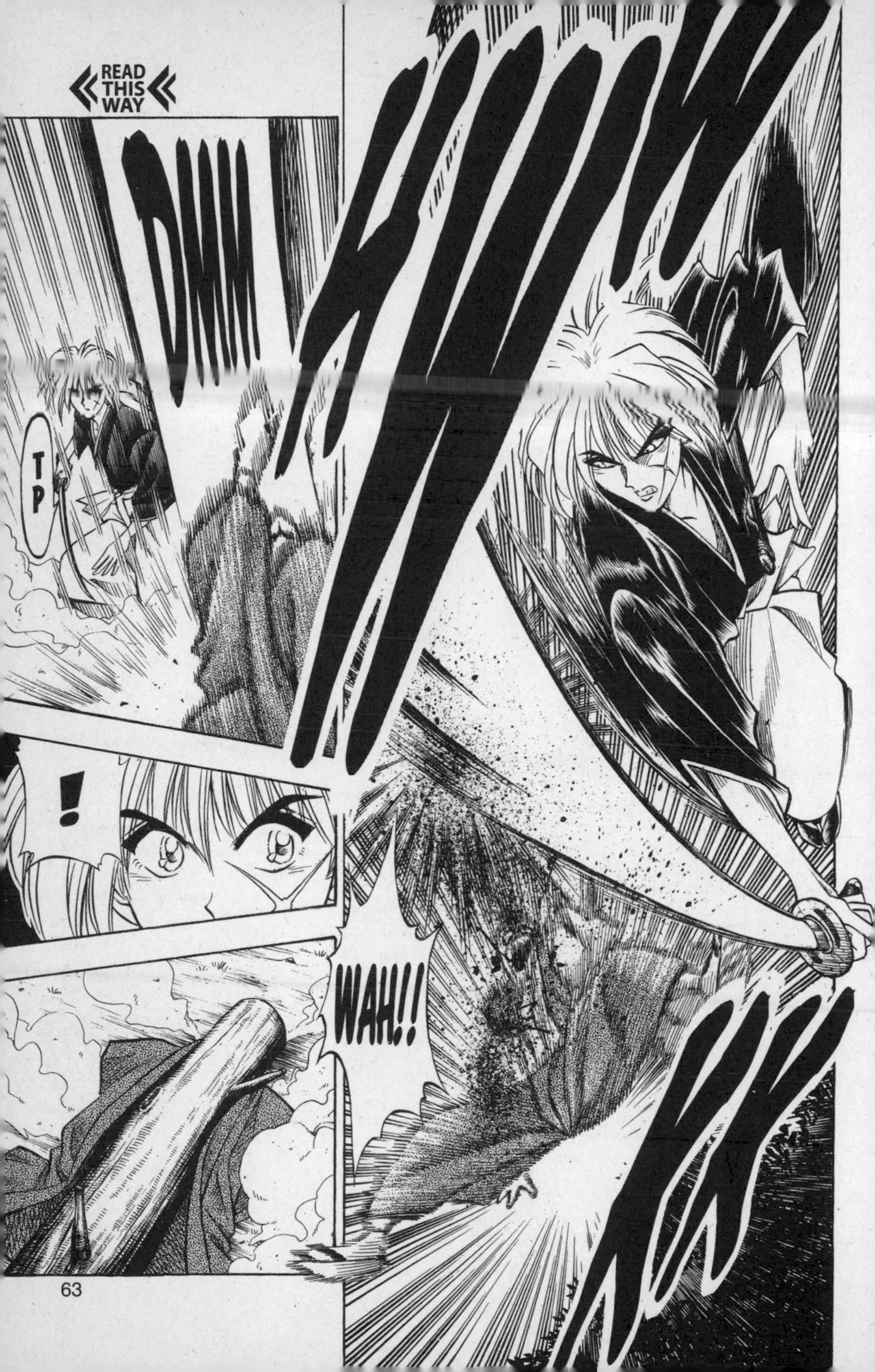
WAH!!
TP
!

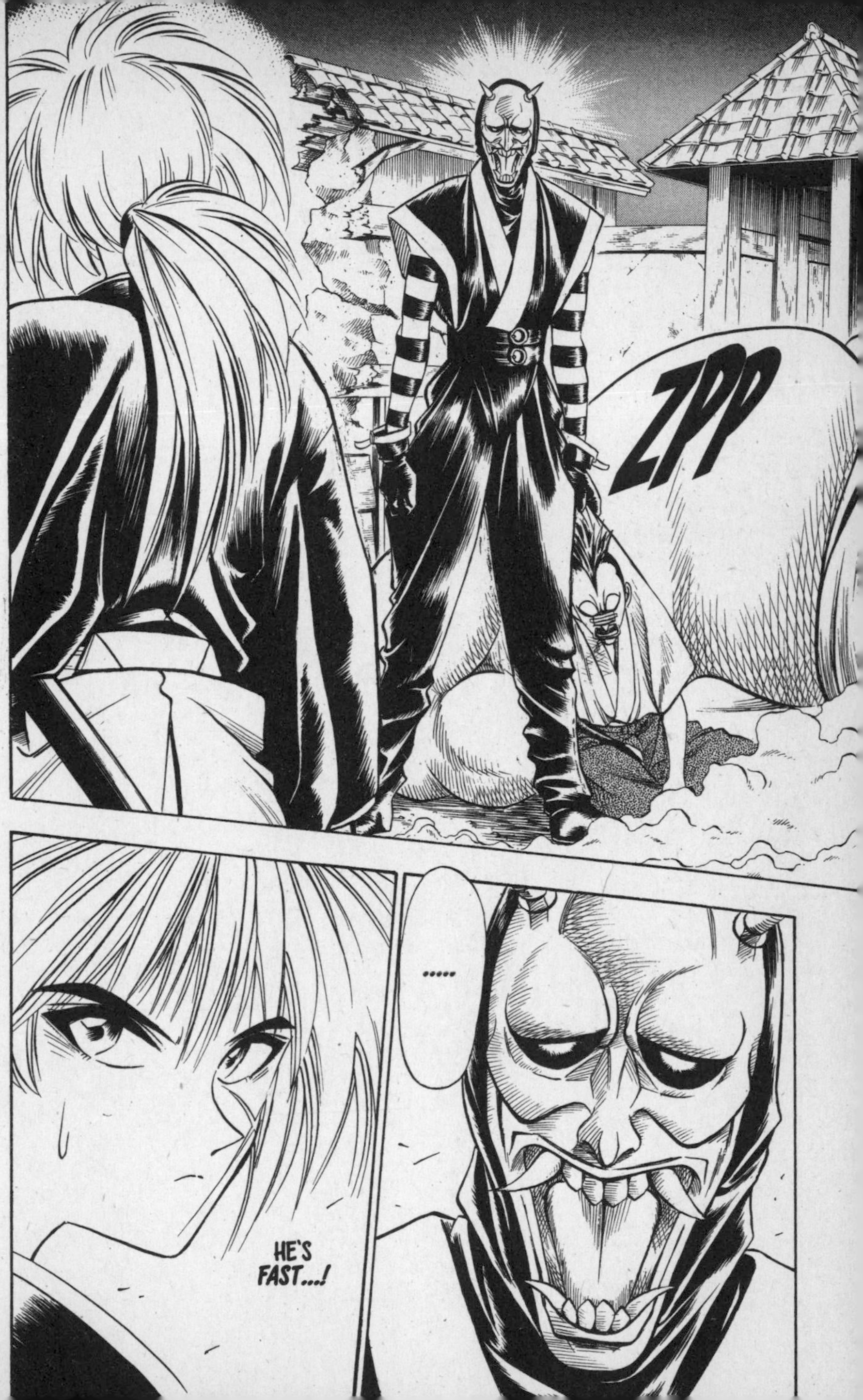
ZPP
......
HE'S FAST...!

READ THIS WAY

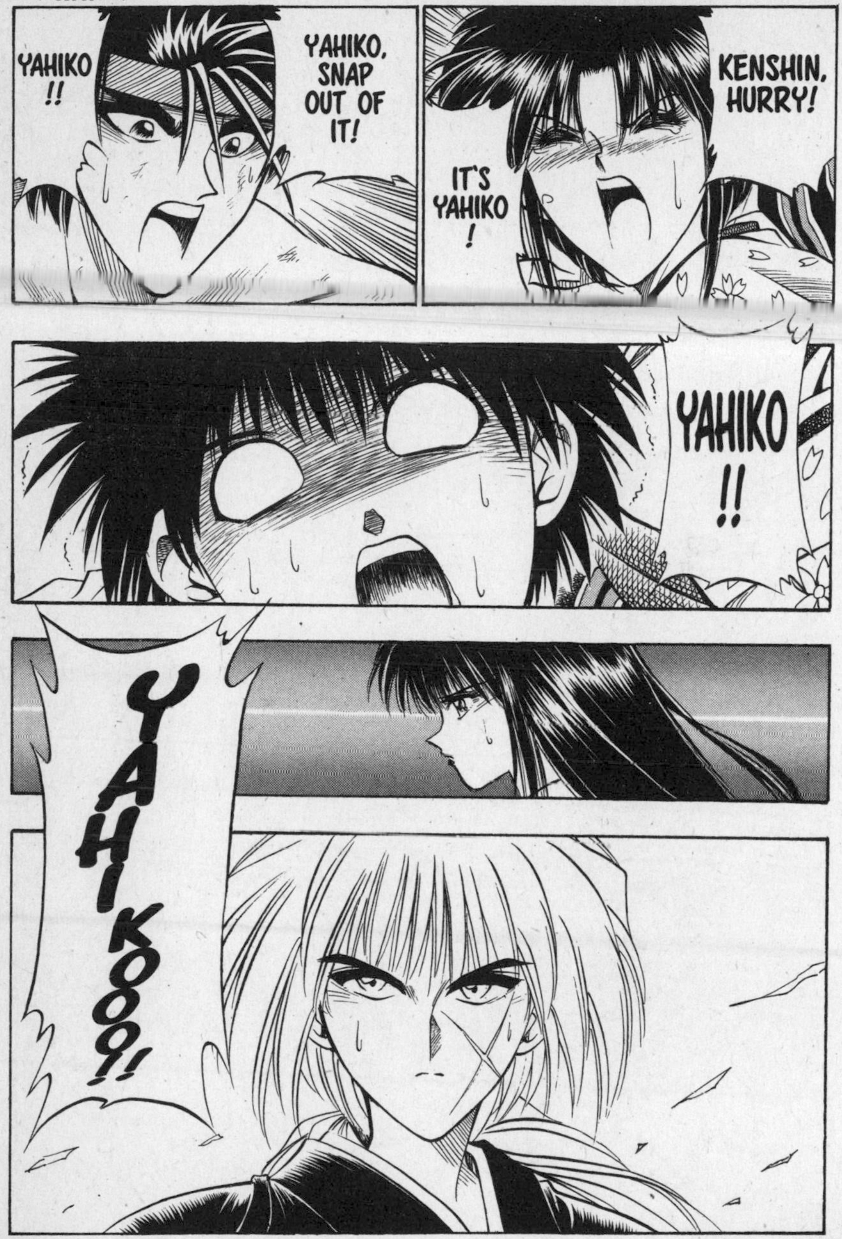
KENSHIN, HURRY!
IT'S YAHIKO!
YAHIKO, SNAP OUT OF IT!
YAHIKO!!
YAHIKO!!
YAHIKOOOO!!

<< READ THIS WAY <<

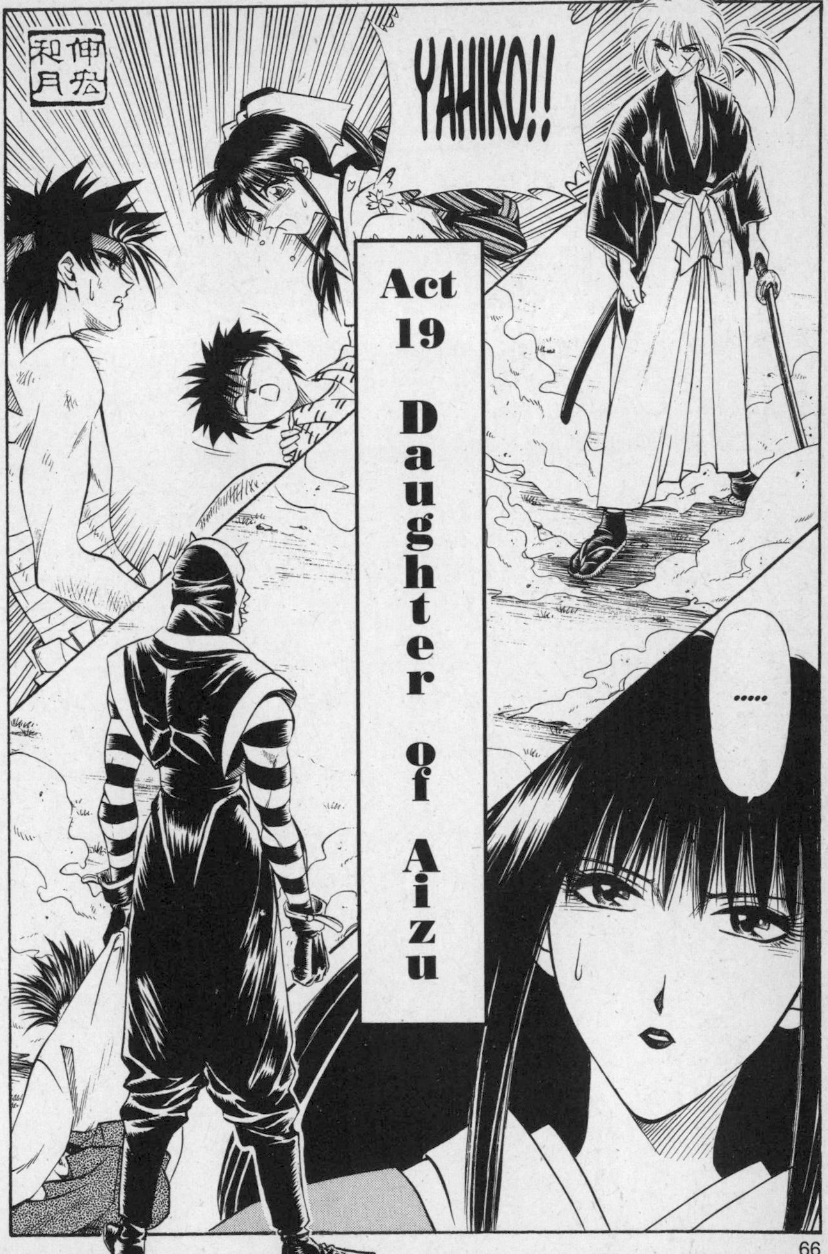

YAHIKO!!
Act 19 Daughter of Aizu
.....

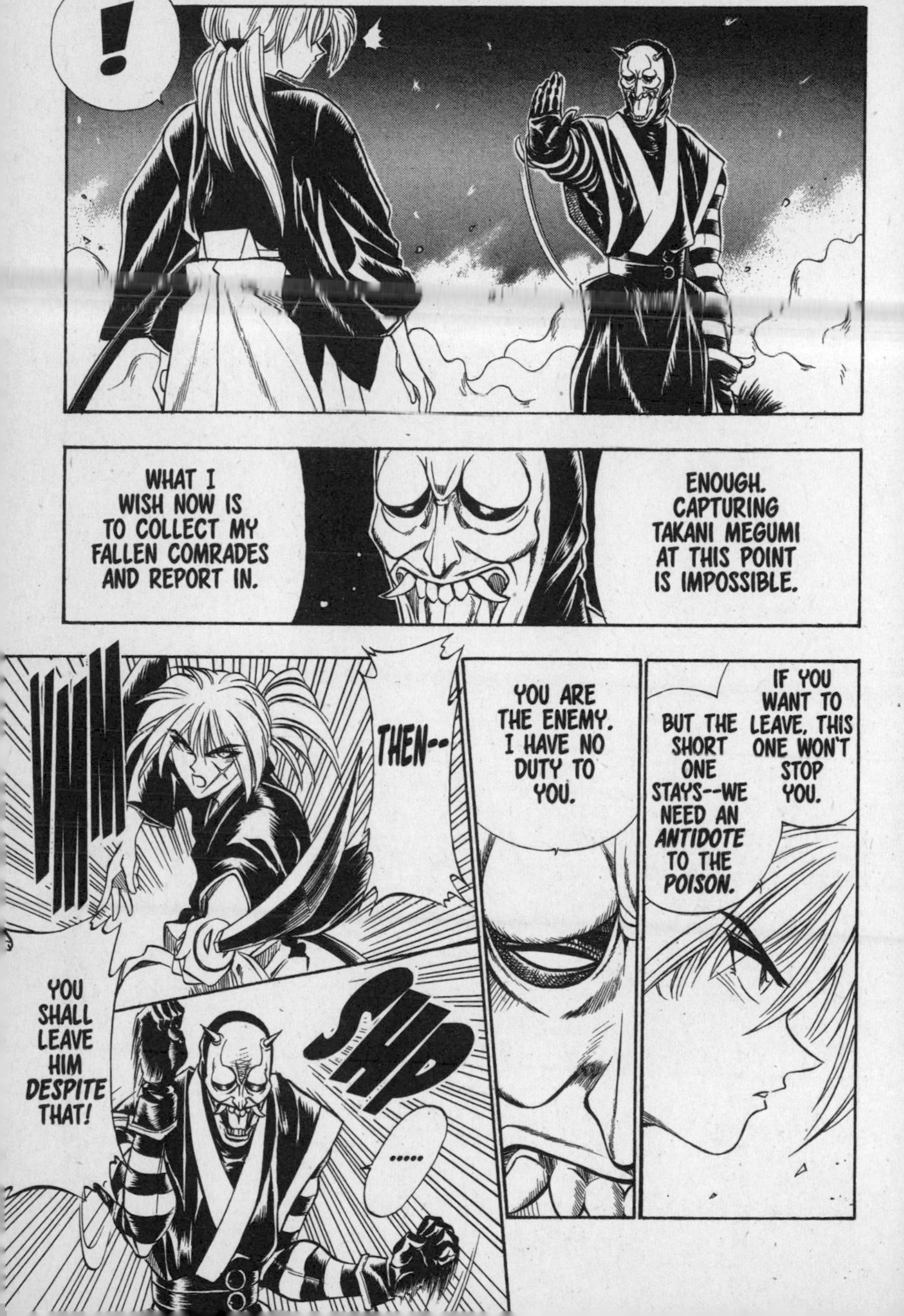
!
ENOUGH. CAPTURING TAKANI MEGUMI AT THIS POINT IS IMPOSSIBLE.
WHAT I WISH NOW IS TO COLLECT MY FALLEN COMRADES AND REPORT IN.
IF YOU WANT TO LEAVE, THIS ONE WON'T STOP YOU.
BUT THE SHORT ONE STAYS--WE NEED AN *ANTIDOTE* TO THE *POISON.*
YOU ARE THE ENEMY. I HAVE NO DUTY TO YOU.
THEN--
VMM
YOU SHALL LEAVE HIM *DESPITE* THAT!
SHP
.....

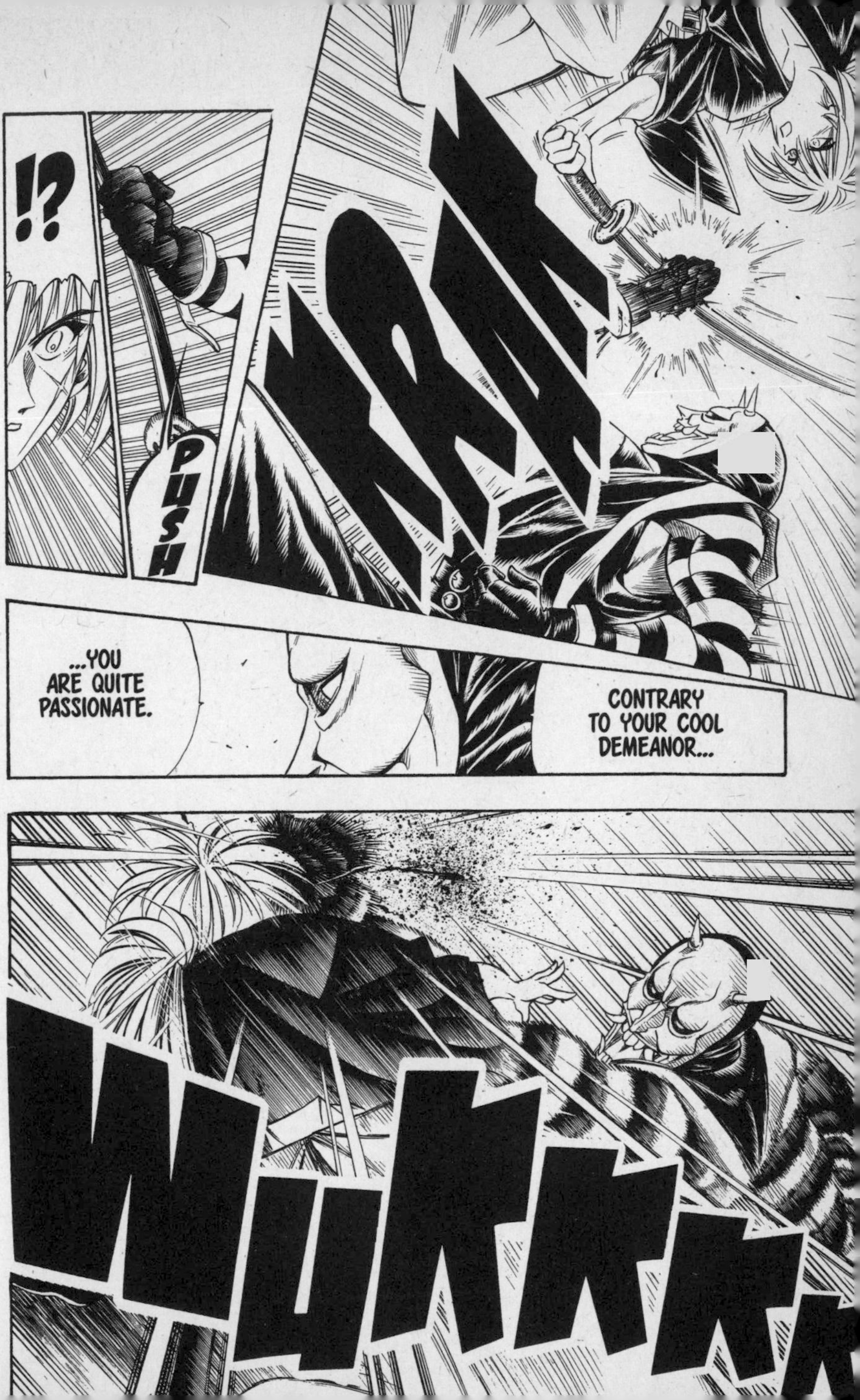
PUSH
!?
CONTRARY TO YOUR COOL DEMEANOR...
...YOU ARE QUITE PASSIONATE.

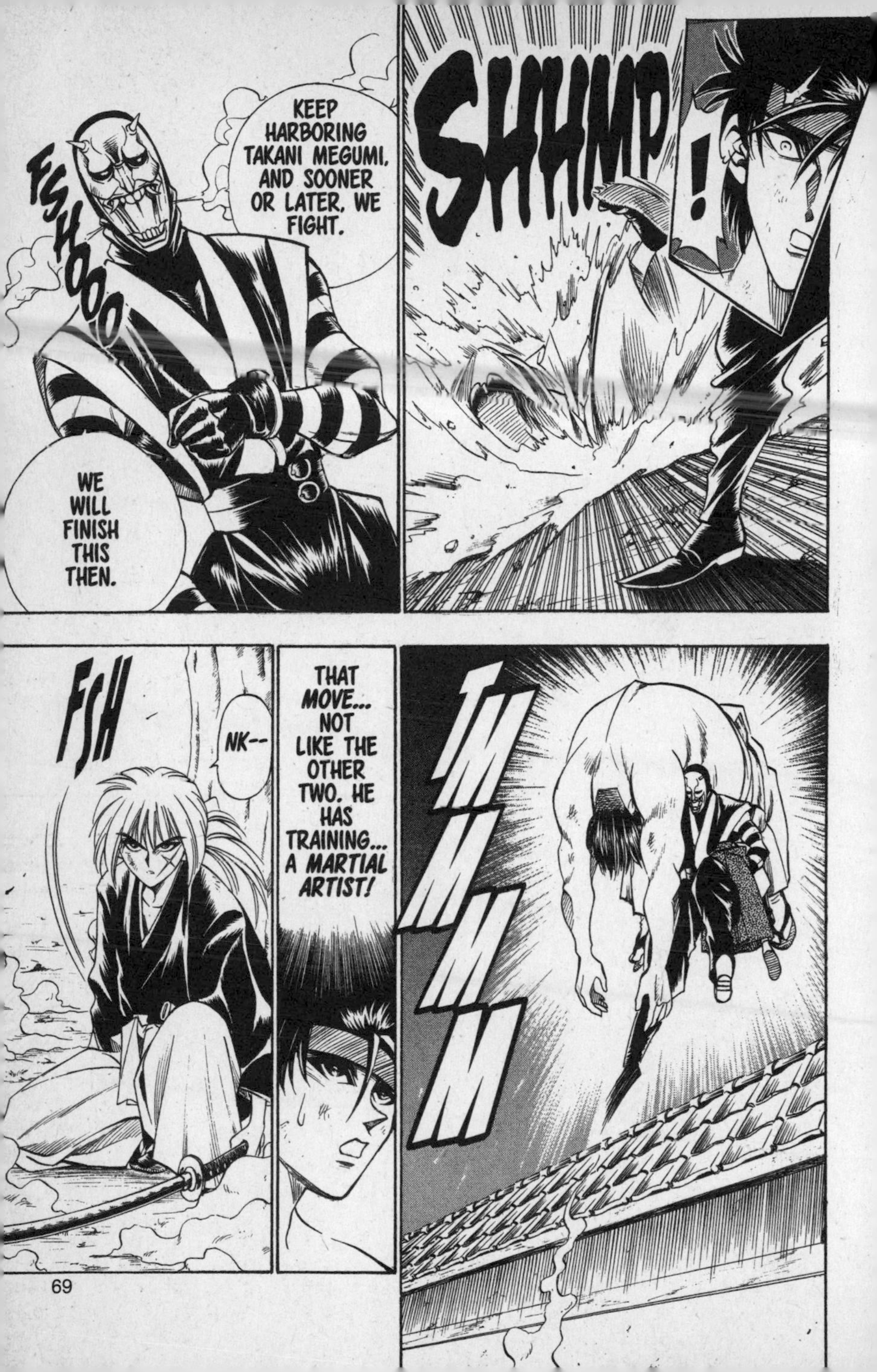
SHHMP
!
KEEP HARBORING TAKANI MEGUMI, AND SOONER OR LATER, WE FIGHT.
FSHOOO
WE WILL FINISH THIS THEN.
THMMMM
THAT *MOVE*... NOT LIKE THE OTHER TWO. HE HAS TRAINING... A *MARTIAL ARTIST!*
NK--
FSH

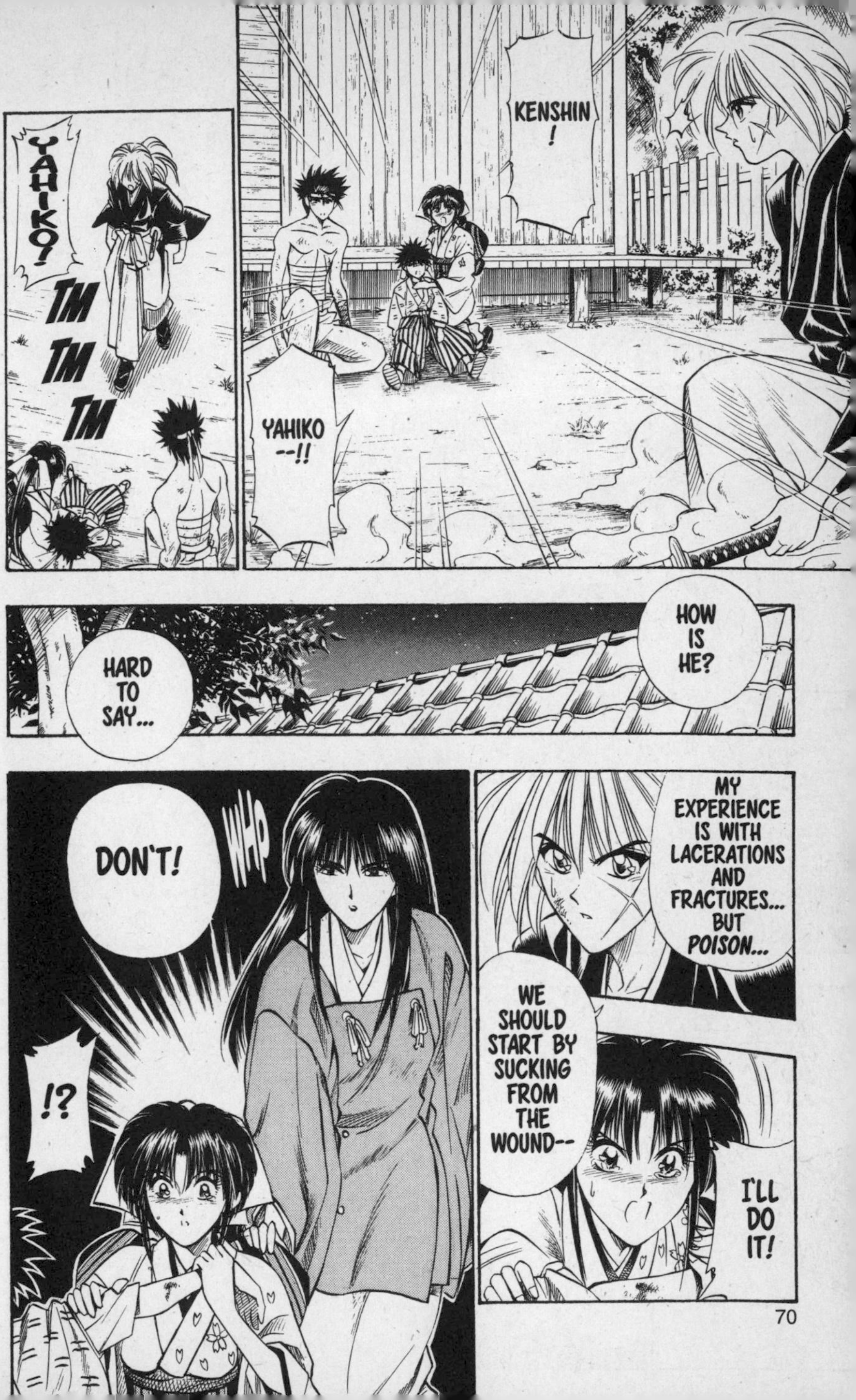
KENSHIN !
YAHIKO --!!
YAHIKO!
TM TM TM
HOW IS HE?
HARD TO SAY...
MY EXPERIENCE IS WITH LACERATIONS AND FRACTURES... BUT POISON...
WE SHOULD START BY SUCKING FROM THE WOUND--
I'LL DO IT!
DON'T!
WHAP
!?

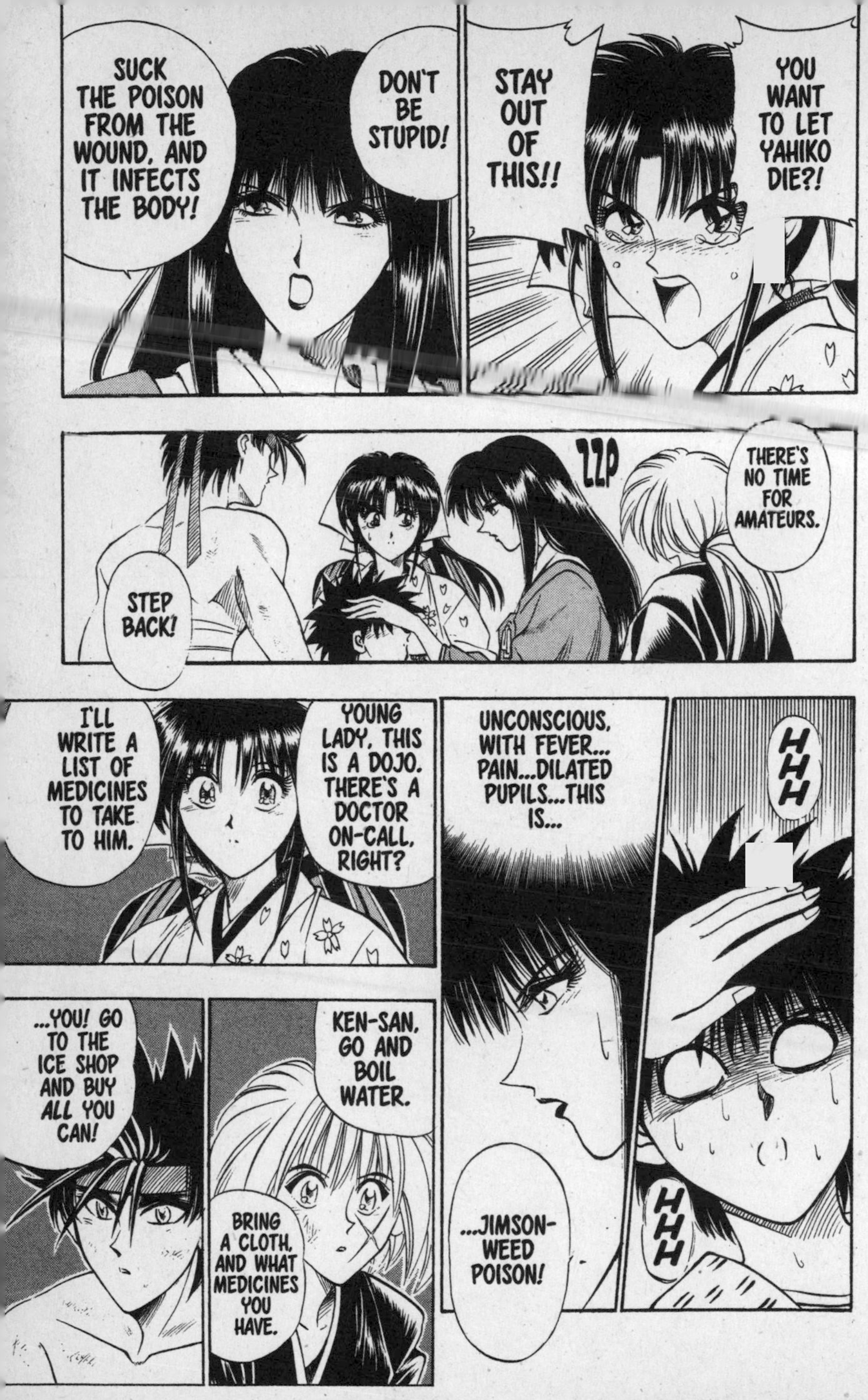
YOU WANT TO LET YAHIKO DIE?!
STAY OUT OF THIS!!
DON'T BE STUPID!
SUCK THE POISON FROM THE WOUND, AND IT INFECTS THE BODY!
THERE'S NO TIME FOR AMATEURS.
ZZP
STEP BACK!
HHH
HHH
UNCONSCIOUS, WITH FEVER... PAIN...DILATED PUPILS...THIS IS...
...JIMSON-WEED POISON!
YOUNG LADY, THIS IS A DOJO. THERE'S A DOCTOR ON-CALL, RIGHT?
I'LL WRITE A LIST OF MEDICINES TO TAKE TO HIM.
KEN-SAN, GO AND BOIL WATER.
BRING A CLOTH, AND WHAT MEDICINES YOU HAVE.
...YOU! GO TO THE ICE SHOP AND BUY ALL YOU CAN!

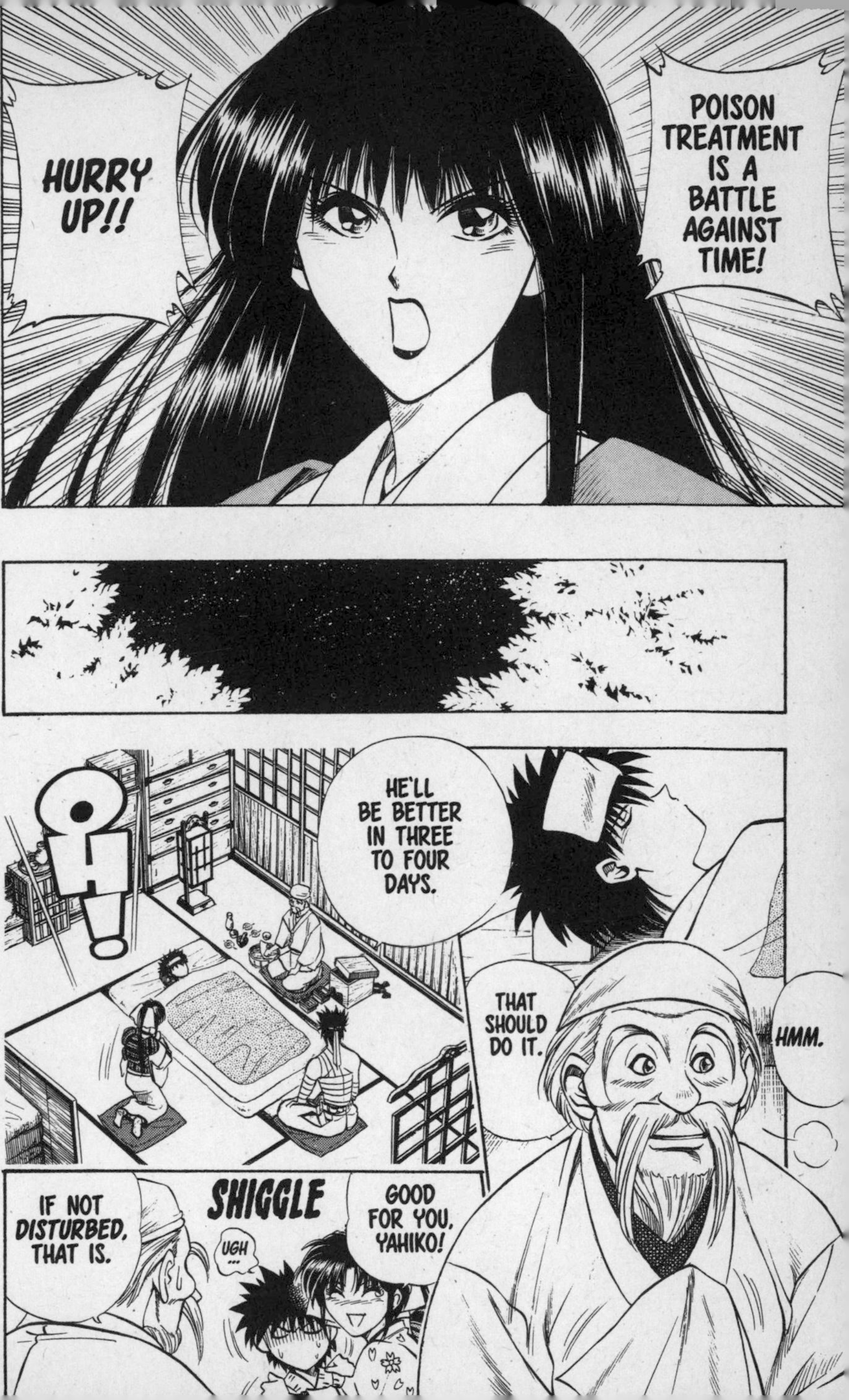
POISON TREATMENT IS A BATTLE AGAINST TIME!
HURRY UP!!
HMM.
THAT SHOULD DO IT.
HE'LL BE BETTER IN THREE TO FOUR DAYS.
OH!
GOOD FOR YOU, YAHIKO!
SHIGGLE
UGH...
IF NOT DISTURBED, THAT IS.

READ THIS WAY

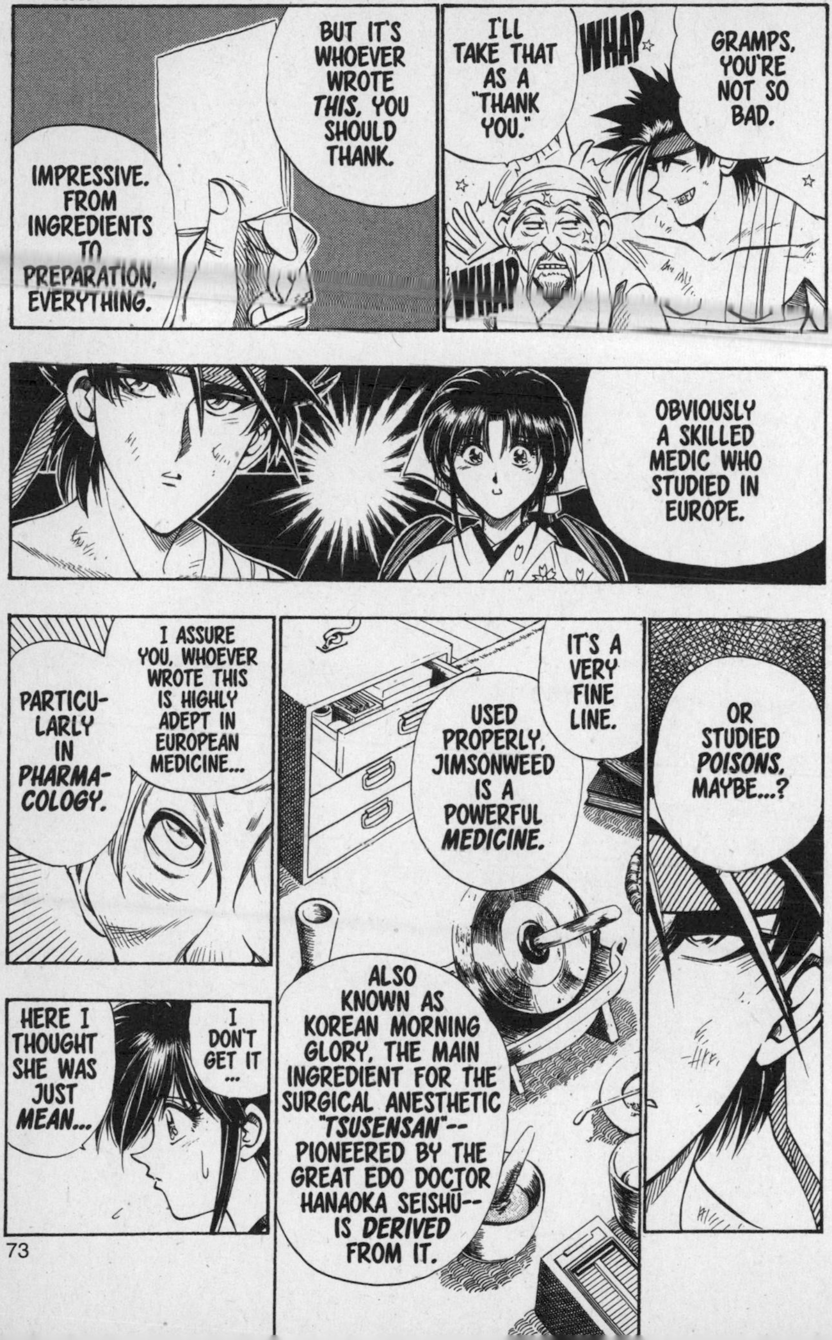
GRAMPS, YOU'RE NOT SO BAD.
WHAP
I'LL TAKE THAT AS A "THANK YOU."
WHAP
BUT IT'S WHOEVER WROTE *THIS*, YOU SHOULD THANK.
IMPRESSIVE. FROM INGREDIENTS TO PREPARATION, EVERYTHING.
OBVIOUSLY A SKILLED MEDIC WHO STUDIED IN EUROPE.
OR STUDIED *POISONS*, MAYBE...?
IT'S A VERY FINE LINE.
USED PROPERLY, JIMSONWEED IS A POWERFUL *MEDICINE*.
ALSO KNOWN AS KOREAN MORNING GLORY, THE MAIN INGREDIENT FOR THE SURGICAL ANESTHETIC *"TSUSENSAN"*-- PIONEERED BY THE GREAT EDO DOCTOR HANAOKA SEISHŪ-- IS *DERIVED* FROM IT.
I ASSURE YOU, WHOEVER WROTE THIS IS HIGHLY ADEPT IN EUROPEAN MEDICINE...
PARTICULARLY IN *PHARMACOLOGY*.
I DON'T GET IT ...
HERE I THOUGHT SHE WAS JUST *MEAN*...

READ THIS WAY

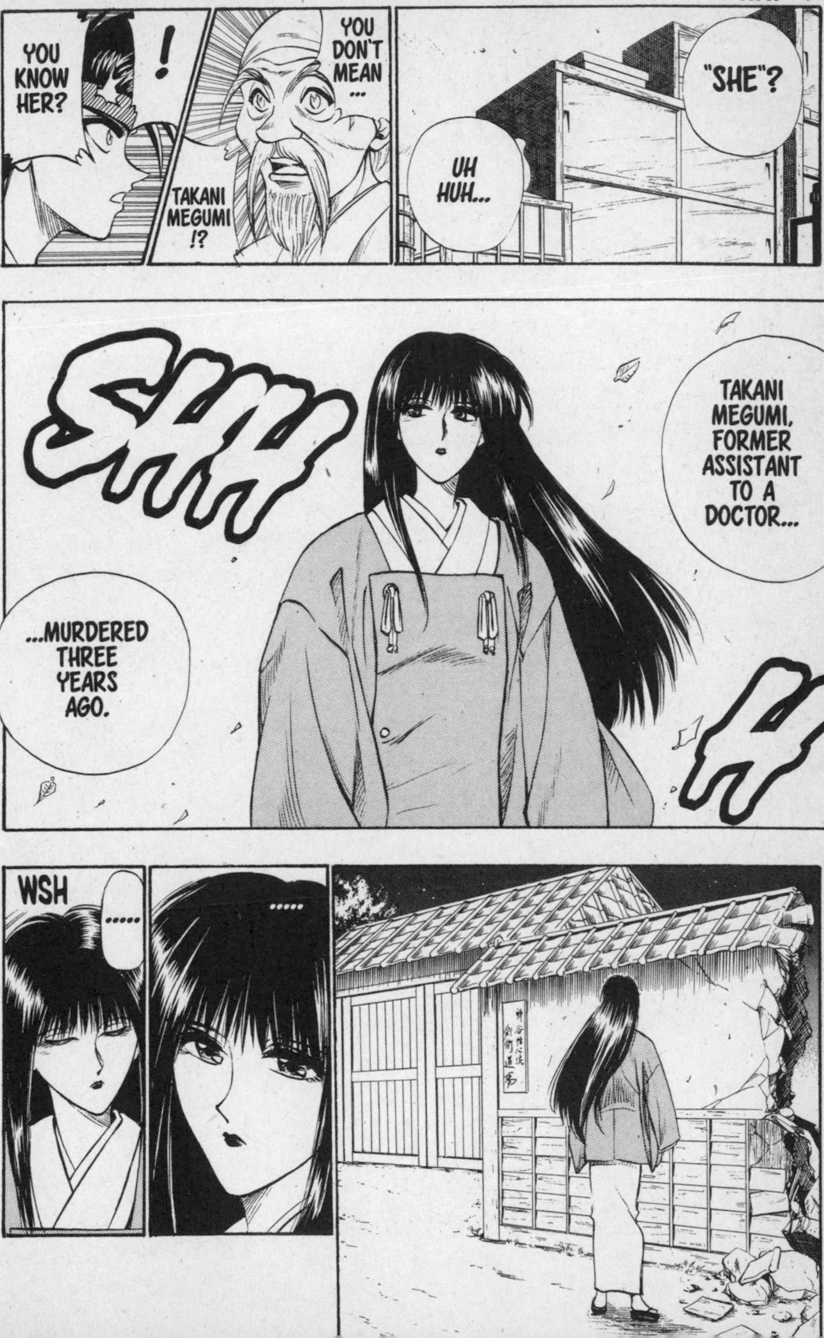
"SHE"?
UH HUH...
YOU DON'T MEAN ...
TAKANI MEGUMI !?
!
YOU KNOW HER?
TAKANI MEGUMI, FORMER ASSISTANT TO A DOCTOR...
SHH
...MURDERED THREE YEARS AGO.
......
WSH
......

READ THIS WAY

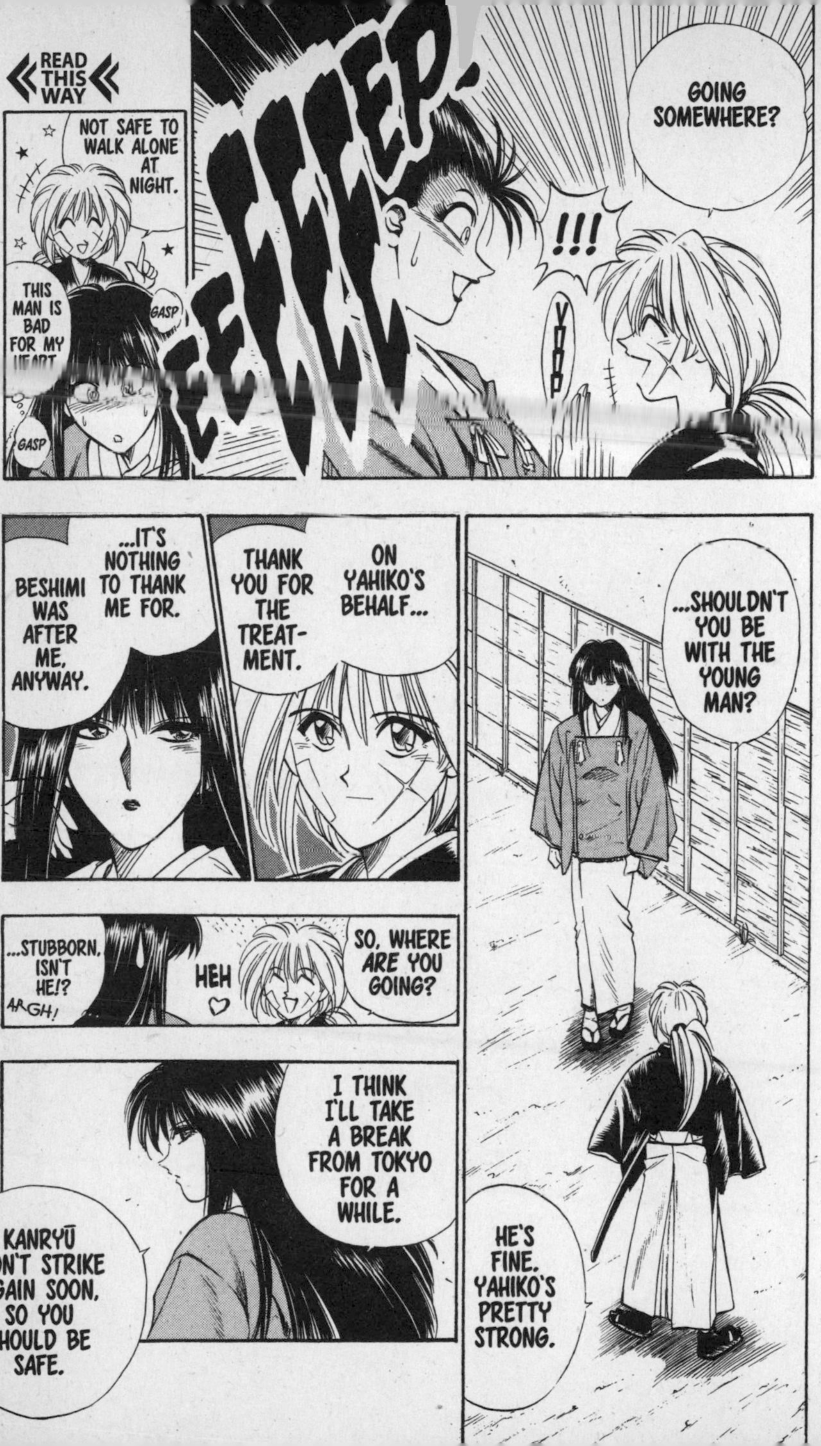

GOING SOMEWHERE?
!!!
VOOP
EEEEP.
NOT SAFE TO WALK ALONE AT NIGHT.
THIS MAN IS BAD FOR MY HEART
GASP
GASP
...SHOULDN'T YOU BE WITH THE YOUNG MAN?
HE'S FINE. YAHIKO'S PRETTY STRONG.
ON YAHIKO'S BEHALF...
THANK YOU FOR THE TREATMENT.
...IT'S NOTHING TO THANK ME FOR.
BESHIMI WAS AFTER ME, ANYWAY.
SO, WHERE ARE YOU GOING?
HEH ♡
...STUBBORN, ISN'T HE!?
ARGH!
I THINK I'LL TAKE A BREAK FROM TOKYO FOR A WHILE.
KANRYŪ WON'T STRIKE AGAIN SOON, SO YOU SHOULD BE SAFE.

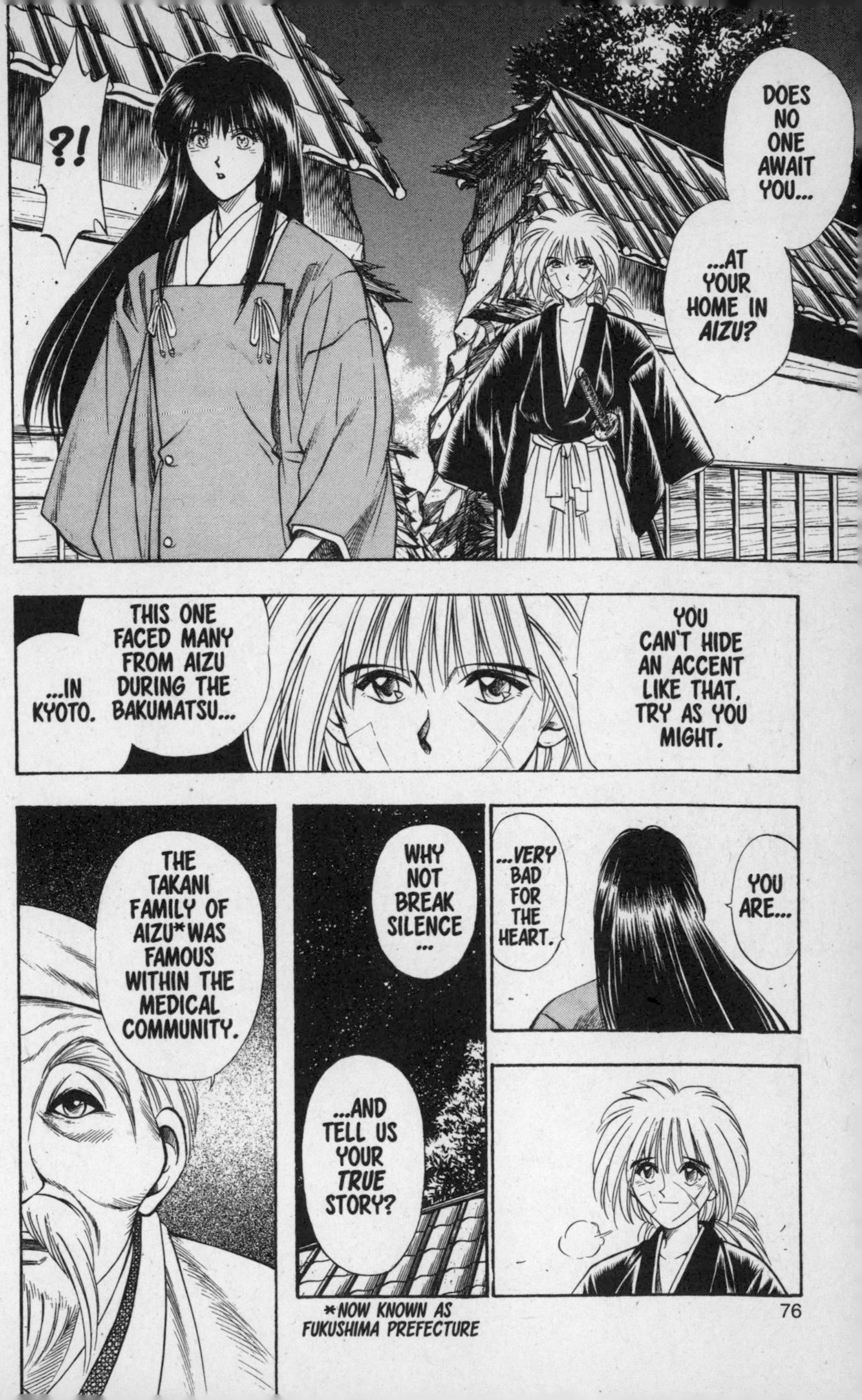
DOES NO ONE AWAIT YOU...
...AT YOUR HOME IN AIZU?
?!
YOU CAN'T HIDE AN ACCENT LIKE THAT, TRY AS YOU MIGHT.
THIS ONE FACED MANY FROM AIZU DURING THE BAKUMATSU...
...IN KYOTO.
YOU ARE...
...VERY BAD FOR THE HEART.
WHY NOT BREAK SILENCE...
...AND TELL US YOUR *TRUE* STORY?
THE TAKANI FAMILY OF AIZU* WAS FAMOUS WITHIN THE MEDICAL COMMUNITY.

*NOW KNOWN AS FUKUSHIMA PREFECTURE

READ THIS WAY

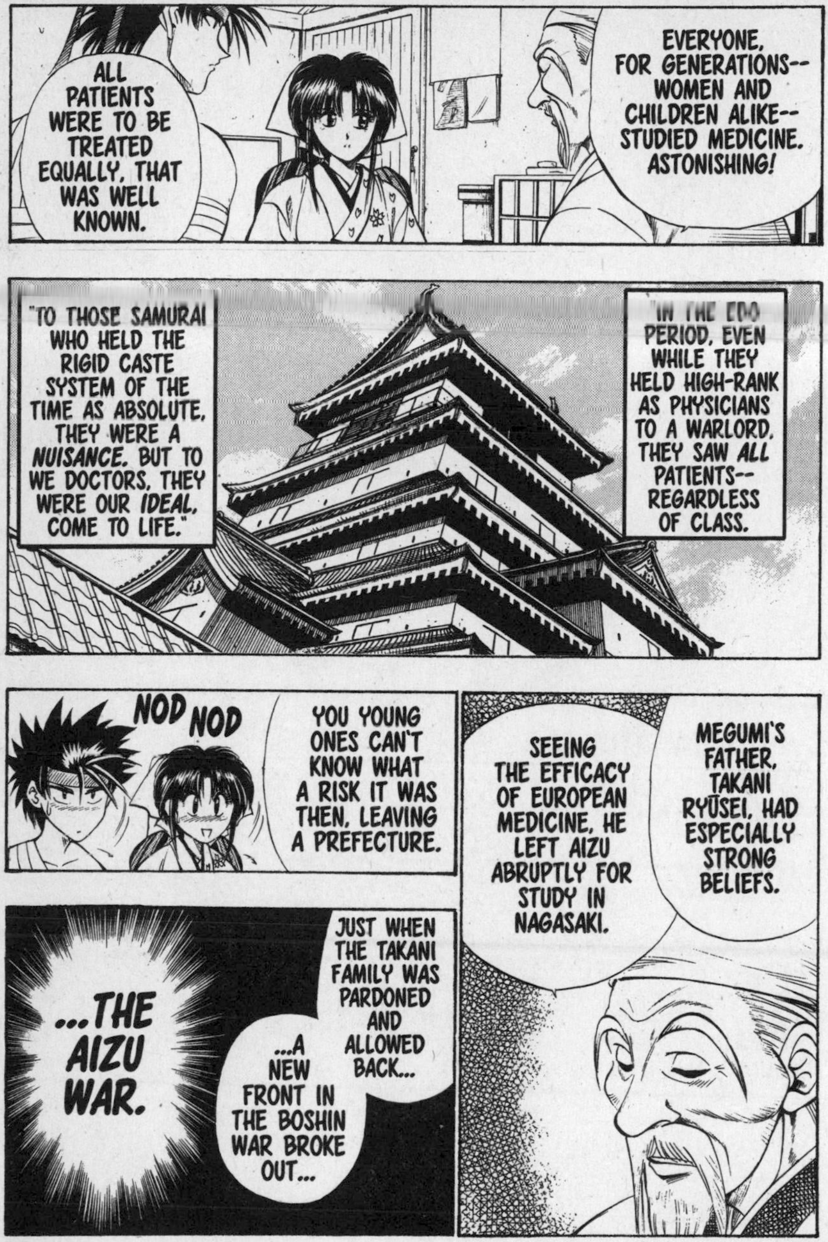
EVERYONE, FOR GENERATIONS-- WOMEN AND CHILDREN ALIKE-- STUDIED MEDICINE. ASTONISHING!
ALL PATIENTS WERE TO BE TREATED EQUALLY, THAT WAS WELL KNOWN.
IN THE EDO PERIOD, EVEN WHILE THEY HELD HIGH-RANK AS PHYSICIANS TO A WARLORD, THEY SAW *ALL* PATIENTS-- REGARDLESS OF CLASS.
"TO THOSE SAMURAI WHO HELD THE RIGID CASTE SYSTEM OF THE TIME AS ABSOLUTE, THEY WERE A *NUISANCE.* BUT TO WE DOCTORS, THEY WERE OUR *IDEAL,* COME TO LIFE."
MEGUMI'S FATHER, TAKANI RYŪSEI, HAD ESPECIALLY STRONG BELIEFS.
SEEING THE EFFICACY OF EUROPEAN MEDICINE, HE LEFT AIZU ABRUPTLY FOR STUDY IN NAGASAKI.
YOU YOUNG ONES CAN'T KNOW WHAT A RISK IT WAS THEN, LEAVING A PREFECTURE.
NOD NOD
JUST WHEN THE TAKANI FAMILY WAS PARDONED AND ALLOWED BACK...
...A NEW FRONT IN THE BOSHIN WAR BROKE OUT...
...THE AIZU WAR.

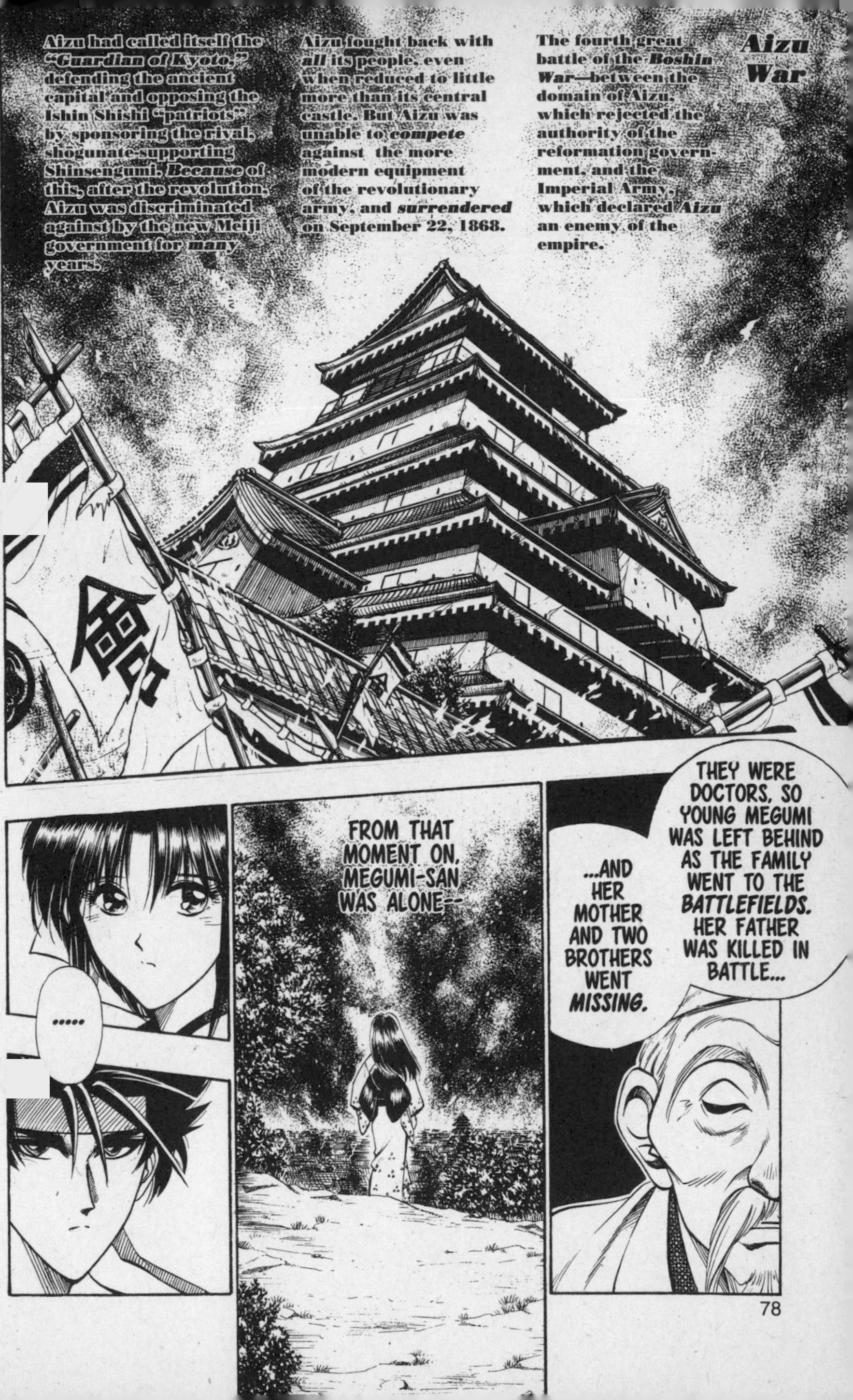
Aizu War
The fourth great battle of the *Boshin War*—between the domain of Aizu, which rejected the authority of the reformation government, and the Imperial Army, which declared *Aizu* an enemy of the empire.
Aizu fought back with *all* its people, even when reduced to little more than its central castle. But Aizu was unable to *compete* against the more modern equipment of the revolutionary army, and *surrendered* on September 22, 1868.
Aizu had called itself the *"Guardian of Kyoto,"* defending the ancient capital and opposing the Ishin Shishi "patriots" by sponsoring the rival, shogunate-supporting Shinsengumi. *Because* of this, after the revolution, Aizu was discriminated against by the new Meiji government for *many* years.
THEY WERE DOCTORS, SO YOUNG MEGUMI WAS LEFT BEHIND AS THE FAMILY WENT TO THE *BATTLEFIELDS*. HER FATHER WAS KILLED IN BATTLE...
...AND HER MOTHER AND TWO BROTHERS WENT *MISSING*.
FROM THAT MOMENT ON, MEGUMI-SAN WAS ALONE--
......

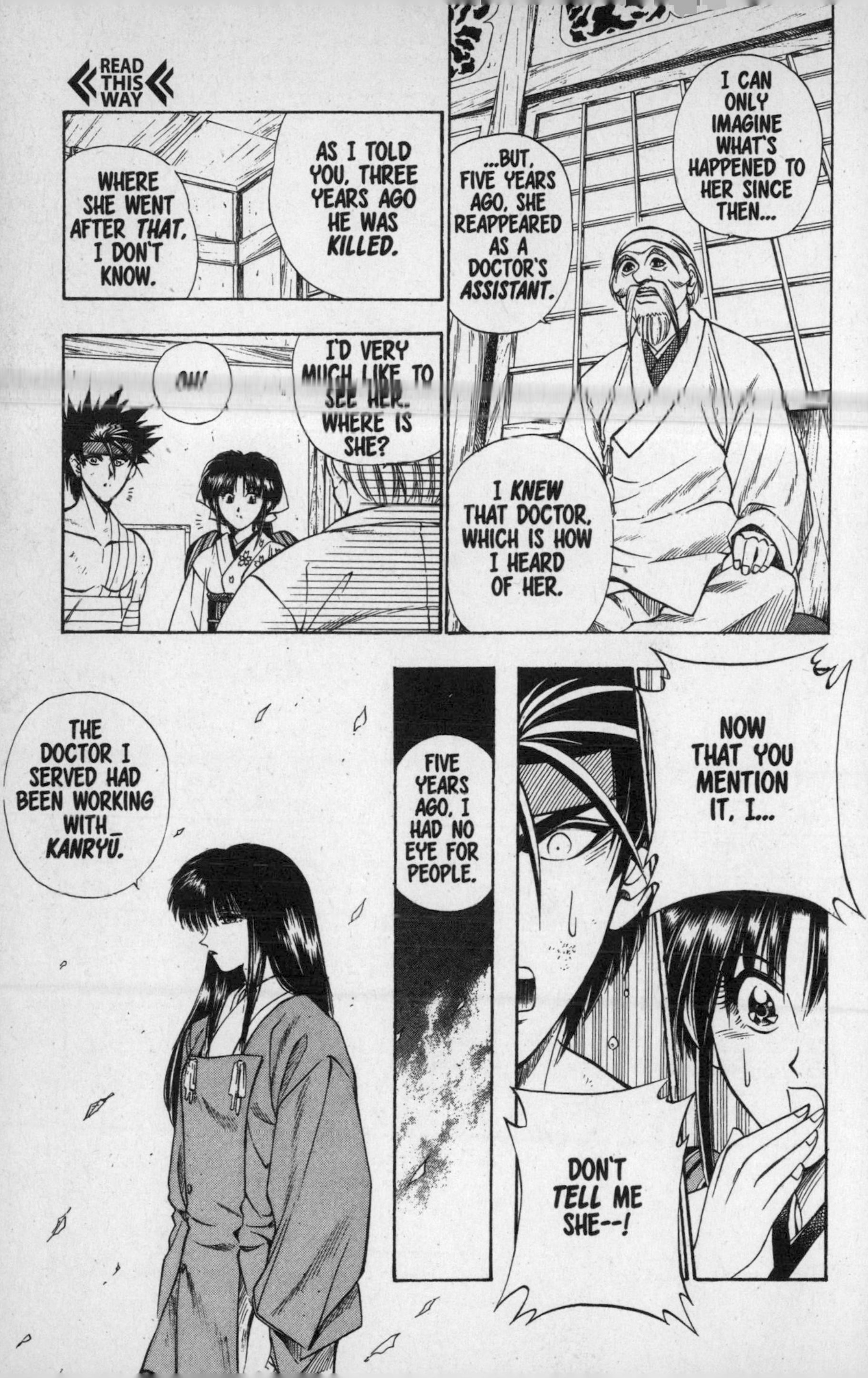
READ THIS WAY
I CAN ONLY IMAGINE WHAT'S HAPPENED TO HER SINCE THEN...
...BUT, FIVE YEARS AGO, SHE REAPPEARED AS A DOCTOR'S *ASSISTANT*.
I *KNEW* THAT DOCTOR, WHICH IS HOW I HEARD OF HER.
AS I TOLD YOU, THREE YEARS AGO HE WAS *KILLED*.
WHERE SHE WENT AFTER *THAT*, I DON'T KNOW.
I'D VERY MUCH LIKE TO SEE HER. WHERE IS SHE?
OH!
NOW THAT YOU MENTION IT, I...
DON'T *TELL* ME SHE--!
FIVE YEARS AGO, I HAD NO EYE FOR PEOPLE.
THE DOCTOR I SERVED HAD BEEN WORKING WITH *KANRYŪ*.

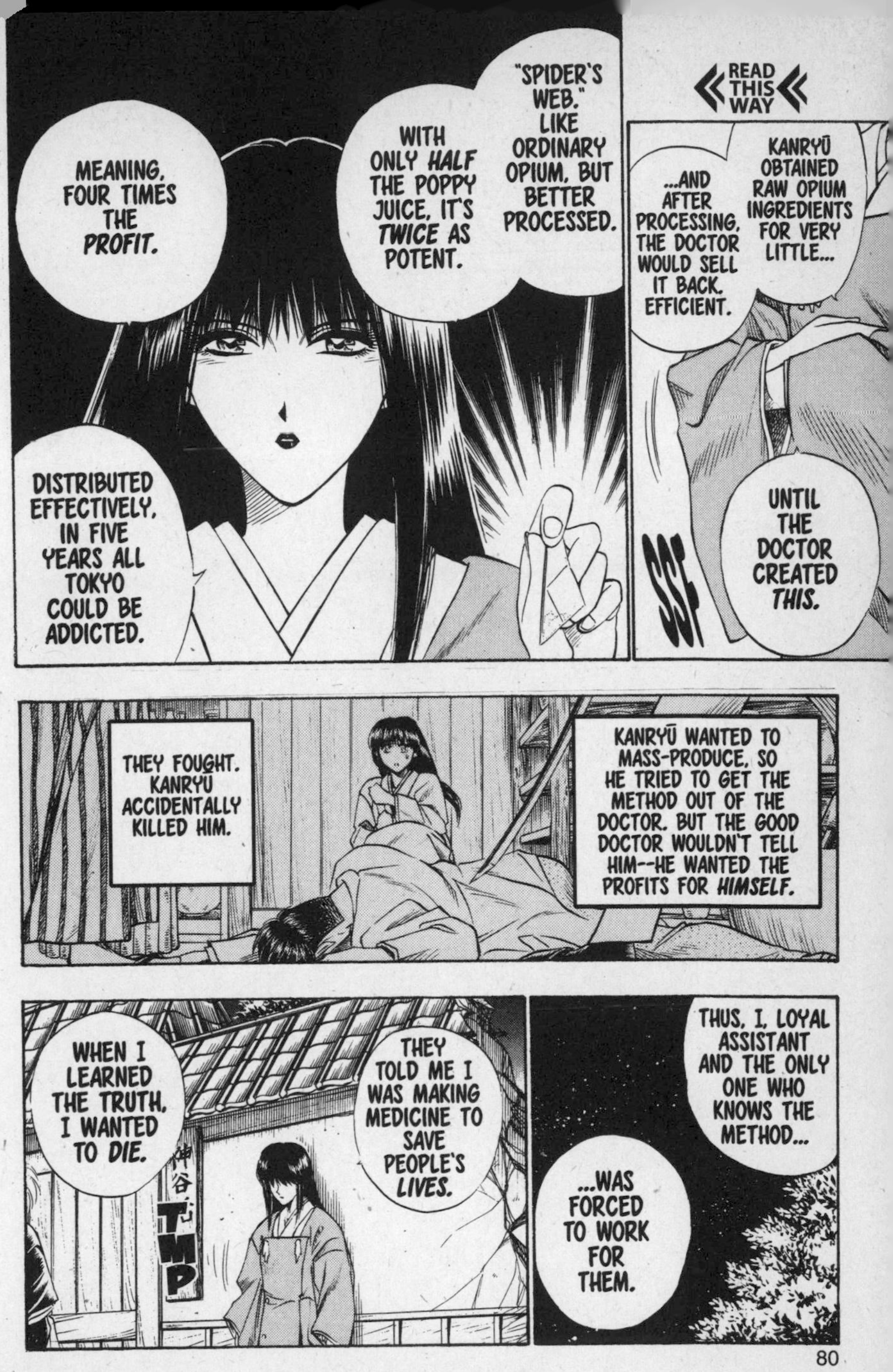
READ THIS WAY
KANRYŪ OBTAINED RAW OPIUM INGREDIENTS FOR VERY LITTLE...
...AND AFTER PROCESSING, THE DOCTOR WOULD SELL IT BACK. EFFICIENT.
UNTIL THE DOCTOR CREATED THIS.
SSP
"SPIDER'S WEB." LIKE ORDINARY OPIUM, BUT BETTER PROCESSED.
WITH ONLY HALF THE POPPY JUICE, IT'S TWICE AS POTENT.
MEANING, FOUR TIMES THE PROFIT.
DISTRIBUTED EFFECTIVELY, IN FIVE YEARS ALL TOKYO COULD BE ADDICTED.
KANRYŪ WANTED TO MASS-PRODUCE, SO HE TRIED TO GET THE METHOD OUT OF THE DOCTOR. BUT THE GOOD DOCTOR WOULDN'T TELL HIM--HE WANTED THE PROFITS FOR HIMSELF.
THEY FOUGHT. KANRYŪ ACCIDENTALLY KILLED HIM.
THUS, I, LOYAL ASSISTANT AND THE ONLY ONE WHO KNOWS THE METHOD...
...WAS FORCED TO WORK FOR THEM.
THEY TOLD ME I WAS MAKING MEDICINE TO SAVE PEOPLE'S LIVES.
WHEN I LEARNED THE TRUTH, I WANTED TO DIE.
神谷
TMP

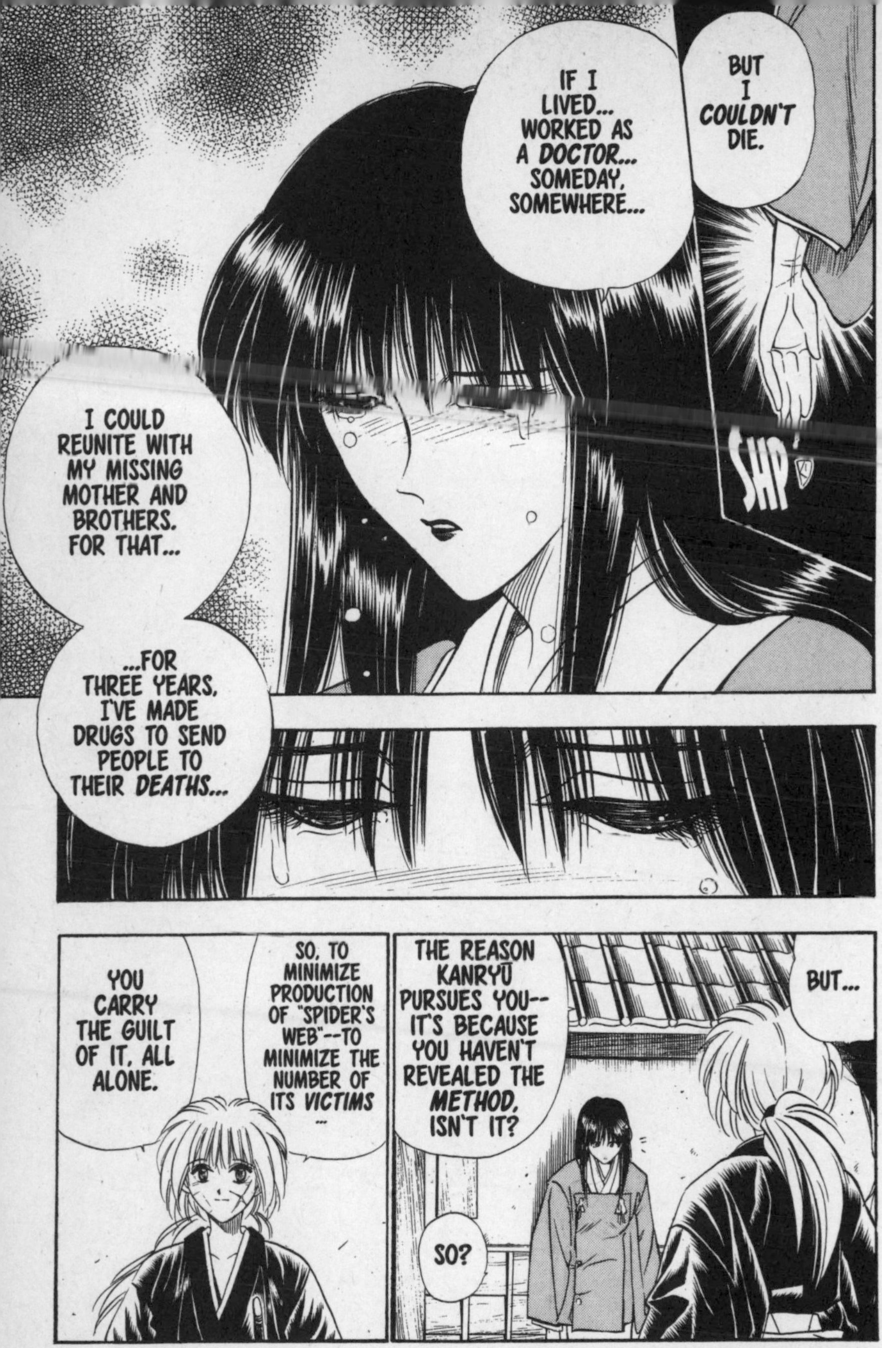
BUT I COULDN'T DIE.
IF I LIVED... WORKED AS A DOCTOR... SOMEDAY, SOMEWHERE...
SHP
I COULD REUNITE WITH MY MISSING MOTHER AND BROTHERS. FOR THAT...
...FOR THREE YEARS, I'VE MADE DRUGS TO SEND PEOPLE TO THEIR DEATHS...
BUT...
THE REASON KANRYŪ PURSUES YOU-- IT'S BECAUSE YOU HAVEN'T REVEALED THE METHOD, ISN'T IT?
SO?
SO, TO MINIMIZE PRODUCTION OF "SPIDER'S WEB"--TO MINIMIZE THE NUMBER OF ITS VICTIMS...
YOU CARRY THE GUILT OF IT, ALL ALONE.

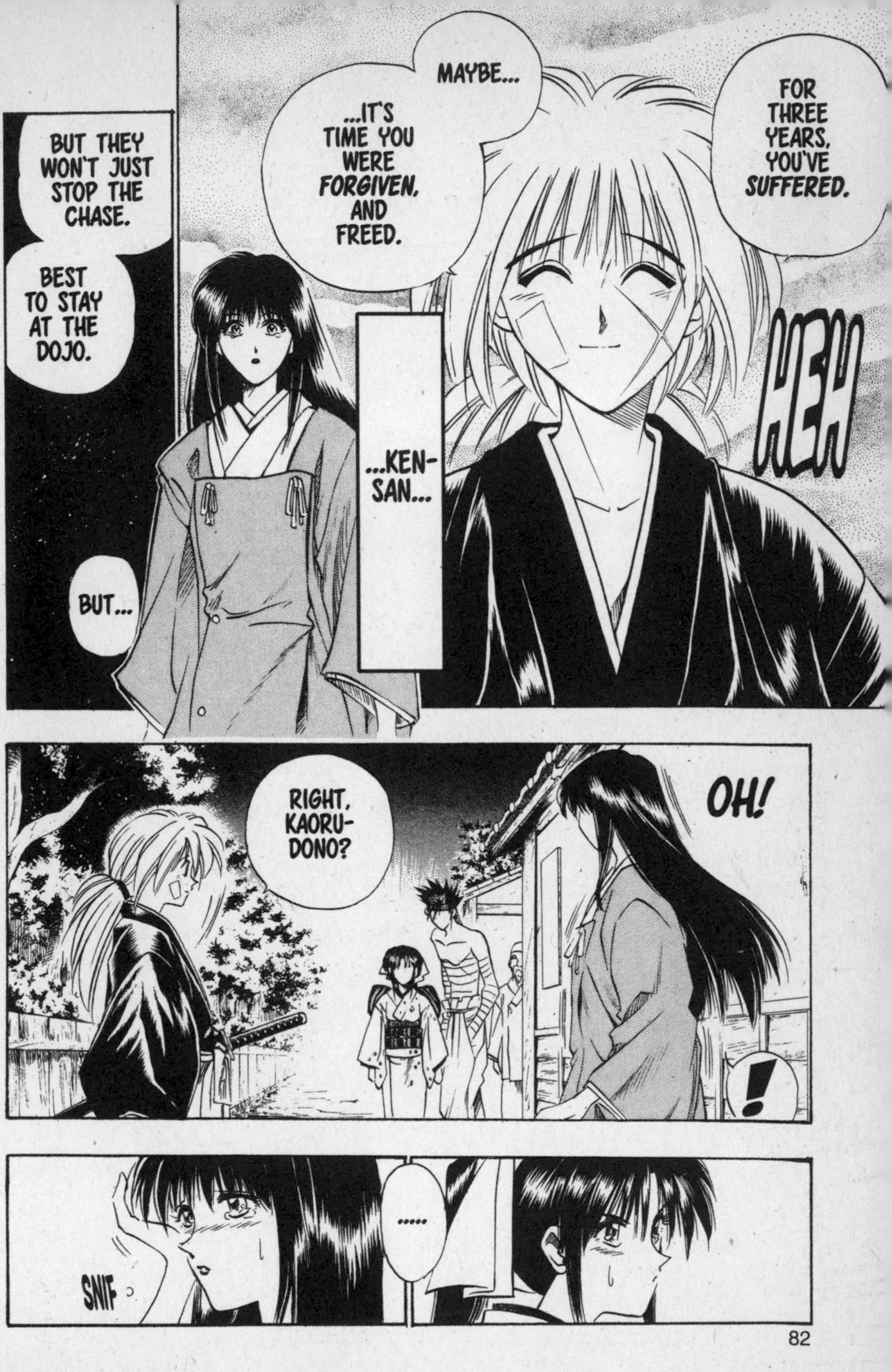

FOR THREE YEARS, YOU'VE SUFFERED.
HEH
MAYBE...
...IT'S TIME YOU WERE FORGIVEN, AND FREED.
...KEN-SAN...
BUT THEY WON'T JUST STOP THE CHASE.
BEST TO STAY AT THE DOJO.
BUT...
OH!
!
RIGHT, KAORU-DONO?
......
SNIF

READ THIS WAY

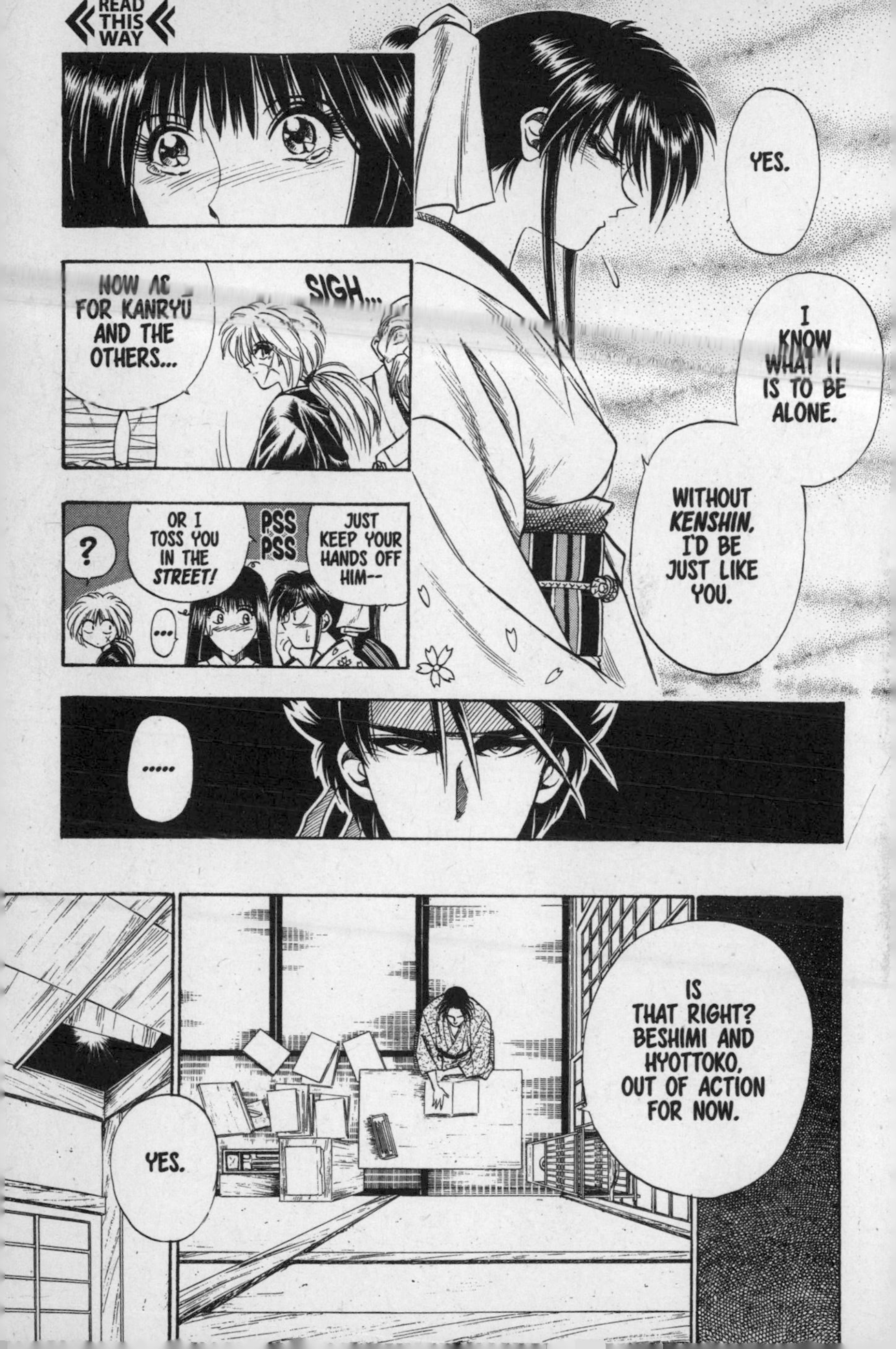
YES.
I KNOW WHAT IT IS TO BE ALONE.
WITHOUT *KENSHIN,* I'D BE JUST LIKE YOU.
SIGH...
NOW AS FOR KANRYŪ AND THE OTHERS...
JUST KEEP YOUR HANDS OFF HIM--
PSS PSS
OR I TOSS YOU IN THE *STREET!*
?
...
......
IS THAT RIGHT? BESHIMI AND HYOTTOKO, OUT OF ACTION FOR NOW.
YES.

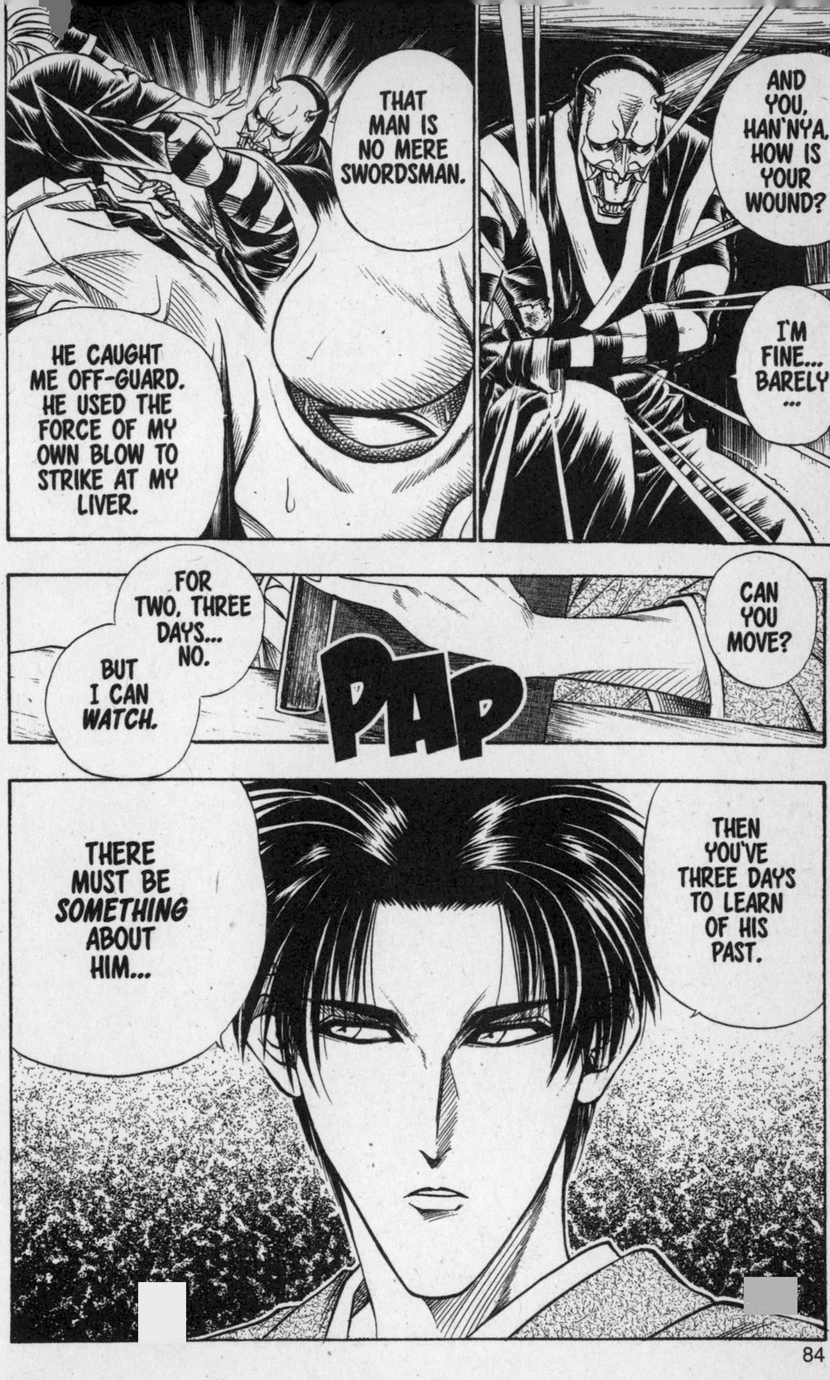
AND YOU, HAN'NYA, HOW IS YOUR WOUND?
I'M FINE... BARELY...
THAT MAN IS NO MERE SWORDSMAN.
HE CAUGHT ME OFF-GUARD. HE USED THE FORCE OF MY OWN BLOW TO STRIKE AT MY LIVER.
CAN YOU MOVE?
PAP
FOR TWO, THREE DAYS... NO.
BUT I CAN WATCH.
THEN YOU'VE THREE DAYS TO LEARN OF HIS PAST.
THERE MUST BE SOMETHING ABOUT HIM...

READ THIS WAY

Act 20
A Reason to Act

伸宏和月

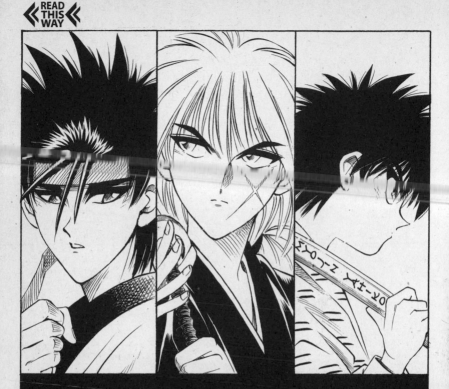

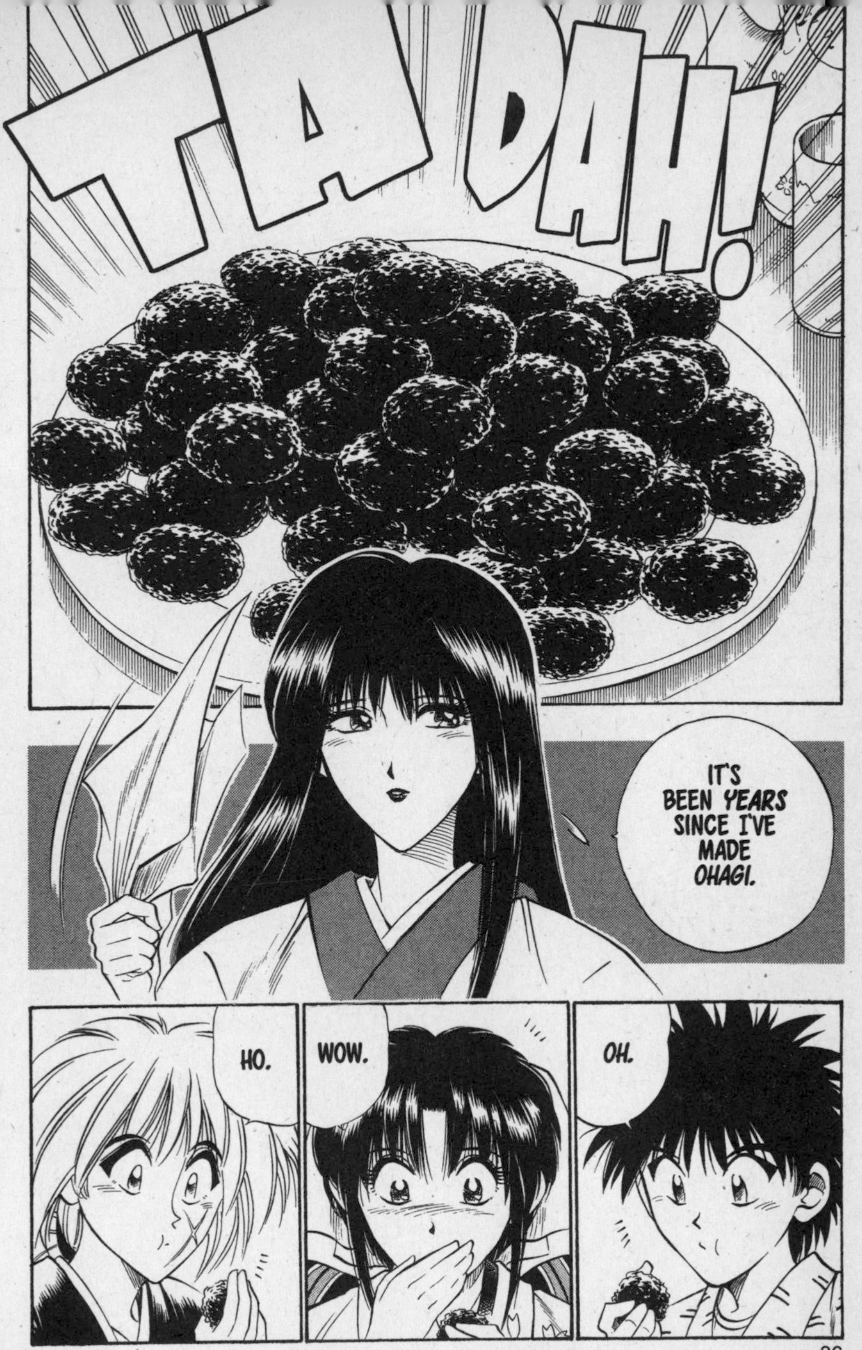
TA DAH!
IT'S BEEN YEARS SINCE I'VE MADE OHAGI.
OH.
WOW.
HO.

READ THIS WAY

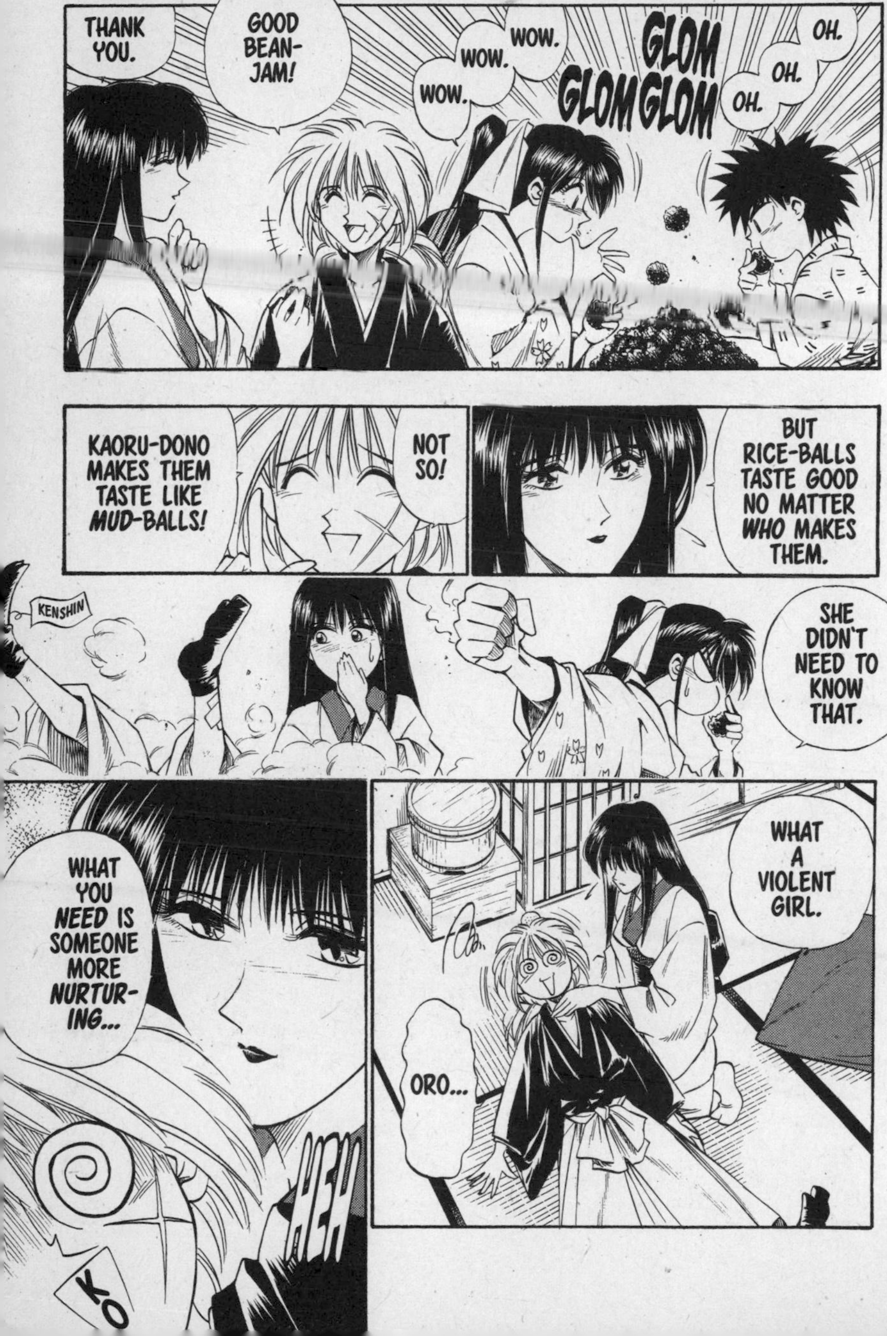
OH. OH. OH.
GLOM GLOMGLOM
WOW. WOW. WOW.
GOOD BEAN-JAM!
THANK YOU.
BUT RICE-BALLS TASTE GOOD NO MATTER WHO MAKES THEM.
NOT SO!
KAORU-DONO MAKES THEM TASTE LIKE MUD-BALLS!
SHE DIDN'T NEED TO KNOW THAT.
KENSHIN
WHAT A VIOLENT GIRL.
ORO...
WHAT YOU NEED IS SOMEONE MORE NURTURING...
HEH
KO

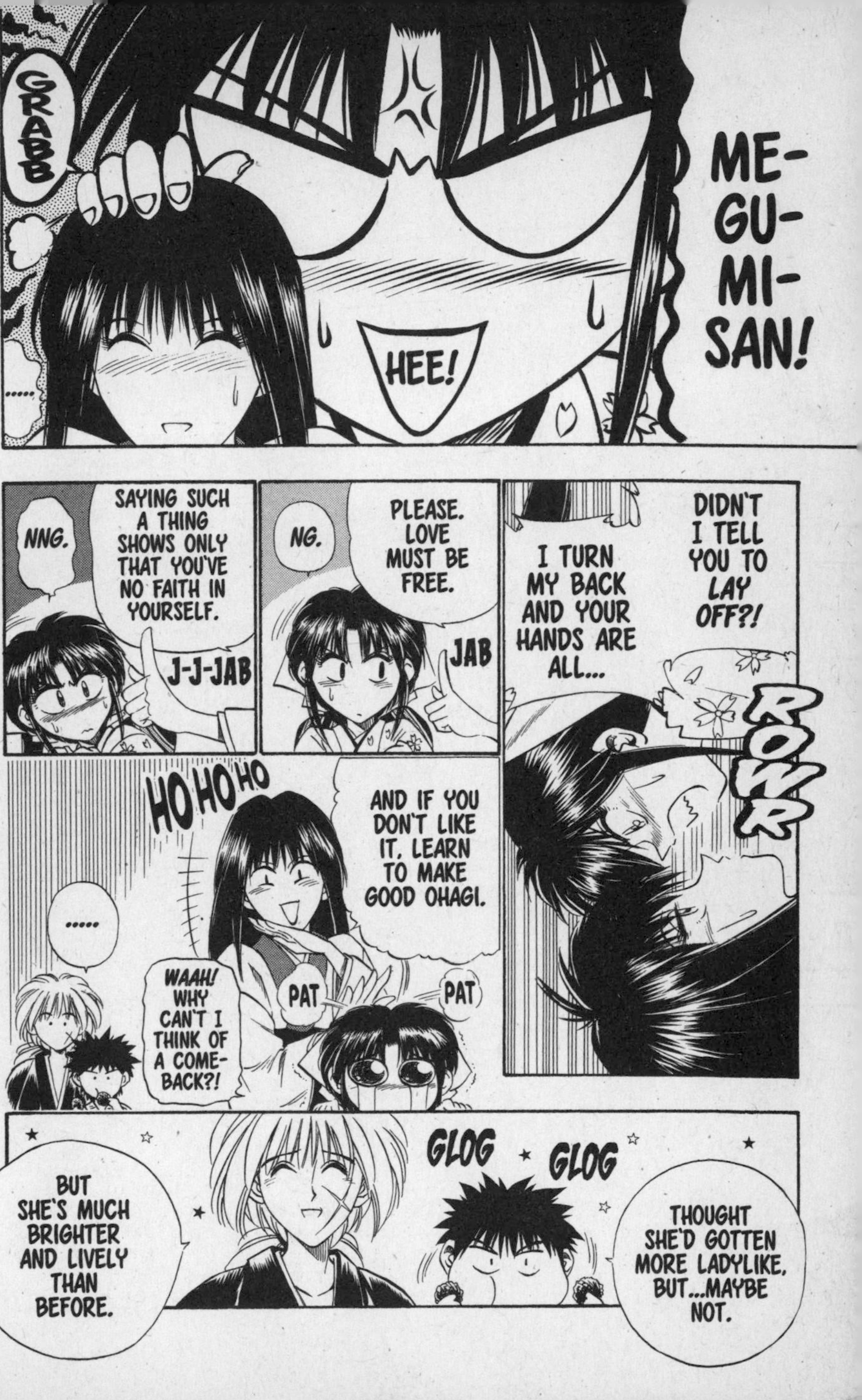
ME-GU-MI-SAN!
HEE!
GRABB
......
DIDN'T I TELL YOU TO LAY OFF?!
I TURN MY BACK AND YOUR HANDS ARE ALL...
ROWR
PLEASE. LOVE MUST BE FREE.
NG.
JAB
SAYING SUCH A THING SHOWS ONLY THAT YOU'VE NO FAITH IN YOURSELF.
NNG.
J-J-JAB
AND IF YOU DON'T LIKE IT, LEARN TO MAKE GOOD OHAGI.
HO HO HO
PAT
PAT
WAAH! WHY CAN'T I THINK OF A COME-BACK?!
......
THOUGHT SHE'D GOTTEN MORE LADYLIKE, BUT...MAYBE NOT.
GLOG
GLOG
BUT SHE'S MUCH BRIGHTER AND LIVELY THAN BEFORE.

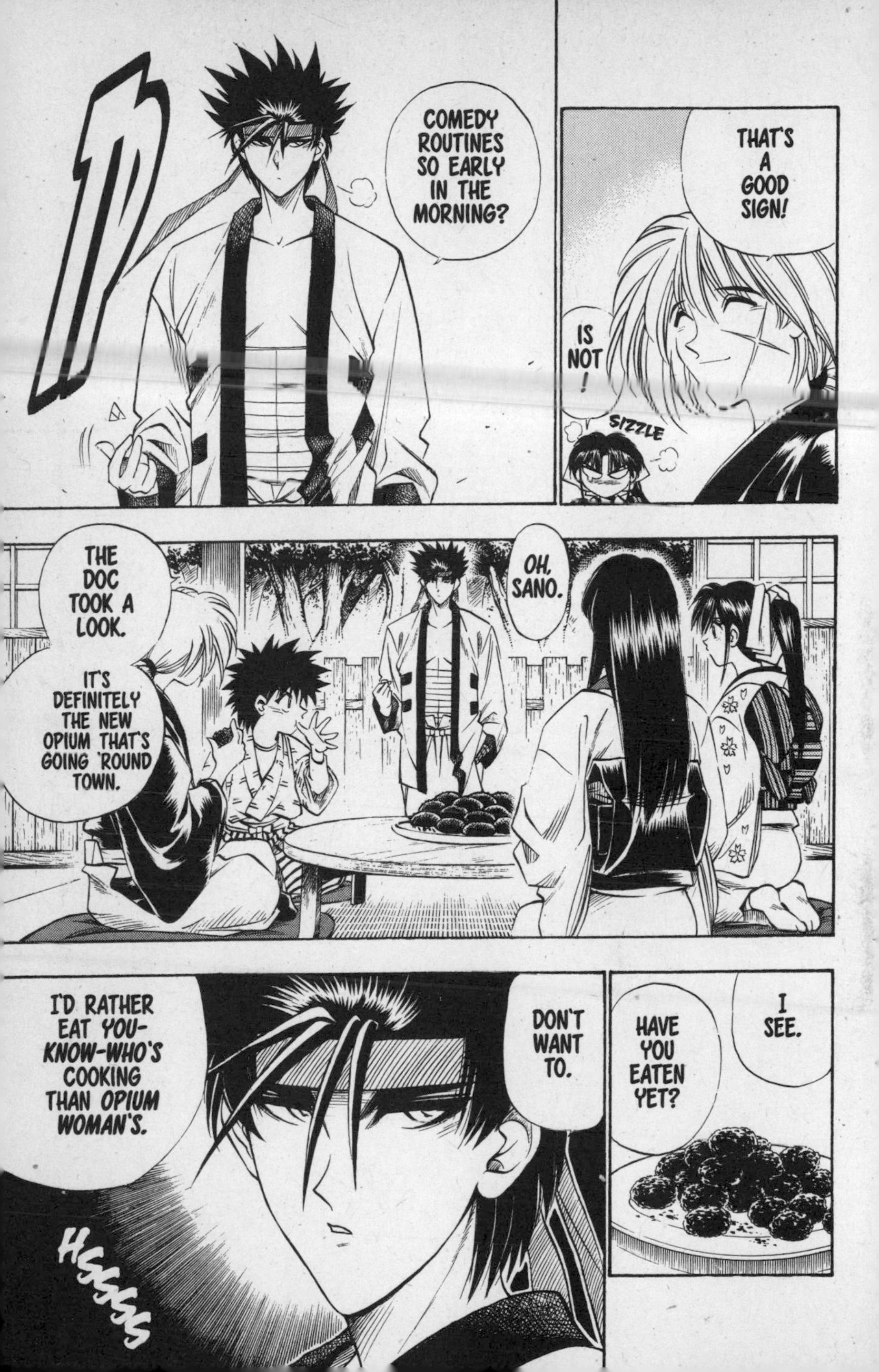
THAT'S A GOOD SIGN!
IS NOT!
SIZZLE
COMEDY ROUTINES SO EARLY IN THE MORNING?
OH, SANO.
THE DOC TOOK A LOOK.
IT'S DEFINITELY THE NEW OPIUM THAT'S GOING 'ROUND TOWN.
I SEE.
HAVE YOU EATEN YET?
DON'T WANT TO.
I'D RATHER EAT YOU-KNOW-WHO'S COOKING THAN OPIUM WOMAN'S.
HSSSSS

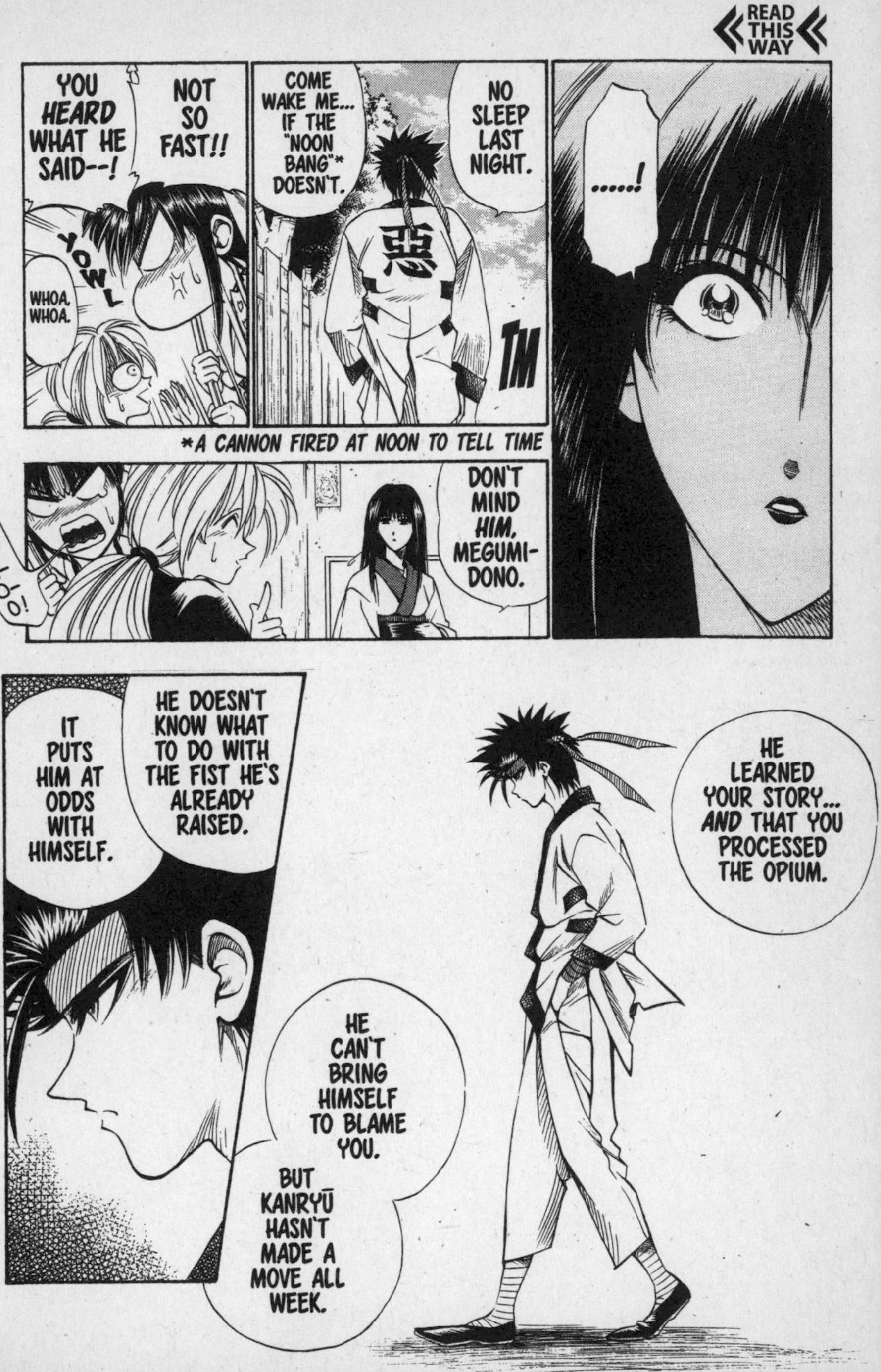
READ THIS WAY
......!
NO SLEEP LAST NIGHT.
COME WAKE ME... IF THE "NOON BANG"* DOESN'T.
TM
NOT SO FAST!!
YOU HEARD WHAT HE SAID--!
YOWL
WHOA, WHOA.
*A CANNON FIRED AT NOON TO TELL TIME
DON'T MIND HIM, MEGUMI-DONO.
HE LEARNED YOUR STORY... AND THAT YOU PROCESSED THE OPIUM.
HE CAN'T BRING HIMSELF TO BLAME YOU.
BUT KANRYŪ HASN'T MADE A MOVE ALL WEEK.
HE DOESN'T KNOW WHAT TO DO WITH THE FIST HE'S ALREADY RAISED.
IT PUTS HIM AT ODDS WITH HIMSELF.

READ THIS WAY

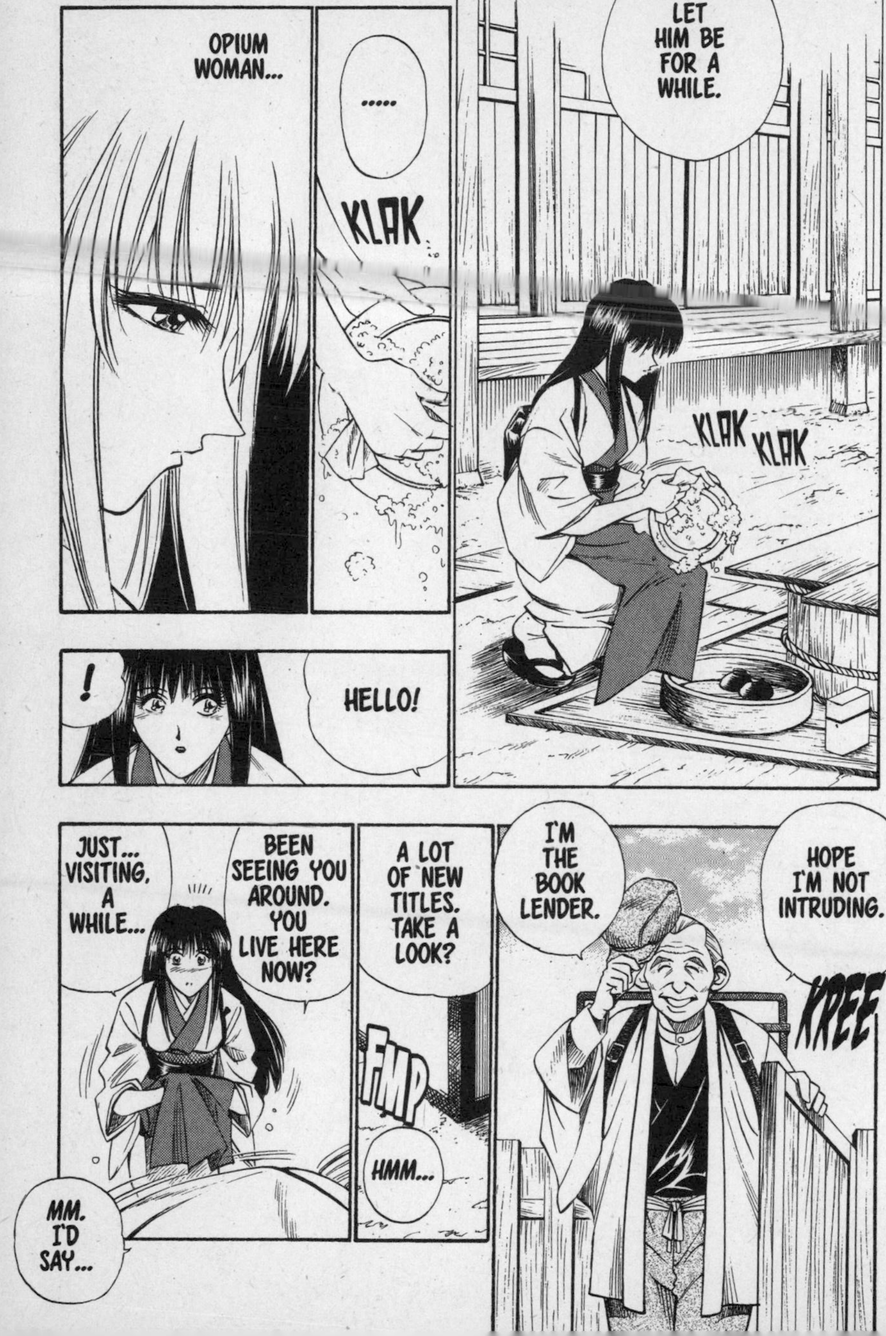

LET HIM BE FOR A WHILE.
KLAK KLAK
......
KLAK
OPIUM WOMAN...
HELLO!
!
HOPE I'M NOT INTRUDING.
I'M THE BOOK LENDER.
KREE
A LOT OF NEW TITLES. TAKE A LOOK?
FMP
HMM...
BEEN SEEING YOU AROUND. YOU LIVE HERE NOW?
JUST... VISITING, A WHILE...
MM. I'D SAY...

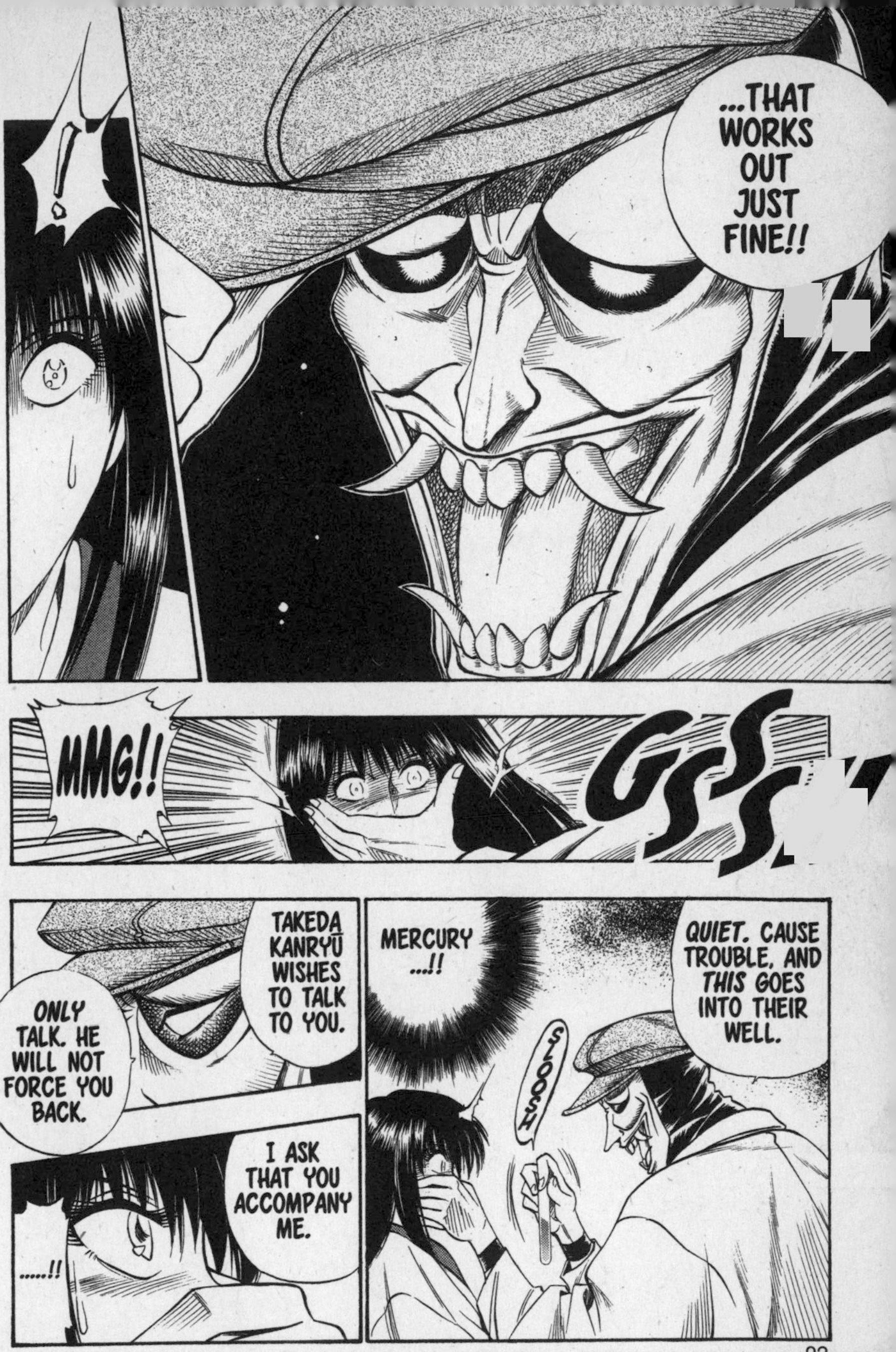
...THAT WORKS OUT JUST FINE!!
!
GSS
MMG!!
QUIET. CAUSE TROUBLE, AND THIS GOES INTO THEIR WELL.
SLOOSH
MERCURY ...!!
TAKEDA KANRYŪ WISHES TO TALK TO YOU.
ONLY TALK. HE WILL NOT FORCE YOU BACK.
I ASK THAT YOU ACCOMPANY ME.
......!!

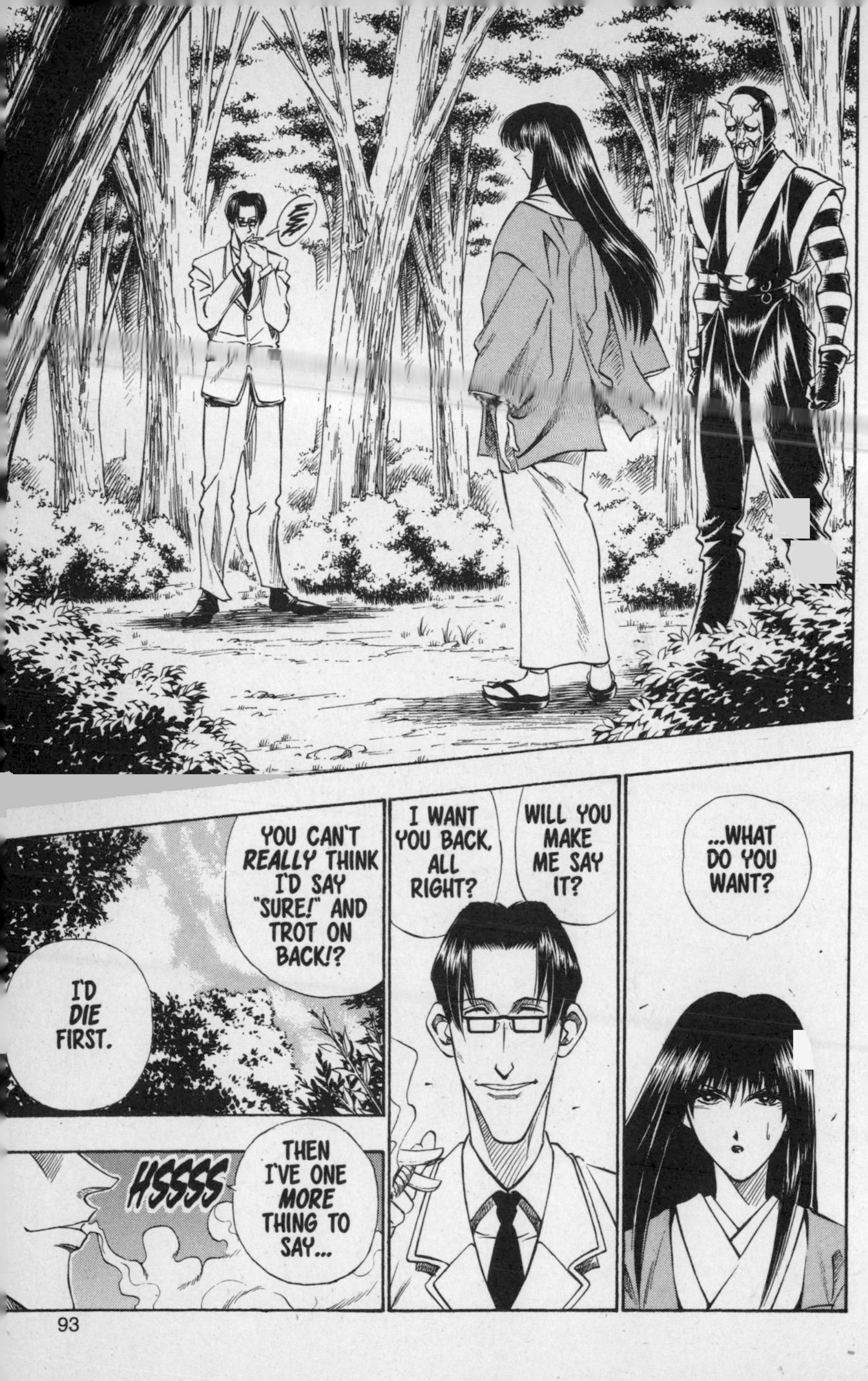
...WHAT DO YOU WANT?
WILL YOU MAKE ME SAY IT?
I WANT YOU BACK, ALL RIGHT?
YOU CAN'T *REALLY* THINK I'D SAY "SURE!" AND TROT ON BACK!?
I'D *DIE* FIRST.
THEN I'VE ONE *MORE* THING TO SAY...
HSSSS

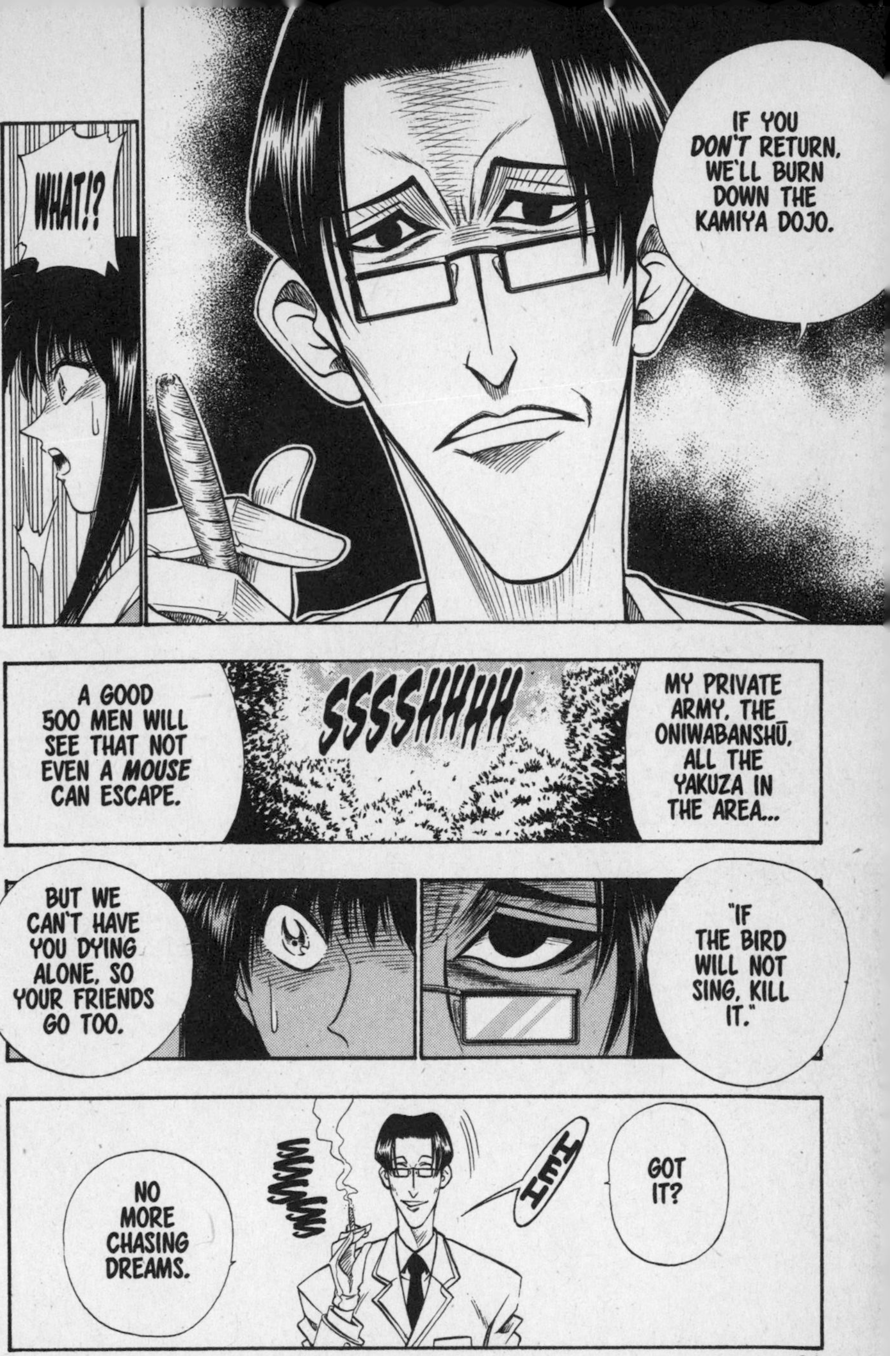
IF YOU *DON'T* RETURN, WE'LL BURN DOWN THE KAMIYA DOJO.
WHAT!?
MY PRIVATE ARMY, THE ONIWABANSHŪ, ALL THE YAKUZA IN THE AREA...
SSSSHHHH
A GOOD 500 MEN WILL SEE THAT NOT EVEN A *MOUSE* CAN ESCAPE.
"IF THE BIRD WILL NOT SING, KILL IT."
BUT WE CAN'T HAVE YOU DYING ALONE, SO YOUR FRIENDS GO TOO.
GOT IT?
HEH
NO MORE CHASING DREAMS.

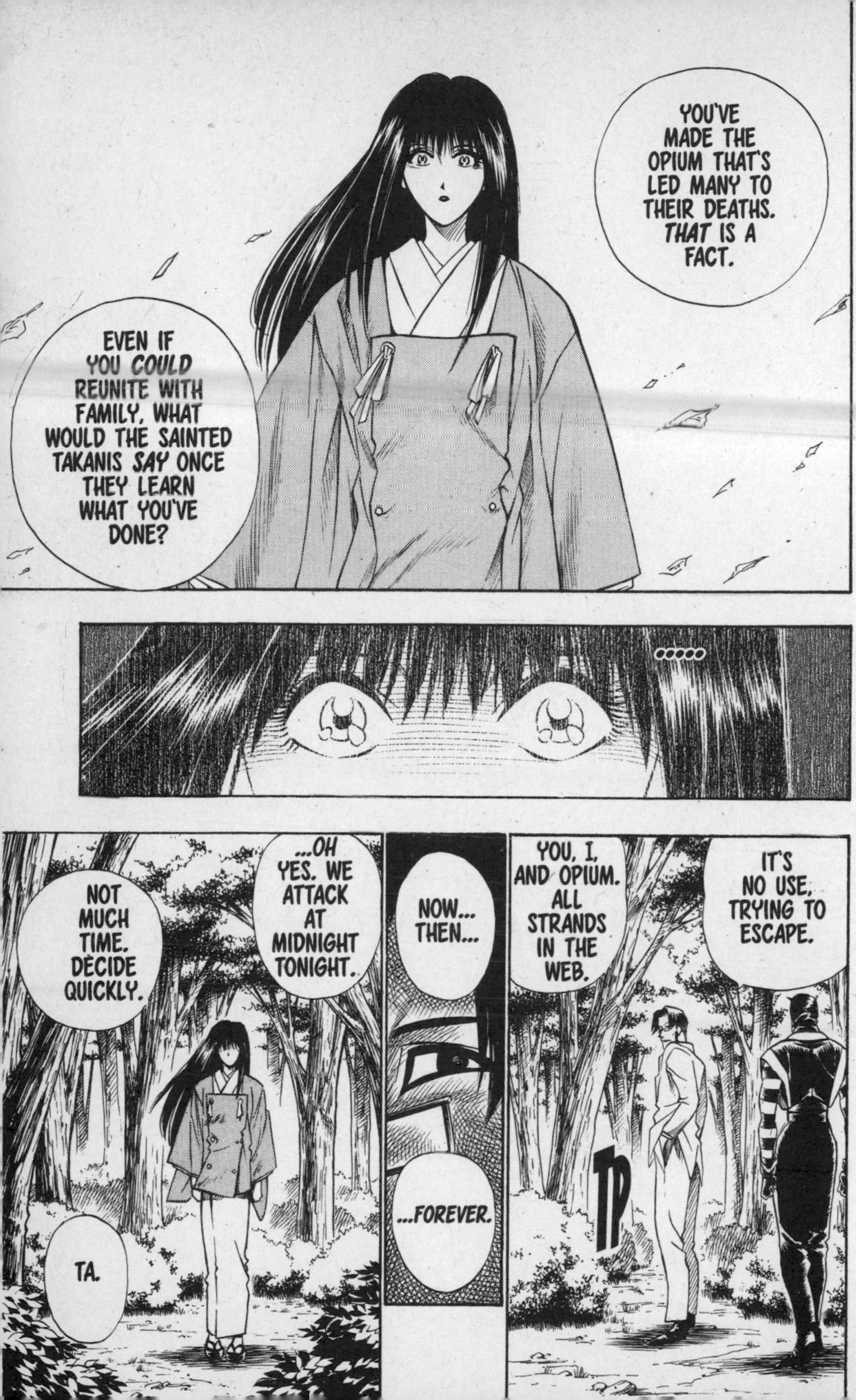
YOU'VE MADE THE OPIUM THAT'S LED MANY TO THEIR DEATHS. *THAT* IS A FACT.
EVEN IF YOU *COULD* REUNITE WITH FAMILY, WHAT WOULD THE SAINTED TAKANIS *SAY* ONCE THEY LEARN WHAT YOU'VE DONE?
IT'S NO USE, TRYING TO ESCAPE.
YOU, I, AND OPIUM. ALL STRANDS IN THE WEB.
TP
NOW... THEN...
...FOREVER.
...OH YES. WE ATTACK AT MIDNIGHT TONIGHT.
NOT MUCH TIME. DECIDE QUICKLY.
TA.

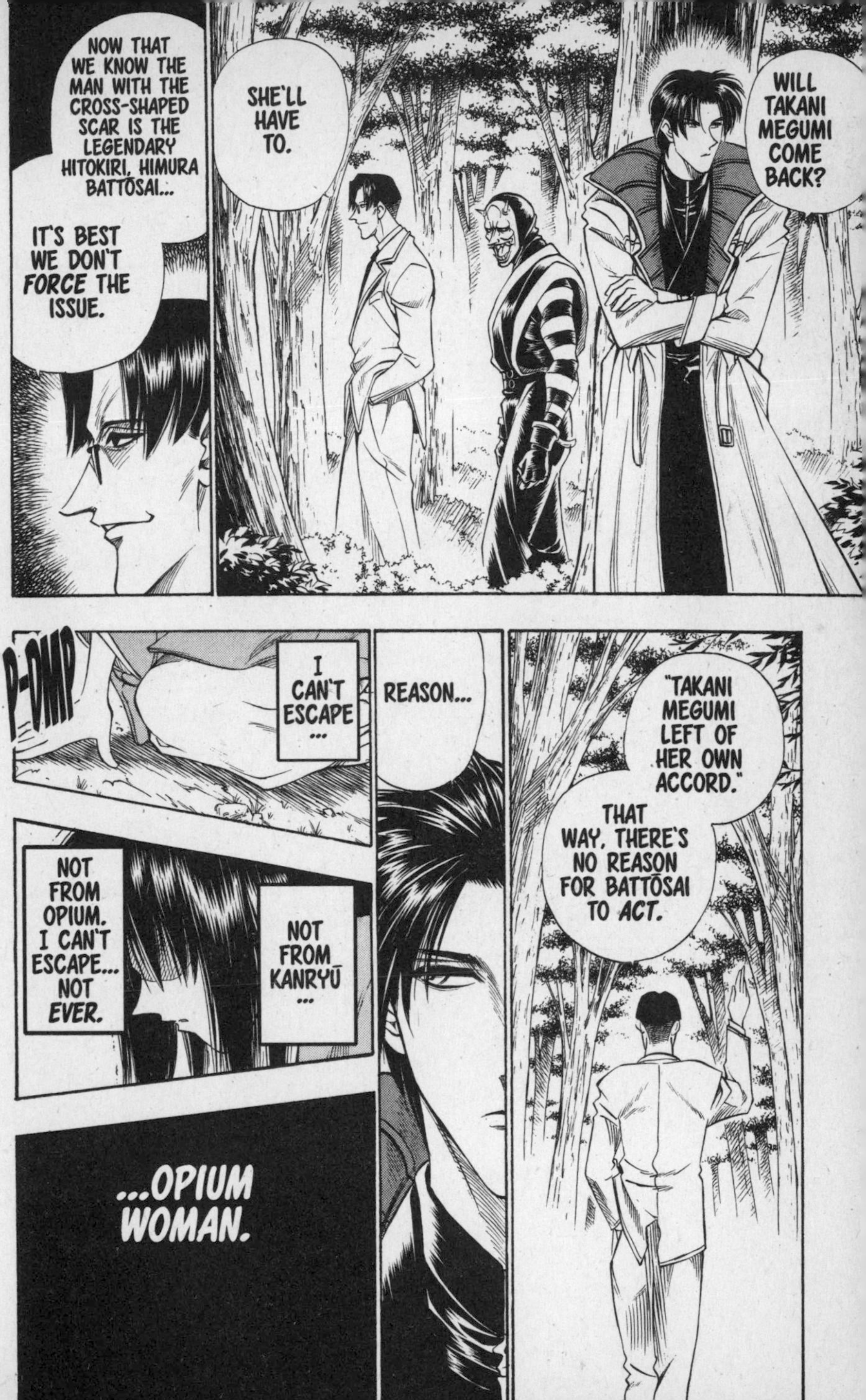
WILL TAKANI MEGUMI COME BACK?
SHE'LL HAVE TO.
NOW THAT WE KNOW THE MAN WITH THE CROSS-SHAPED SCAR IS THE LEGENDARY HITOKIRI, HIMURA BATTŌSAI...
IT'S BEST WE DON'T *FORCE* THE ISSUE.
"TAKANI MEGUMI LEFT OF HER OWN ACCORD."
THAT WAY, THERE'S NO REASON FOR BATTŌSAI TO *ACT*.
REASON...
P-DMP
I CAN'T ESCAPE...
NOT FROM KANRYŪ...
NOT FROM OPIUM. I CAN'T ESCAPE... NOT *EVER*.
...OPIUM WOMAN.

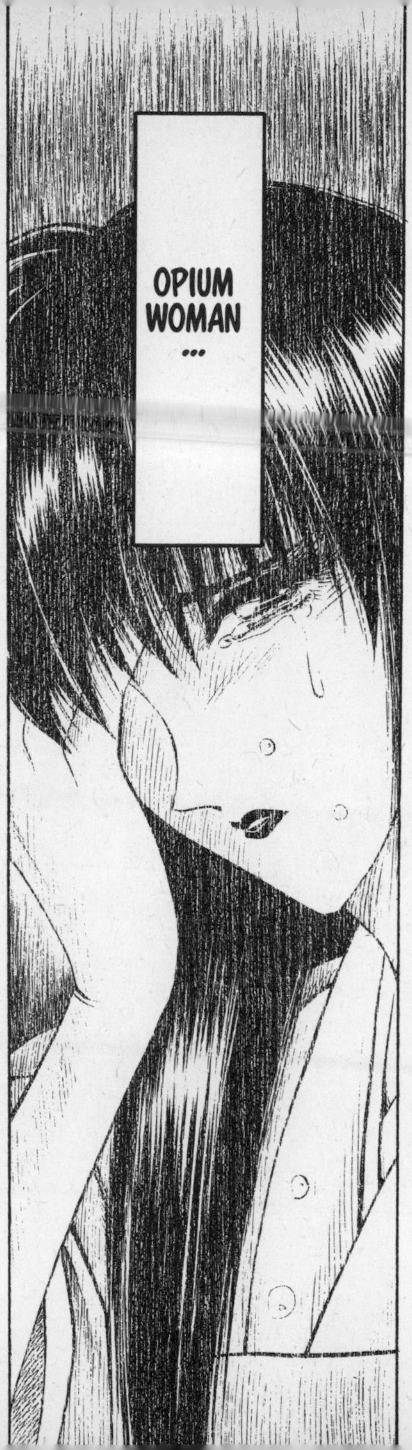
OPIUM WOMAN ...

READ THIS WAY

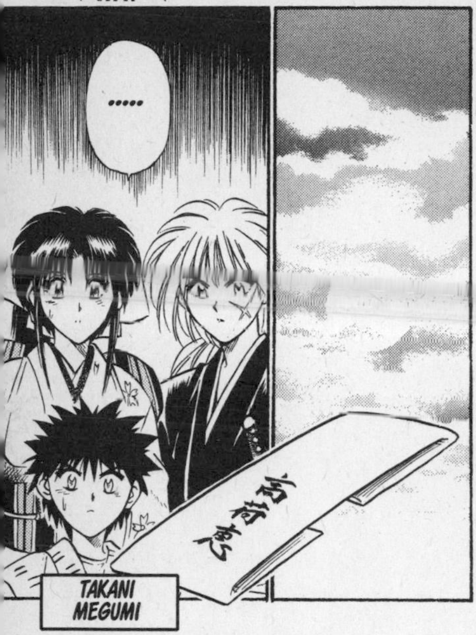
高荷恵
......
TAKANI MEGUMI

Long time no see! Watsuki here. About those fan letters, again— I've been getting more and more from you guys. We're becoming more like a "young men's" magazine, but even so, the ratio is still running 7:3, females over males. I do still plan to reply to you, so please be patient, just a bit longer—especially those of you who've sent multiple letters already. (I'm so sorry!)

Watsuki

伸宏和月

READ THIS WAY

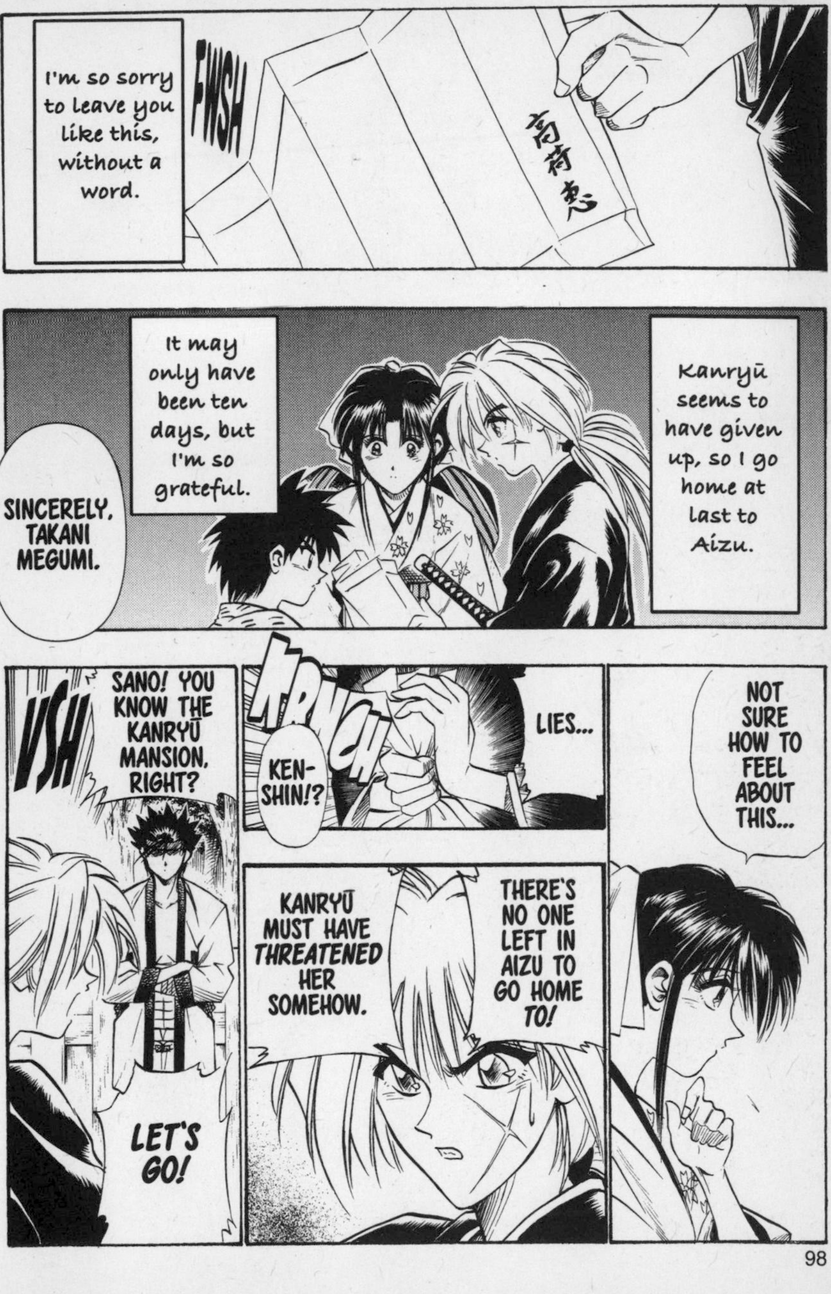
FWSH
I'm so sorry to leave you like this, without a word.
高荷恵
Kanryū seems to have given up, so I go home at last to Aizu.
It may only have been ten days, but I'm so grateful.
SINCERELY, TAKANI MEGUMI.
NOT SURE HOW TO FEEL ABOUT THIS...
LIES...
KRUNCH
KEN-SHIN!?
THERE'S NO ONE LEFT IN AIZU TO GO HOME TO!
KANRYŪ MUST HAVE THREATENED HER SOMEHOW.
VSH
SANO! YOU KNOW THE KANRYŪ MANSION, RIGHT?
LET'S GO!

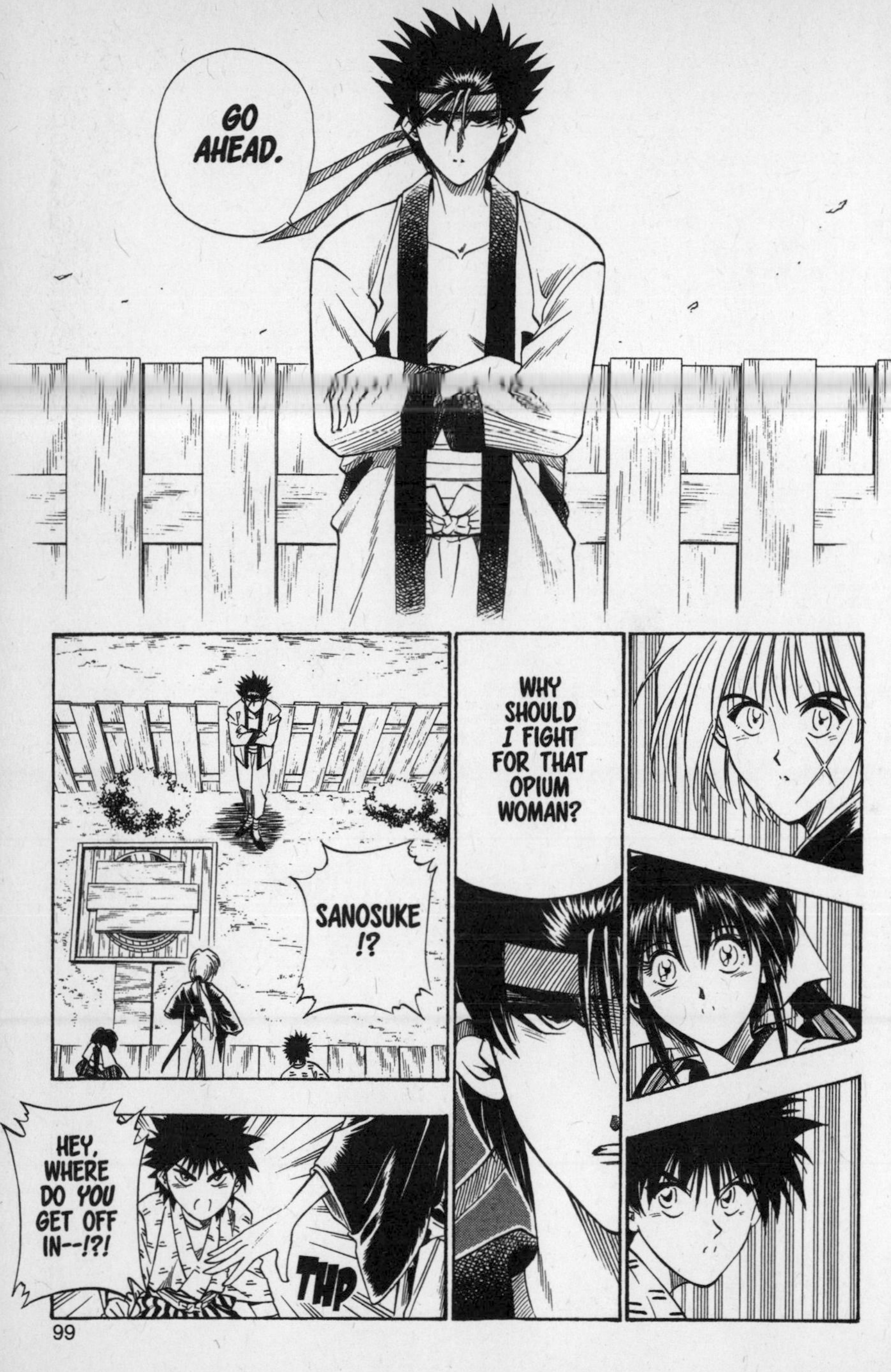
GO AHEAD.
WHY SHOULD I FIGHT FOR THAT OPIUM WOMAN?
SANOSUKE !?
HEY, WHERE DO YOU GET OFF IN--!?!
THP

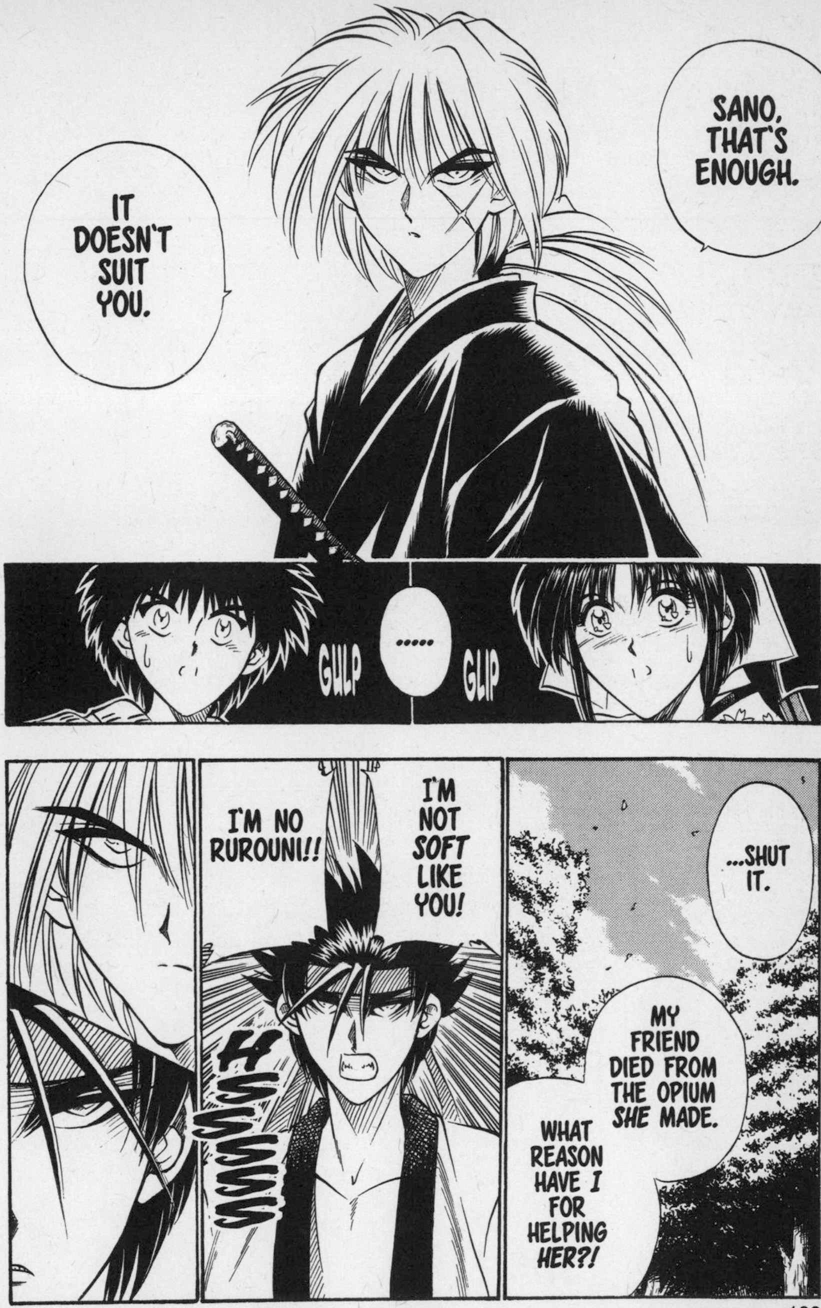
SANO, THAT'S ENOUGH.
IT DOESN'T SUIT YOU.
GLIP
......
GULP
...SHUT IT.
MY FRIEND DIED FROM THE OPIUM *SHE* MADE.
WHAT REASON HAVE *I* FOR HELPING *HER*?!
I'M NOT *SOFT* LIKE YOU!
I'M NO RUROUNI!!
HSSSSSS

READ THIS WAY

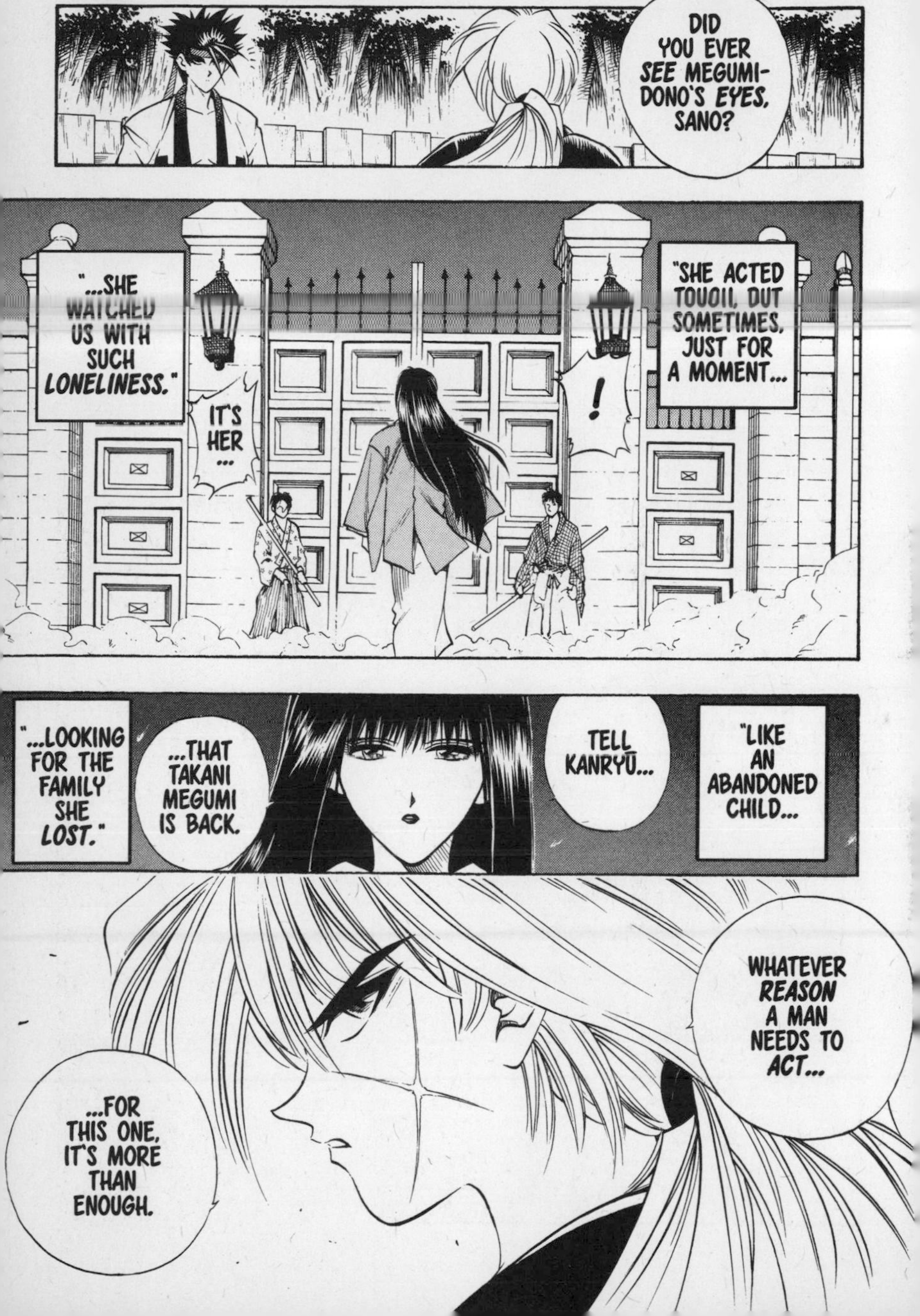

DID YOU EVER SEE MEGUMI-DONO'S EYES, SANO?
"SHE ACTED TOUGH, BUT SOMETIMES, JUST FOR A MOMENT...
!
IT'S HER...
"...SHE WATCHED US WITH SUCH LONELINESS."
"LIKE AN ABANDONED CHILD...
TELL KANRYŪ...
...THAT TAKANI MEGUMI IS BACK.
"...LOOKING FOR THE FAMILY SHE LOST."
WHATEVER REASON A MAN NEEDS TO ACT...
...FOR THIS ONE, IT'S MORE THAN ENOUGH.

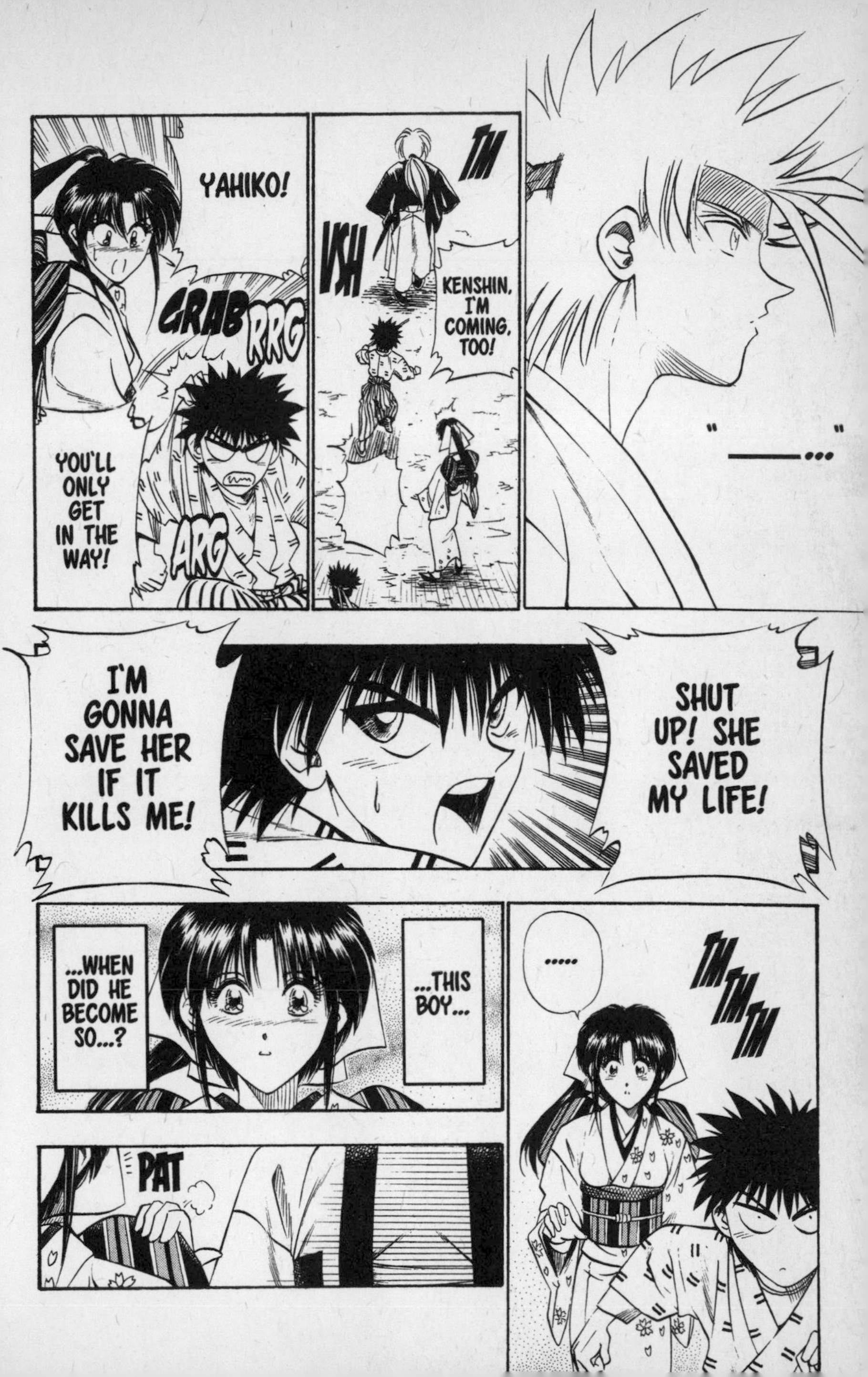
"——..."
TH
VSH
KENSHIN, I'M COMING, TOO!
YAHIKO!
GRAB
RRG
YOU'LL ONLY GET IN THE WAY!
ARG
SHUT UP! SHE SAVED MY LIFE!
I'M GONNA SAVE HER IF IT KILLS ME!
.....
TH TH TH
...THIS BOY...
...WHEN DID HE BECOME SO...?
PAT

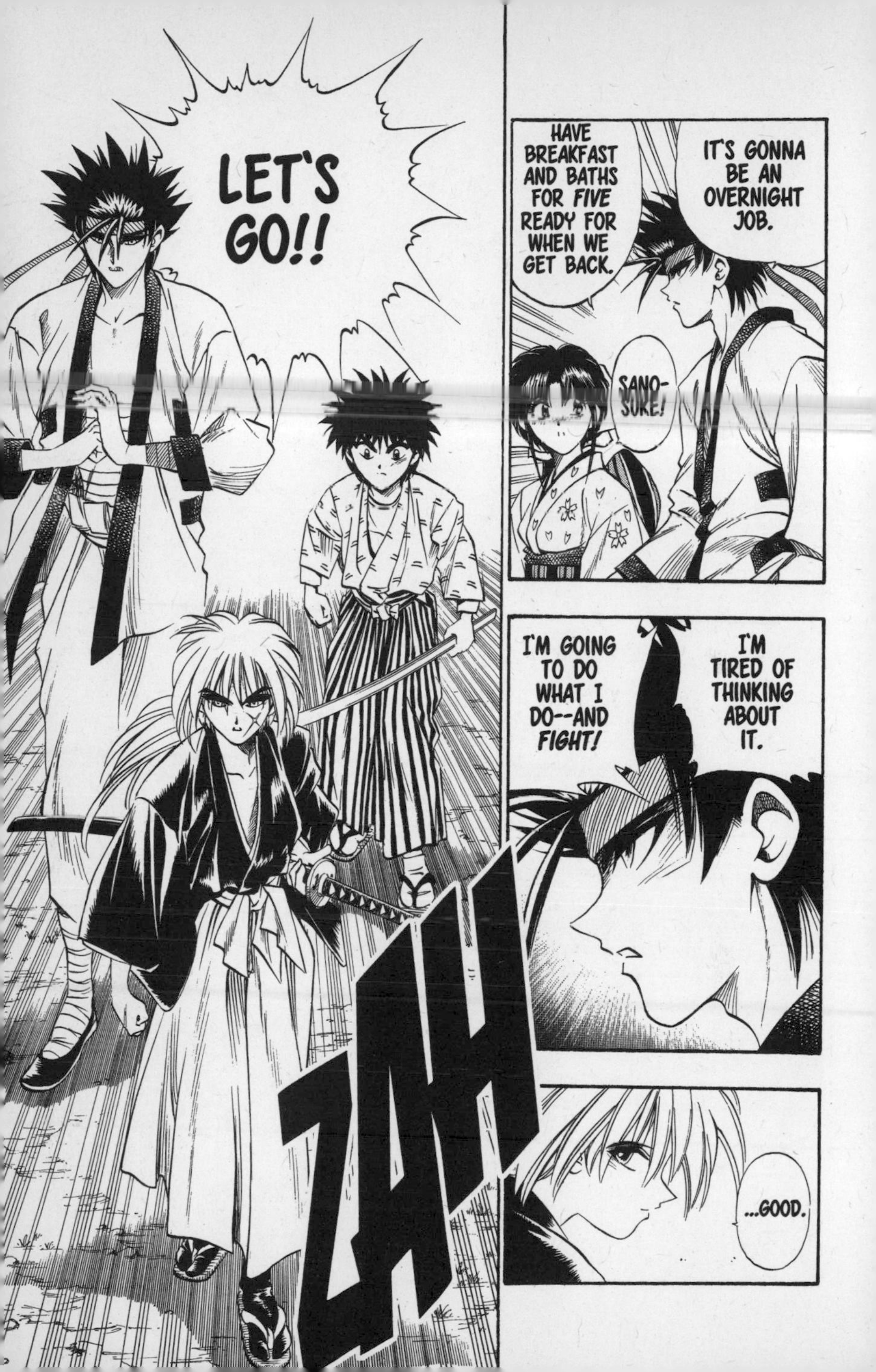
IT'S GONNA BE AN OVERNIGHT JOB.
HAVE BREAKFAST AND BATHS FOR *FIVE* READY FOR WHEN WE GET BACK.
SANO-SUKE!
I'M TIRED OF THINKING ABOUT IT.
I'M GOING TO DO WHAT I DO--AND *FIGHT!*
...GOOD.
LET'S GO!!
ZAH

READ THIS WAY

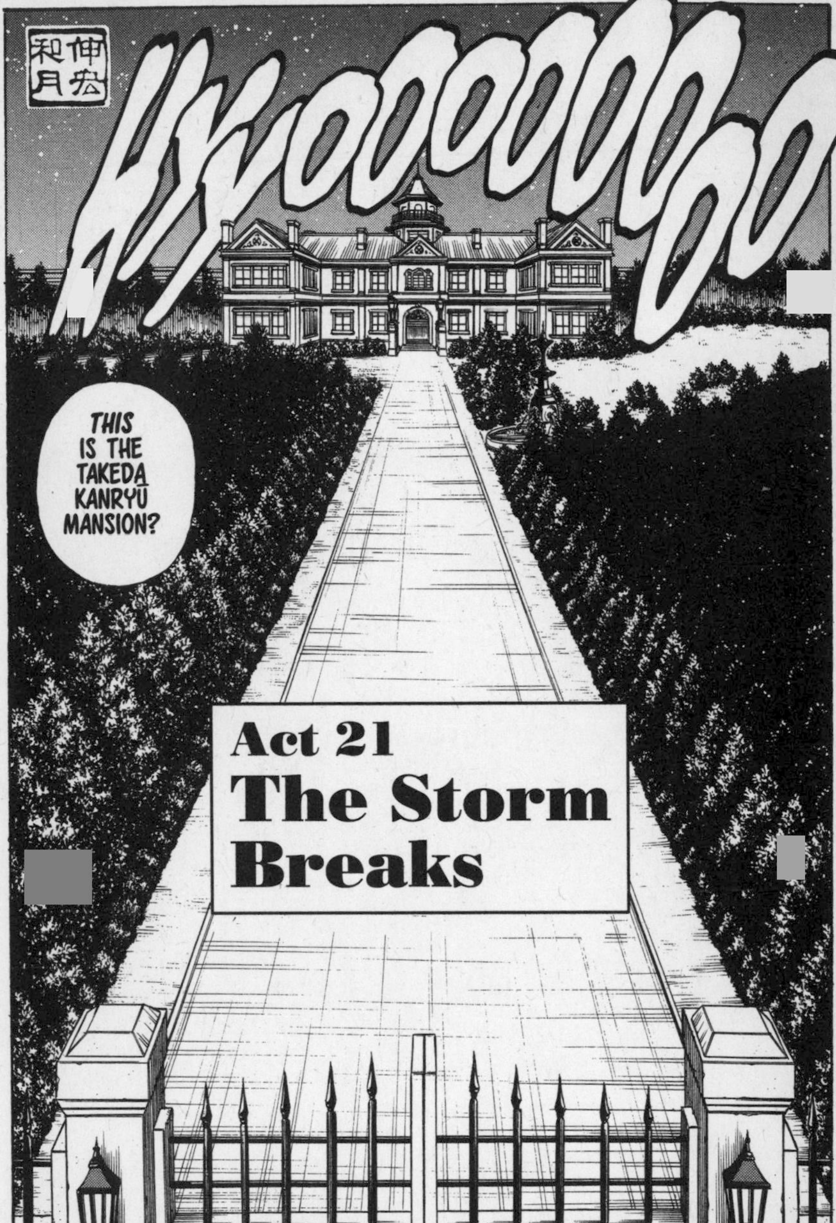

伸宏和月
THIS IS THE TAKEDA KANRYŪ MANSION?

Act 21 The Storm Breaks

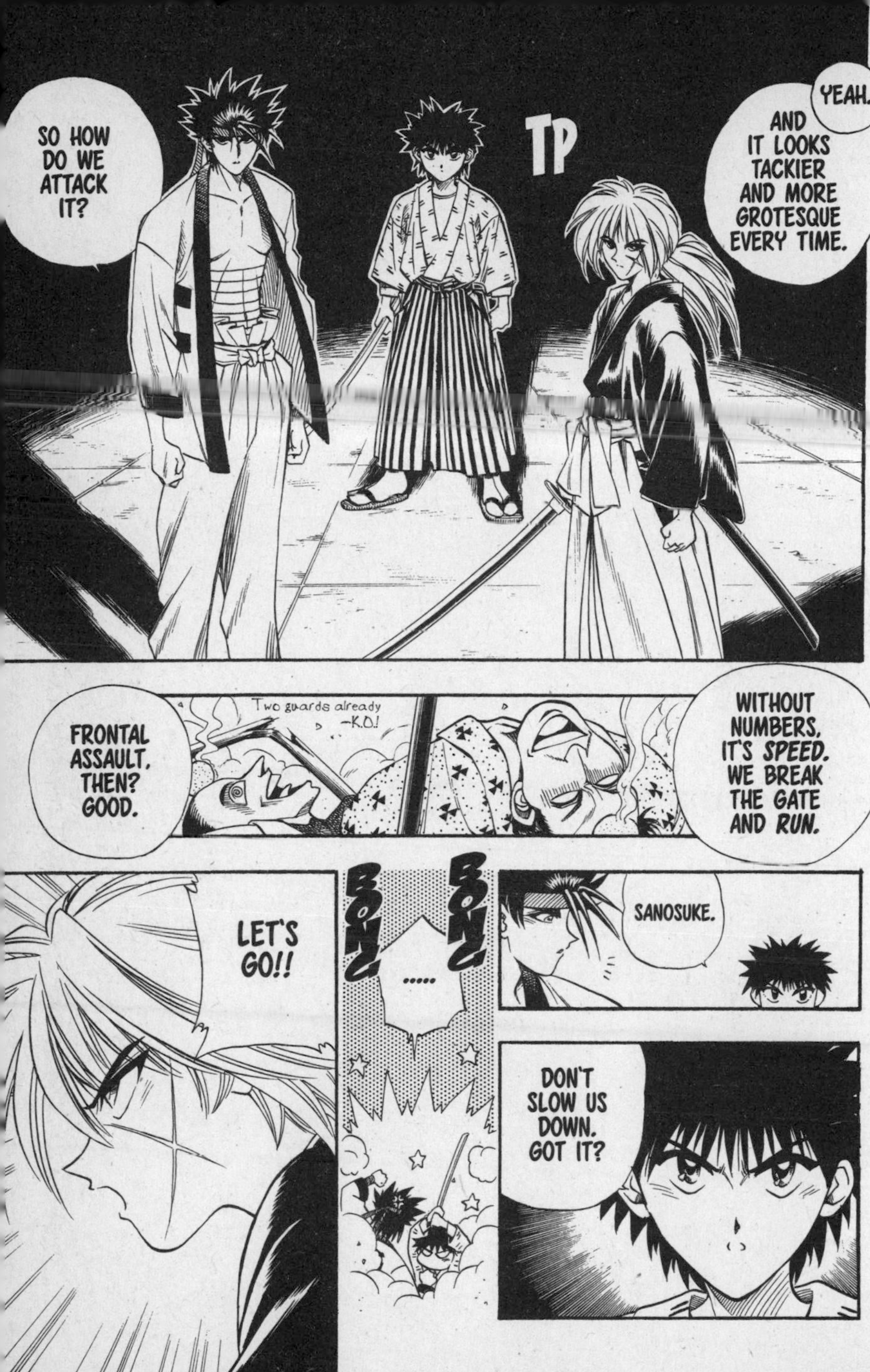
YEAH.
AND IT LOOKS TACKIER AND MORE GROTESQUE EVERY TIME.
TP
SO HOW DO WE ATTACK IT?
WITHOUT NUMBERS, IT'S SPEED. WE BREAK THE GATE AND RUN.
Two guards already —K.O.!
FRONTAL ASSAULT, THEN? GOOD.
SANOSUKE.
DON'T SLOW US DOWN. GOT IT?
BONG
BONG
.....
LET'S GO!!

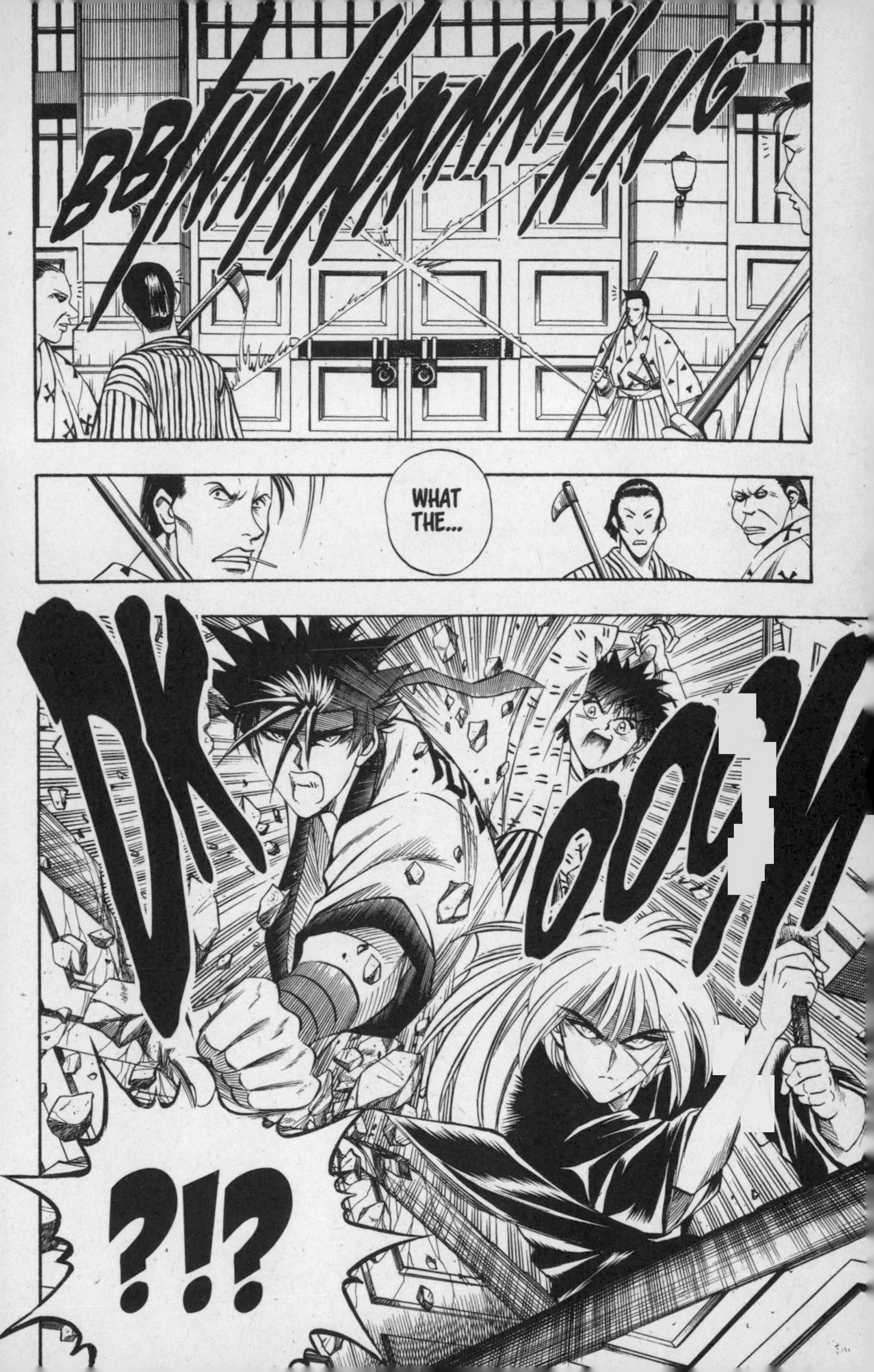
WHAT THE...
?!?

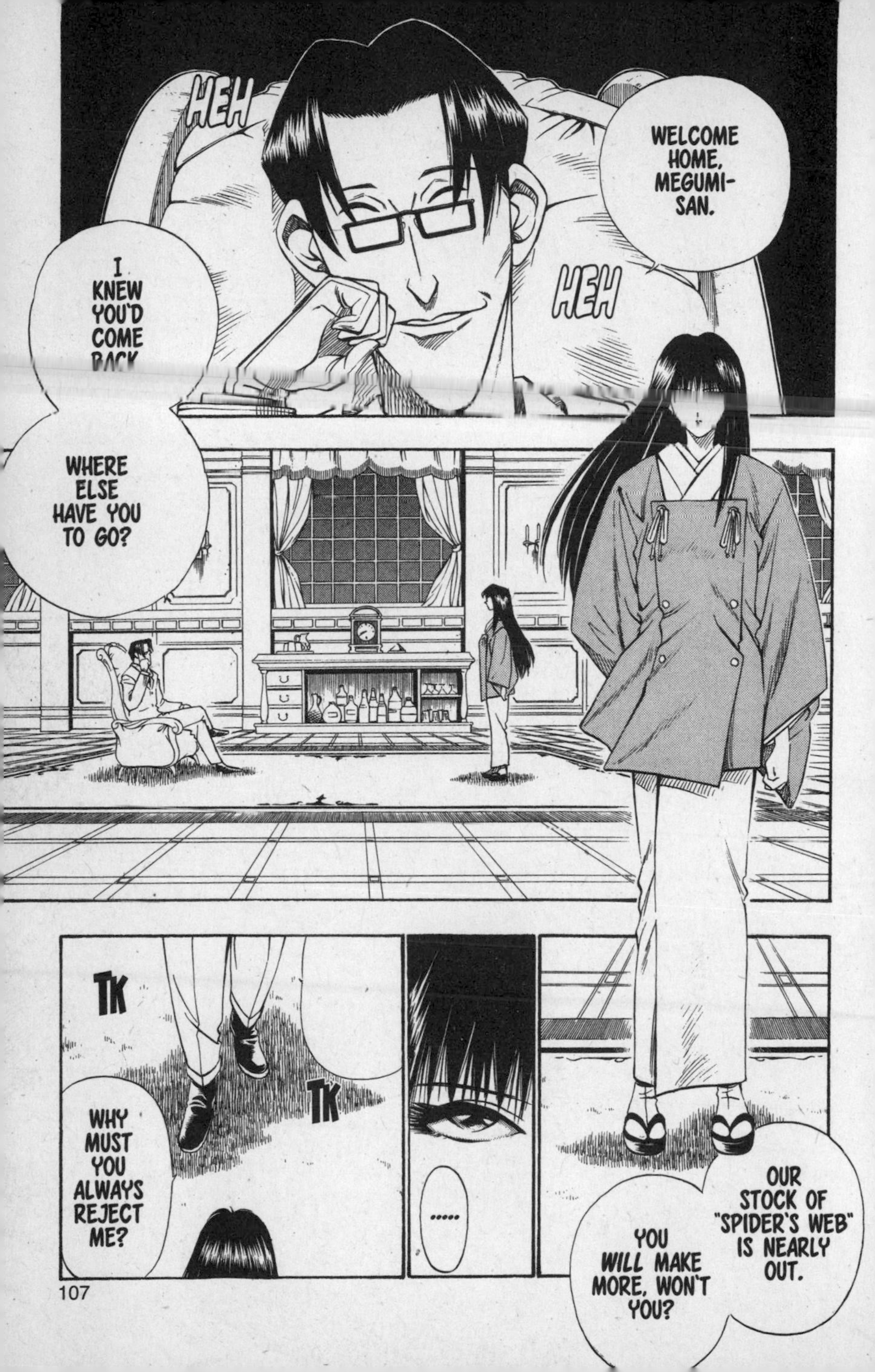
WELCOME HOME, MEGUMI-SAN.
HEH
HEH
I KNEW YOU'D COME BACK
WHERE ELSE HAVE YOU TO GO?
OUR STOCK OF "SPIDER'S WEB" IS NEARLY OUT.
YOU *WILL* MAKE MORE, WON'T YOU?
......
TK
TK
WHY MUST YOU ALWAYS REJECT ME?

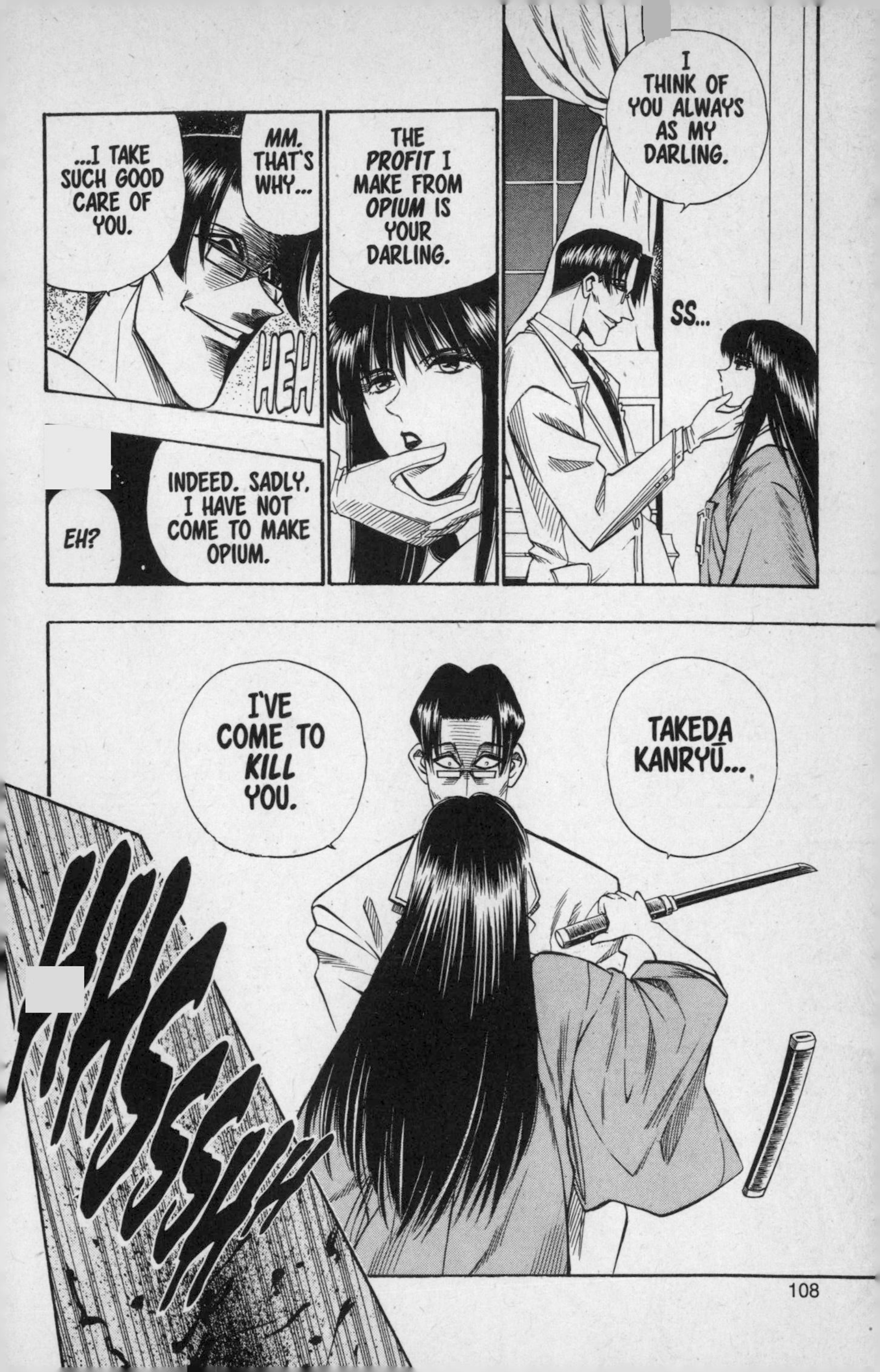
I THINK OF YOU ALWAYS AS MY DARLING.
SS...
THE *PROFIT* I MAKE FROM *OPIUM* IS YOUR DARLING.
MM. THAT'S WHY...
...I TAKE SUCH GOOD CARE OF YOU.
HEH
INDEED. SADLY, I HAVE NOT COME TO MAKE OPIUM.
EH?
TAKEDA KANRYŪ...
I'VE COME TO *KILL* YOU.

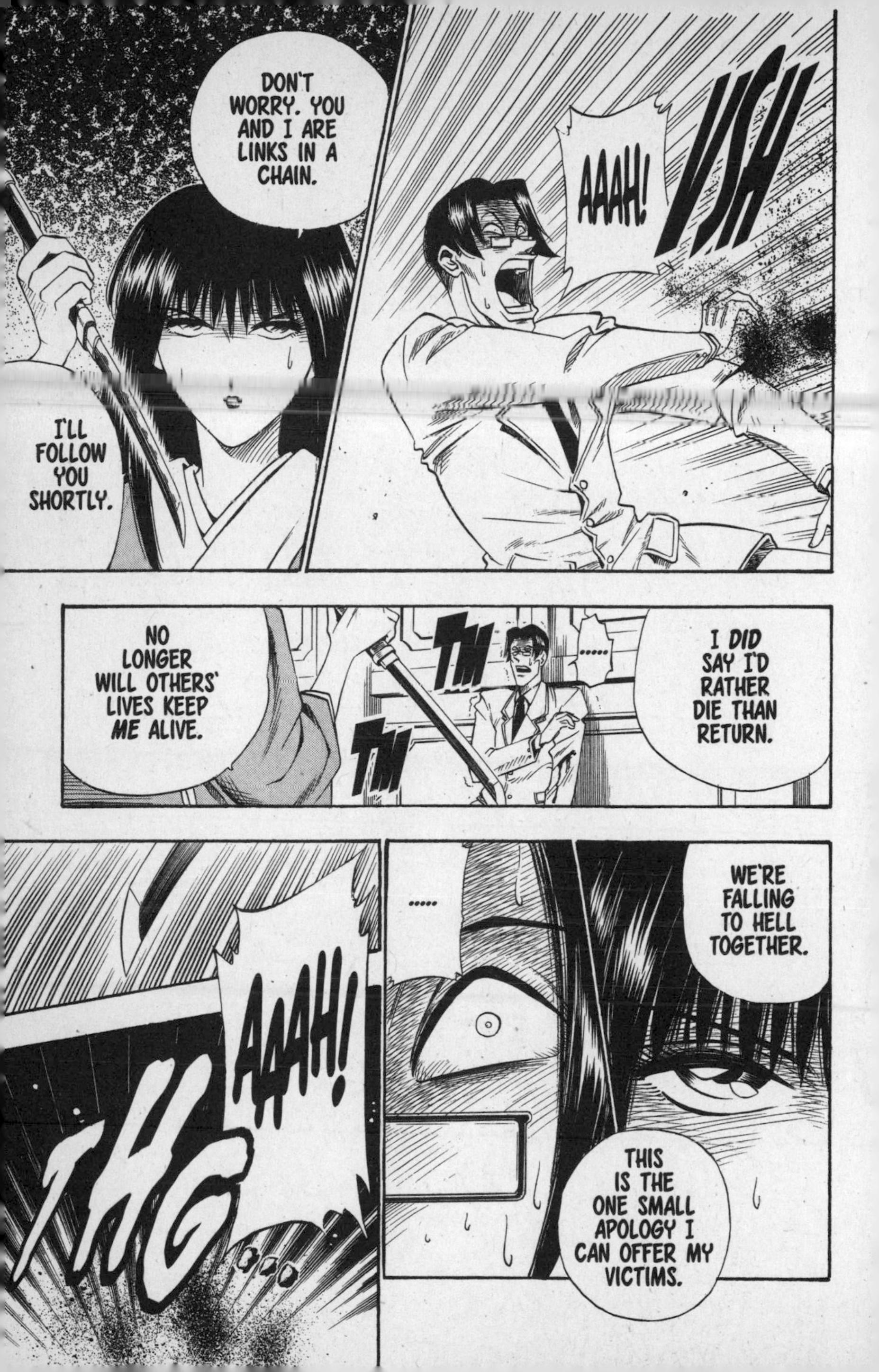
AAAH!
VSH
DON'T WORRY. YOU AND I ARE LINKS IN A CHAIN.
I'LL FOLLOW YOU SHORTLY.
I *DID* SAY I'D RATHER DIE THAN RETURN.
.....
TM
TM
NO LONGER WILL OTHERS' LIVES KEEP *ME* ALIVE.
WE'RE FALLING TO HELL TOGETHER.
.....
THIS IS THE ONE SMALL APOLOGY I CAN OFFER MY VICTIMS.
AAAH!
THG

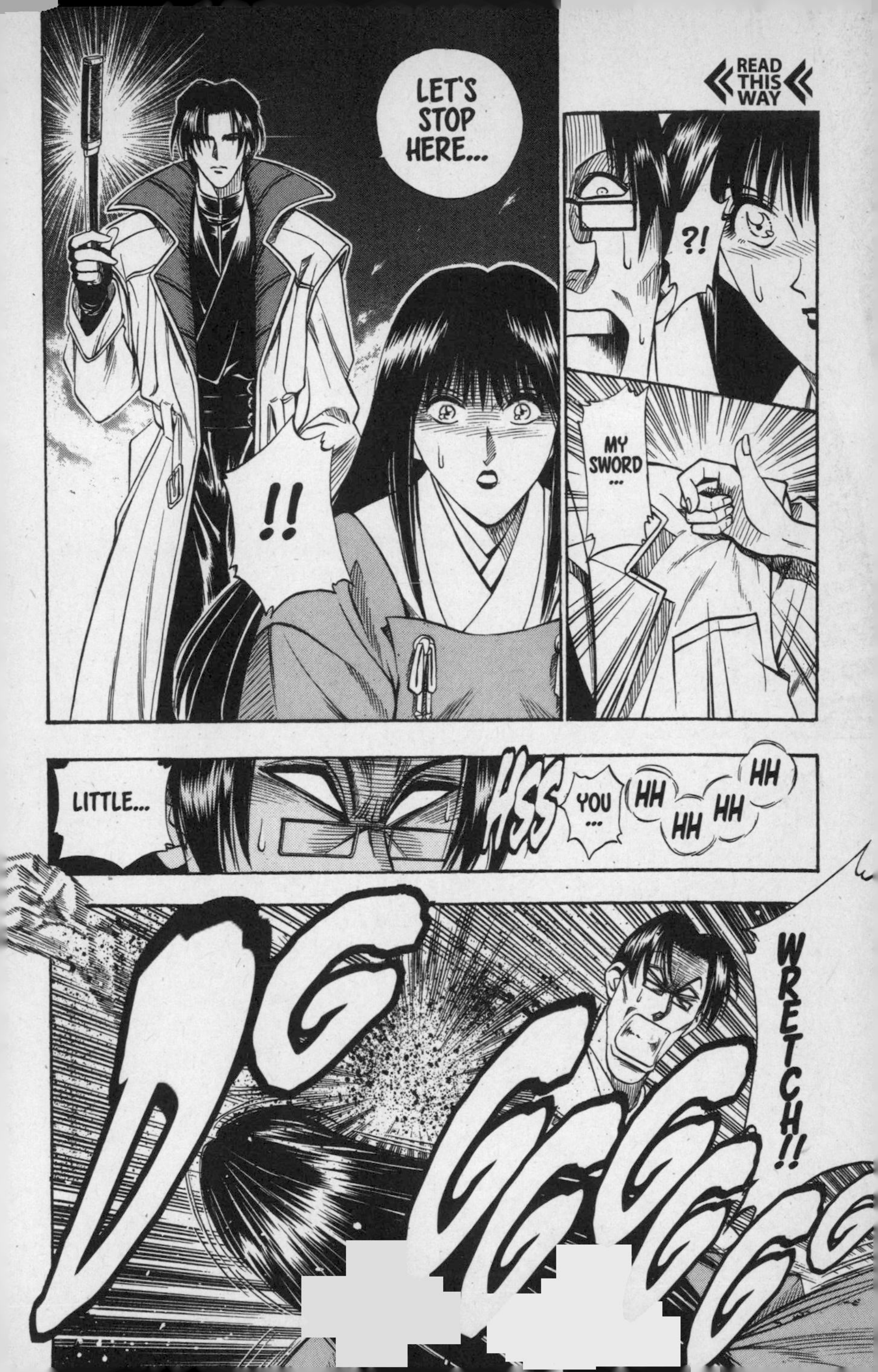
READ THIS WAY
?!
MY SWORD ...
LET'S STOP HERE...
!!
HH
HH
HH
HH
YOU ...
HSS
LITTLE...
WRETCH!!

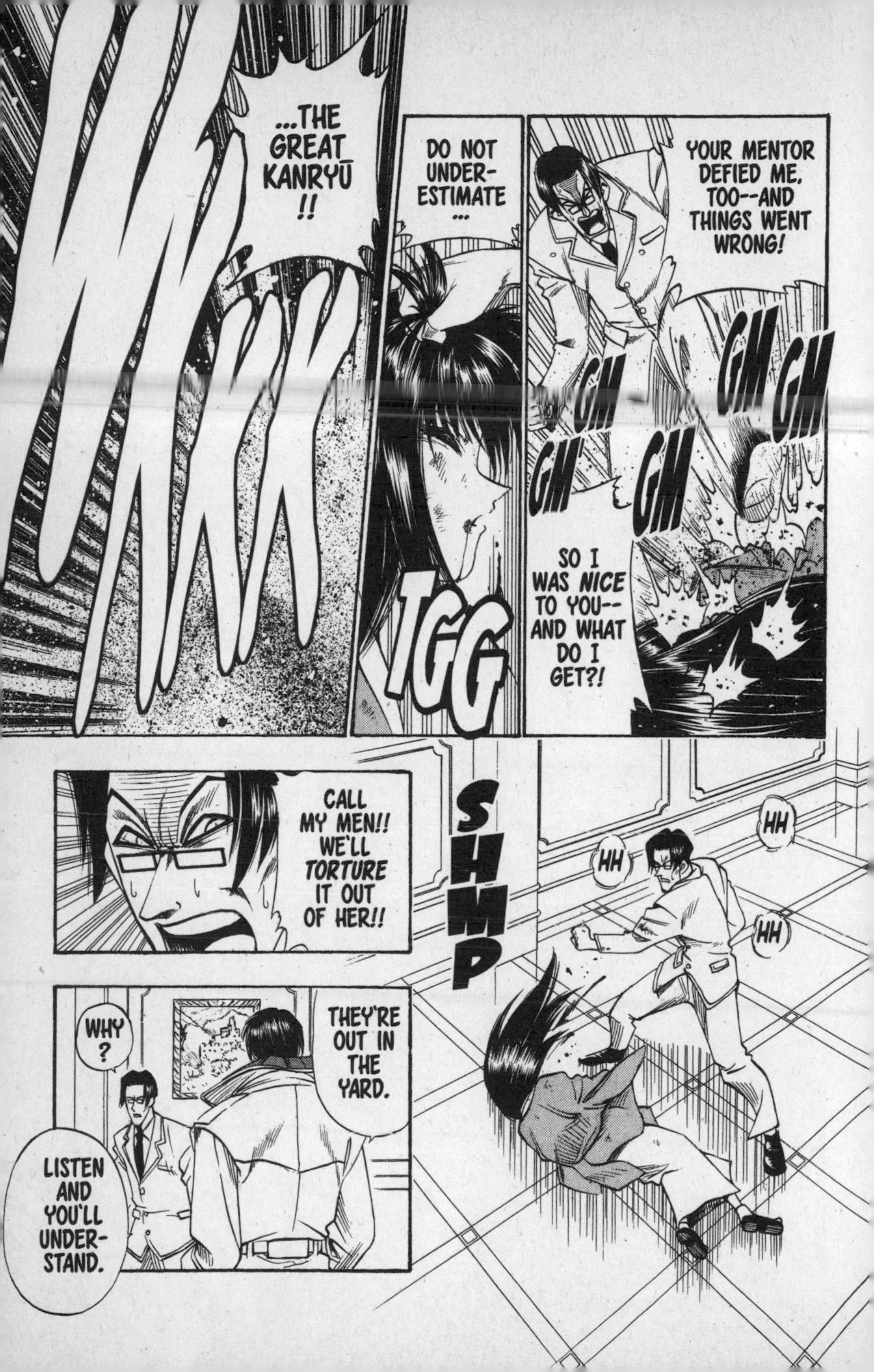
YOUR MENTOR DEFIED ME, TOO--AND THINGS WENT WRONG!
GM GM GM GM GM GM
SO I WAS *NICE* TO YOU--AND WHAT DO I GET?!
DO NOT UNDER-ESTIMATE ...
TGG
...THE GREAT KANRYŪ !!
SHMP
HH
HH
HH
CALL MY MEN!! WE'LL *TORTURE* IT OUT OF HER!!
THEY'RE OUT IN THE YARD.
WHY ?
LISTEN AND YOU'LL UNDER-STAND.

READ THIS WAY

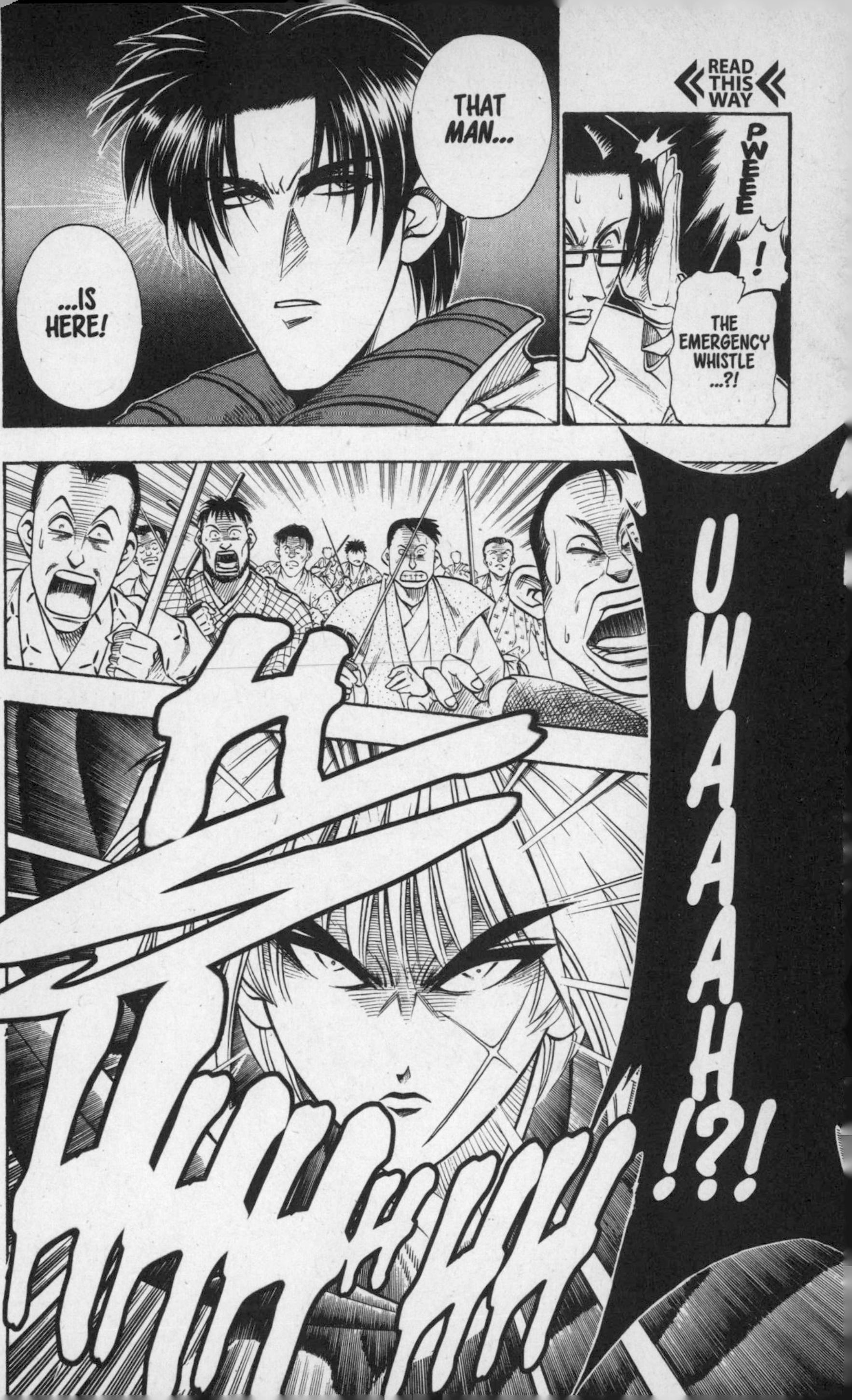
PWEEE!
THE EMERGENCY WHISTLE ...?!
THAT MAN...
...IS HERE!
UWAAAAH!?!

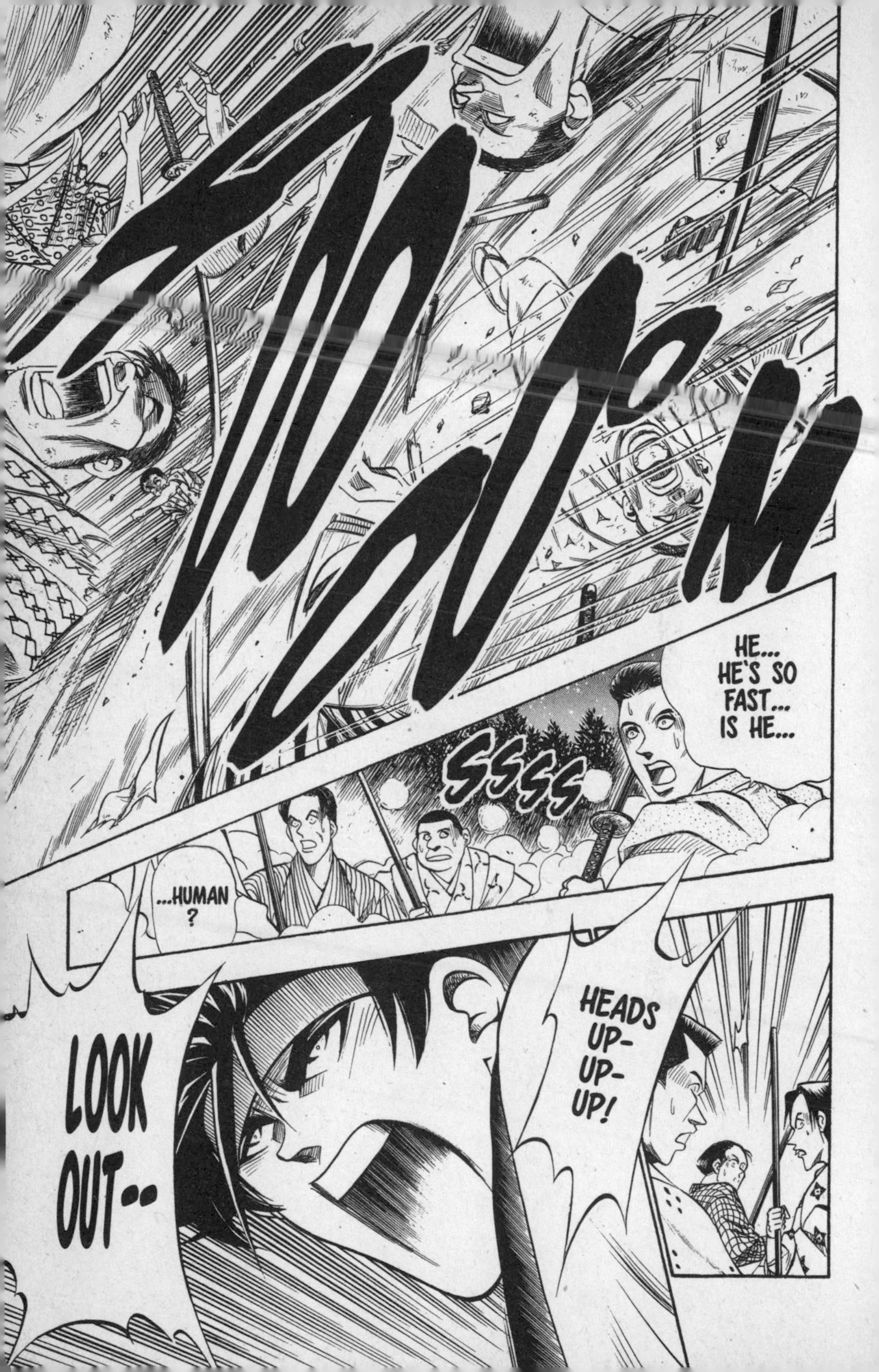
HE... HE'S SO FAST... IS HE...
SSSS
...HUMAN ?
HEADS UP-UP-UP!
LOOK OUT--

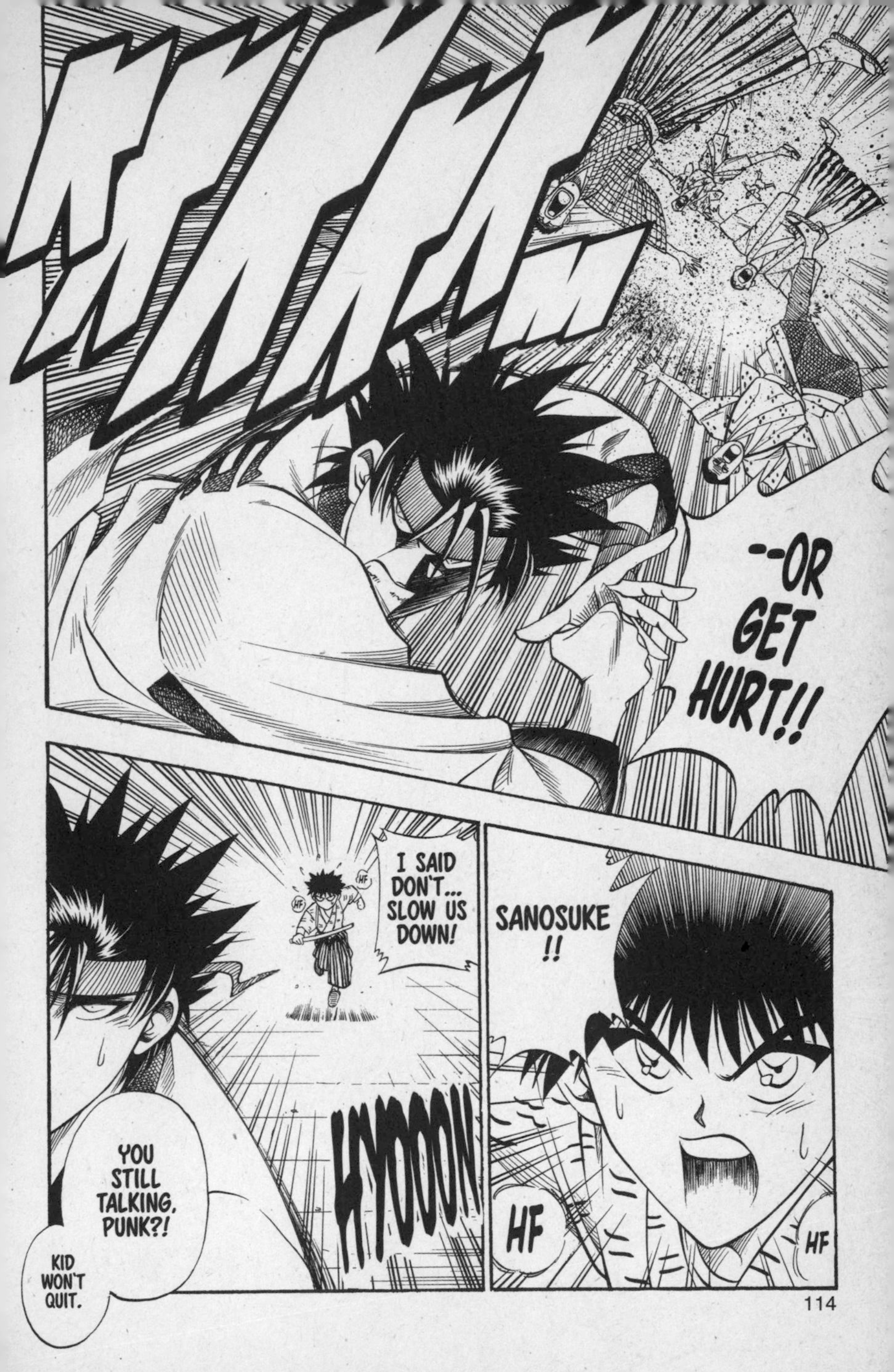
--OR GET HURT!!
SANOSUKE !!
HF
HF
I SAID DON'T... SLOW US DOWN!
HF
HF
HYOOON
YOU STILL TALKING, PUNK?!
KID WON'T QUIT.

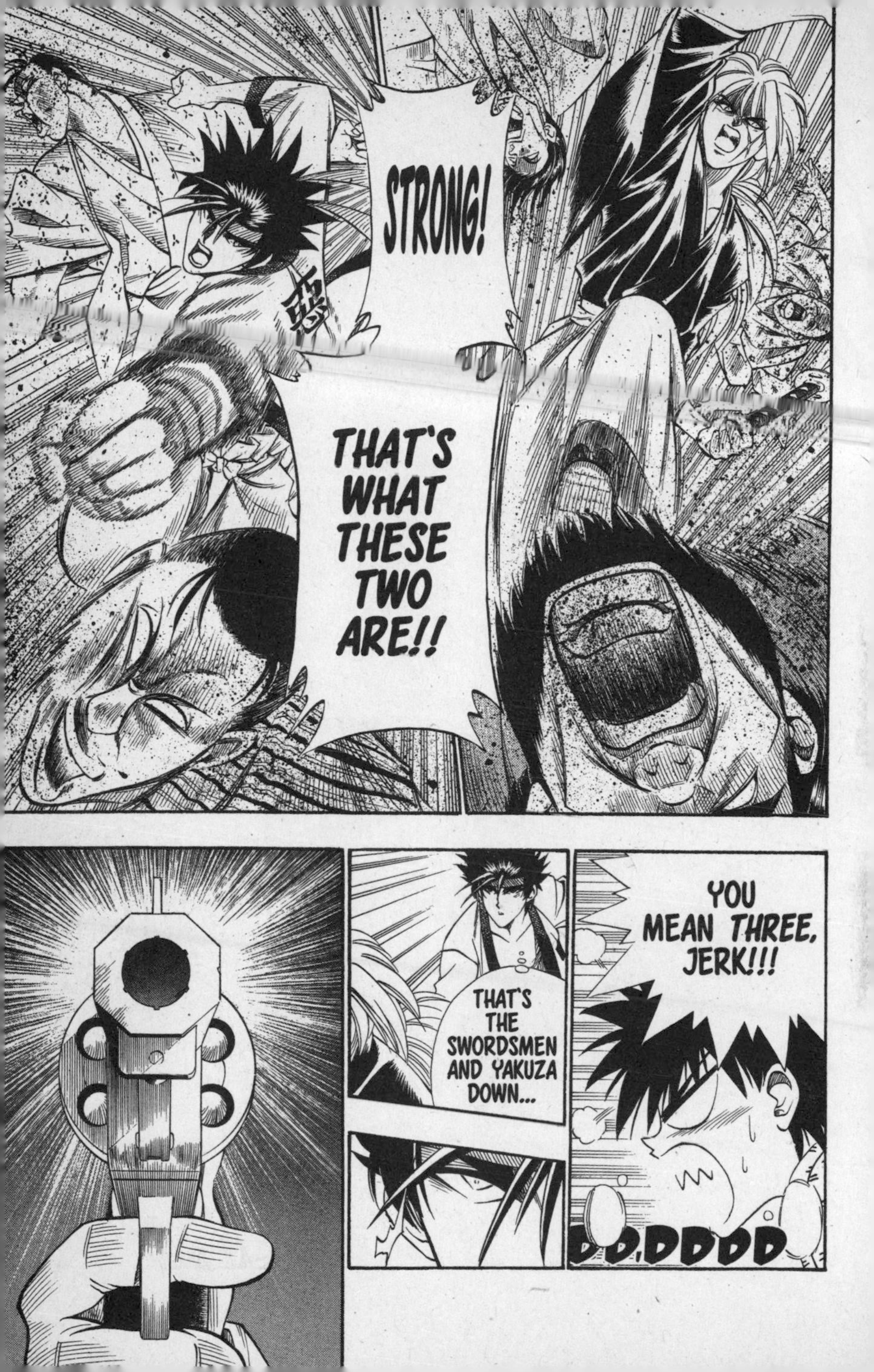
STRONG!
THAT'S WHAT THESE TWO ARE!!
YOU MEAN THREE, JERK!!!
DDDDDD
THAT'S THE SWORDSMEN AND YAKUZA DOWN...

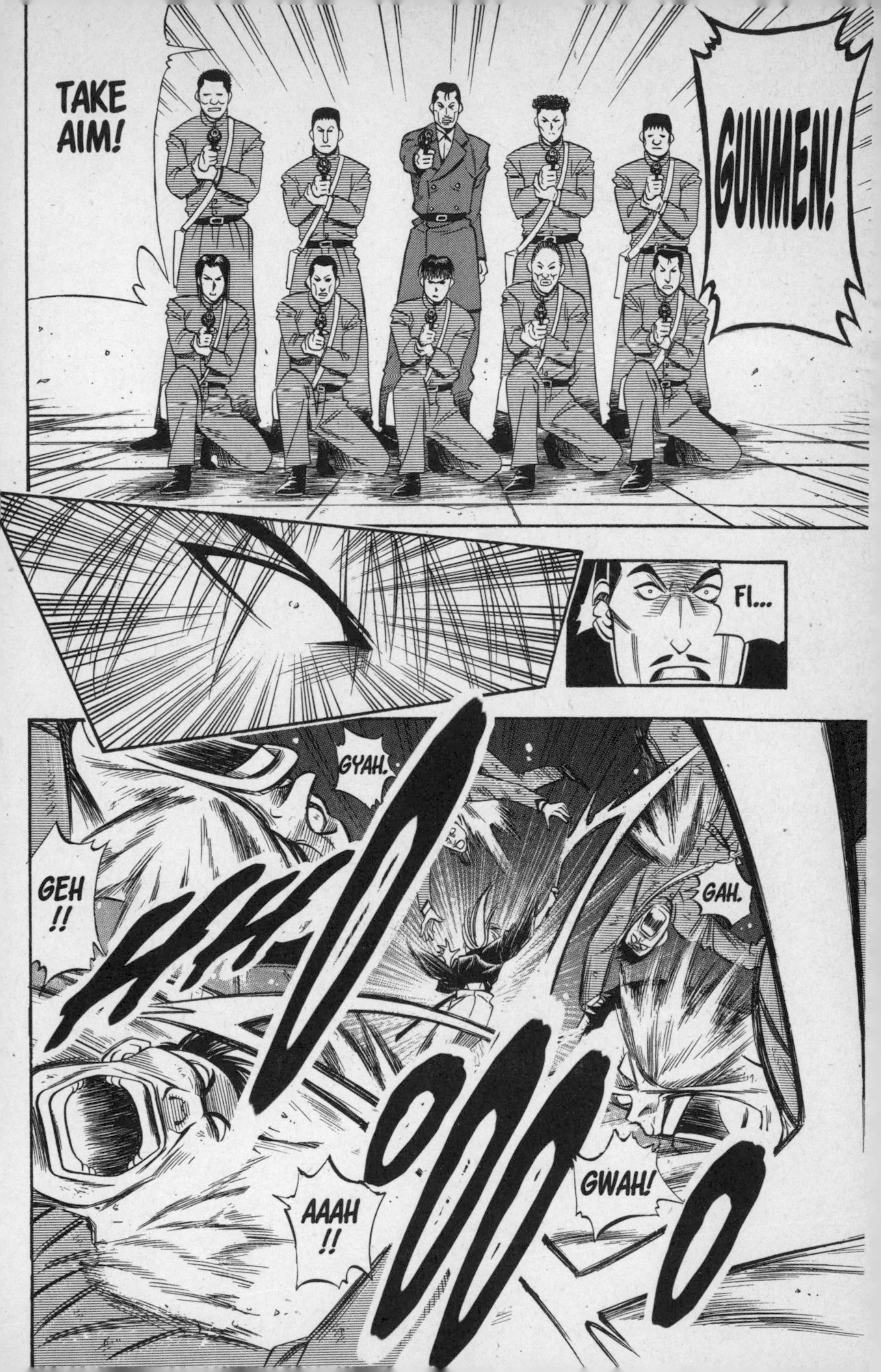
GUNMEN!
TAKE AIM!
FI...
GAH.
GYAH.
GEH !!
GWAH!
AAAH !!

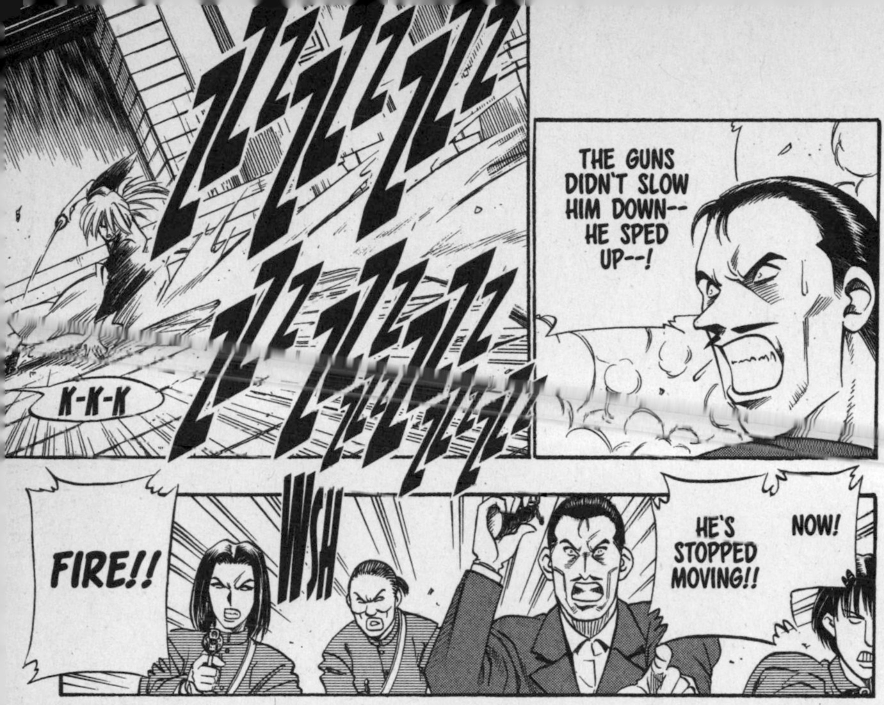
THE GUNS DIDN'T SLOW HIM DOWN-- HE SPED UP--!
K-K-K
NOW!
HE'S STOPPED MOVING!!
WSH
FIRE!!

Sure, you may THINK I'm behind the times, but lately I'm hooked on "Samurai Damashi'i" (Samurai Spirits, also known in the U.S. as "Samurai Shodown"). I even bought a NEO*GEO CD to play it!

So now you're thinking I'm a gamer, maybe, but that wouldn't be true. Watsuki has been to an arcade, like, five times in his life, and THAT's only because of his assistants, so I seriously suck. Even on "Easy Mode," I lose all the time, and Haohmaru is always dying. Worse, because I can play no more than one or two hours a week, I never get any better at it.

As I write this, I have yet to get my hands on "Shin (New) Samurai Damashi'i" ("Samurai Shodown II), but as you READ this, most likely Kibagami Genjuro has already begun dying his endless deaths by my hand. (Apologies to those of you who have no interest in video games, and have no idea what this is all about.)

和月伸宏

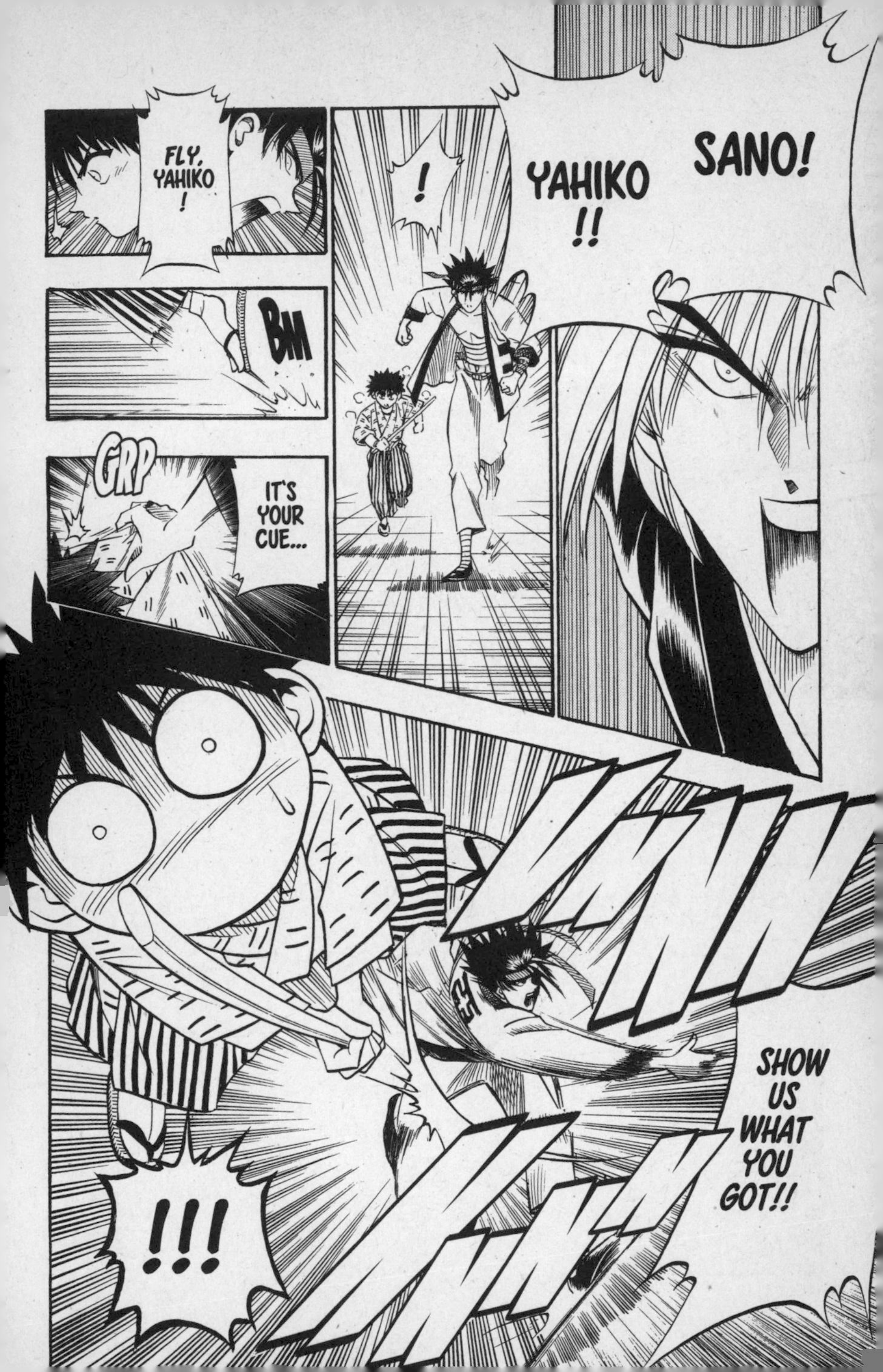
SANO!
YAHIKO !!
!
FLY, YAHIKO !
BM
GRP
IT'S YOUR CUE...
SHOW US WHAT YOU GOT!!
!!!

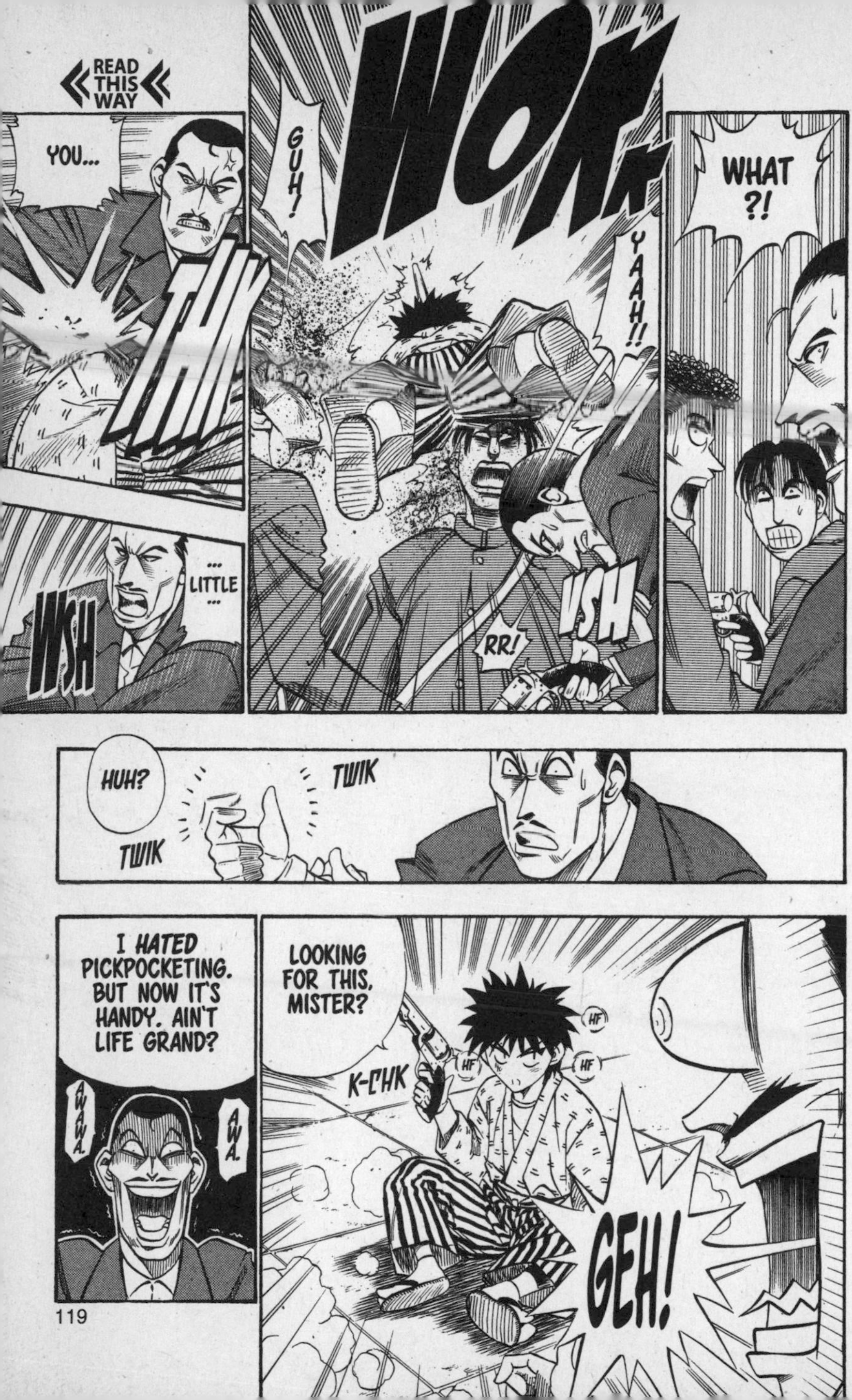
READ THIS WAY
WHAT ?!
WOK
YAAAH!!
GUH!
VSH
RR!
YOU...
THK
...LITTLE...
VSH
TWIK
HUH?
TWIK
GEH!
LOOKING FOR THIS, MISTER?
HF
HF
HF
K-CHK
I HATED PICKPOCKETING. BUT NOW IT'S HANDY. AIN'T LIFE GRAND?
AWA.
AWAWA.

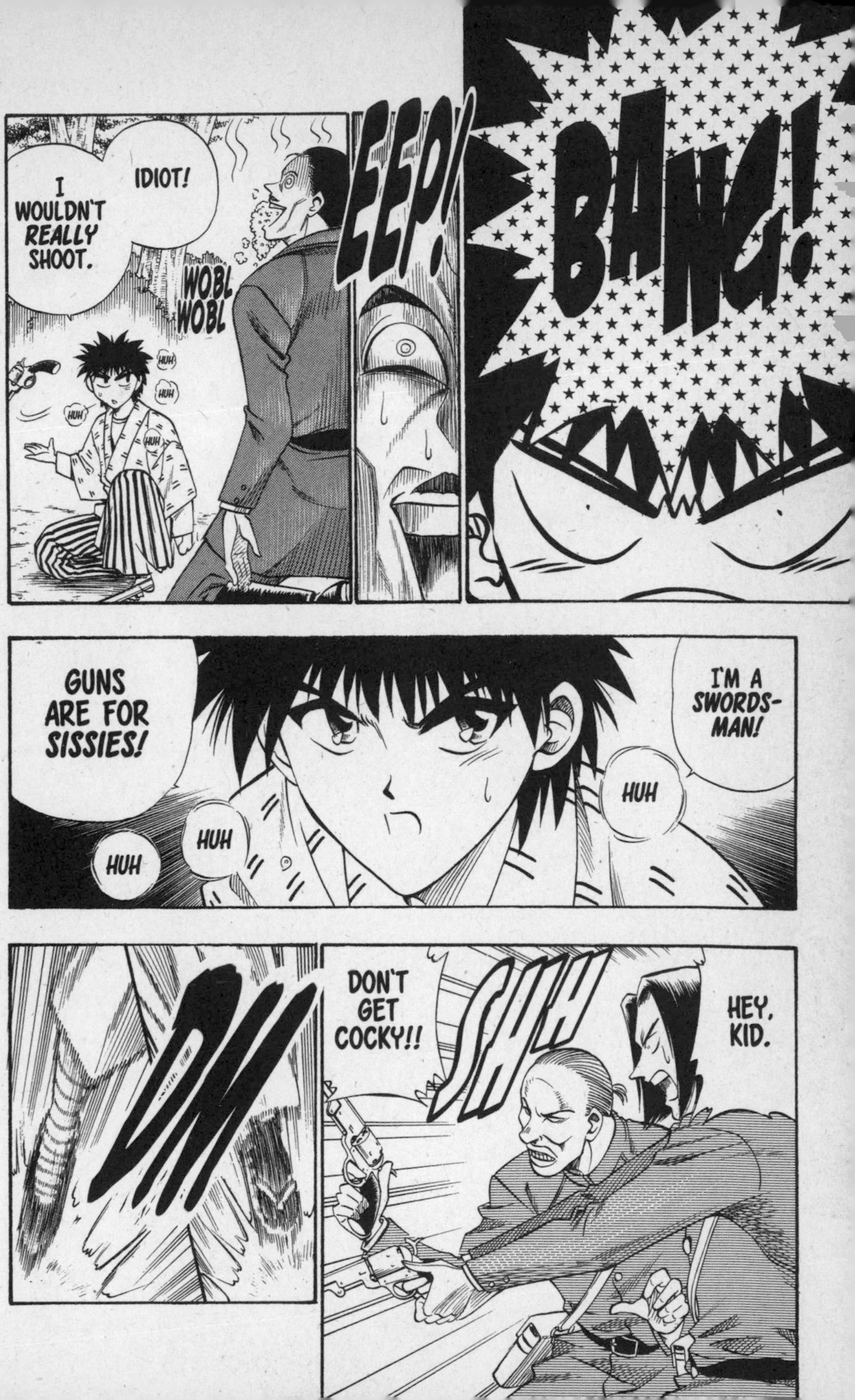
BANG!
EEP!!
IDIOT!
I WOULDN'T REALLY SHOOT.
WOBL WOBL
HUH
HUH
HUH
HUH
I'M A SWORDS-MAN!
HUH
GUNS ARE FOR SISSIES!
HUH
HUH
HEY, KID.
DON'T GET COCKY!!

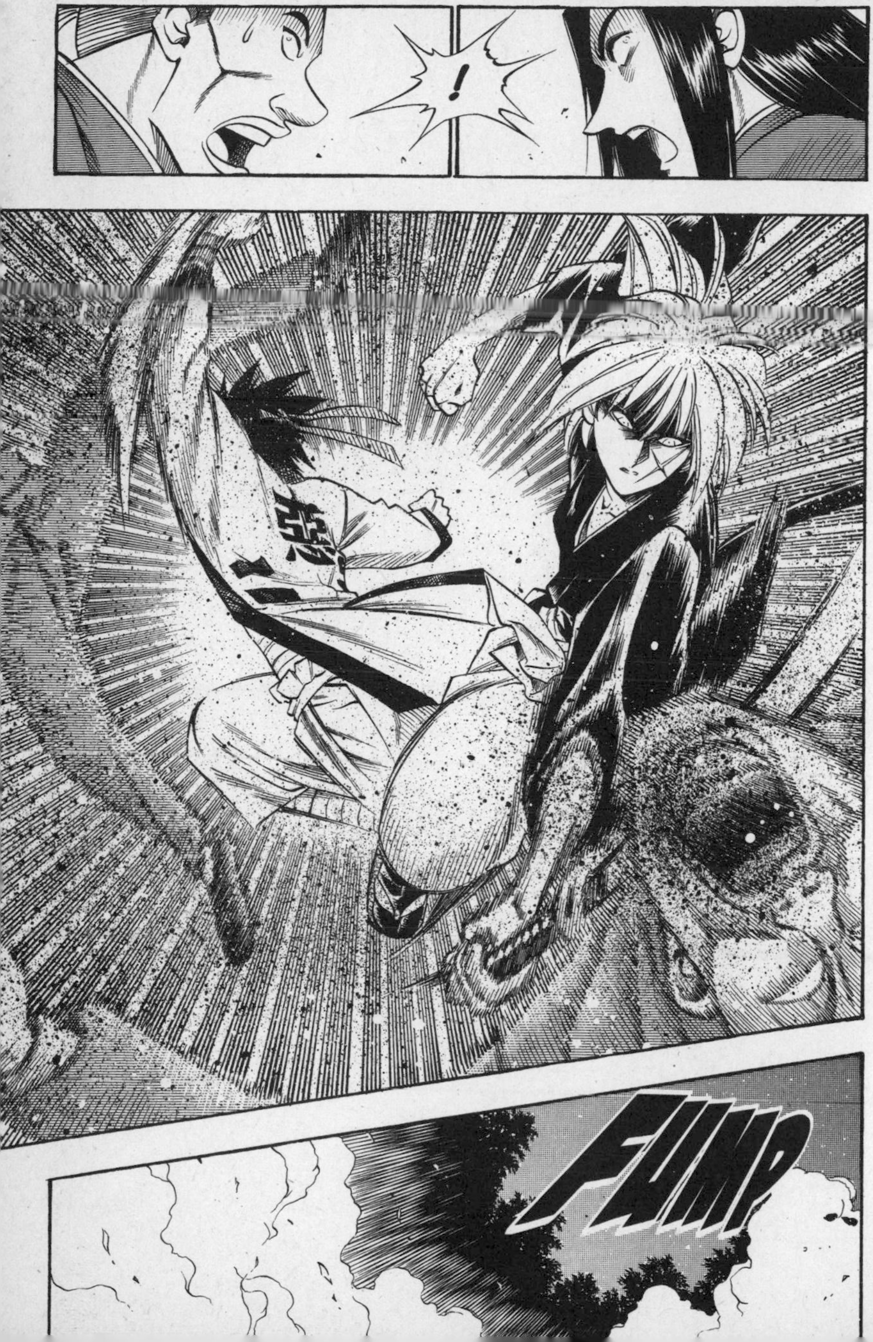
!
FUMP

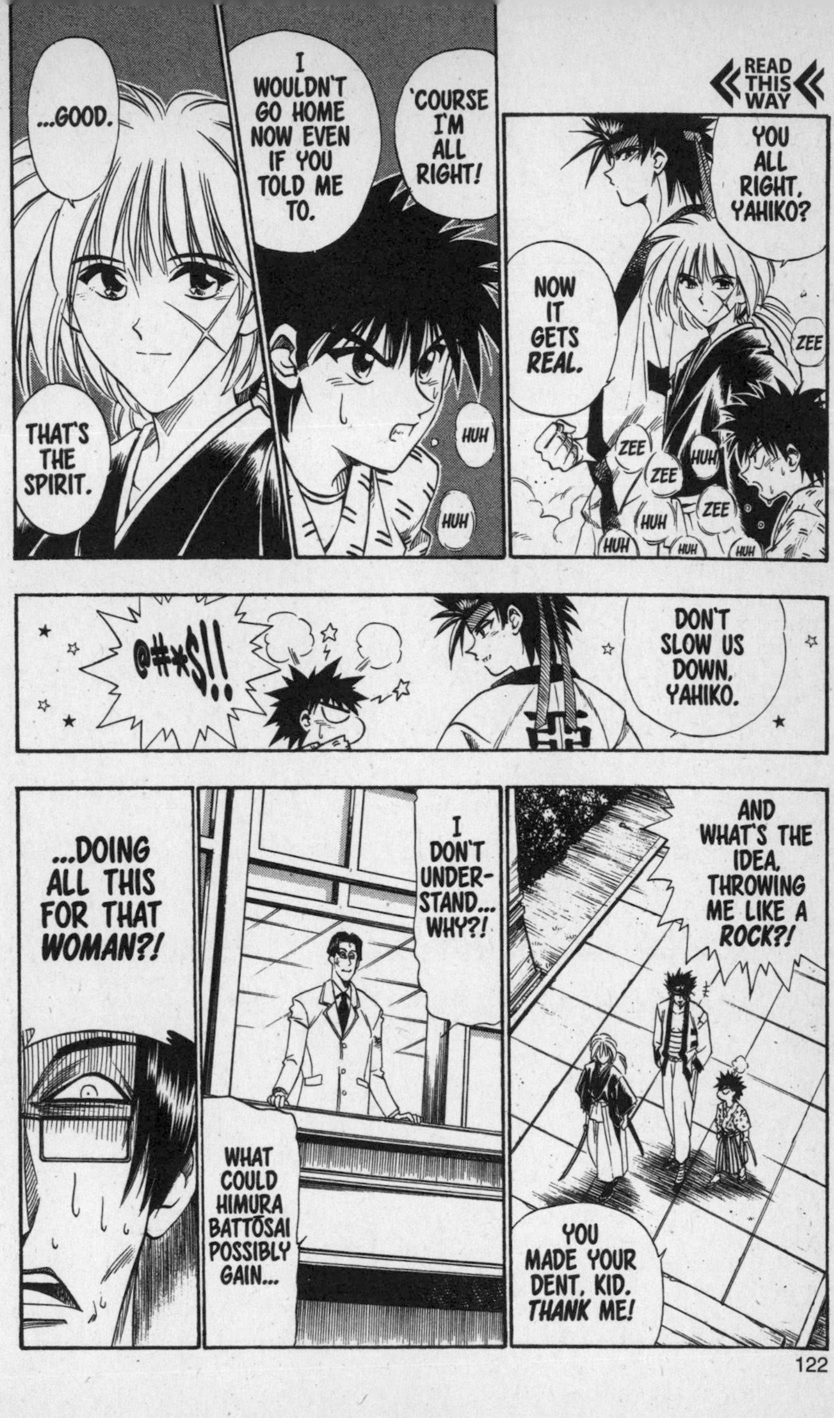
READ THIS WAY
YOU ALL RIGHT, YAHIKO?
NOW IT GETS REAL.
ZEE
ZEE HUH ZEE ZEE HUH HUH HUH HUH
`COURSE I'M ALL RIGHT!
I WOULDN'T GO HOME NOW EVEN IF YOU TOLD ME TO.
HUH
HUH
...GOOD.
THAT'S THE SPIRIT.
DON'T SLOW US DOWN, YAHIKO.
@#*$!!
AND WHAT'S THE IDEA, THROWING ME LIKE A ROCK?!
YOU MADE YOUR DENT, KID. THANK ME!
I DON'T UNDER-STAND... WHY?!
WHAT COULD HIMURA BATTŌSAI POSSIBLY GAIN...
...DOING ALL THIS FOR THAT WOMAN?!

READ THIS WAY

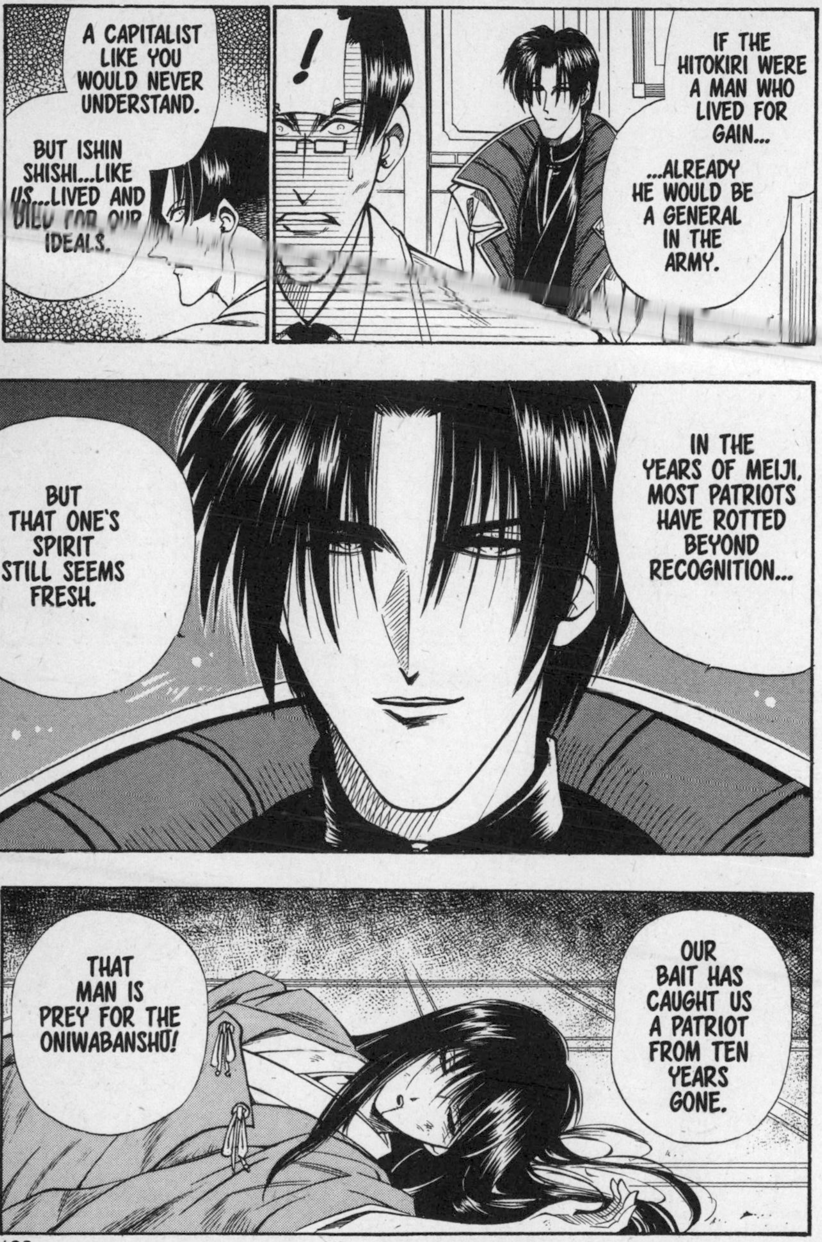
IF THE HITOKIRI WERE A MAN WHO LIVED FOR GAIN...
...ALREADY HE WOULD BE A GENERAL IN THE ARMY.
!
A CAPITALIST LIKE YOU WOULD NEVER UNDERSTAND.
BUT ISHIN SHISHI...LIKE US...LIVED AND DIED FOR OUR IDEALS.
IN THE YEARS OF MEIJI, MOST PATRIOTS HAVE ROTTED BEYOND RECOGNITION...
BUT THAT ONE'S SPIRIT STILL SEEMS FRESH.
OUR BAIT HAS CAUGHT US A PATRIOT FROM TEN YEARS GONE.
THAT MAN IS PREY FOR THE ONIWABANSHŪ!

Rurouni Kenshin

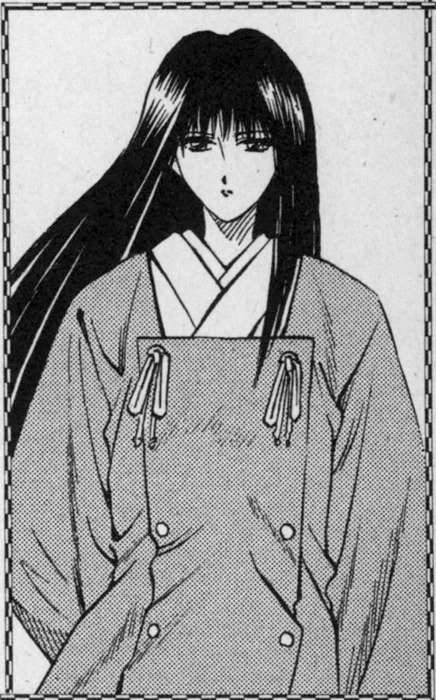

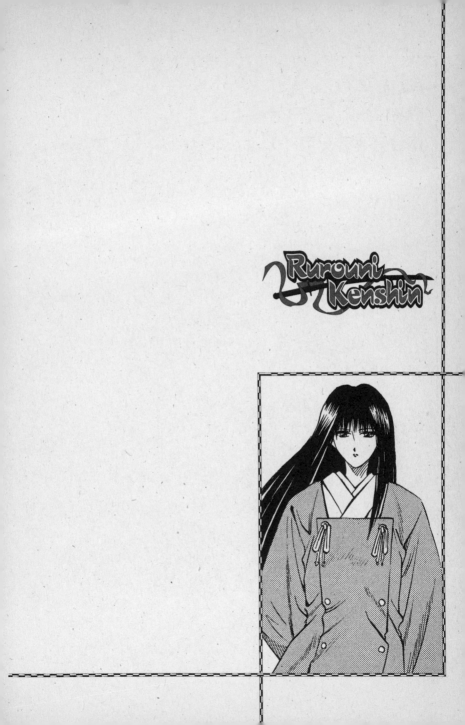

Act 22
Attack on Kanryū Mansion

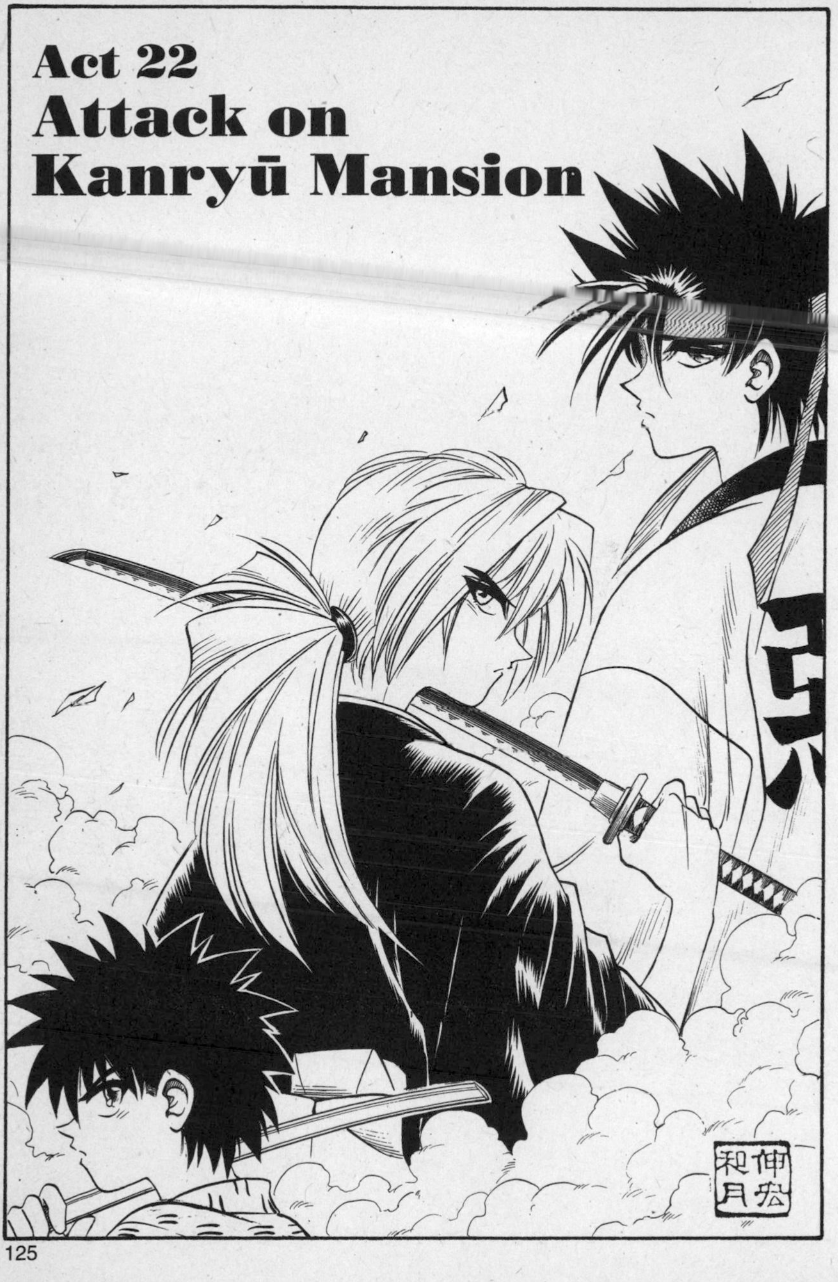
伸宏
和月

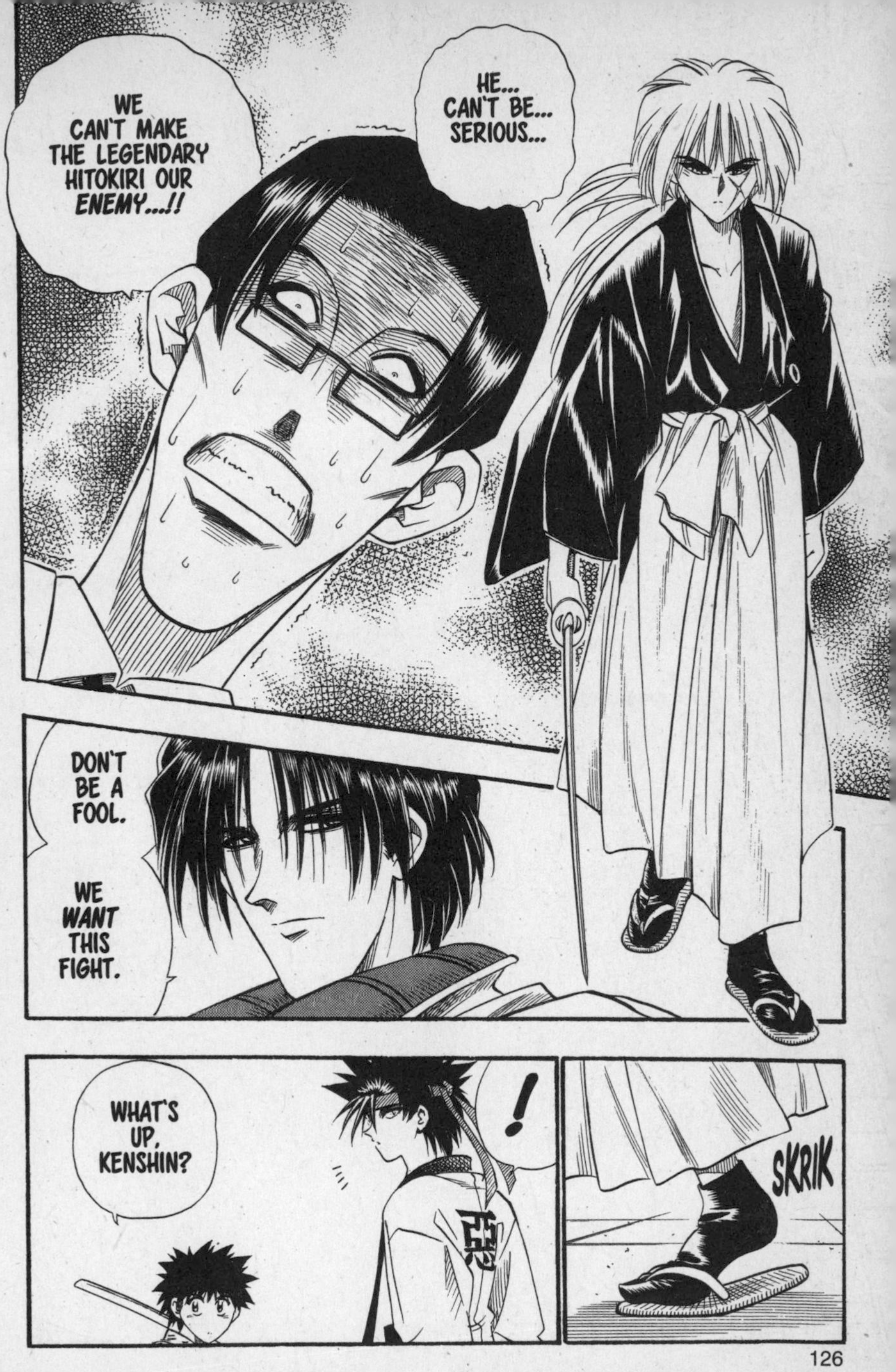
HE... CAN'T BE... SERIOUS...
WE CAN'T MAKE THE LEGENDARY HITOKIRI OUR ENEMY...!!
DON'T BE A FOOL.
WE WANT THIS FIGHT.
SKRIK
!
WHAT'S UP, KENSHIN?

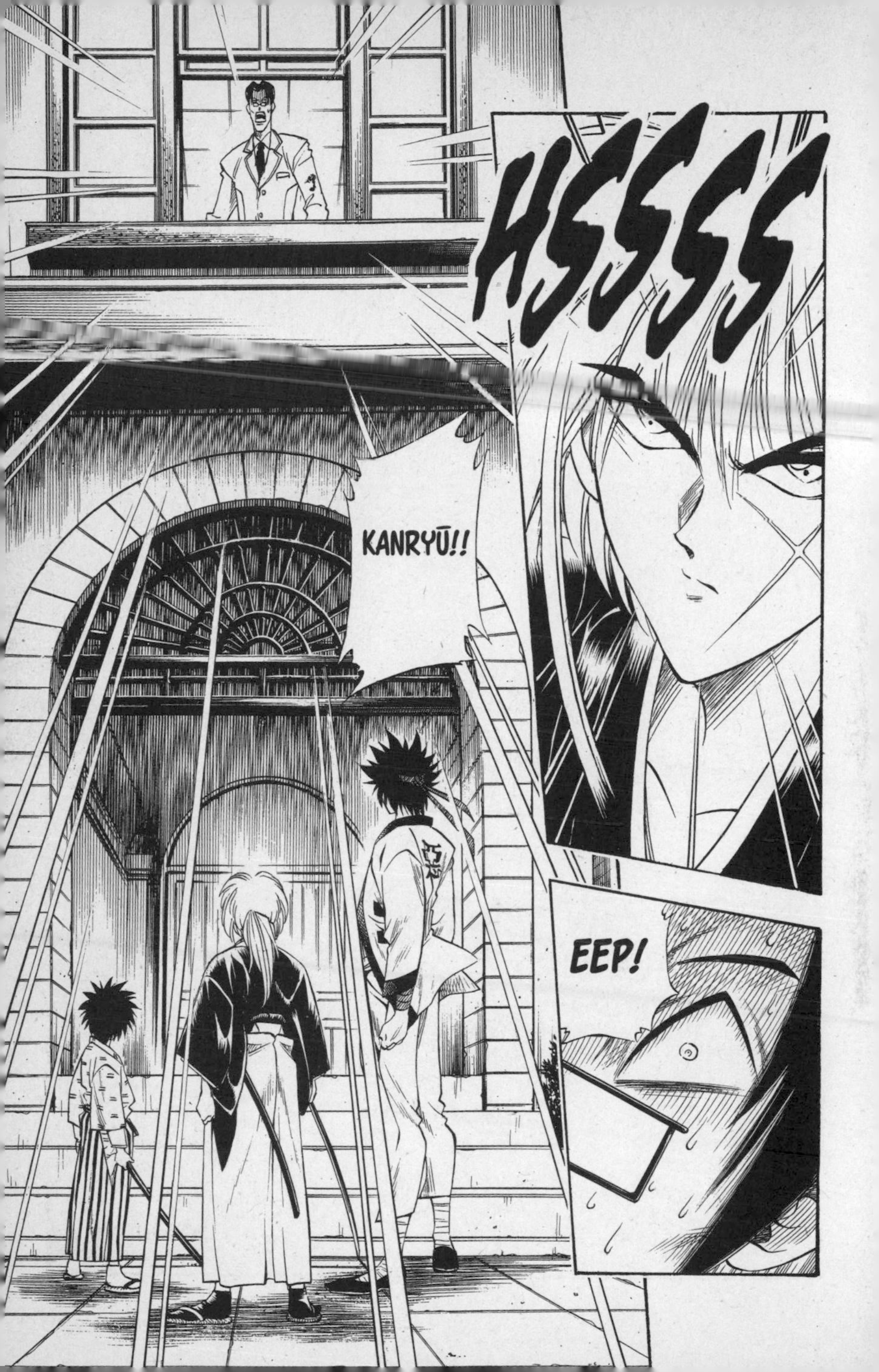
HSSSS
EEP!
KANRYŪ!!

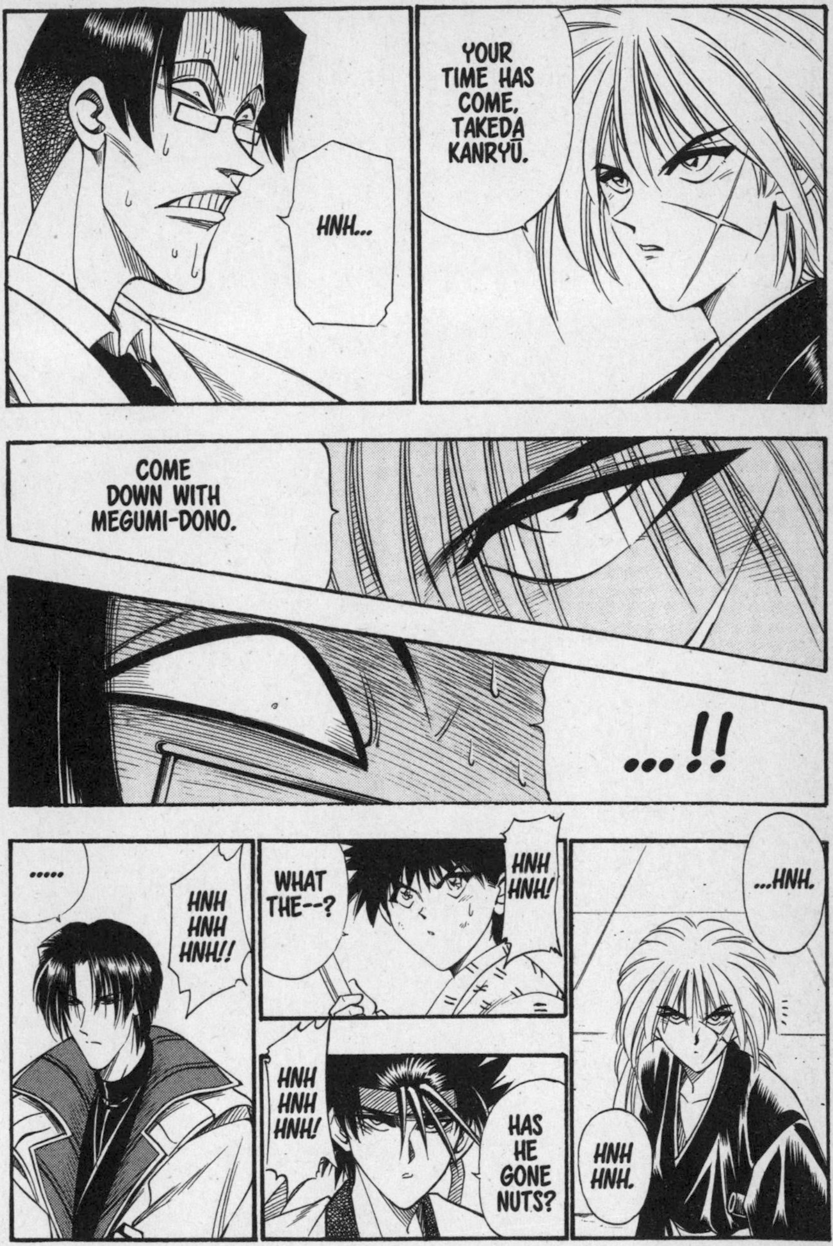
YOUR TIME HAS COME, TAKEDA KANRYŪ.
HNH...
COME DOWN WITH MEGUMI-DONO.
...!!
...HNH.
HNH HNH.
HNH HNH!
WHAT THE--?
HNH HNH HNH!
HAS HE GONE NUTS?
HNH HNH HNH!!
.....

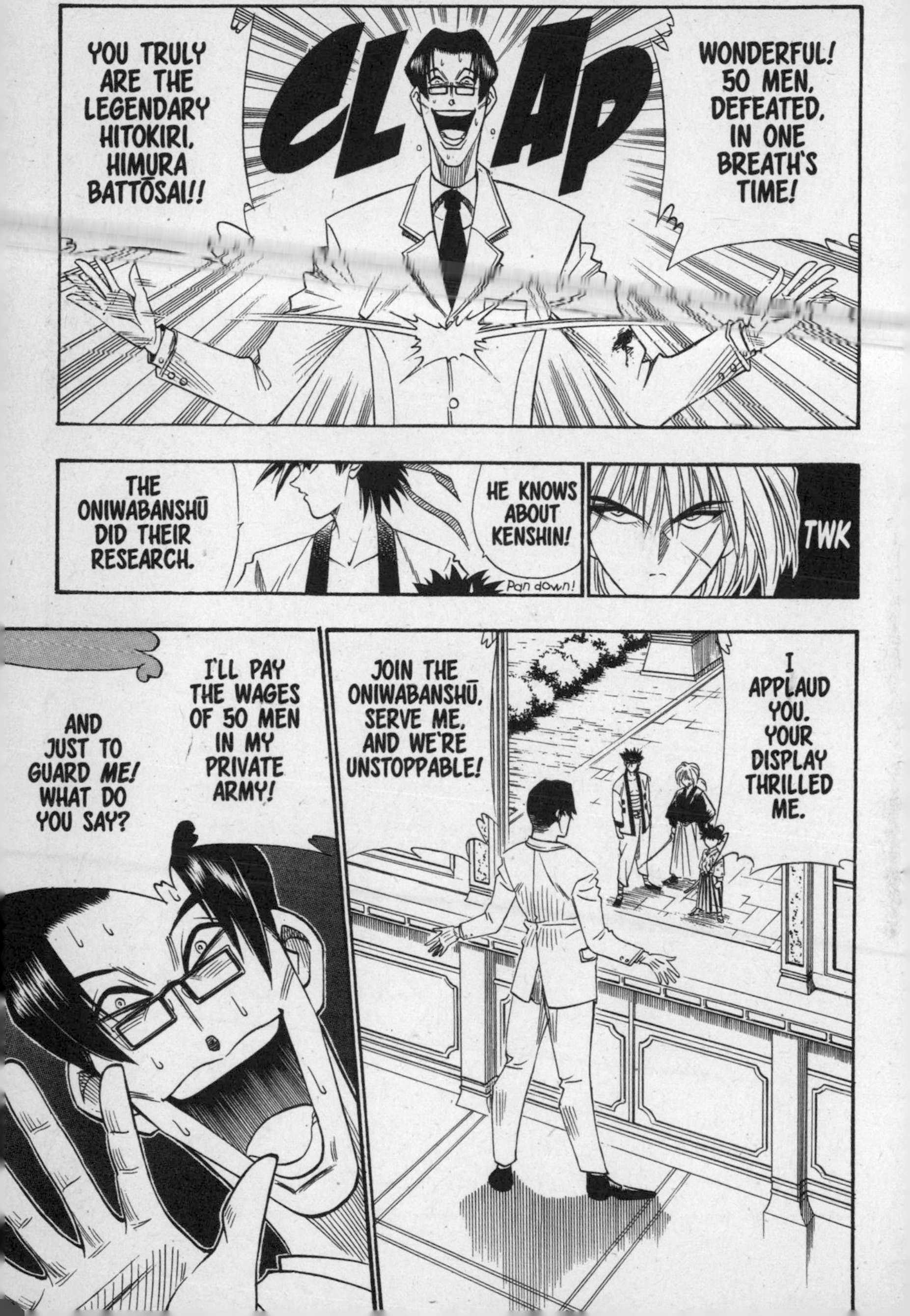
WONDERFUL! 50 MEN, DEFEATED, IN ONE BREATH'S TIME!
CLAP
YOU TRULY ARE THE LEGENDARY HITOKIRI, HIMURA BATTŌSAI!!
TWK
HE KNOWS ABOUT KENSHIN!
Pan down!
THE ONIWABANSHŪ DID THEIR RESEARCH.
I APPLAUD YOU. YOUR DISPLAY THRILLED ME.
JOIN THE ONIWABANSHŪ, SERVE ME, AND WE'RE UNSTOPPABLE!
I'LL PAY THE WAGES OF 50 MEN IN MY PRIVATE ARMY!
AND JUST TO GUARD ME! WHAT DO YOU SAY?

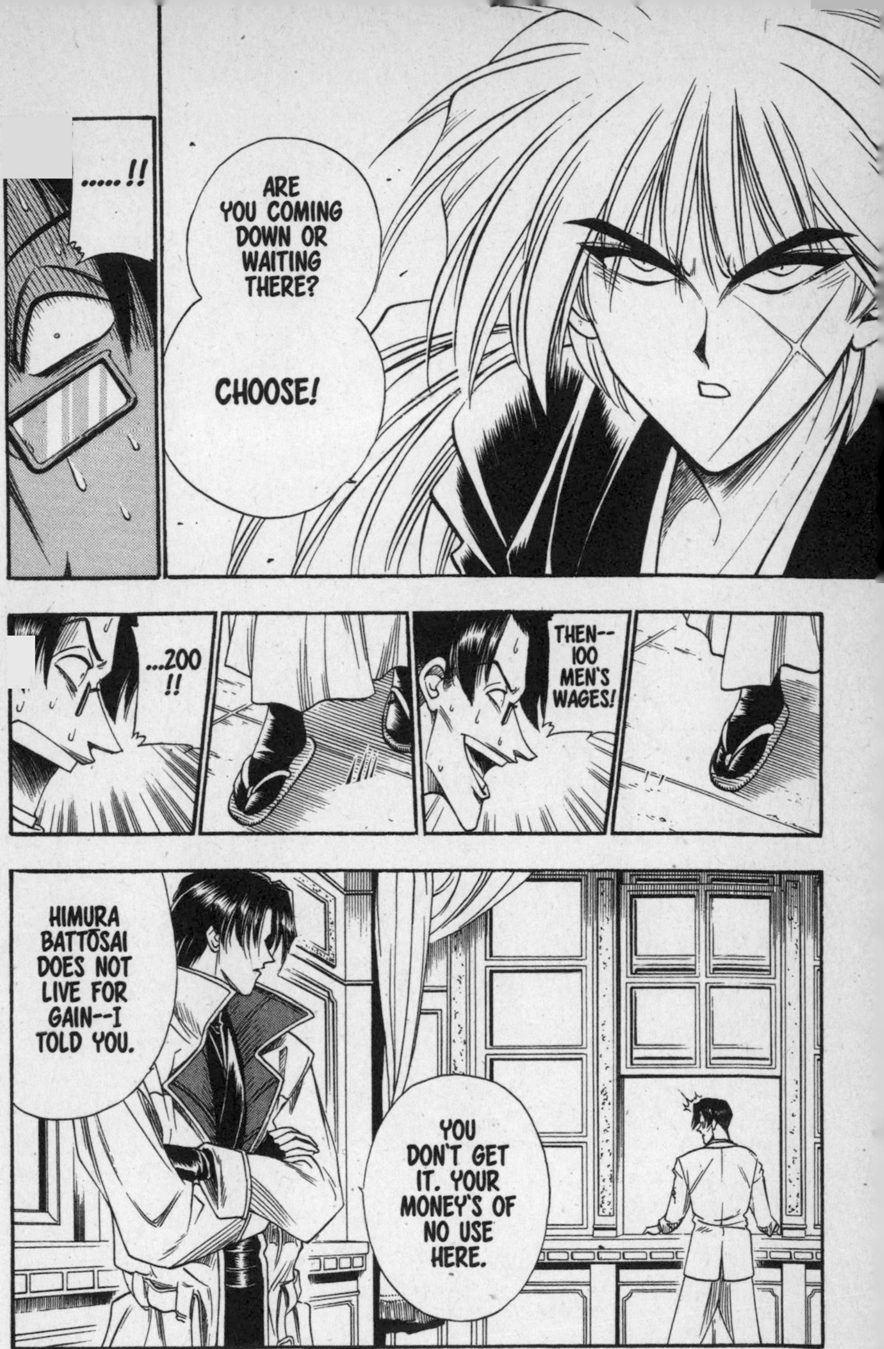
ARE YOU COMING DOWN OR WAITING THERE?
CHOOSE!
......!!
THEN-- 100 MEN'S WAGES!
...200 !!
YOU DON'T GET IT. YOUR MONEY'S OF NO USE HERE.
HIMURA BATTŌSAI DOES NOT LIVE FOR GAIN--I TOLD YOU.

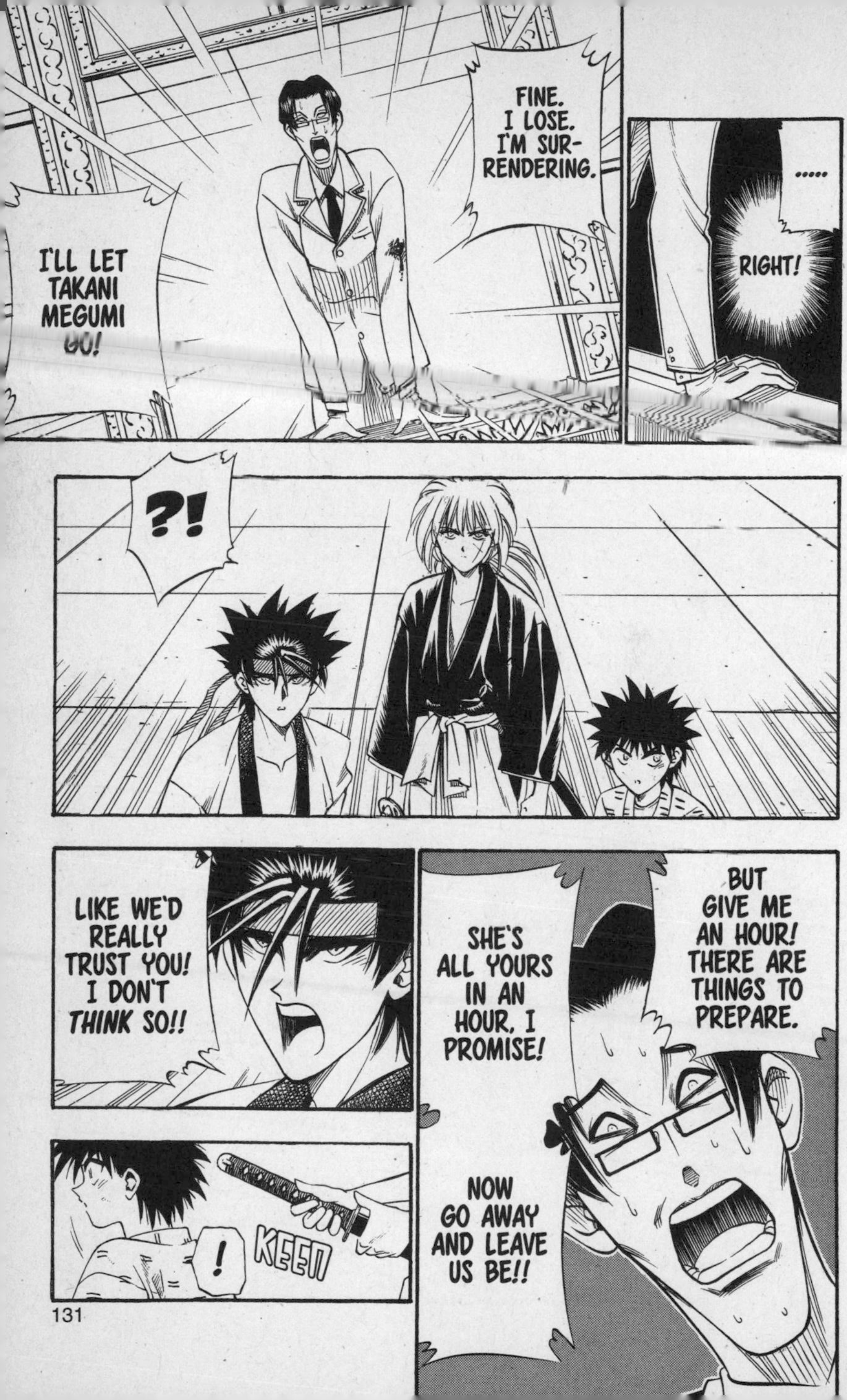
.....
RIGHT!
FINE. I LOSE. I'M SURRENDERING.
I'LL LET TAKANI MEGUMI GO!
?!
BUT GIVE ME AN HOUR! THERE ARE THINGS TO PREPARE.
SHE'S ALL YOURS IN AN HOUR, I PROMISE!
NOW GO AWAY AND LEAVE US BE!!
LIKE WE'D REALLY TRUST YOU! I DON'T THINK SO!!
!
KEEN

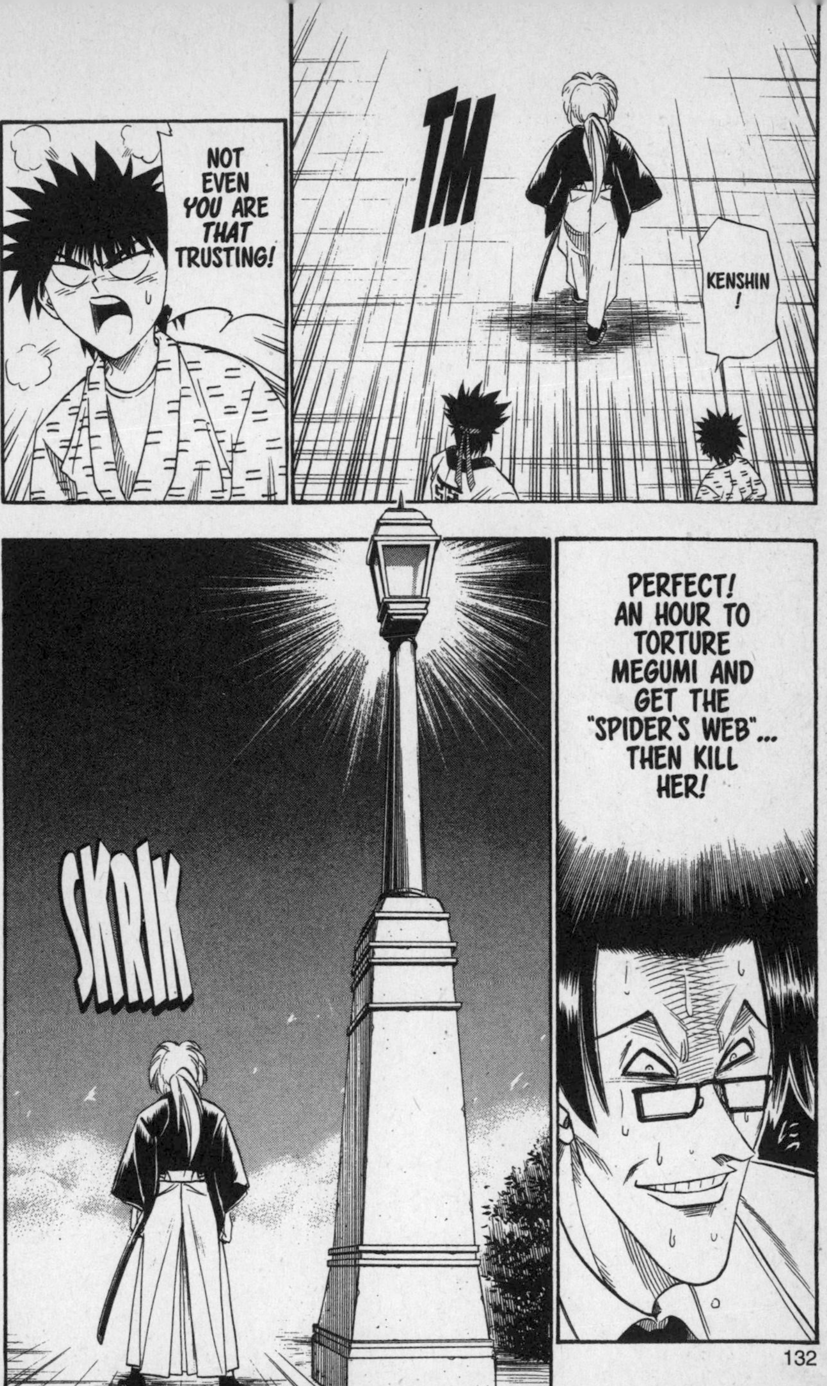
TM
KENSHIN!
NOT EVEN YOU ARE THAT TRUSTING!
PERFECT! AN HOUR TO TORTURE MEGUMI AND GET THE "SPIDER'S WEB"... THEN KILL HER!
SKRIK

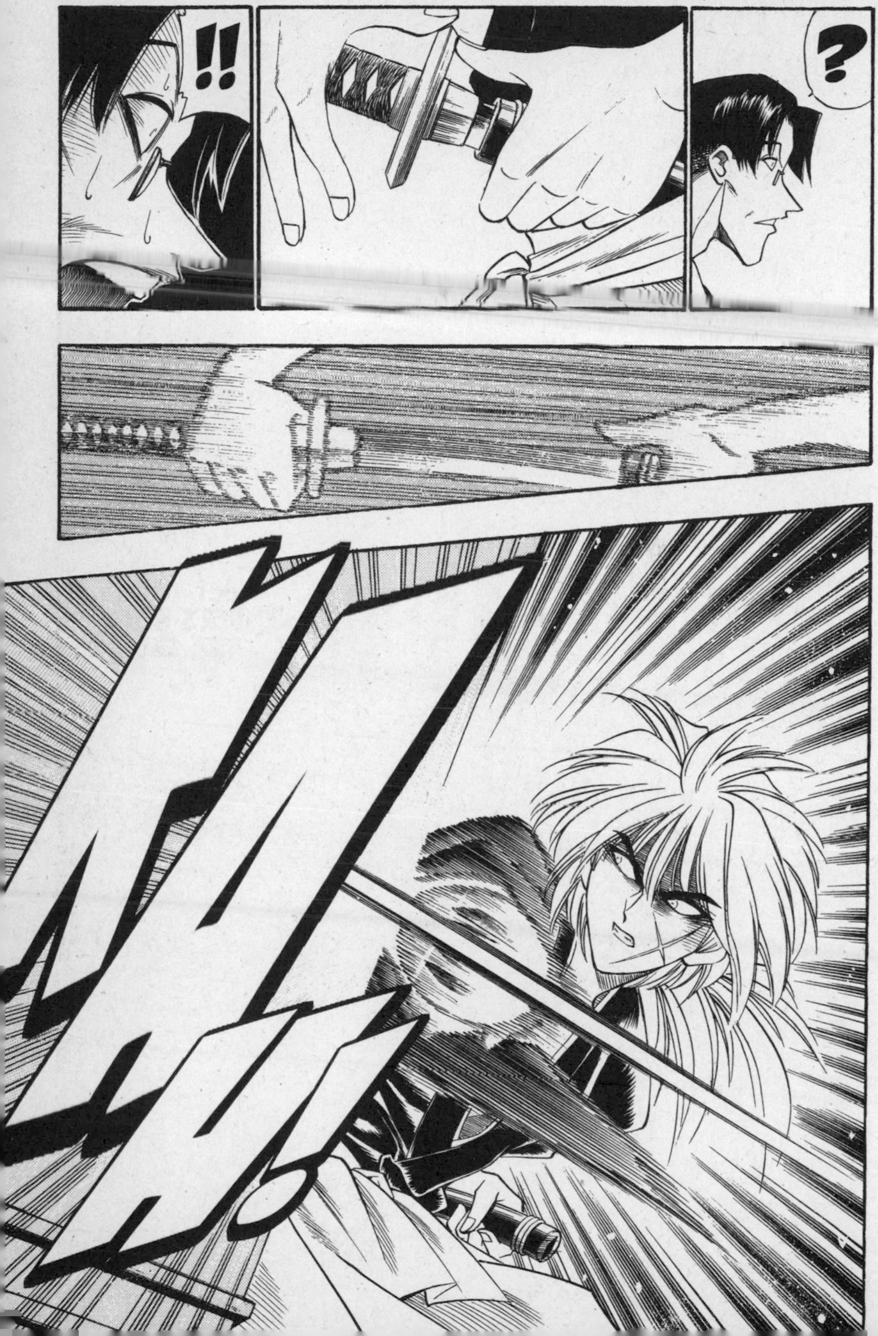
?
!!

READ THIS WAY

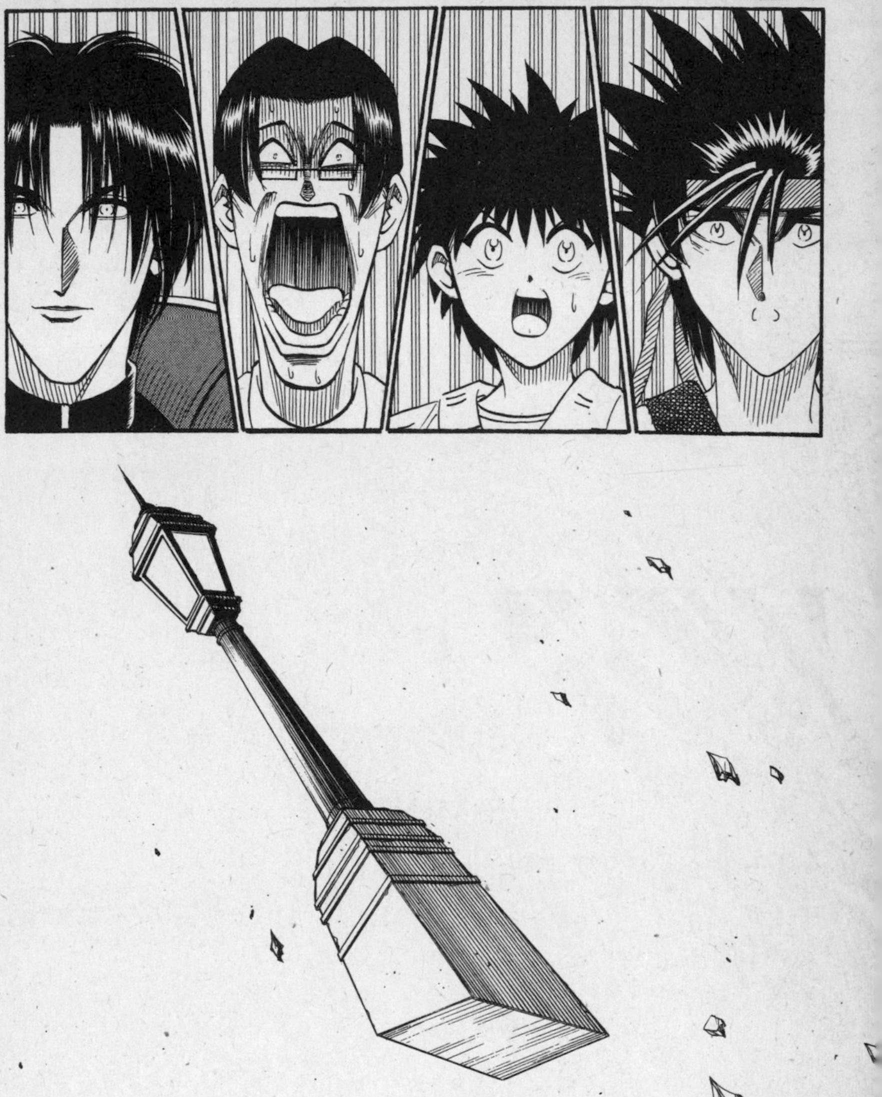

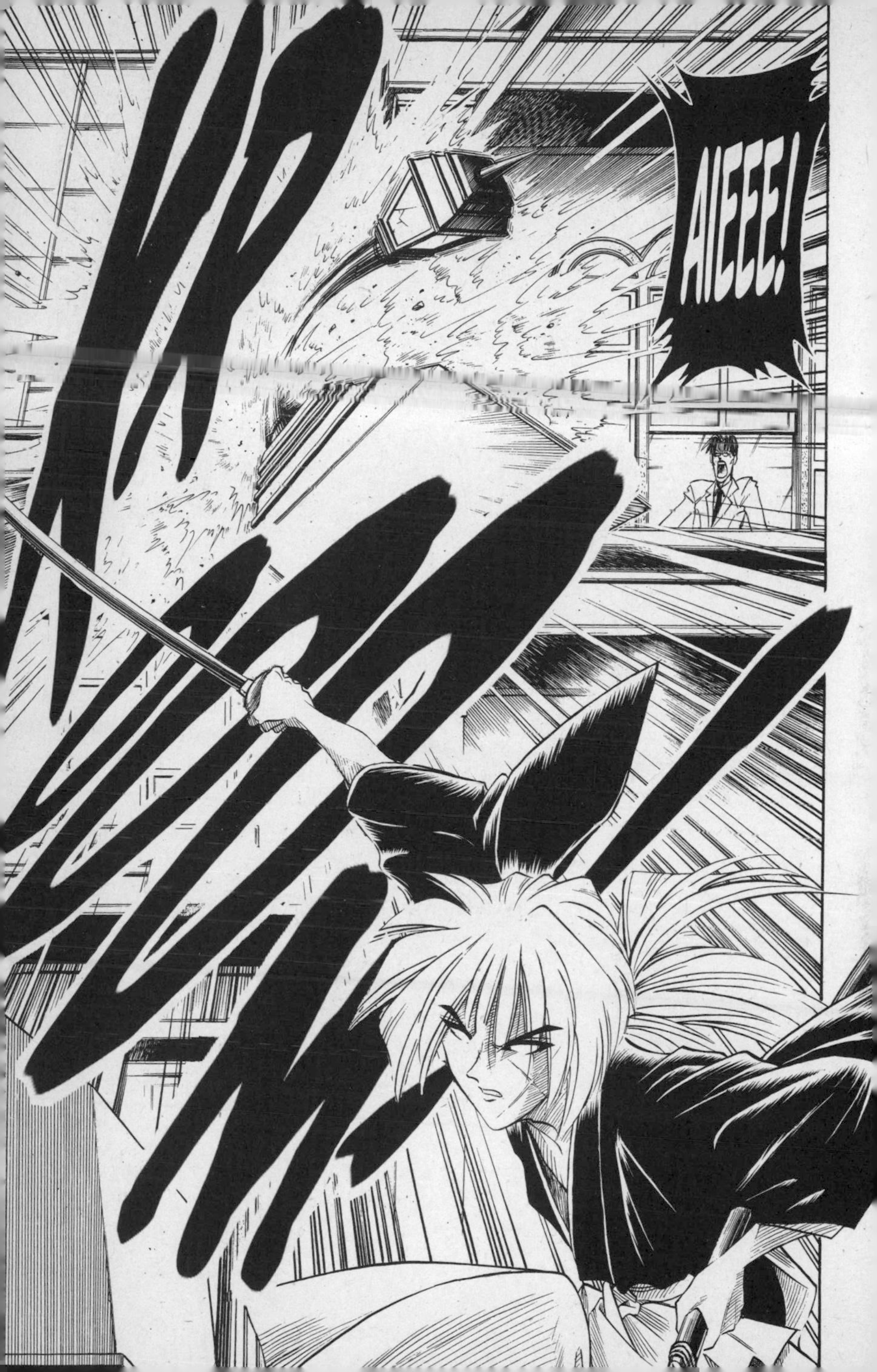
AIEEE!

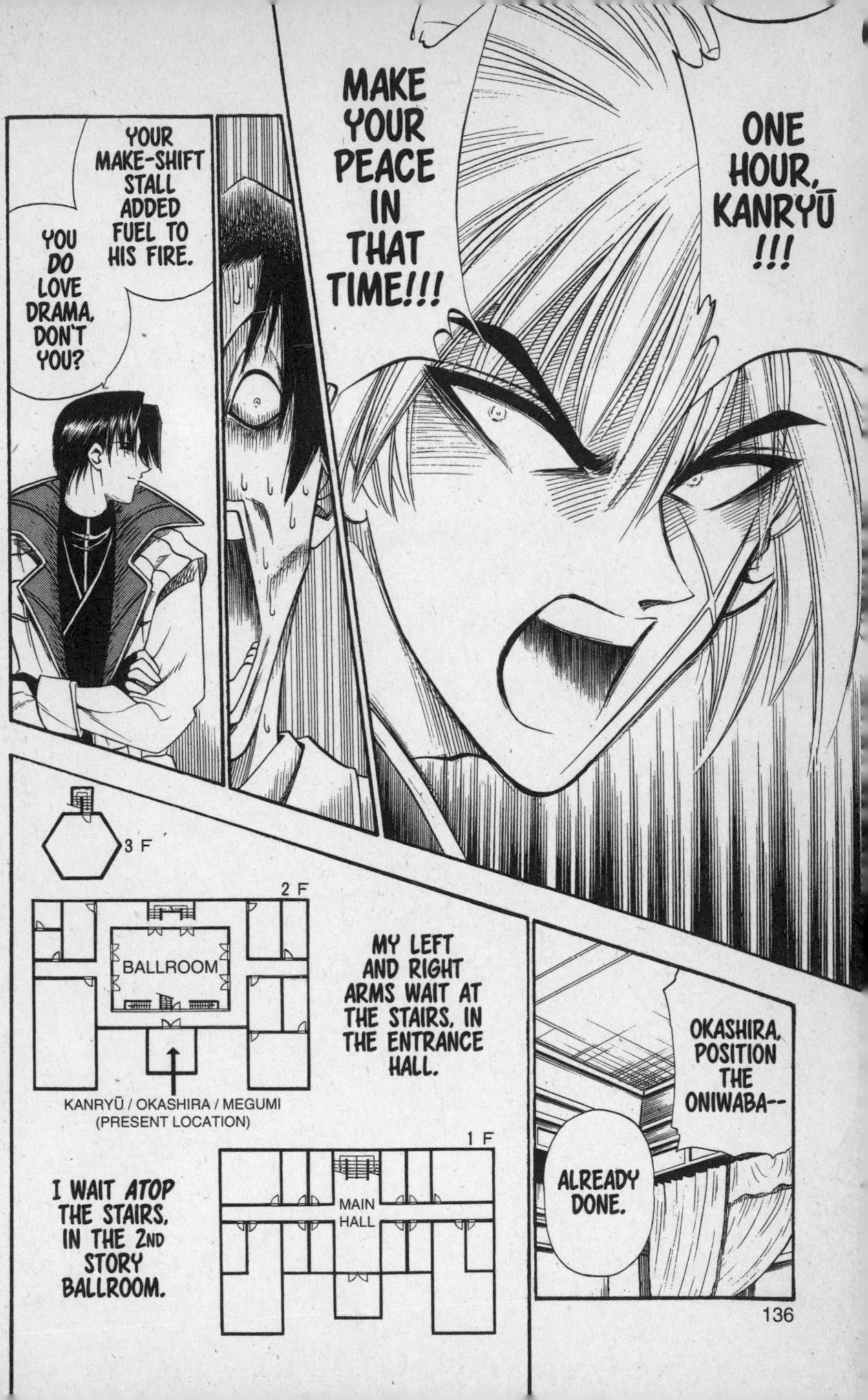
ONE HOUR, KANRYŪ!!!
MAKE YOUR PEACE IN THAT TIME!!!
YOUR MAKE-SHIFT STALL ADDED FUEL TO HIS FIRE.
YOU DO LOVE DRAMA, DON'T YOU?
OKASHIRA, POSITION THE ONIWABA--
ALREADY DONE.
MY LEFT AND RIGHT ARMS WAIT AT THE STAIRS, IN THE ENTRANCE HALL.
3 F
2 F
BALLROOM
KANRYŪ / OKASHIRA / MEGUMI (PRESENT LOCATION)
1 F
MAIN HALL
I WAIT ATOP THE STAIRS, IN THE 2ND STORY BALLROOM.

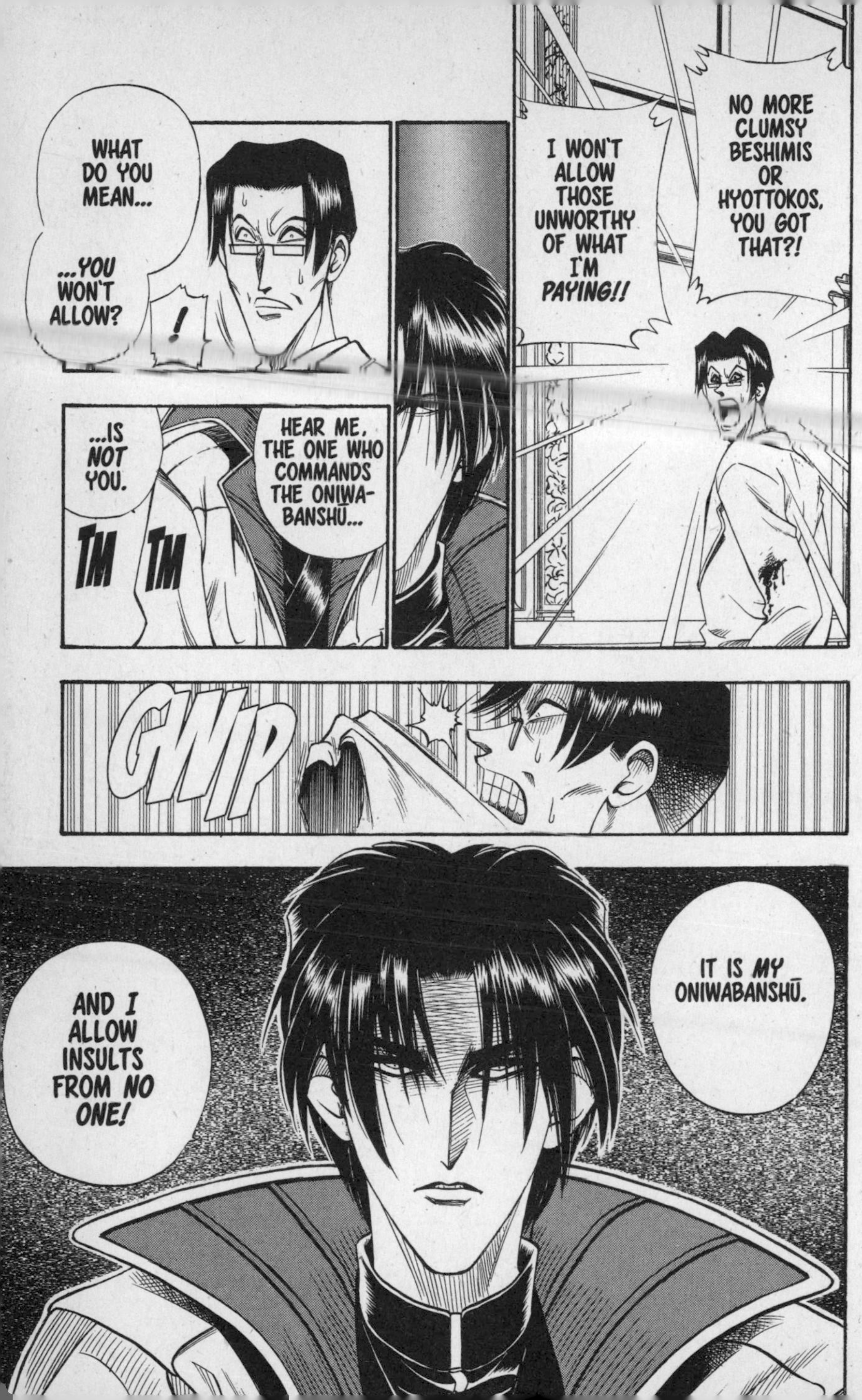
NO MORE CLUMSY BESHIMIS OR HYOTTOKOS, YOU GOT THAT?!
I WON'T ALLOW THOSE UNWORTHY OF WHAT I'M *PAYING!!*
WHAT DO YOU MEAN...
...YOU WON'T ALLOW?
!
HEAR ME, THE ONE WHO COMMANDS THE ONIWA-BANSHŪ...
...IS *NOT* YOU.
TM TM
GNIP
IT IS *MY* ONIWABANSHŪ.
AND *I* ALLOW INSULTS FROM *NO ONE!*

READ THIS WAY

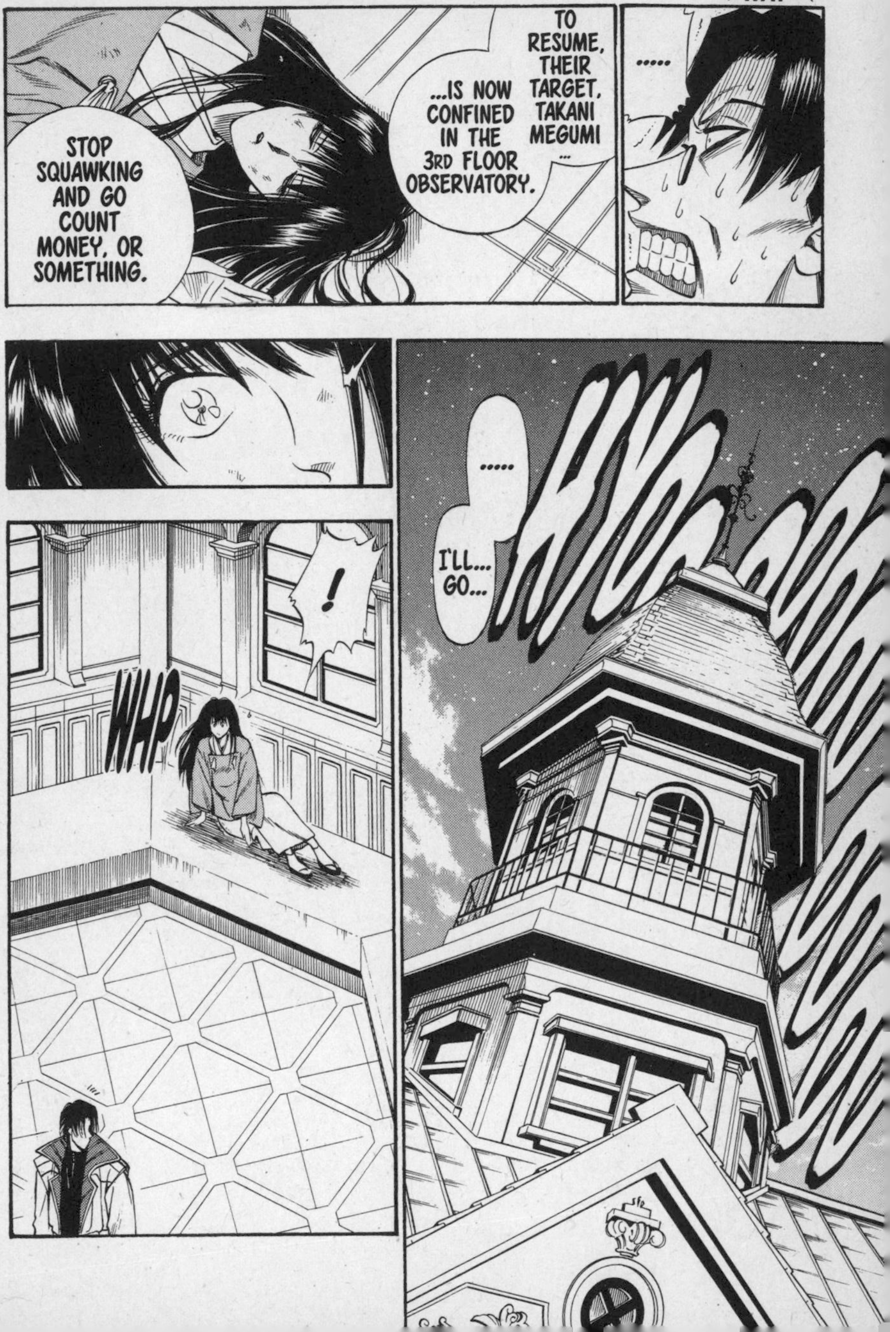
.....
TO RESUME, THEIR TARGET, TAKANI MEGUMI ...
...IS NOW CONFINED IN THE 3RD FLOOR OBSERVATORY.
STOP SQUAWKING AND GO COUNT MONEY, OR SOMETHING.
.....
I'LL... GO...
!
WHP

READ THIS WAY

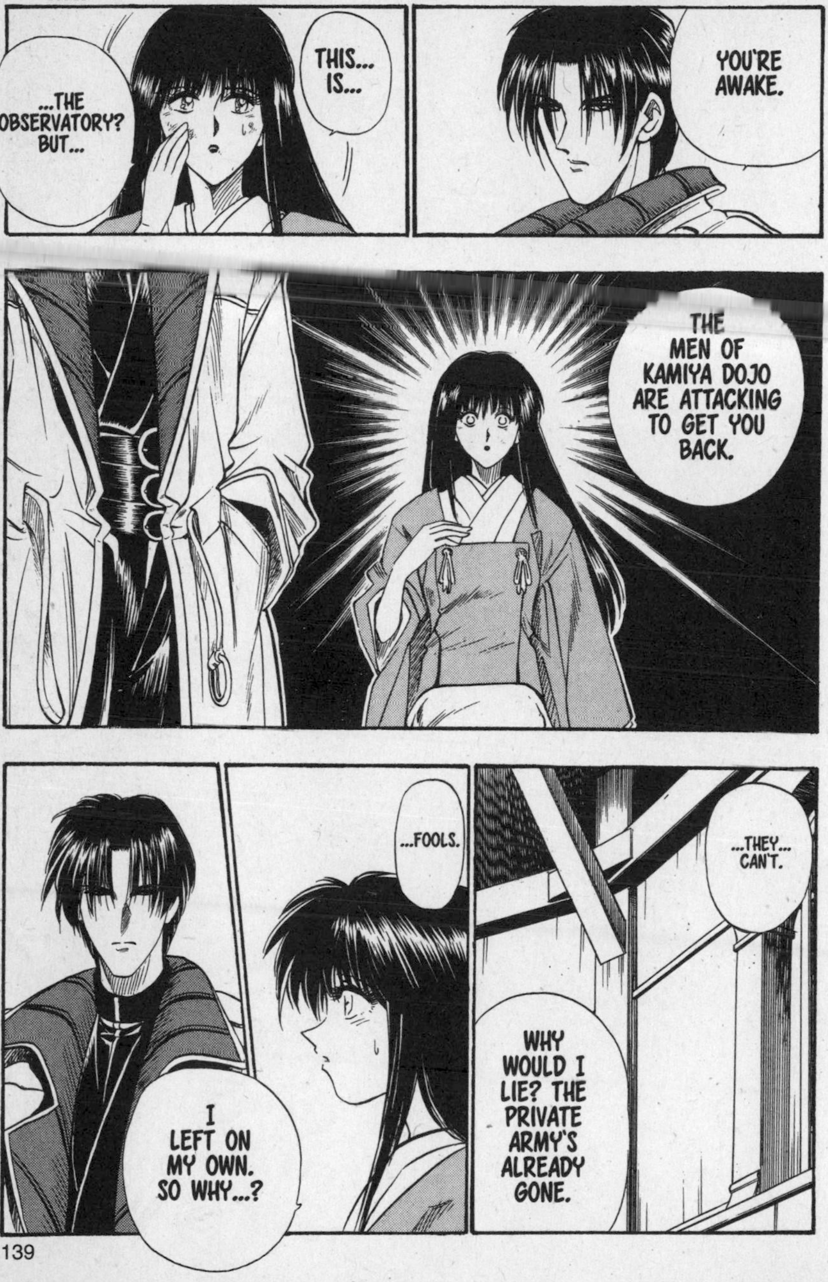
YOU'RE AWAKE.
THIS... IS...
...THE OBSERVATORY? BUT...
THE MEN OF KAMIYA DOJO ARE ATTACKING TO GET YOU BACK.
...THEY... CAN'T.
WHY WOULD I LIE? THE PRIVATE ARMY'S ALREADY GONE.
...FOOLS.
I LEFT ON MY OWN. SO WHY...?

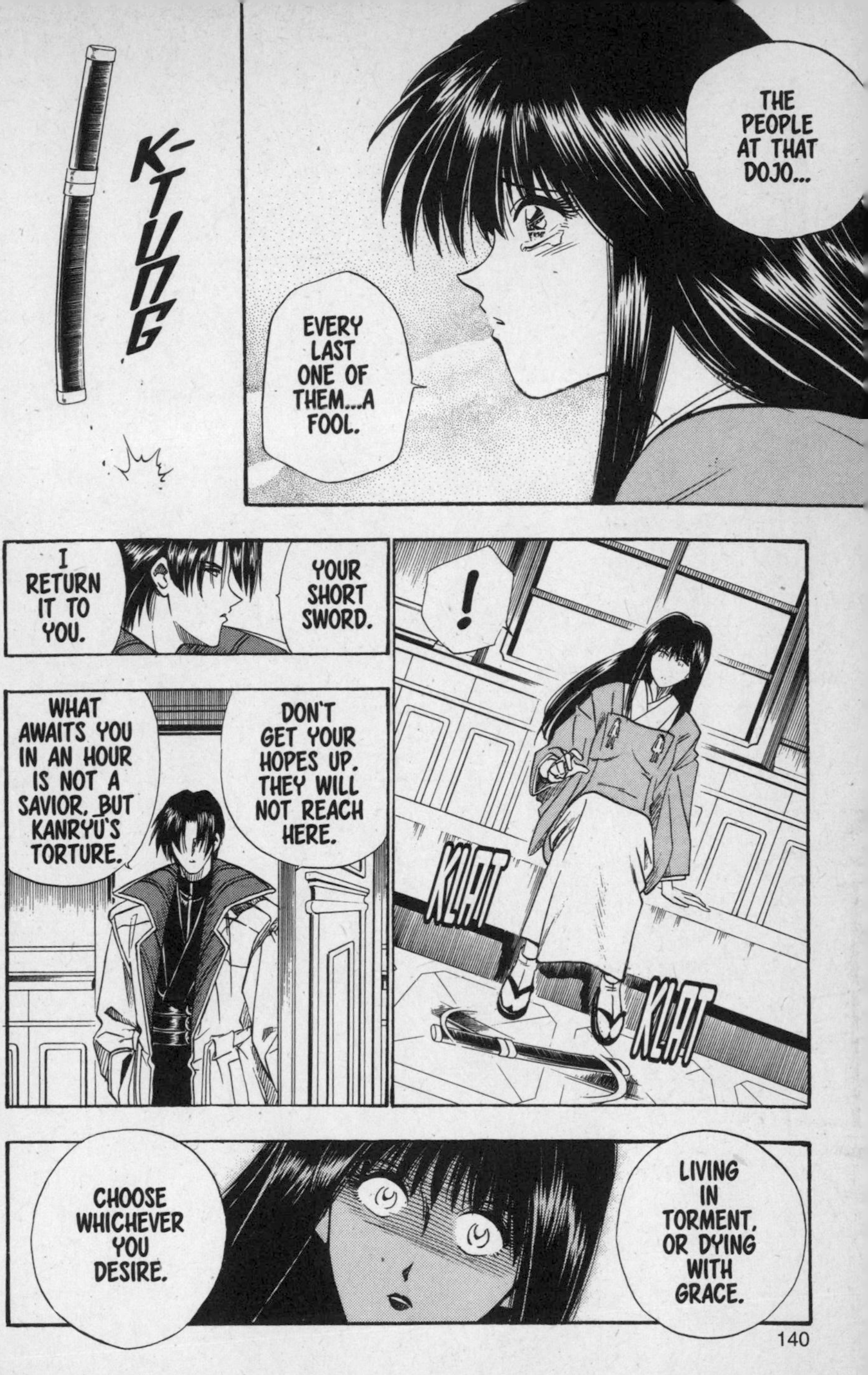
THE PEOPLE AT THAT DOJO...
EVERY LAST ONE OF THEM...A FOOL.
K-TUNG
!
KLAT
KLAT
YOUR SHORT SWORD.
I RETURN IT TO YOU.
DON'T GET YOUR HOPES UP. THEY WILL NOT REACH HERE.
WHAT AWAITS YOU IN AN HOUR IS NOT A SAVIOR, BUT KANRYU'S TORTURE.
LIVING IN TORMENT, OR DYING WITH GRACE.
CHOOSE WHICHEVER YOU DESIRE.

READ THIS WAY

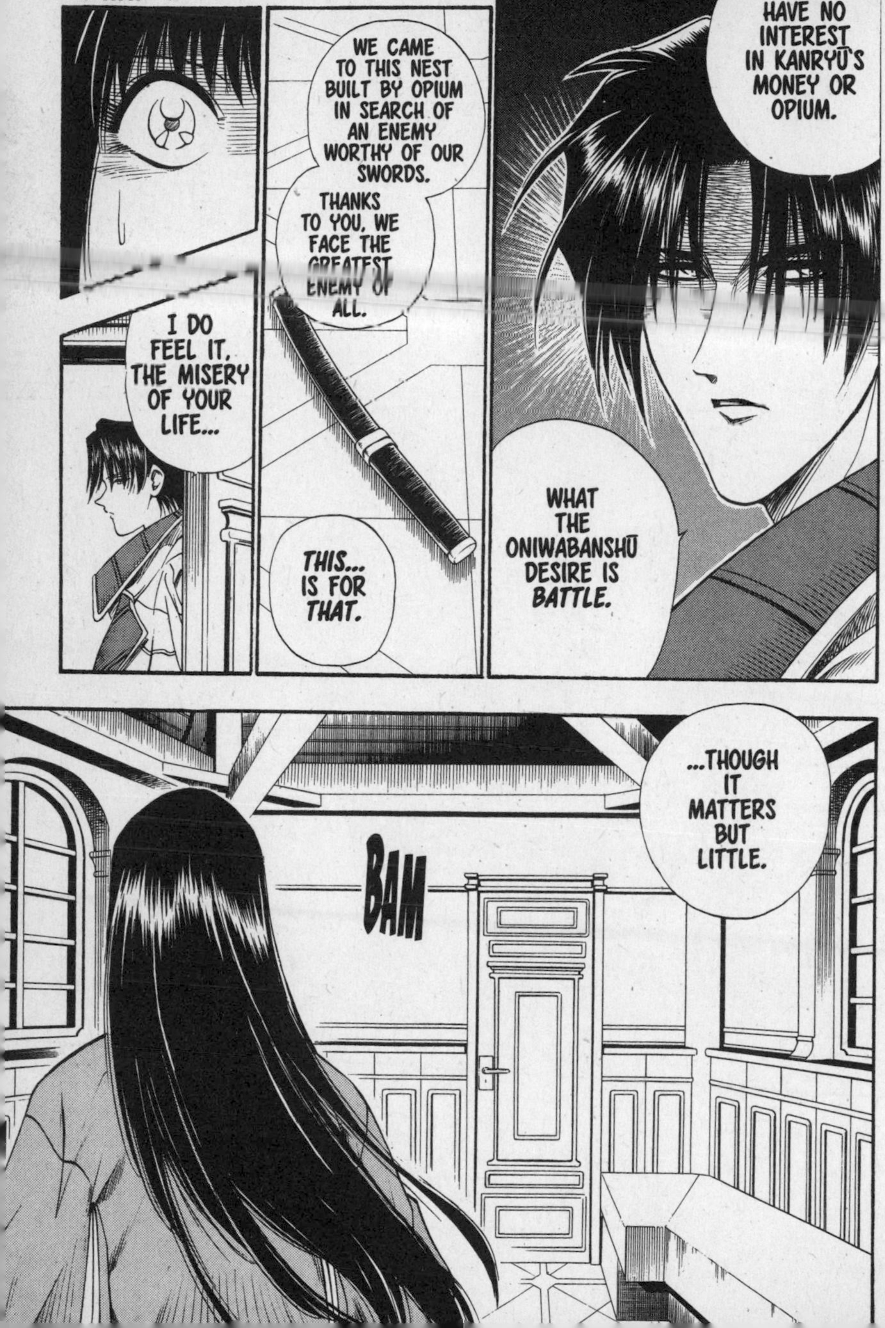
WE HAVE NO INTEREST IN KANRYŪ'S MONEY OR OPIUM.
WHAT THE ONIWABANSHŪ DESIRE IS BATTLE.
WE CAME TO THIS NEST BUILT BY OPIUM IN SEARCH OF AN ENEMY WORTHY OF OUR SWORDS.
THANKS TO YOU, WE FACE THE GREATEST ENEMY OF ALL.
THIS... IS FOR THAT.
I DO FEEL IT, THE MISERY OF YOUR LIFE...
...THOUGH IT MATTERS BUT LITTLE.
BAM

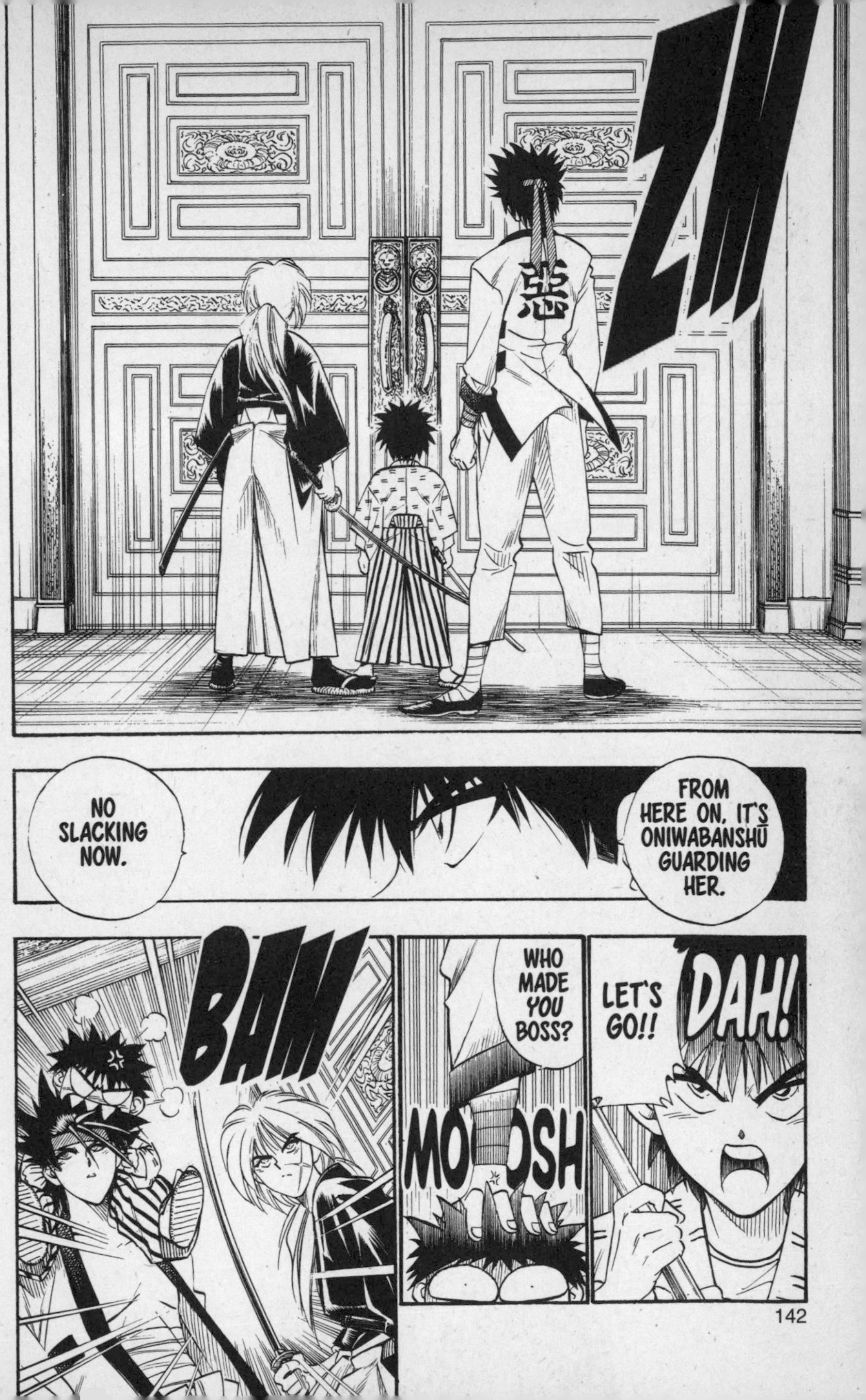
ZAH
FROM HERE ON, IT'S ONIWABANSHŪ GUARDING HER.
NO SLACKING NOW.
DAH!
LET'S GO!!
WHO MADE YOU BOSS?
MO OSH
BAM

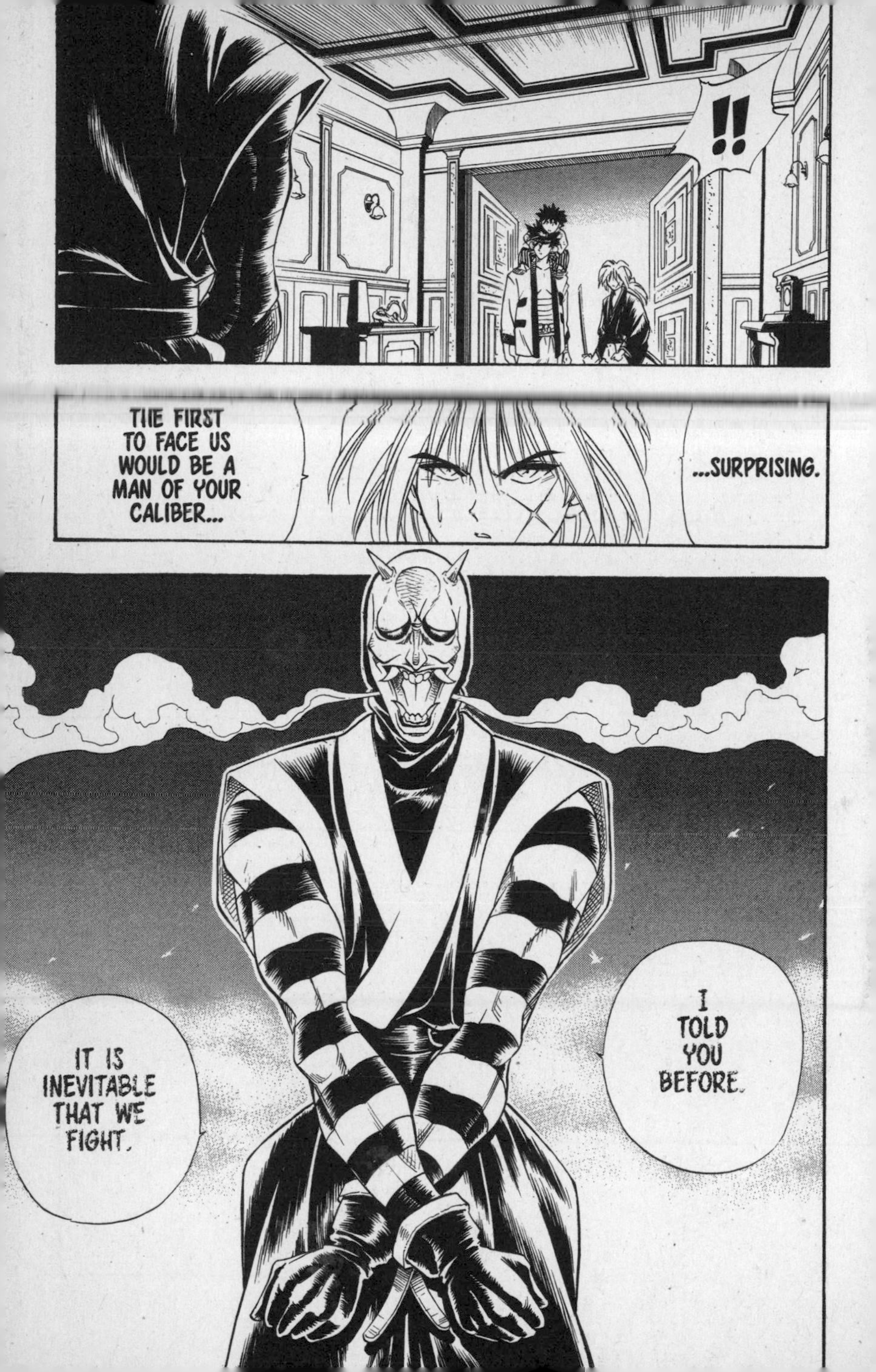
!!
THE FIRST TO FACE US WOULD BE A MAN OF YOUR CALIBER...
...SURPRISING.
I TOLD YOU BEFORE.
IT IS INEVITABLE THAT WE FIGHT.

READ THIS WAY

Rurouni Kenshin

What you're about to read is the very first *Rurouni,* published half a year before the story included at the end of Volume 1. If we think of that story as a "side-story," we can think of this one as the series "pilot"—with some of the details being different between then and now. This early story loosely echoes the later "Megumi Arc," as will become clear once you start reading—though, in this version, Megumi, Kaoru and Yahiko are all siblings. (Megumi's personality is also completely changed.)

One thing about it I can now tell you is that the *Rurouni Kenshin* series wasn't begun entirely of Watsuki's own will. Having had some positive feedback with a "historical" debut work, still there was no getting around the fact that historical stories were *hard.* I'd thought to do my next work—what ended up becoming this story—in a contemporary setting, but my editor said to me, "You're a new, up-and-coming artist who's achieved some success (in historical genres); why not make your next one the same? If that proves popular as well, you can run with it." That's how I wound up doing *Rurouni.*

My goal was to take the time-period (Bakumatsu) from *Moeyo Ken*—Watsuki's bible—and combine it with a *Sugata Sanshirō*-type story. Complicating things further was the title, which went through many revisions. It started as "Nishin (Two-Hearts) Kenshin," went to "Yorozuya (Jack-of-All-Trades) Kenshin," then to several variations of "Rurouni" and "Kenshin"—sometimes with different *kanji*—ending up, eventually, as "Rurouni, Meiji Swordsman Romantic Story." It took me eight months to do a 45-page story...only for it to fall to the tender editorial mercies of a selection committee. Suffice it to say, the process was *not* easy.

A year and a half to age, and eventually the *Rurouni Kenshin* series we know today was born. Once again, let me take this opportunity to thank all you fans, who've given me such support.

GLOOOOOM
Oh, man, looking back now, this art BITES.
What was I thinking, leaving it in here...??

伸宏和月

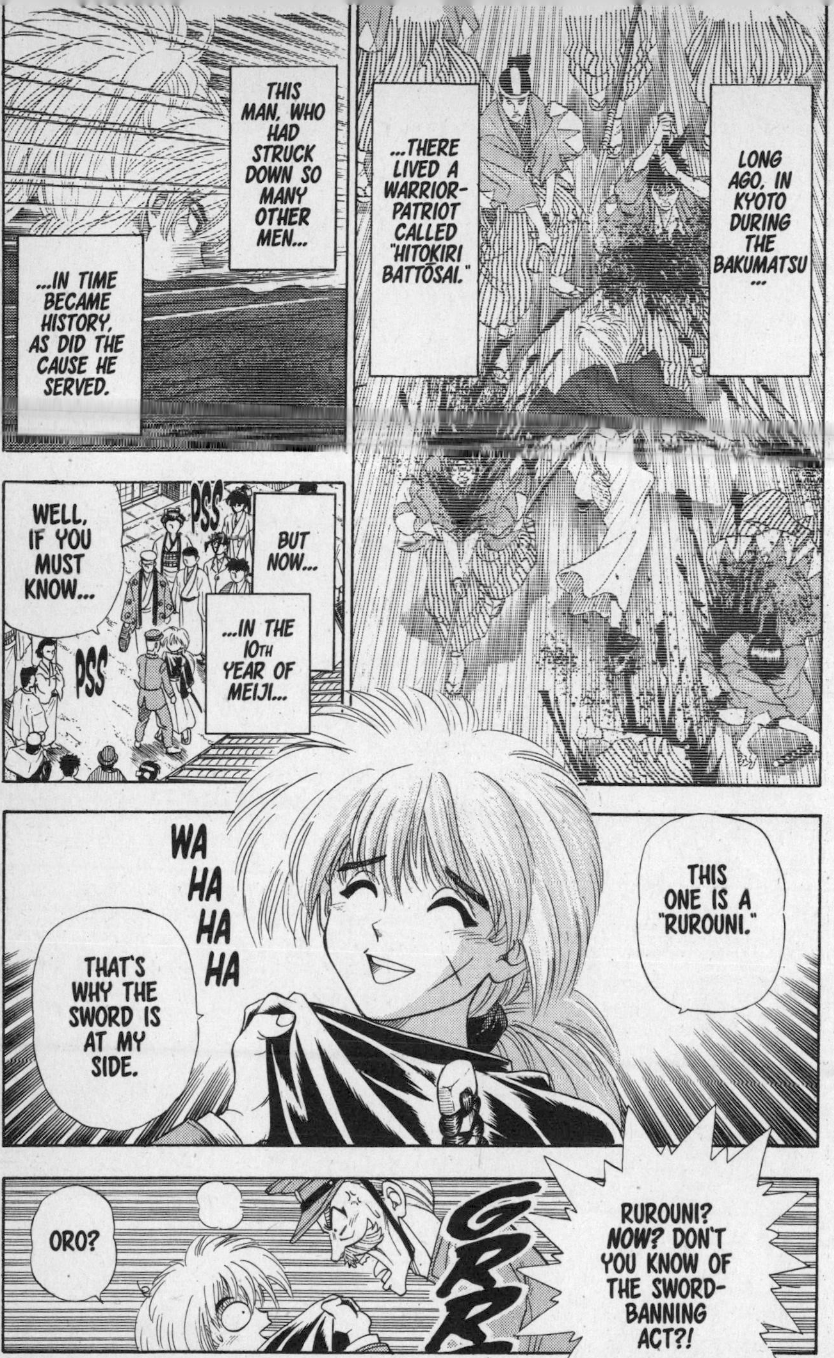
LONG AGO, IN KYOTO DURING THE BAKUMATSU...
...THERE LIVED A WARRIOR-PATRIOT CALLED "HITOKIRI BATTŌSAI."
THIS MAN, WHO HAD STRUCK DOWN SO MANY OTHER MEN...
...IN TIME BECAME HISTORY, AS DID THE CAUSE HE SERVED.
BUT NOW...
...IN THE 10TH YEAR OF MEIJI...
PSS
PSS
WELL, IF YOU MUST KNOW...
THIS ONE IS A "RUROUNI."
WA HA HA HA
THAT'S WHY THE SWORD IS AT MY SIDE.
RUROUNI? NOW? DON'T YOU KNOW OF THE SWORD-BANNING ACT?!
GRR
ORO?

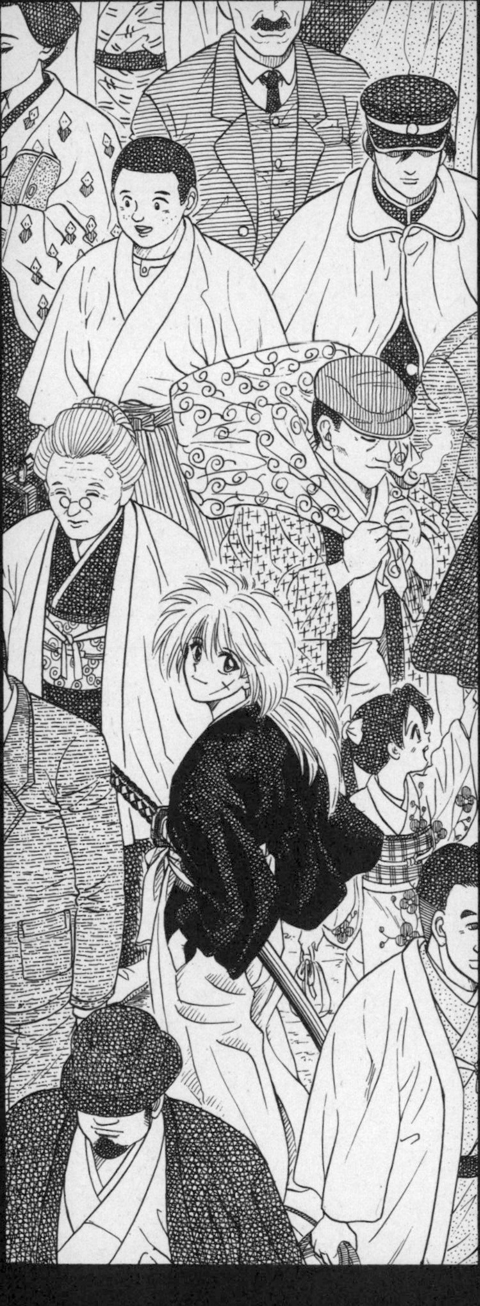

END-OF-VOLUME SPECIAL (2)

RUROUNI

MEIJI SWORDSMAN ROMANTIC STORY

READ THIS WAY

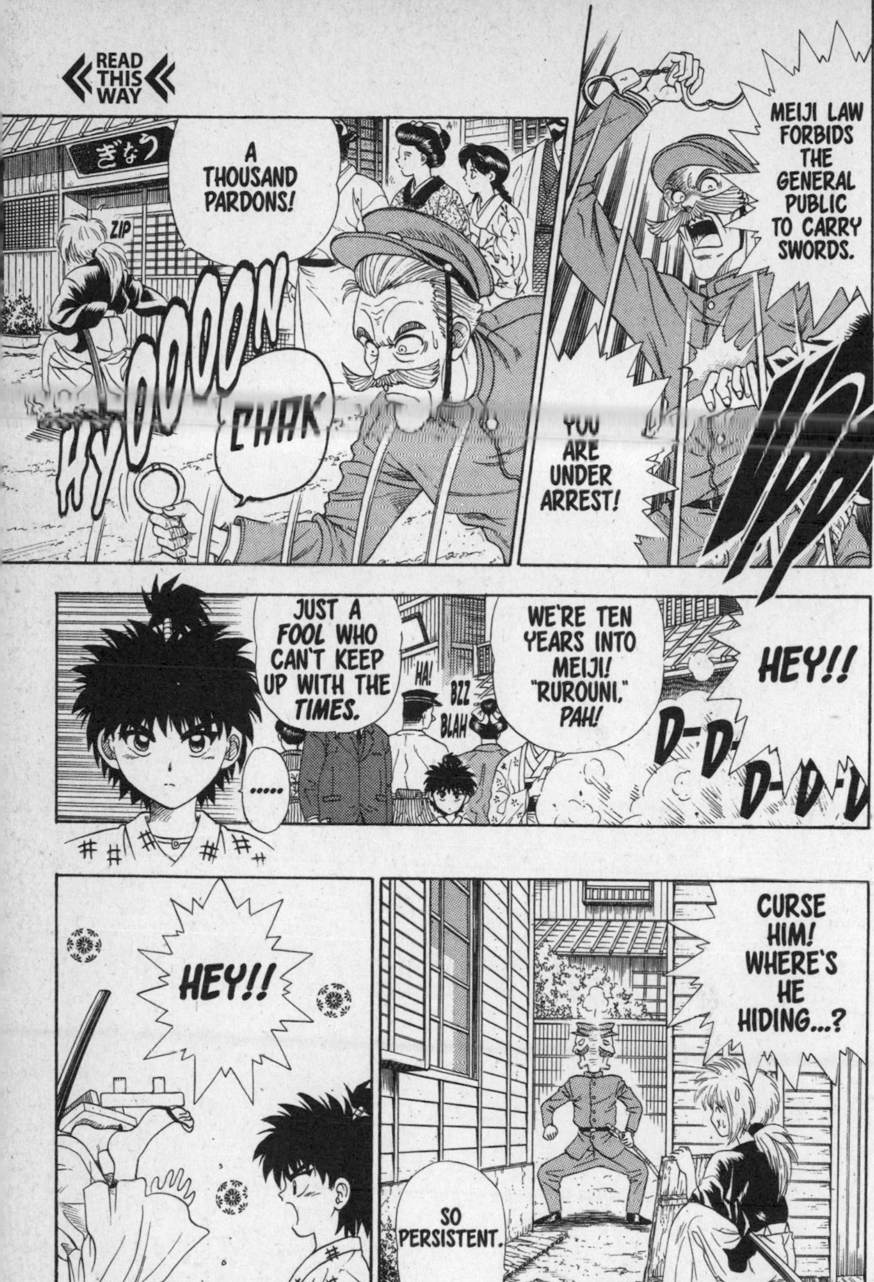
MEIJI LAW FORBIDS THE GENERAL PUBLIC TO CARRY SWORDS.
YOU ARE UNDER ARREST!
A THOUSAND PARDONS!
ぎなう
ZIP
HYOOOON
CHAK
HEY!!
D-D-D-D-D
WE'RE TEN YEARS INTO MEIJI! "RUROUNI," PAH!
BZZ
BLAH
HA!
JUST A FOOL WHO CAN'T KEEP UP WITH THE TIMES.
......
CURSE HIM! WHERE'S HE HIDING...?
SO PERSISTENT.
HEY!!

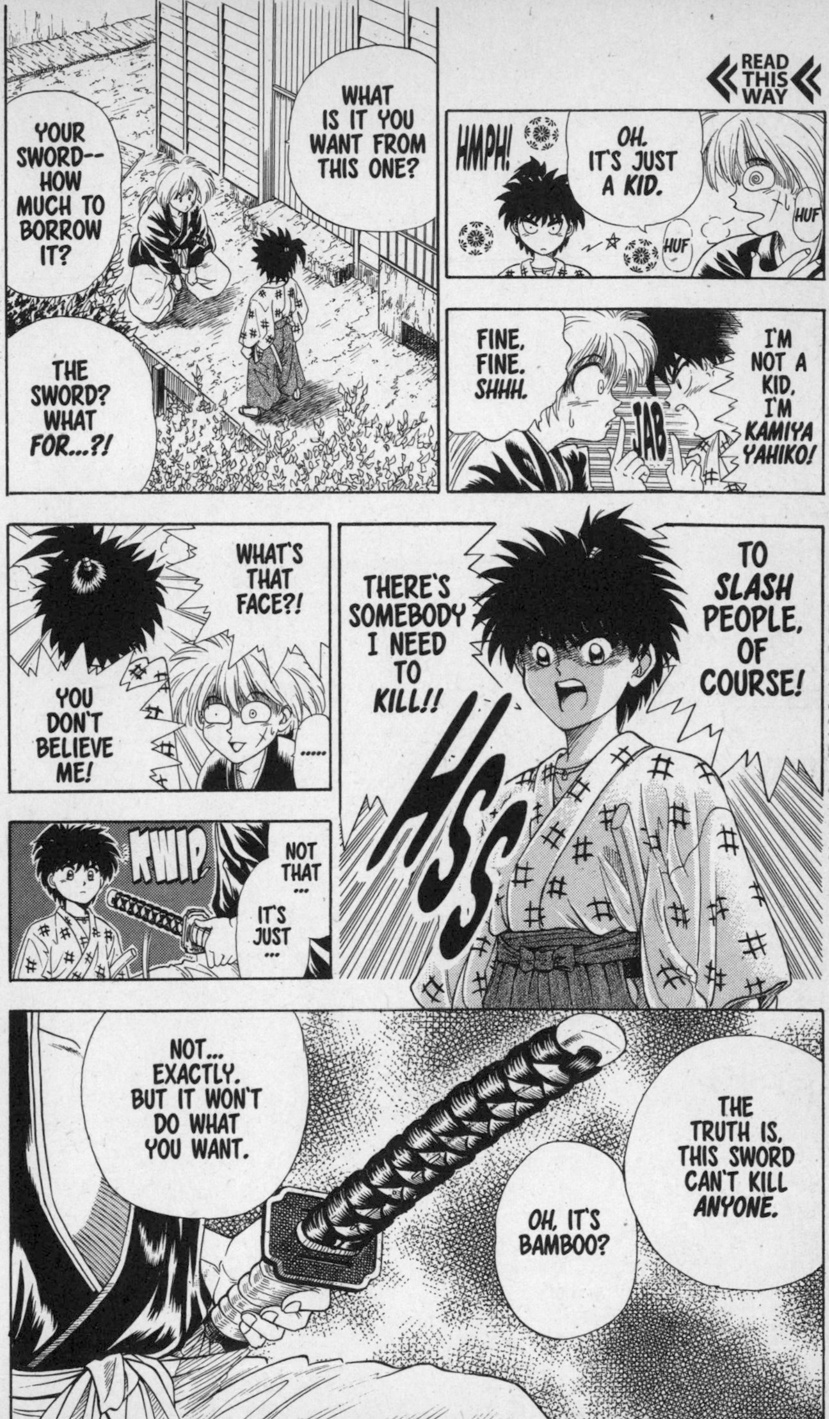
READ THIS WAY
OH. IT'S JUST A KID.
HUF
HUF
HMPH!
I'M NOT A KID, I'M KAMIYA YAHIKO!
JAB
FINE, FINE. SHHH.
WHAT IS IT YOU WANT FROM THIS ONE?
YOUR SWORD-- HOW MUCH TO BORROW IT?
THE SWORD? WHAT FOR...?!
TO SLASH PEOPLE, OF COURSE!
THERE'S SOMEBODY I NEED TO KILL!!
HSS
WHAT'S THAT FACE?!
.....
YOU DON'T BELIEVE ME!
NOT THAT ...
IT'S JUST ...
KWIP
THE TRUTH IS, THIS SWORD CAN'T KILL ANYONE.
OH, IT'S BAMBOO?
NOT... EXACTLY. BUT IT WON'T DO WHAT YOU WANT.

READ THIS WAY

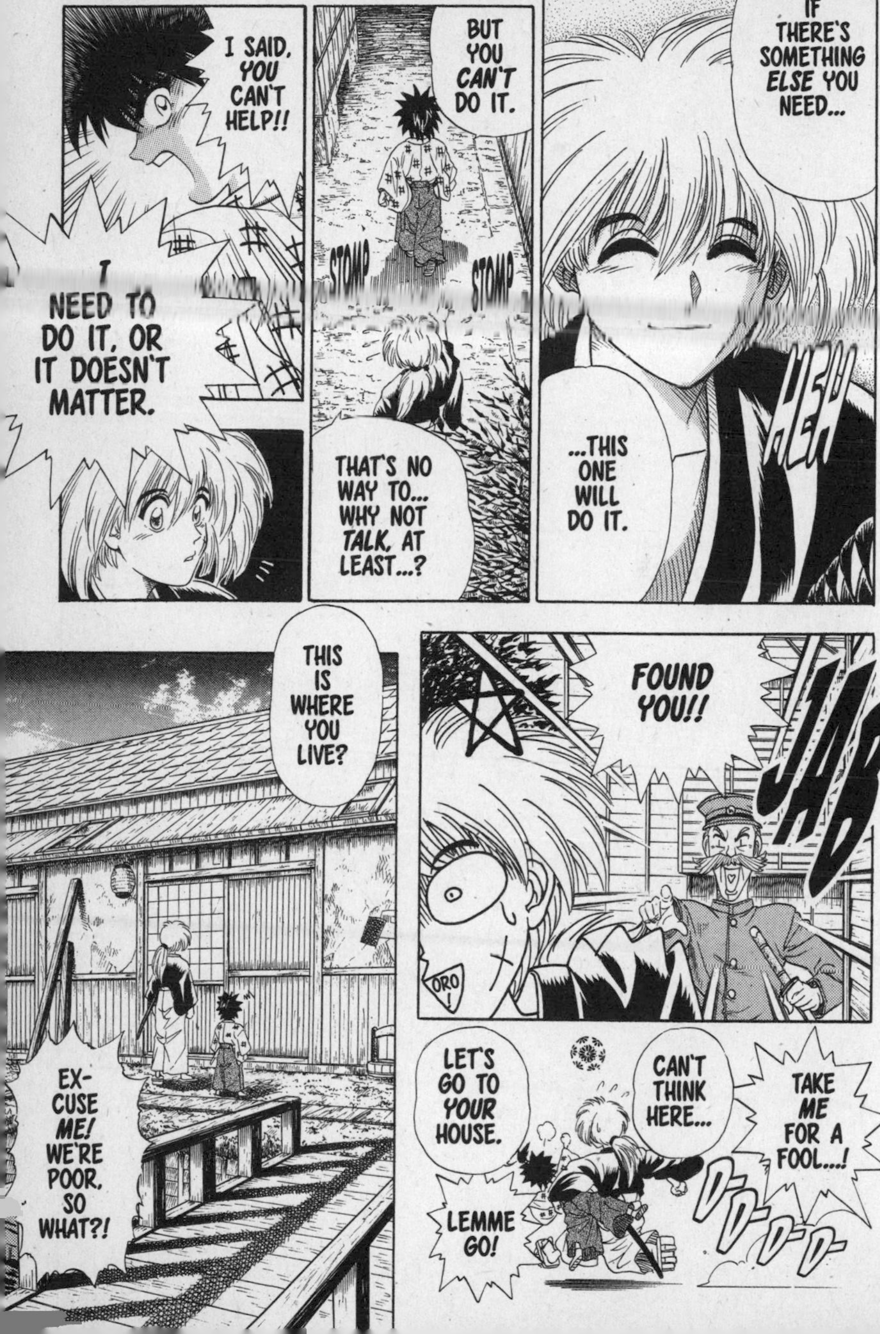
IF THERE'S SOMETHING ELSE YOU NEED...
...THIS ONE WILL DO IT.
HEH
BUT YOU CAN'T DO IT.
STOMP
STOMP
THAT'S NO WAY TO... WHY NOT TALK, AT LEAST...?
I SAID, YOU CAN'T HELP!!
I NEED TO DO IT, OR IT DOESN'T MATTER.
FOUND YOU!!
JAB
ORO!
TAKE ME FOR A FOOL...!
CAN'T THINK HERE...
LET'S GO TO YOUR HOUSE.
LEMME GO!
D-D-D-D-
THIS IS WHERE YOU LIVE?
EX-CUSE ME! WE'RE POOR, SO WHAT?!

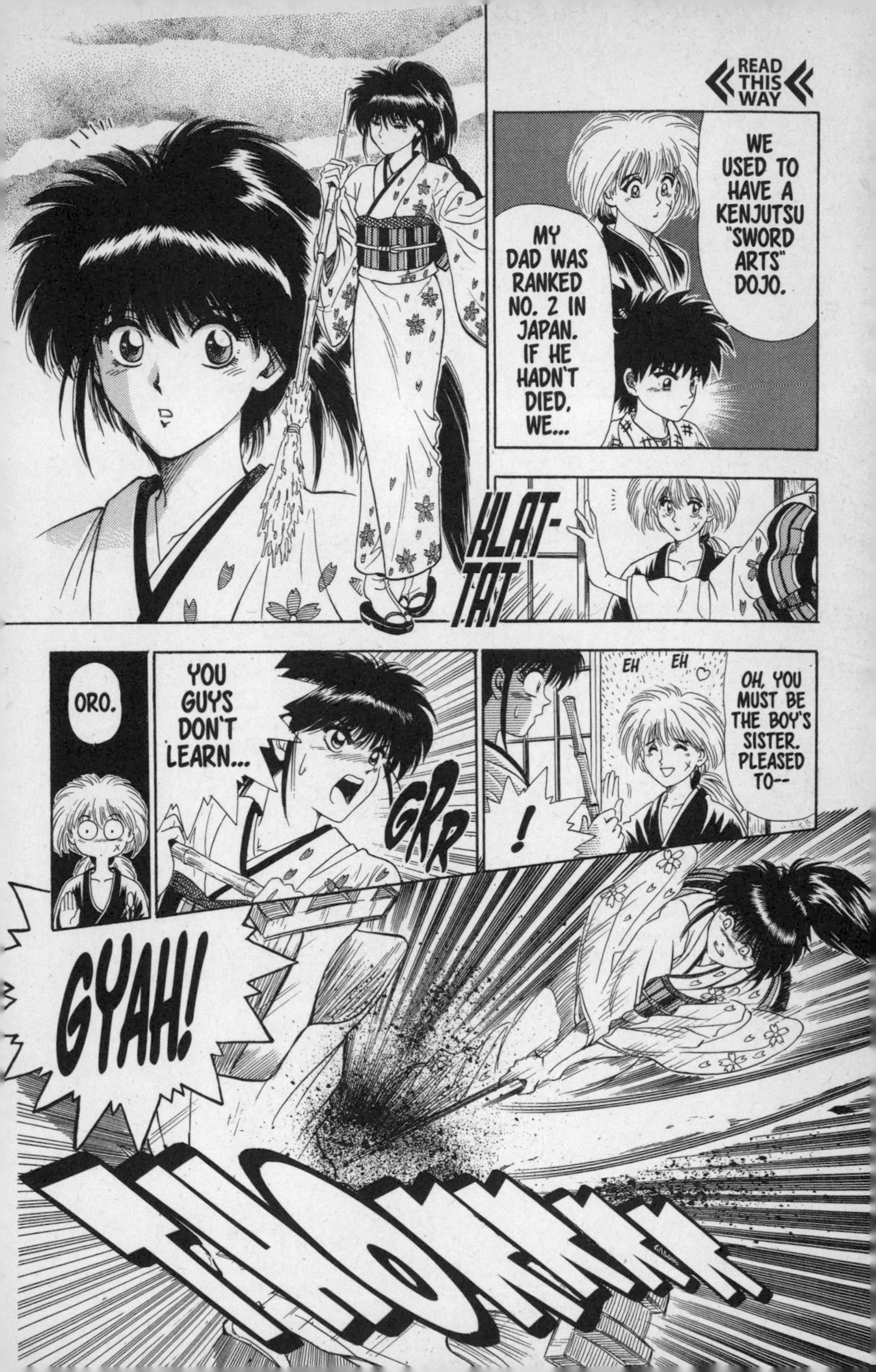
READ THIS WAY
WE USED TO HAVE A KENJUTSU "SWORD ARTS" DOJO.
MY DAD WAS RANKED NO. 2 IN JAPAN. IF HE HADN'T DIED, WE...
KLAT-TAT
OH, YOU MUST BE THE BOY'S SISTER. PLEASED TO--
EH EH
!
YOU GUYS DON'T LEARN...
GRR
ORO.
GYAH!

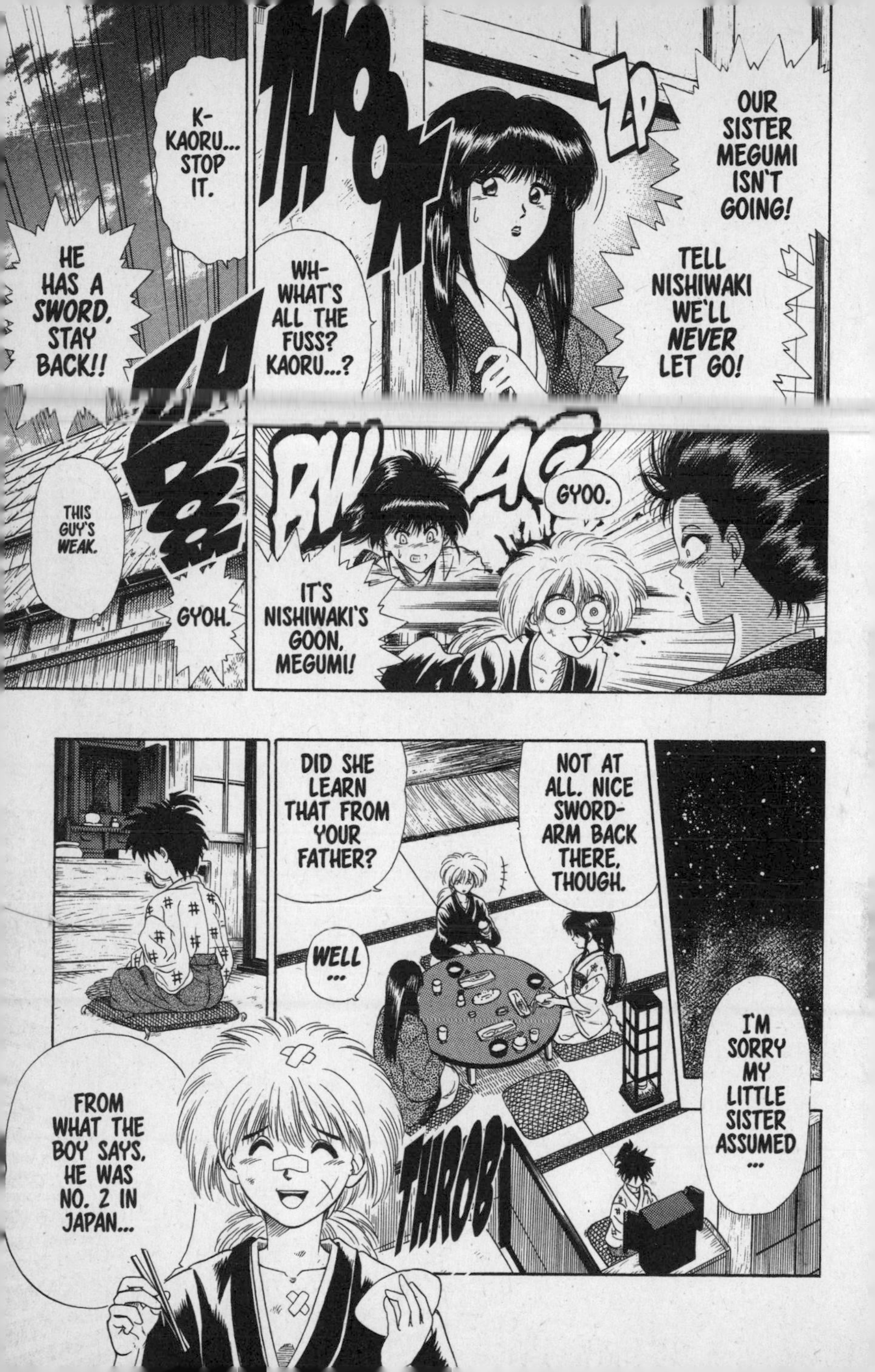
OUR SISTER MEGUMI ISN'T GOING!
TELL NISHIWAKI WE'LL NEVER LET GO!
ZP
WH-WHAT'S ALL THE FUSS? KAORU...?
K-KAORU... STOP IT.
HE HAS A SWORD, STAY BACK!!
GYOO.
IT'S NISHIWAKI'S GOON, MEGUMI!
THIS GUY'S WEAK.
GYOH.
I'M SORRY MY LITTLE SISTER ASSUMED...
NOT AT ALL. NICE SWORD-ARM BACK THERE, THOUGH.
DID SHE LEARN THAT FROM YOUR FATHER?
WELL...
THROB
FROM WHAT THE BOY SAYS, HE WAS NO. 2 IN JAPAN...

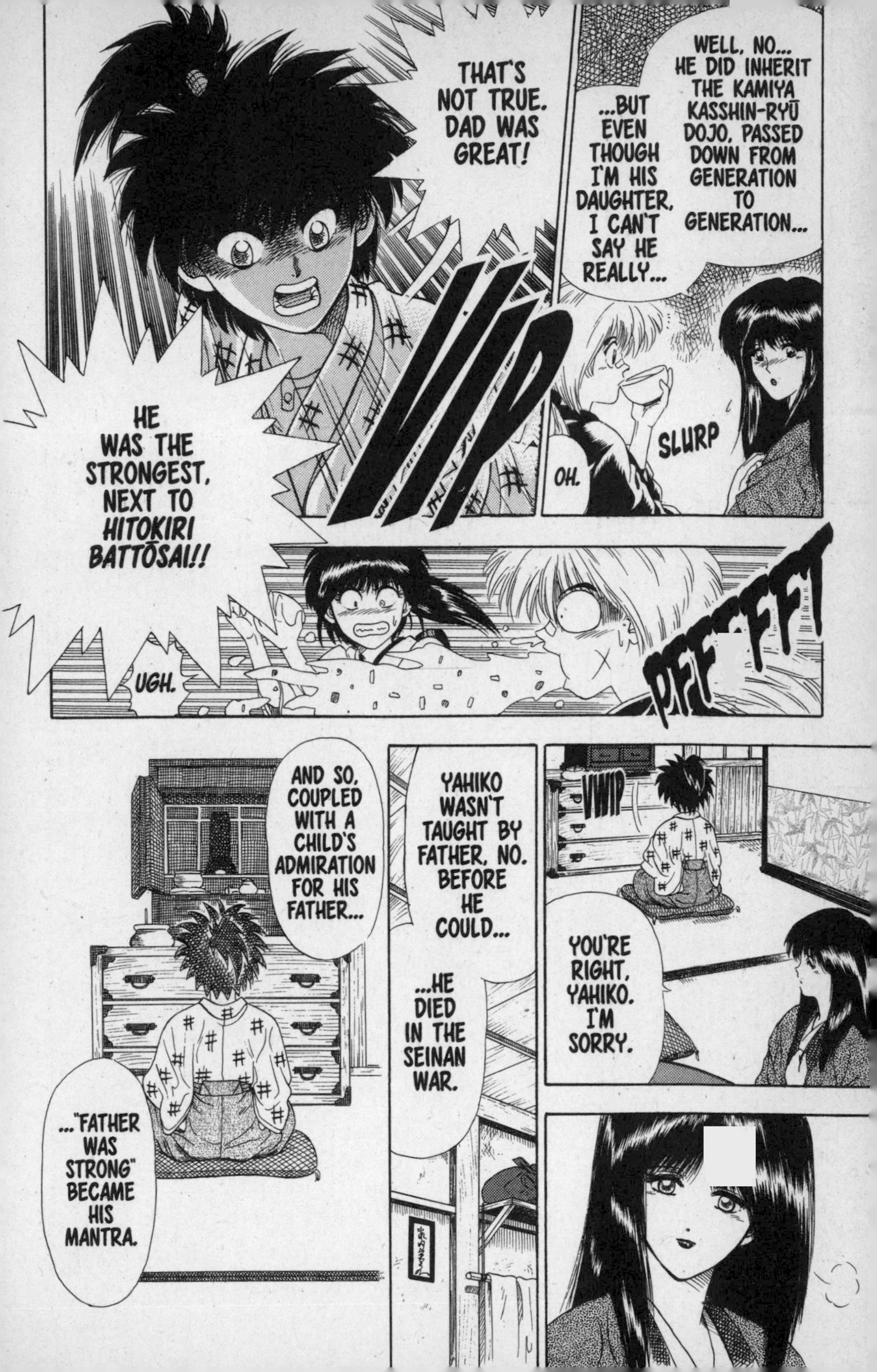
WELL, NO... HE DID INHERIT THE KAMIYA KASSHIN-RYŪ DOJO, PASSED DOWN FROM GENERATION TO GENERATION...
...BUT EVEN THOUGH I'M HIS DAUGHTER, I CAN'T SAY HE REALLY...
SLURP
OH.
THAT'S NOT TRUE. DAD WAS GREAT!
HE WAS THE STRONGEST, NEXT TO HITOKIRI BATTŌSAI!!
UGH.
VWIP
YOU'RE RIGHT, YAHIKO. I'M SORRY.
YAHIKO WASN'T TAUGHT BY FATHER, NO. BEFORE HE COULD...
...HE DIED IN THE SEINAN WAR.
AND SO, COUPLED WITH A CHILD'S ADMIRATION FOR HIS FATHER...
..."FATHER WAS STRONG" BECAME HIS MANTRA.

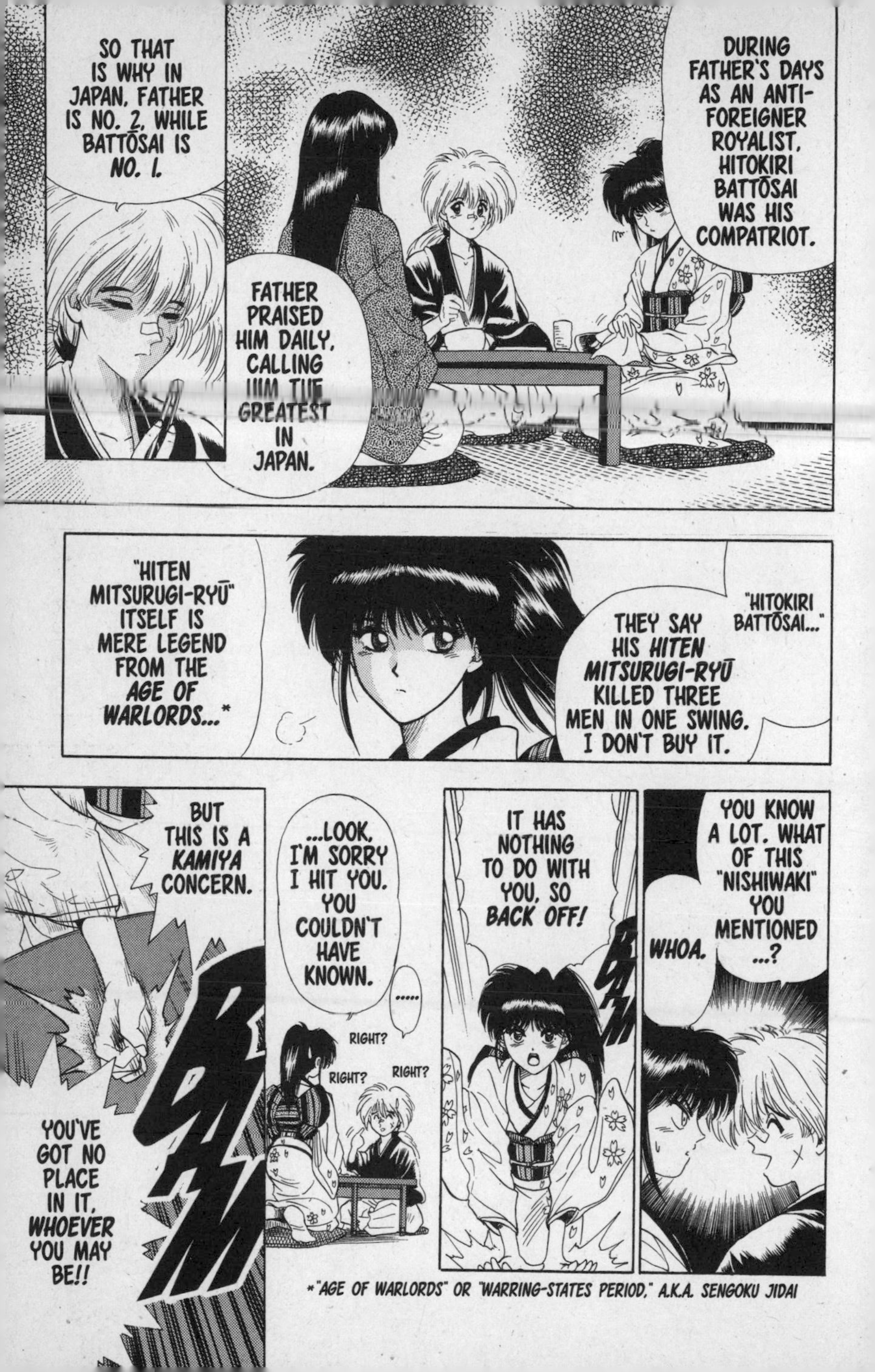
DURING FATHER'S DAYS AS AN ANTI-FOREIGNER ROYALIST, HITOKIRI BATTŌSAI WAS HIS COMPATRIOT.
FATHER PRAISED HIM DAILY, CALLING HIM THE GREATEST IN JAPAN.
SO THAT IS WHY IN JAPAN, FATHER IS NO. 2, WHILE BATTŌSAI IS NO. 1.
"HITOKIRI BATTŌSAI..."
THEY SAY HIS HITEN MITSURUGI-RYŪ KILLED THREE MEN IN ONE SWING. I DON'T BUY IT.
"HITEN MITSURUGI-RYŪ" ITSELF IS MERE LEGEND FROM THE AGE OF WARLORDS...*
YOU KNOW A LOT. WHAT OF THIS "NISHIWAKI" YOU MENTIONED ...?
WHOA.
IT HAS NOTHING TO DO WITH YOU, SO BACK OFF!
...LOOK, I'M SORRY I HIT YOU. YOU COULDN'T HAVE KNOWN.
......
RIGHT?
RIGHT?
RIGHT?
BUT THIS IS A KAMIYA CONCERN.
YOU'VE GOT NO PLACE IN IT, WHOEVER YOU MAY BE!!

*"AGE OF WARLORDS" OR "WARRING-STATES PERIOD," A.K.A. SENGOKU JIDAI

READ THIS WAY

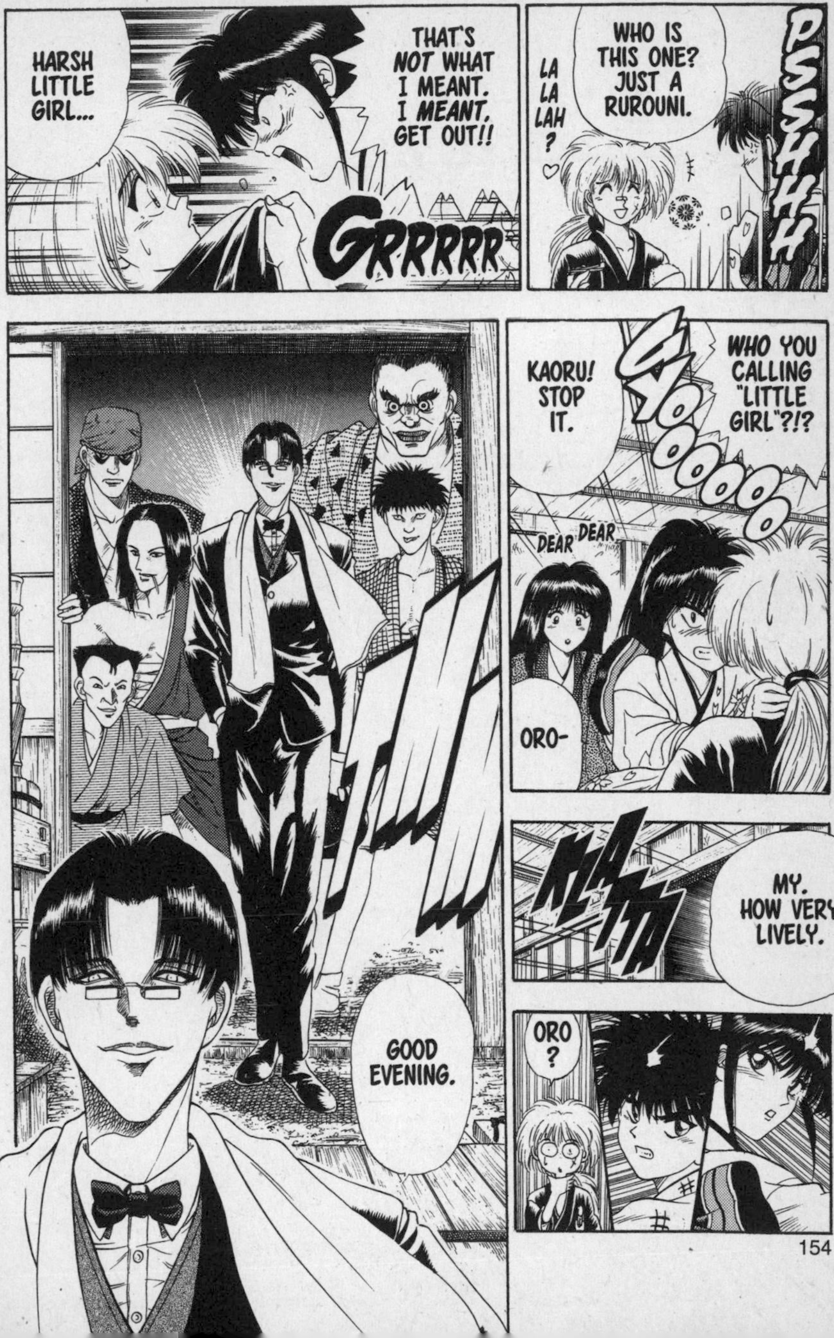
PSSHHH
WHO IS THIS ONE? JUST A RUROUNI.
LA LA LAH ?
THAT'S *NOT* WHAT I MEANT. I *MEANT*, GET OUT!!
GRRRRR
HARSH LITTLE GIRL...
WHO YOU CALLING "LITTLE GIRL"?!?
KAORU! STOP IT.
DEAR DEAR
ORO-
MY. HOW VERY LIVELY.
ORO ?
GOOD EVENING.

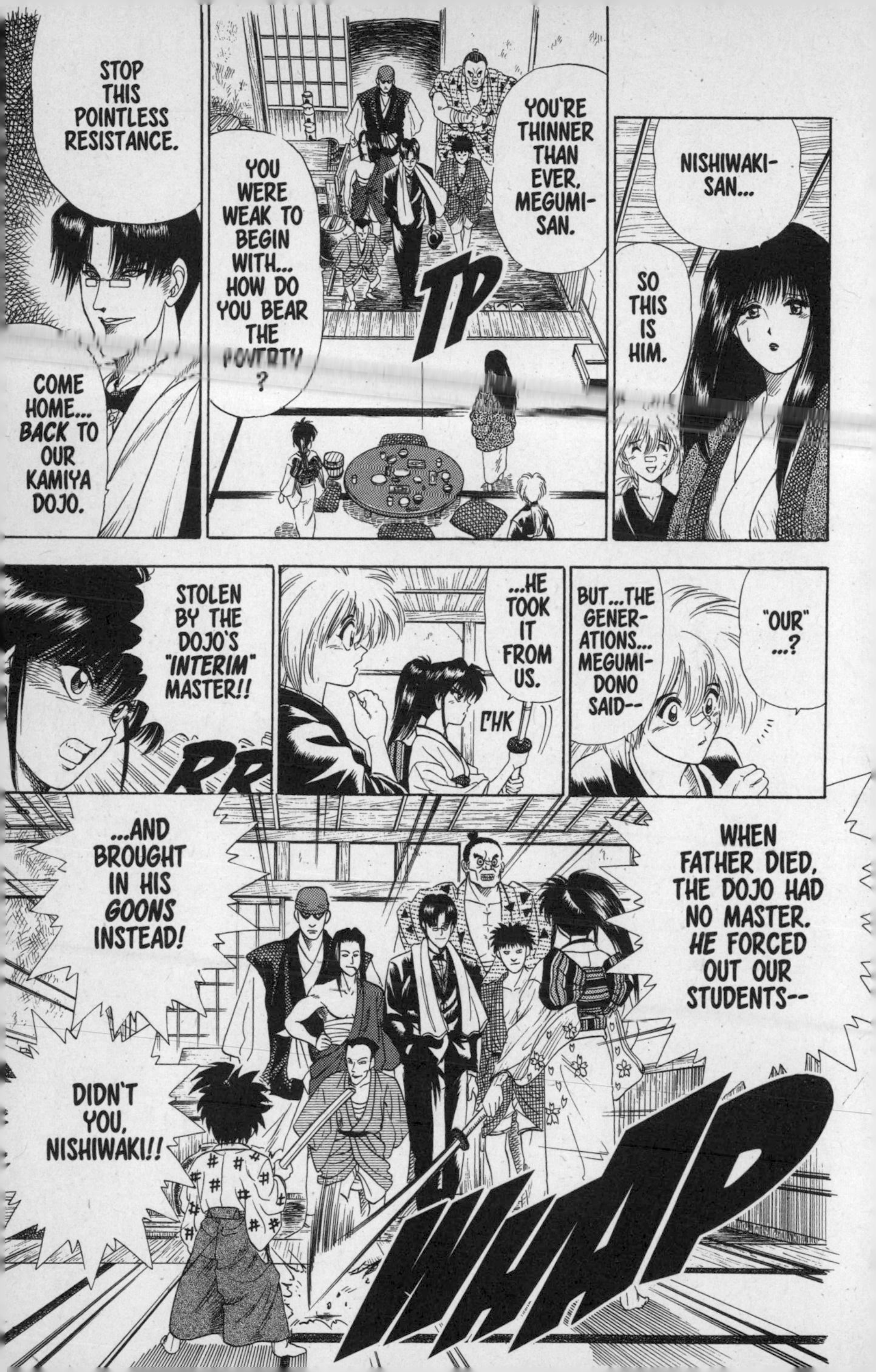
NISHIWAKI-SAN...
SO THIS IS HIM.
YOU'RE THINNER THAN EVER, MEGUMI-SAN.
YOU WERE WEAK TO BEGIN WITH... HOW DO YOU BEAR THE POVERTY?
TP
STOP THIS POINTLESS RESISTANCE.
COME HOME... BACK TO OUR KAMIYA DOJO.
"OUR" ...?
BUT...THE GENERATIONS... MEGUMI-DONO SAID--
...HE TOOK IT FROM US.
CHK
STOLEN BY THE DOJO'S "INTERIM" MASTER!!
RR
WHEN FATHER DIED, THE DOJO HAD NO MASTER. HE FORCED OUT OUR STUDENTS--
...AND BROUGHT IN HIS GOONS INSTEAD!
DIDN'T YOU, NISHIWAKI!!
WHAP

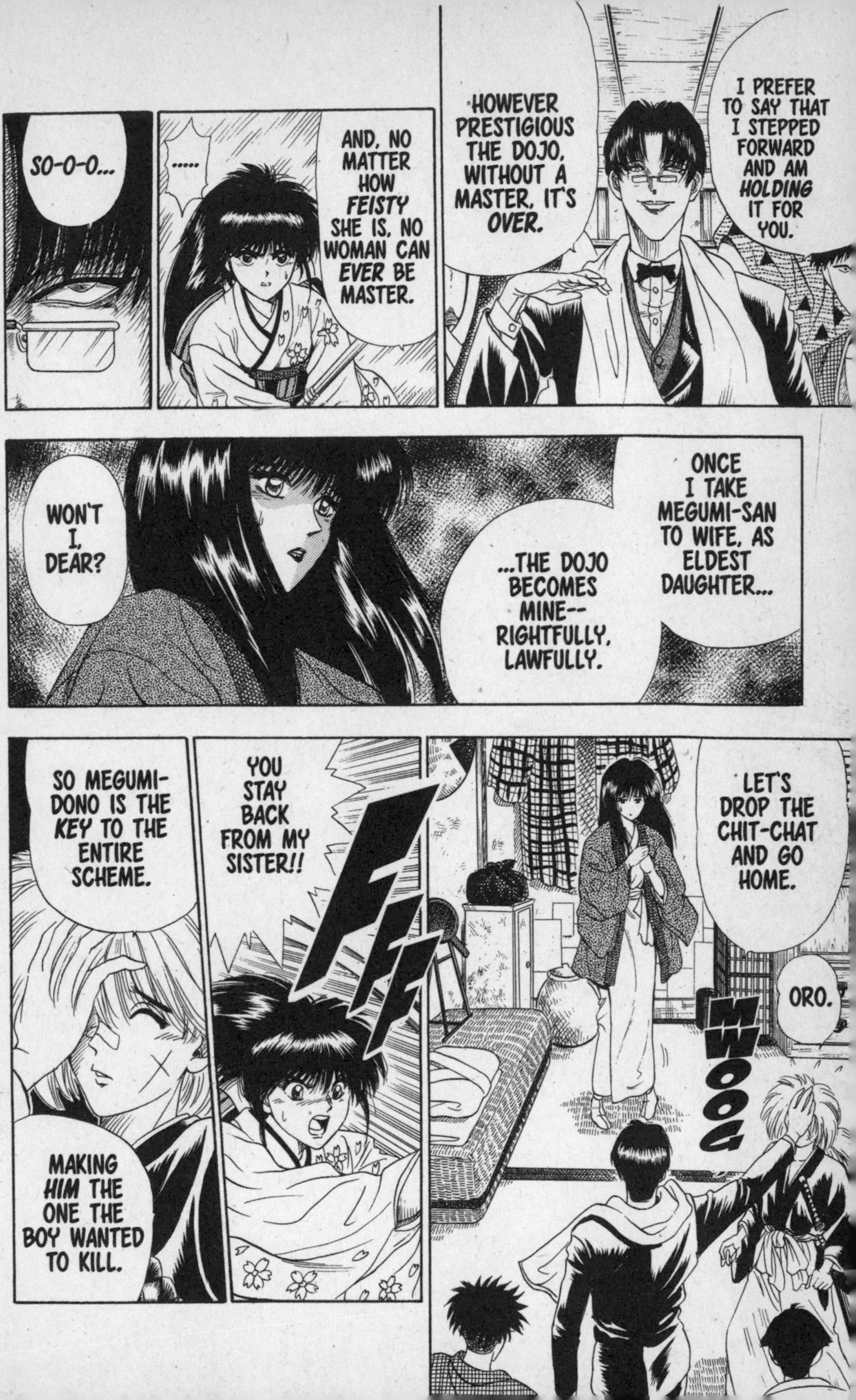
I PREFER TO SAY THAT I STEPPED FORWARD AND AM HOLDING IT FOR YOU.
HOWEVER PRESTIGIOUS THE DOJO, WITHOUT A MASTER, IT'S OVER.
AND, NO MATTER HOW FEISTY SHE IS, NO WOMAN CAN EVER BE MASTER.
.....
SO-O-O...
ONCE I TAKE MEGUMI-SAN TO WIFE, AS ELDEST DAUGHTER...
...THE DOJO BECOMES MINE-- RIGHTFULLY, LAWFULLY.
WON'T I, DEAR?
LET'S DROP THE CHIT-CHAT AND GO HOME.
ORO.
WWOOG
YOU STAY BACK FROM MY SISTER!!
SO MEGUMI-DONO IS THE KEY TO THE ENTIRE SCHEME.
MAKING HIM THE ONE THE BOY WANTED TO KILL.

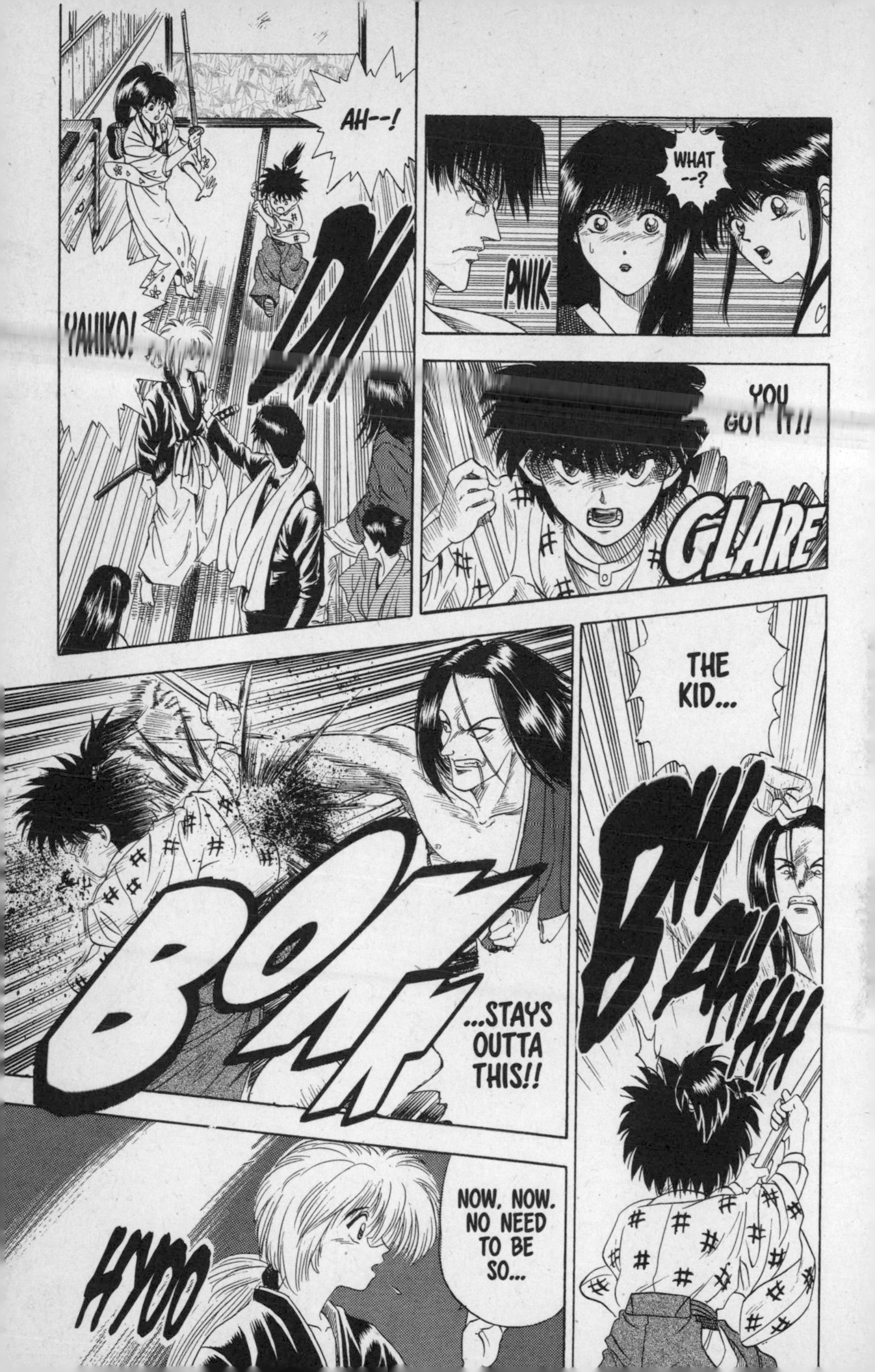
WHAT --?
PWIK
YOU GOT IT!!
GLARE
AH--!
YAHIKO!
THE KID...
BOM
...STAYS OUTTA THIS!!
NOW, NOW. NO NEED TO BE SO...
HYOO

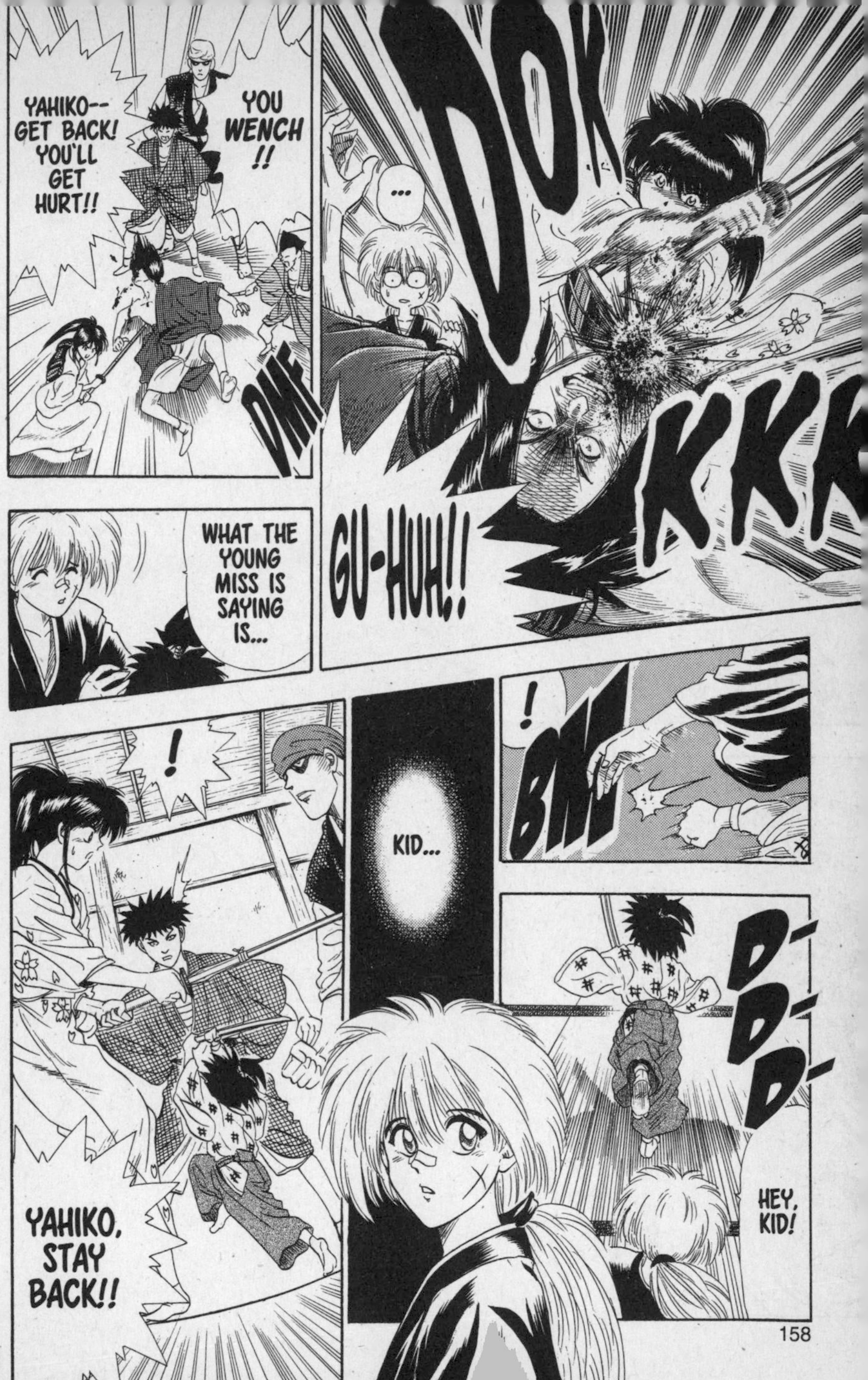
DOK
...
GU-HUH!!
KKK
YOU WENCH!!
YAHIKO-- GET BACK! YOU'LL GET HURT!!
DMF
WHAT THE YOUNG MISS IS SAYING IS...
!
BMM
D-D-D-
HEY, KID!
KID...
!
YAHIKO, STAY BACK!!

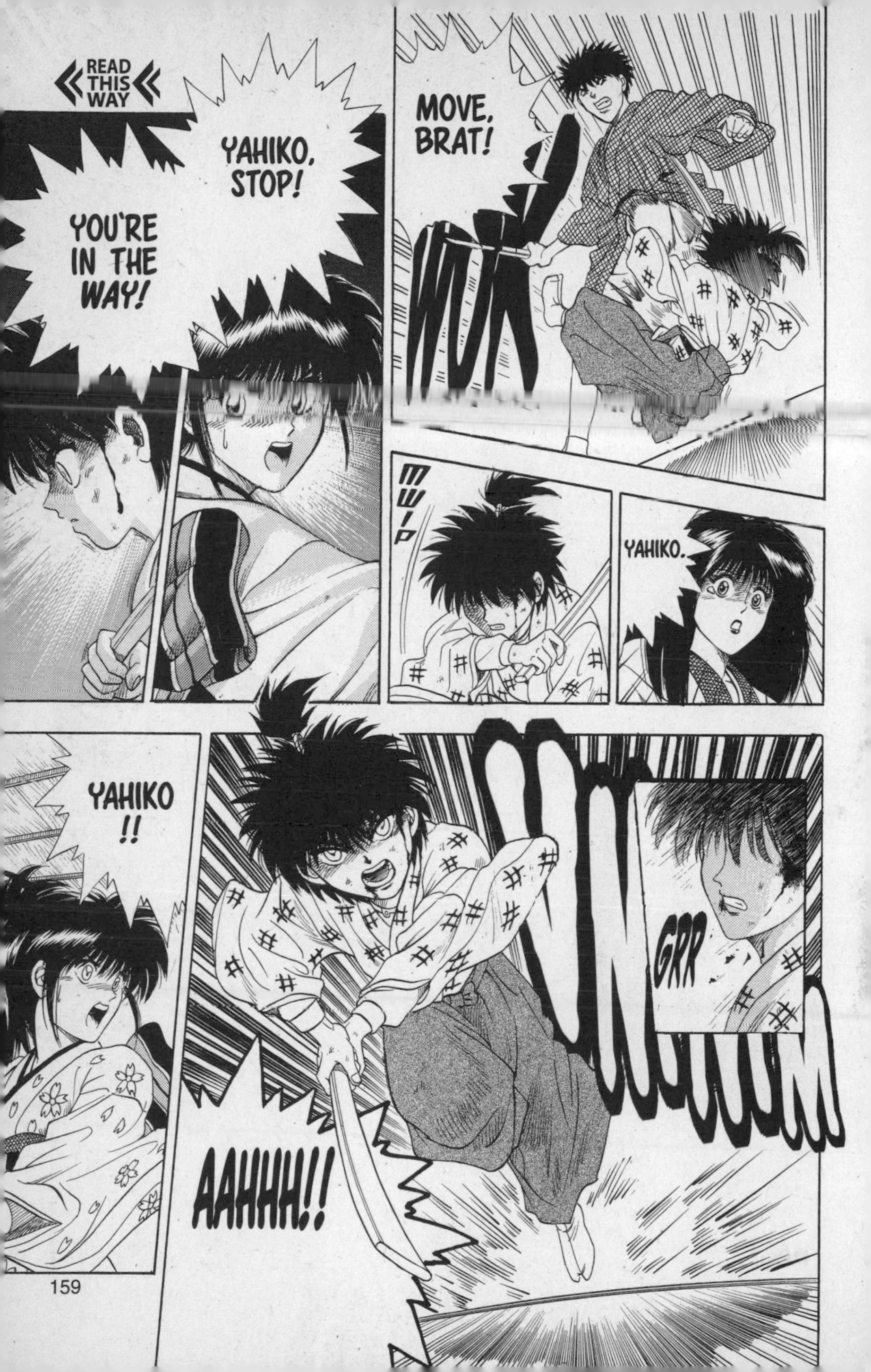
READ THIS WAY
MOVE, BRAT!
YAHIKO.
MWIP
YAHIKO, STOP!
YOU'RE IN THE WAY!
GRR
AAHHH!!
YAHIKO !!

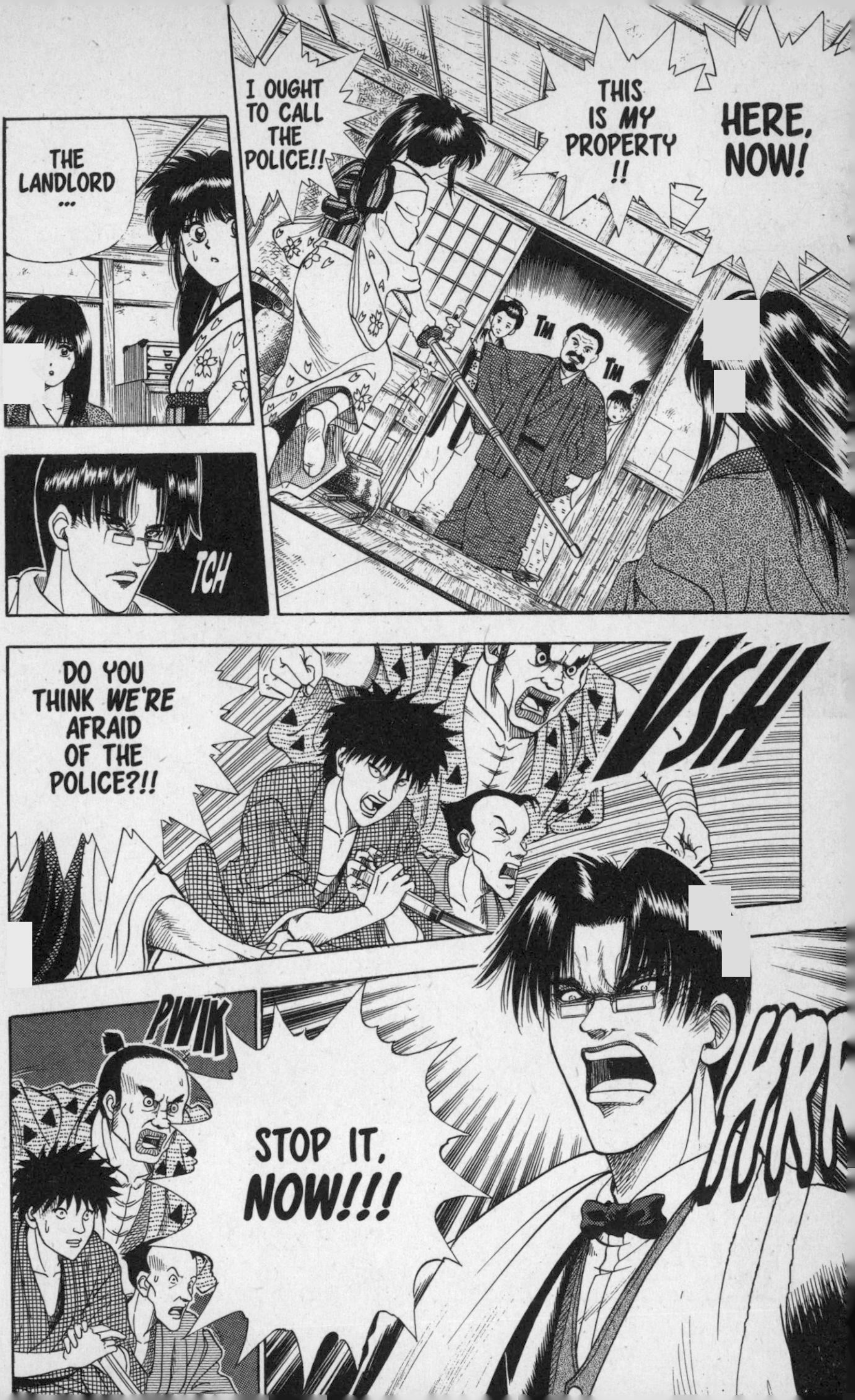
HERE, NOW!
THIS IS MY PROPERTY!!
TM
TM
I OUGHT TO CALL THE POLICE!!
THE LANDLORD...
TCH
VSH
DO YOU THINK WE'RE AFRAID OF THE POLICE?!!
STOP IT, NOW!!!
PWIK

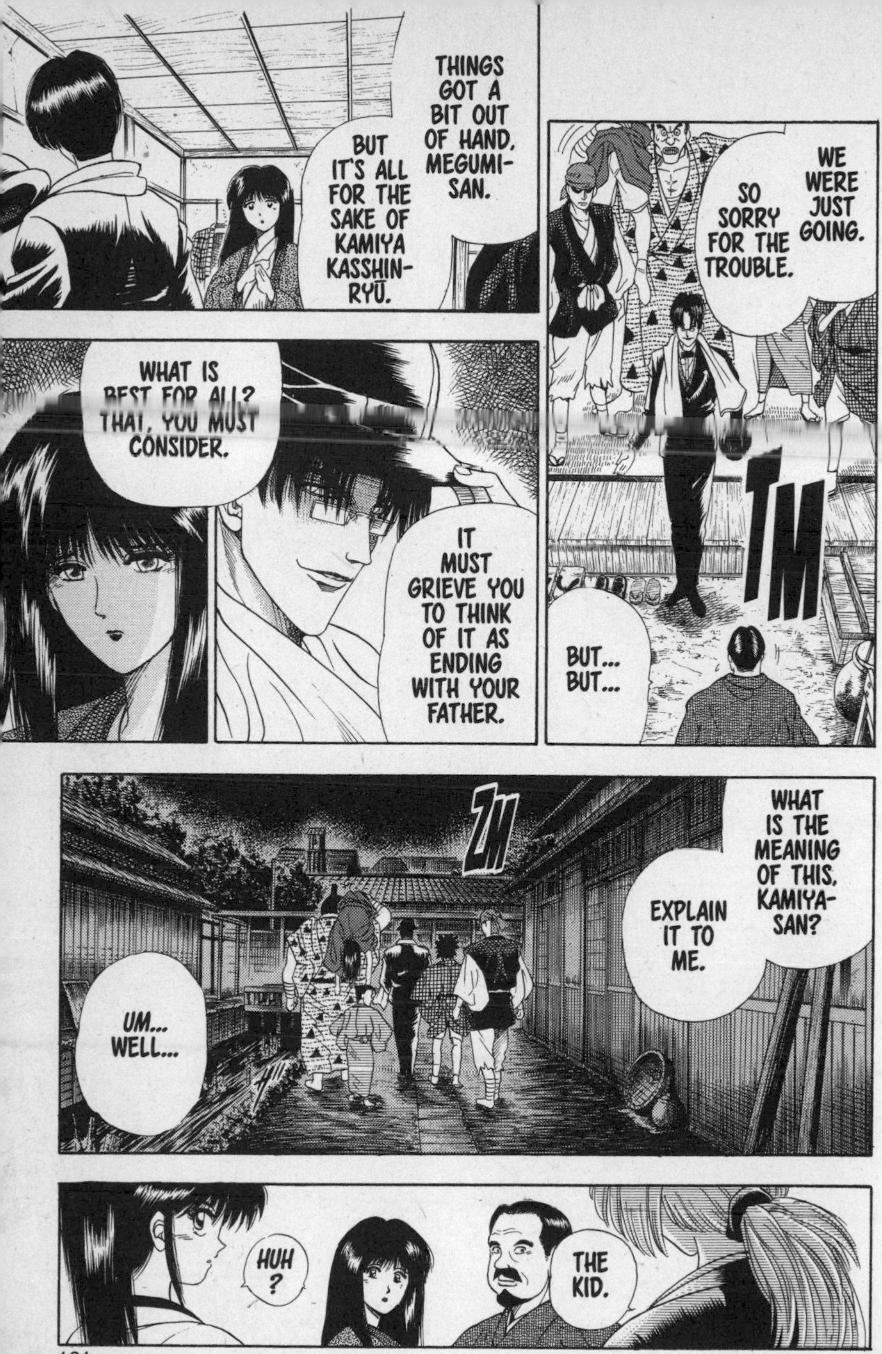
WE WERE JUST GOING.
SO SORRY FOR THE TROUBLE.
TM
BUT... BUT...
THINGS GOT A BIT OUT OF HAND, MEGUMI-SAN.
BUT IT'S ALL FOR THE SAKE OF KAMIYA KASSHIN-RYŪ.
IT MUST GRIEVE YOU TO THINK OF IT AS ENDING WITH YOUR FATHER.
WHAT IS BEST FOR ALL? THAT, YOU MUST CONSIDER.
WHAT IS THE MEANING OF THIS, KAMIYA-SAN?
EXPLAIN IT TO ME.
ZM
UM... WELL...
THE KID.
HUH?

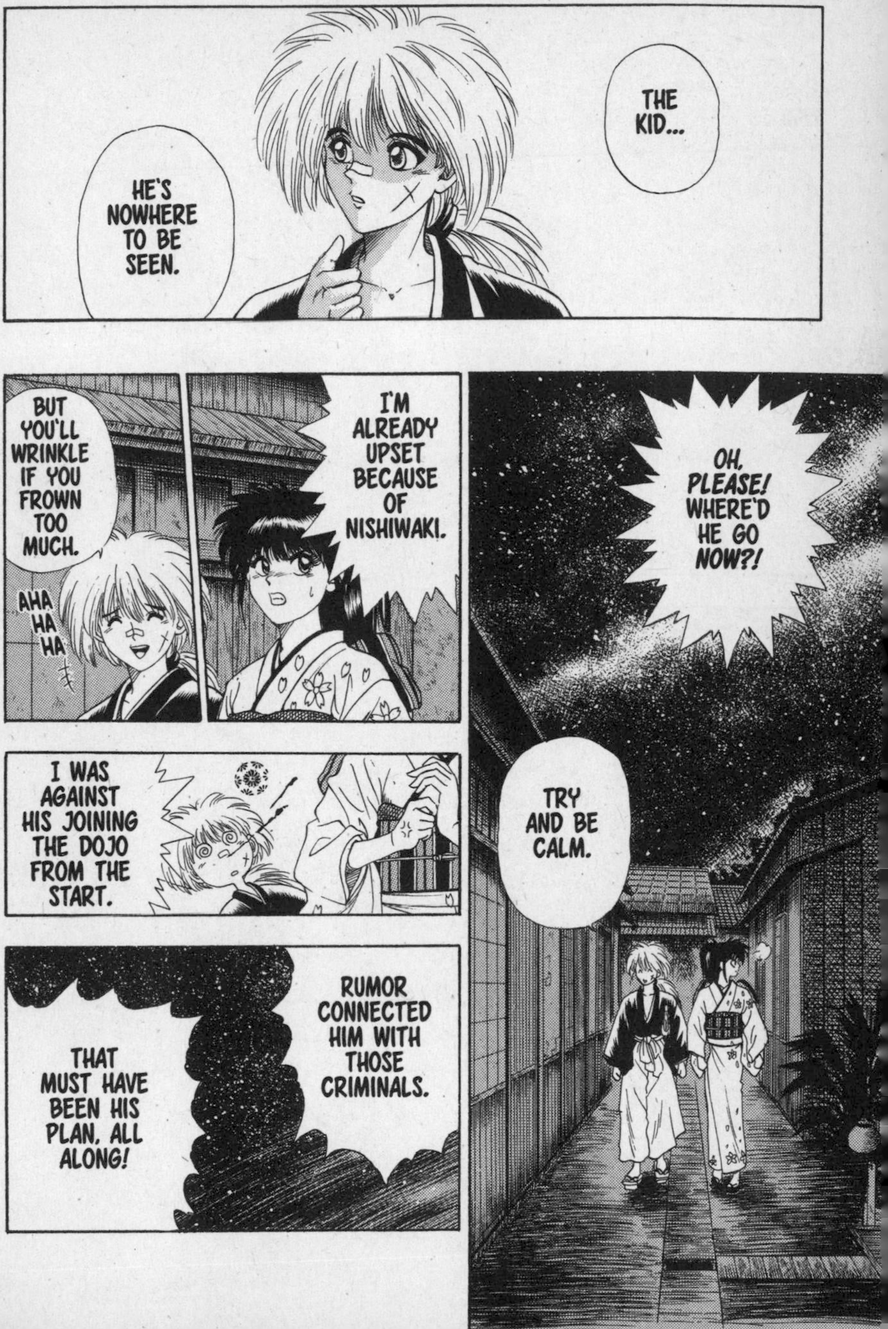
THE KID...
HE'S NOWHERE TO BE SEEN.
OH, PLEASE! WHERE'D HE GO NOW?!
TRY AND BE CALM.
I'M ALREADY UPSET BECAUSE OF NISHIWAKI.
BUT YOU'LL WRINKLE IF YOU FROWN TOO MUCH.
AHA HA HA
I WAS AGAINST HIS JOINING THE DOJO FROM THE START.
RUMOR CONNECTED HIM WITH THOSE CRIMINALS.
THAT MUST HAVE BEEN HIS PLAN, ALL ALONG!

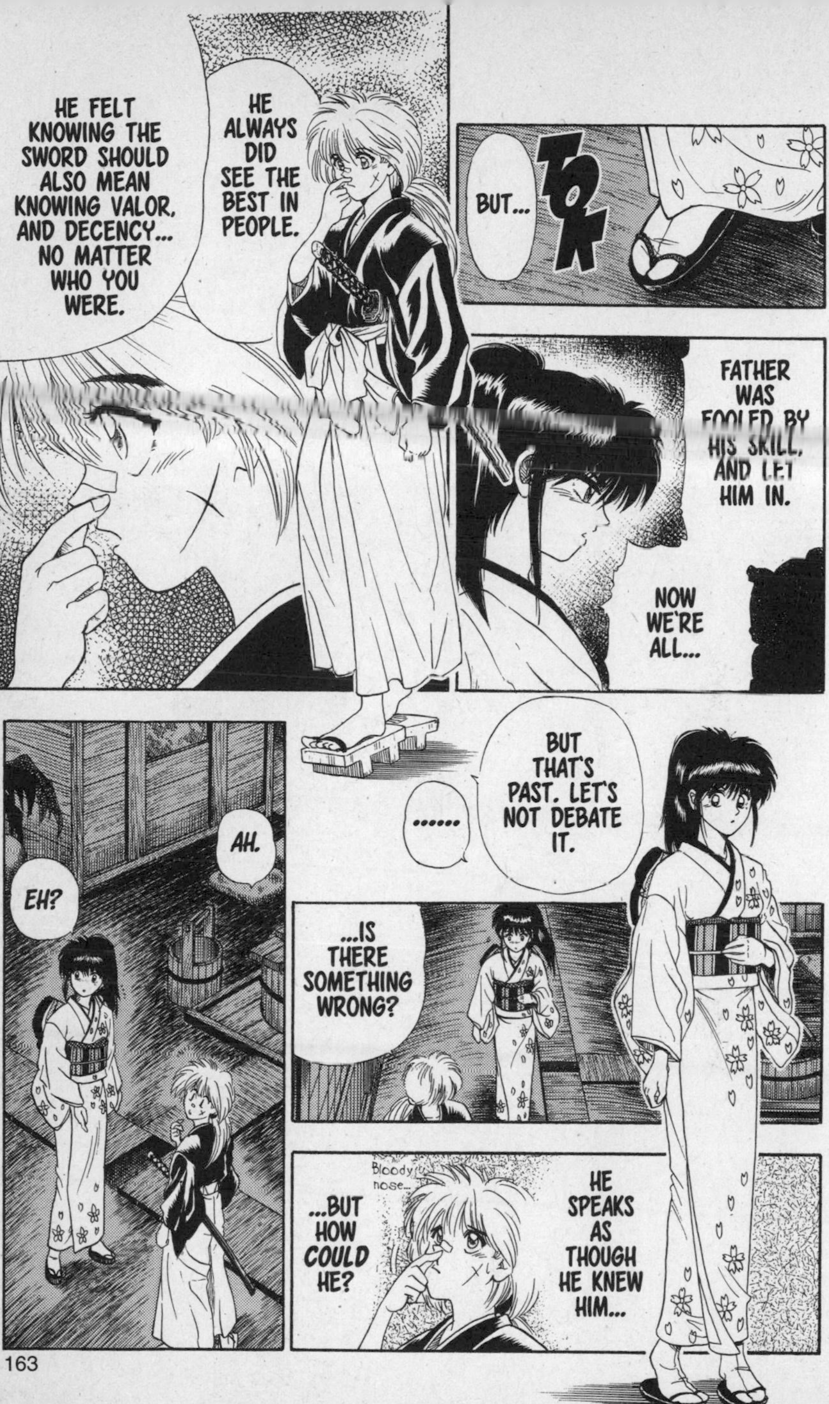
BUT...
TOK
FATHER WAS FOOLED BY HIS SKILL, AND LET HIM IN.
NOW WE'RE ALL...
HE ALWAYS DID SEE THE BEST IN PEOPLE.
HE FELT KNOWING THE SWORD SHOULD ALSO MEAN KNOWING VALOR, AND DECENCY... NO MATTER WHO YOU WERE.
BUT THAT'S PAST. LET'S NOT DEBATE IT.
....
...IS THERE SOMETHING WRONG?
HE SPEAKS AS THOUGH HE KNEW HIM...
Bloody nose...
...BUT HOW COULD HE?
AH.
EH?

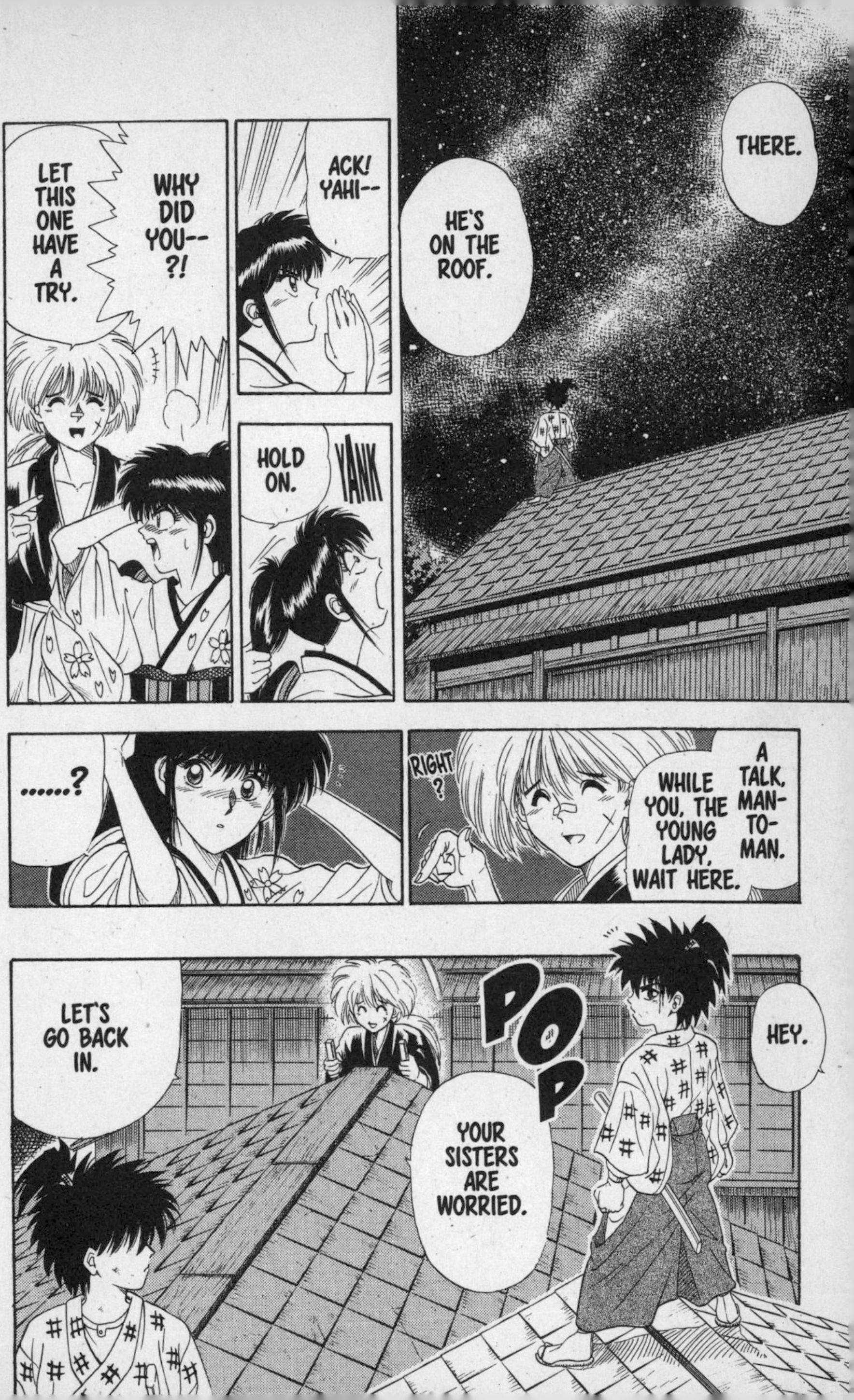
THERE.
HE'S ON THE ROOF.
ACK! YAHI--
HOLD ON.
YANK
WHY DID YOU--?!
LET THIS ONE HAVE A TRY.
A TALK, MAN-TO-MAN.
WHILE YOU, THE YOUNG LADY, WAIT HERE.
RIGHT?
......?
HEY.
POP
YOUR SISTERS ARE WORRIED.
LET'S GO BACK IN.

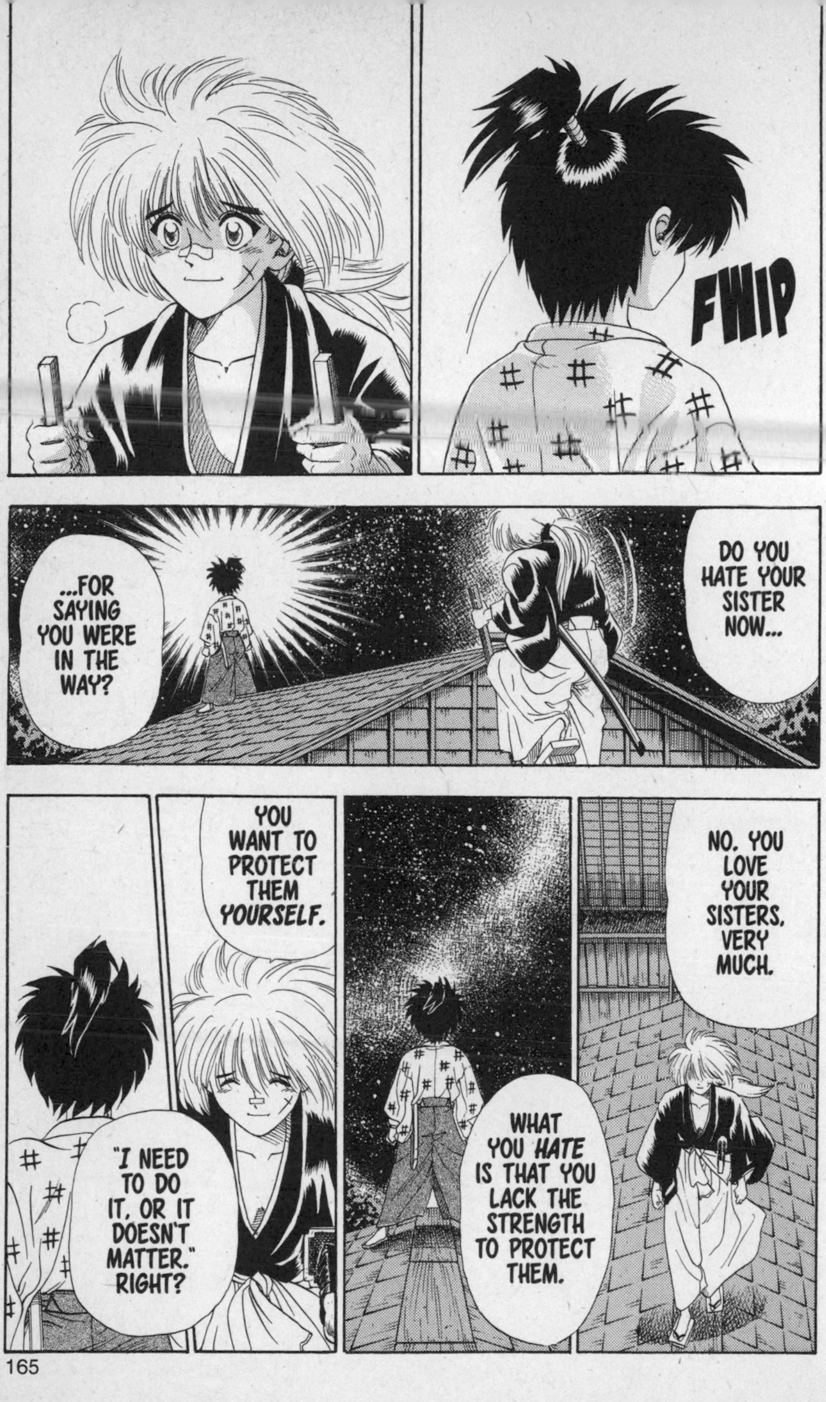
FWIP
DO YOU HATE YOUR SISTER NOW...
...FOR SAYING YOU WERE IN THE WAY?
NO. YOU LOVE YOUR SISTERS, VERY MUCH.
WHAT YOU HATE IS THAT YOU LACK THE STRENGTH TO PROTECT THEM.
YOU WANT TO PROTECT THEM YOURSELF.
"I NEED TO DO IT, OR IT DOESN'T MATTER." RIGHT?

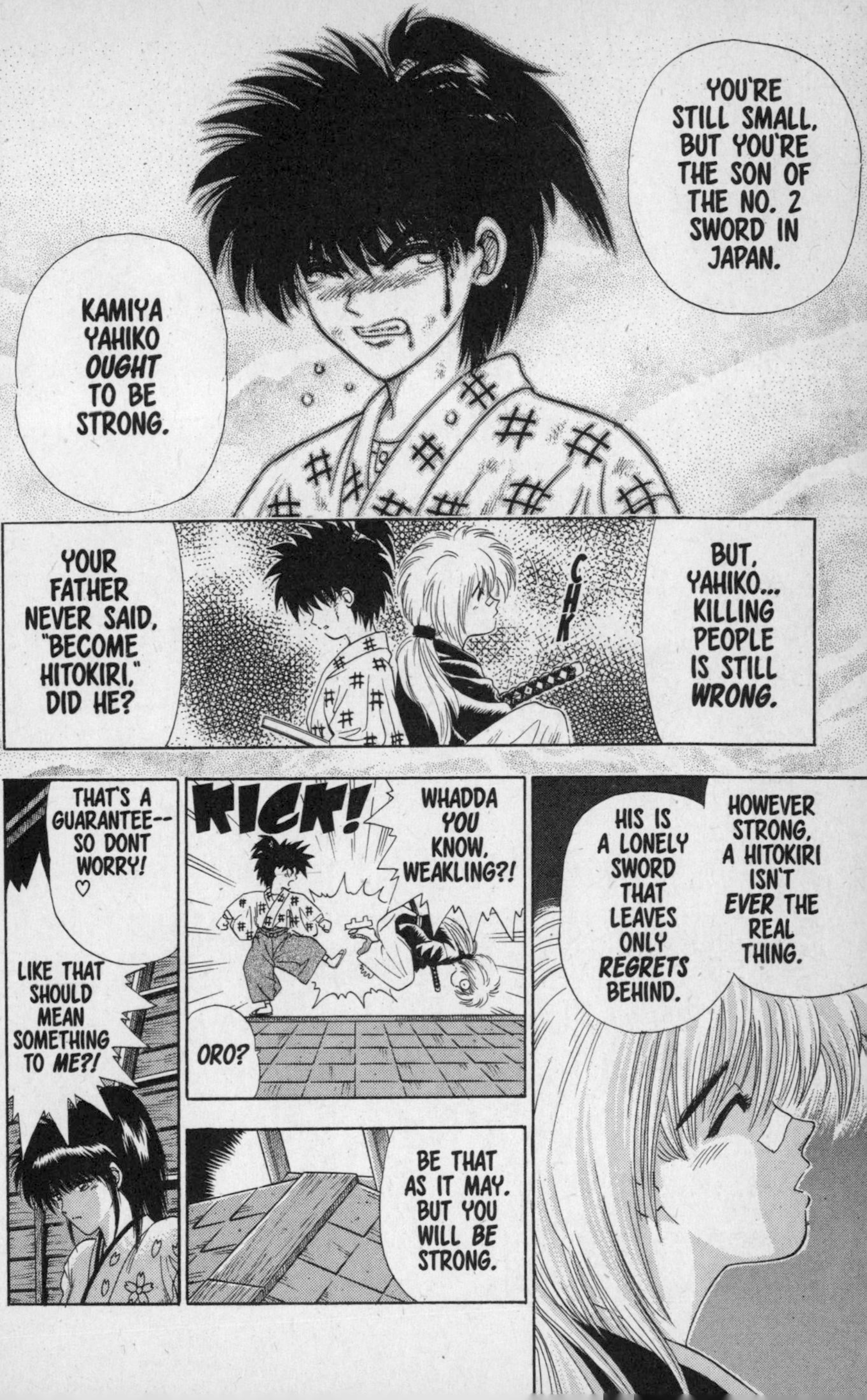

YOU'RE STILL SMALL, BUT YOU'RE THE SON OF THE NO. 2 SWORD IN JAPAN.
KAMIYA YAHIKO *OUGHT* TO BE STRONG.
BUT, YAHIKO... KILLING PEOPLE IS STILL *WRONG.*
CHK
YOUR FATHER NEVER SAID, "BECOME HITOKIRI," DID HE?
HOWEVER STRONG, A HITOKIRI ISN'T *EVER* THE REAL THING.
HIS IS A LONELY SWORD THAT LEAVES ONLY *REGRETS* BEHIND.
WHADDA *YOU* KNOW, WEAKLING?!
KICK!
ORO?
BE THAT AS IT MAY. BUT YOU *WILL* BE STRONG.
THAT'S A GUARANTEE-- SO DONT WORRY! ♡
LIKE THAT SHOULD MEAN SOMETHING TO *ME?!*

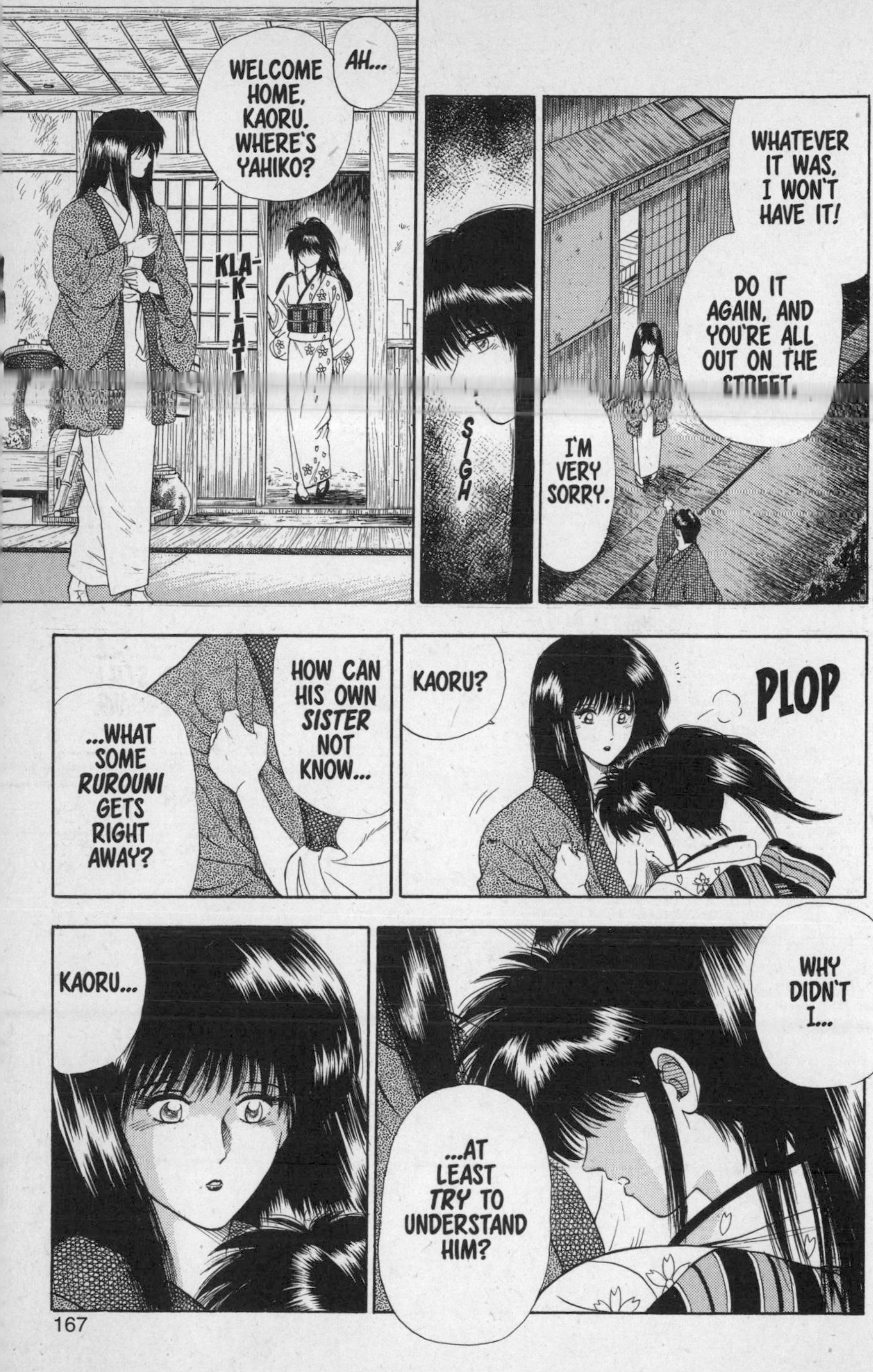
WHATEVER IT WAS, I WON'T HAVE IT!
DO IT AGAIN, AND YOU'RE ALL OUT ON THE STREET.
I'M VERY SORRY.
SIGH
AH...
WELCOME HOME, KAORU. WHERE'S YAHIKO?
KLA-KLAT!
PLOP
KAORU?
HOW CAN HIS OWN SISTER NOT KNOW...
...WHAT SOME RUROUNI GETS RIGHT AWAY?
WHY DIDN'T I...
...AT LEAST TRY TO UNDERSTAND HIM?
KAORU...

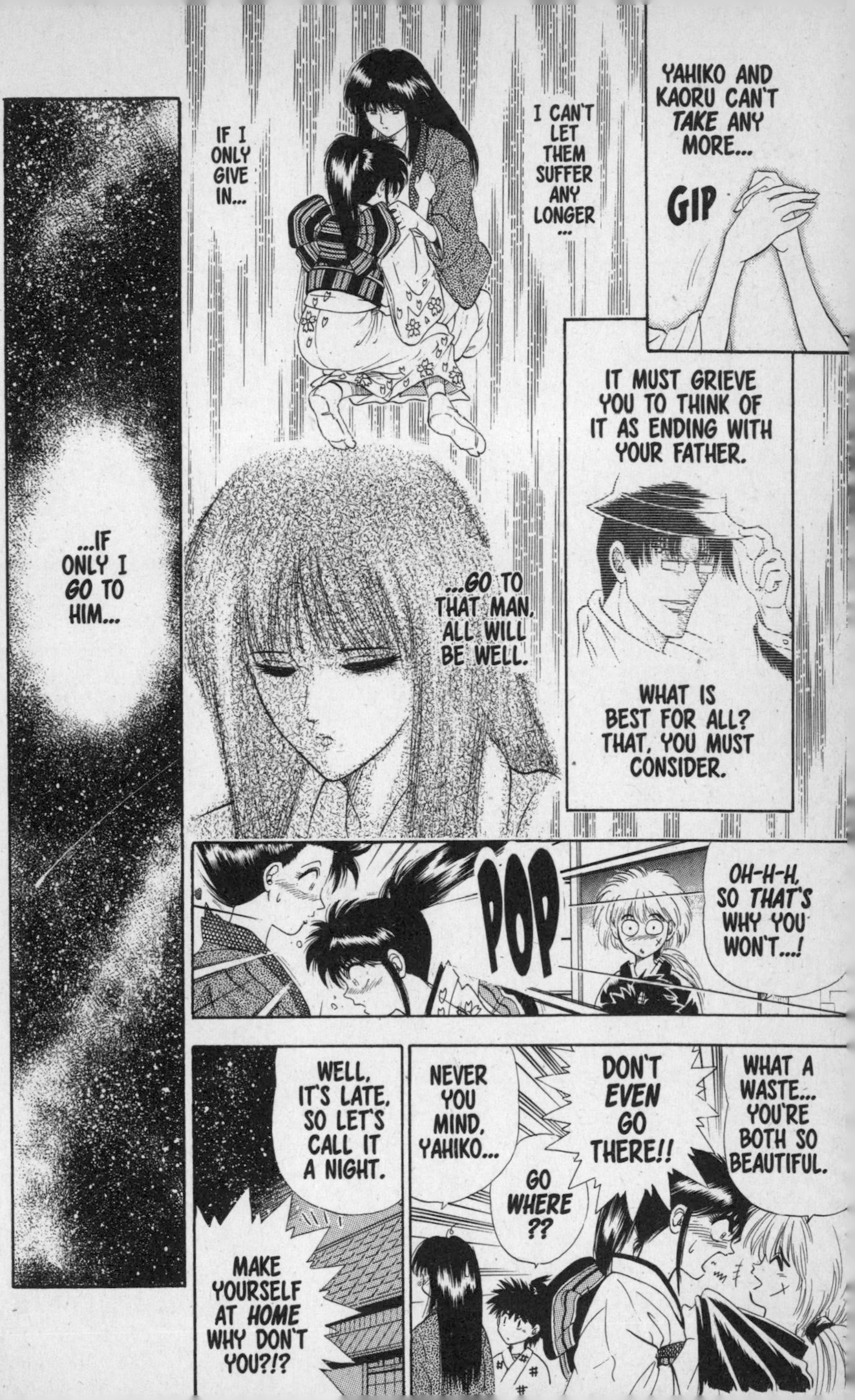
YAHIKO AND KAORU CAN'T *TAKE* ANY MORE...
GIP
I CAN'T LET THEM SUFFER ANY LONGER...
IF I ONLY GIVE IN...
IT MUST GRIEVE YOU TO THINK OF IT AS ENDING WITH YOUR FATHER.
WHAT IS BEST FOR ALL? THAT, YOU MUST CONSIDER.
...GO TO THAT MAN, ALL WILL BE WELL.
OH-H-H, SO *THAT'S* WHY YOU WON'T...!
POP
...IF ONLY I GO TO HIM...
WHAT A WASTE... YOU'RE BOTH SO BEAUTIFUL.
DON'T *EVEN* GO THERE!!
NEVER YOU MIND, YAHIKO...
GO *WHERE* ??
WELL, IT'S LATE, SO LET'S CALL IT A NIGHT.
MAKE YOURSELF AT *HOME* WHY DON'T YOU?!?

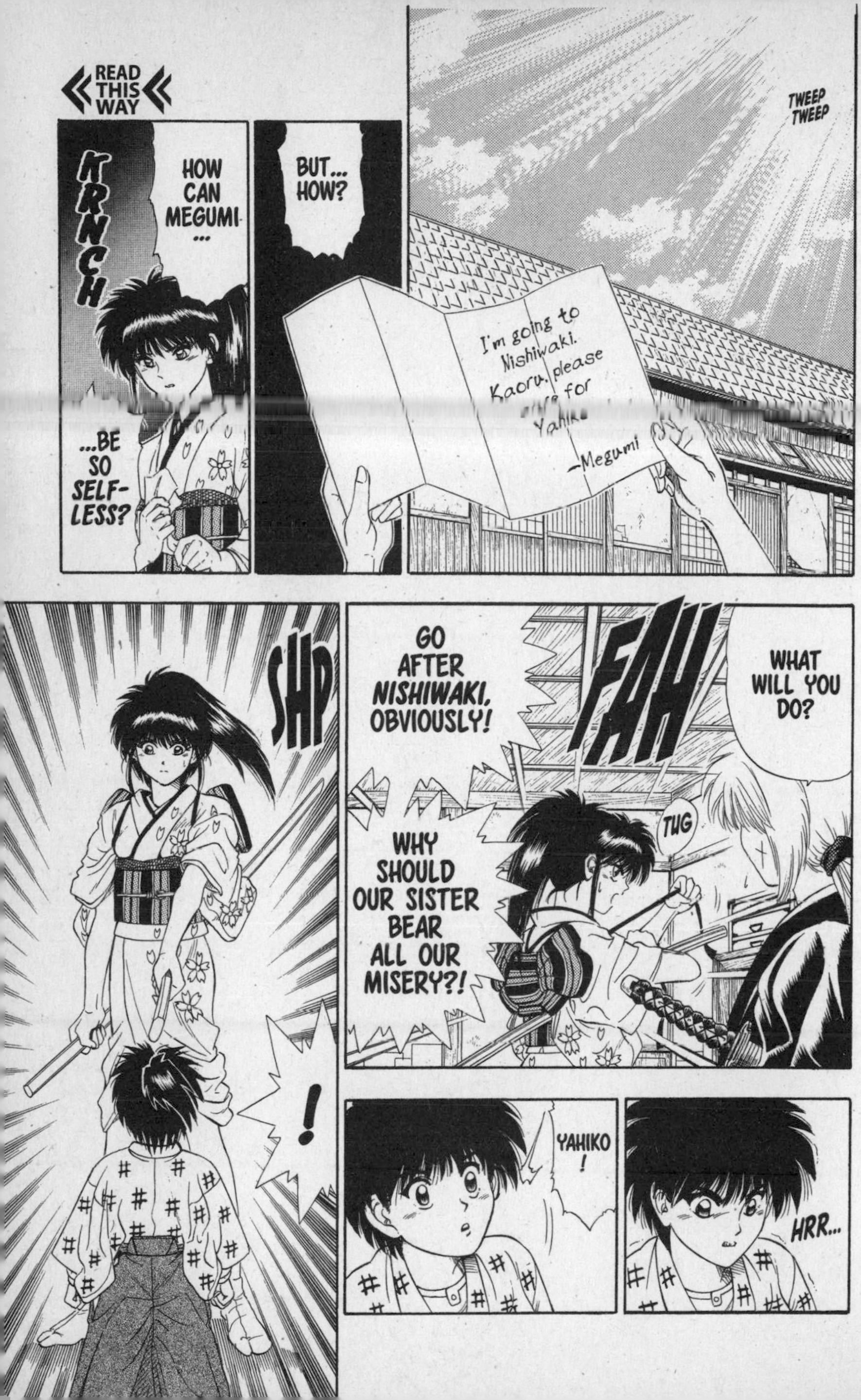
READ THIS WAY
TWEEP TWEEP
I'm going to Nishiwaki. Kaoru, please
for
—Megumi
BUT... HOW?
HOW CAN MEGUMI...
KRNCH
...BE SO SELFLESS?
WHAT WILL YOU DO?
FAH
GO AFTER NISHIWAKI, OBVIOUSLY!
TUG
WHY SHOULD OUR SISTER BEAR ALL OUR MISERY?!
HRR...
YAHIKO!
SHP
!

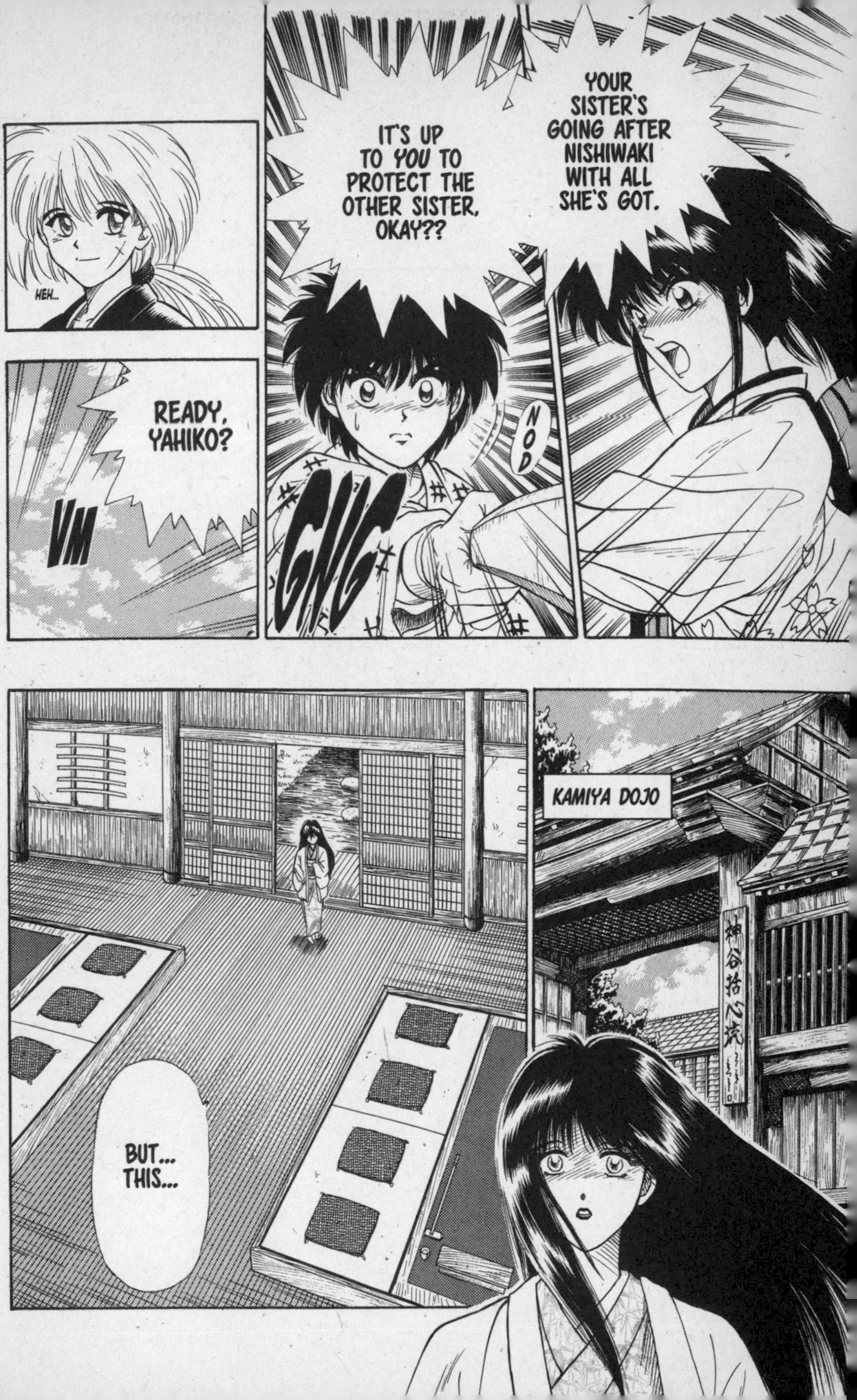
YOUR SISTER'S GOING AFTER NISHIWAKI WITH ALL SHE'S GOT.
IT'S UP TO *YOU* TO PROTECT THE OTHER SISTER, OKAY??
NOD
GNG
HEH...
READY, YAHIKO?
VM
KAMIYA DOJO
BUT... THIS...

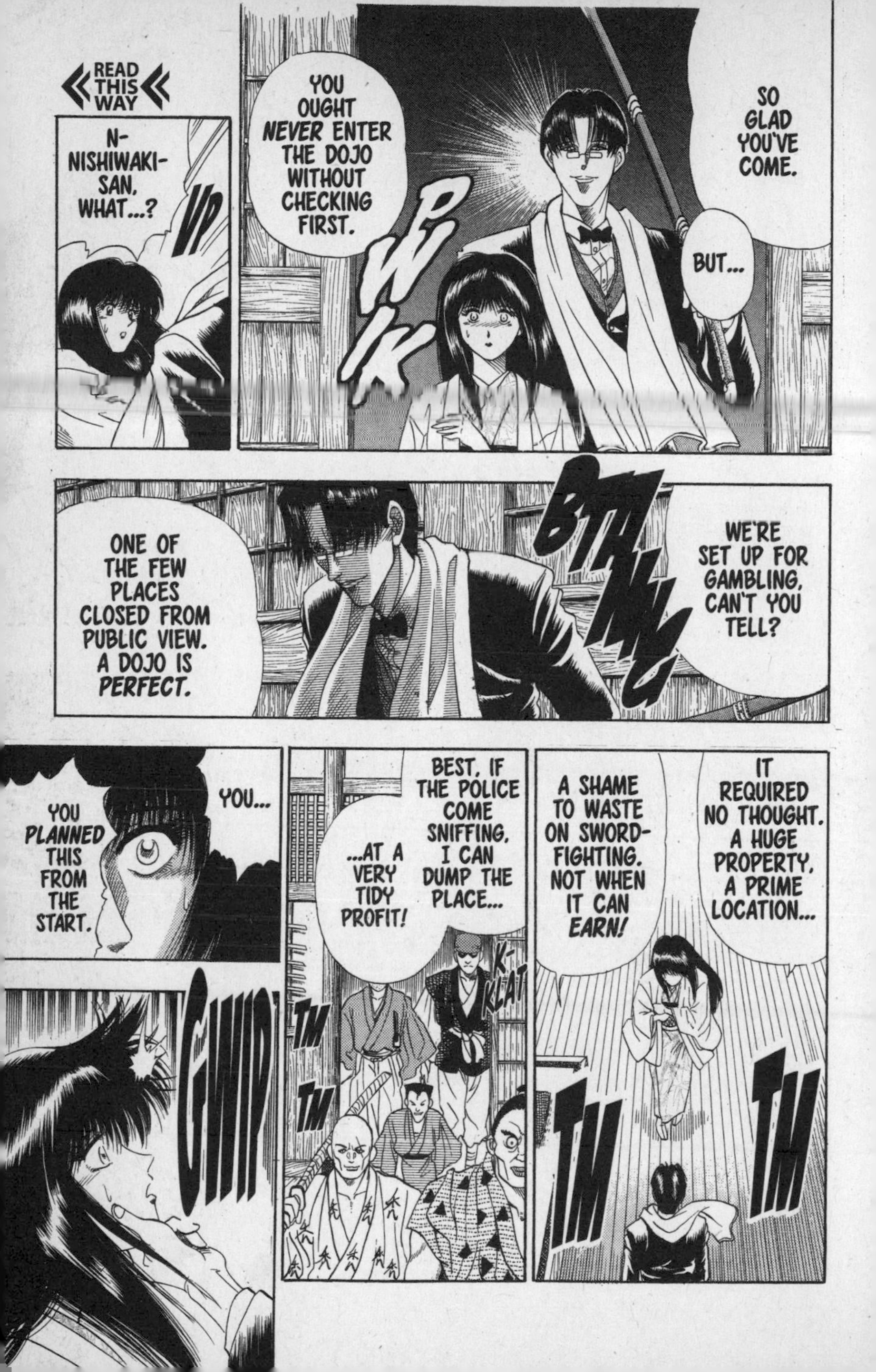
READ THIS WAY
SO GLAD YOU'VE COME.
BUT...
YOU OUGHT NEVER ENTER THE DOJO WITHOUT CHECKING FIRST.
PWIK
N-NISHIWAKI-SAN, WHAT...?
VP
WE'RE SET UP FOR GAMBLING, CAN'T YOU TELL?
ONE OF THE FEW PLACES CLOSED FROM PUBLIC VIEW. A DOJO IS PERFECT.
IT REQUIRED NO THOUGHT. A HUGE PROPERTY, A PRIME LOCATION...
A SHAME TO WASTE ON SWORD-FIGHTING. NOT WHEN IT CAN EARN!
TM
TM
BEST, IF THE POLICE COME SNIFFING, I CAN DUMP THE PLACE...
...AT A VERY TIDY PROFIT!
K-KLAT
TM
TM
YOU...
YOU PLANNED THIS FROM THE START.

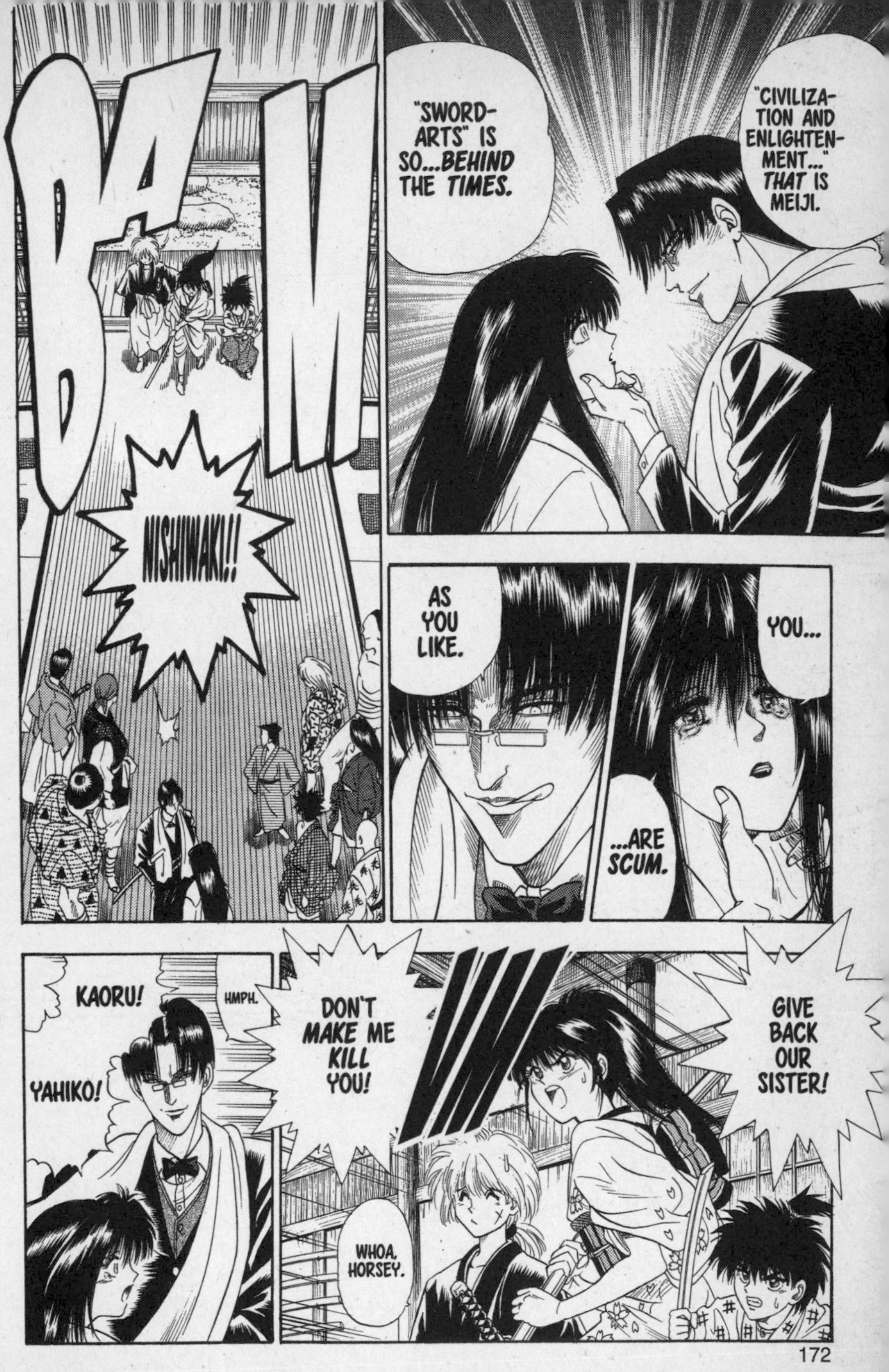
"CIVILIZATION AND ENLIGHTENMENT..." THAT IS MEIJI.
"SWORD-ARTS" IS SO...BEHIND THE TIMES.
YOU...
...ARE SCUM.
AS YOU LIKE.
GAN!
NISHIWAKI!!
GIVE BACK OUR SISTER!
DON'T MAKE ME KILL YOU!
WHOA, HORSEY.
HMPH.
KAORU!
YAHIKO!

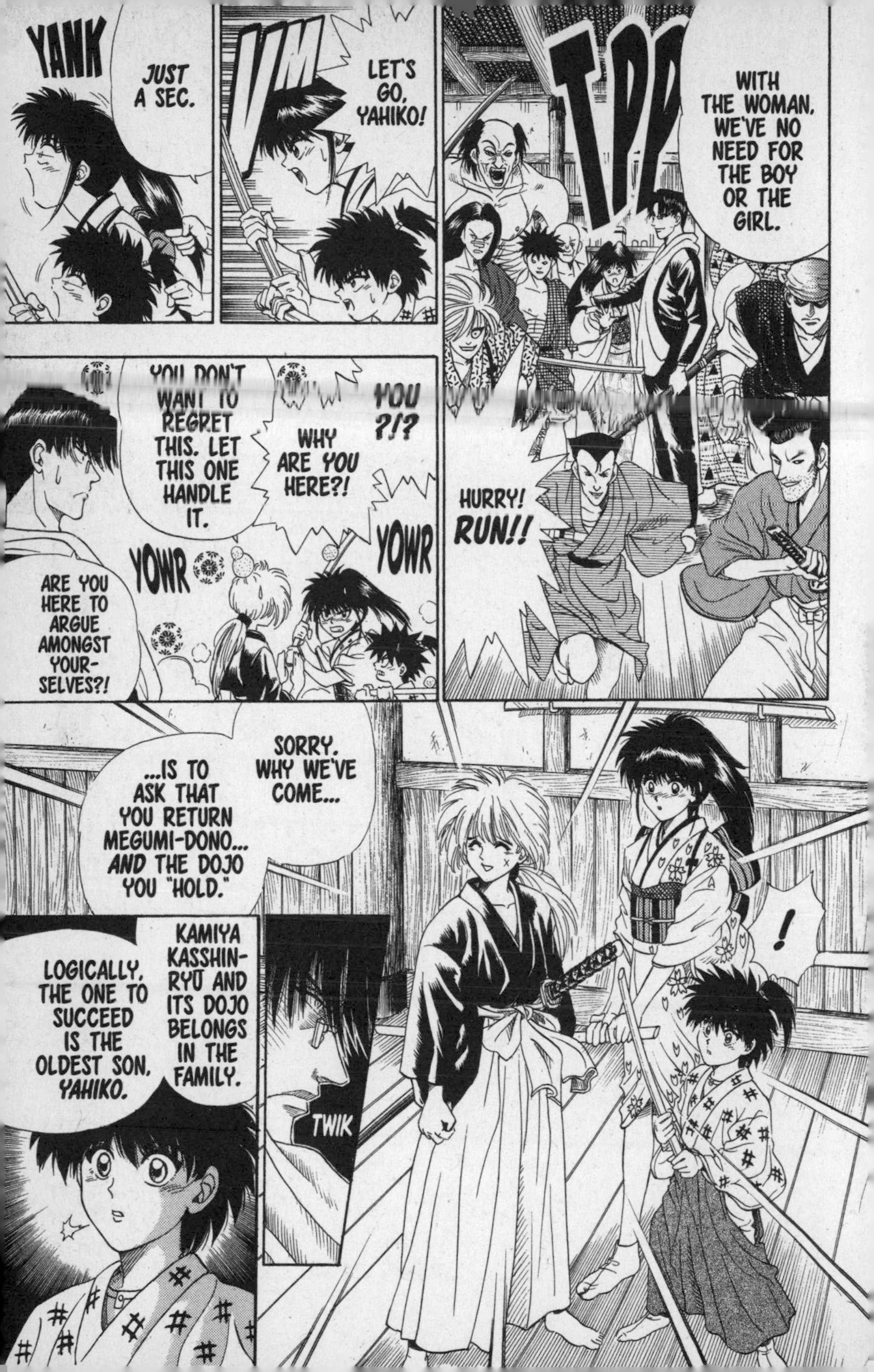
TPP
WITH THE WOMAN, WE'VE NO NEED FOR THE BOY OR THE GIRL.
VUM
LET'S GO, YAHIKO!
YANK
JUST A SEC.
HURRY! RUN!!
YOU ?!?
WHY ARE YOU HERE?!
YOWR
YOU DON'T WANT TO REGRET THIS. LET THIS ONE HANDLE IT.
YOWR
ARE YOU HERE TO ARGUE AMONGST YOURSELVES?!
SORRY. WHY WE'VE COME...
...IS TO ASK THAT YOU RETURN MEGUMI-DONO... AND THE DOJO YOU "HOLD."
!
KAMIYA KASSHIN-RYŪ AND ITS DOJO BELONGS IN THE FAMILY.
TWIK
LOGICALLY, THE ONE TO SUCCEED IS THE OLDEST SON, YAHIKO.

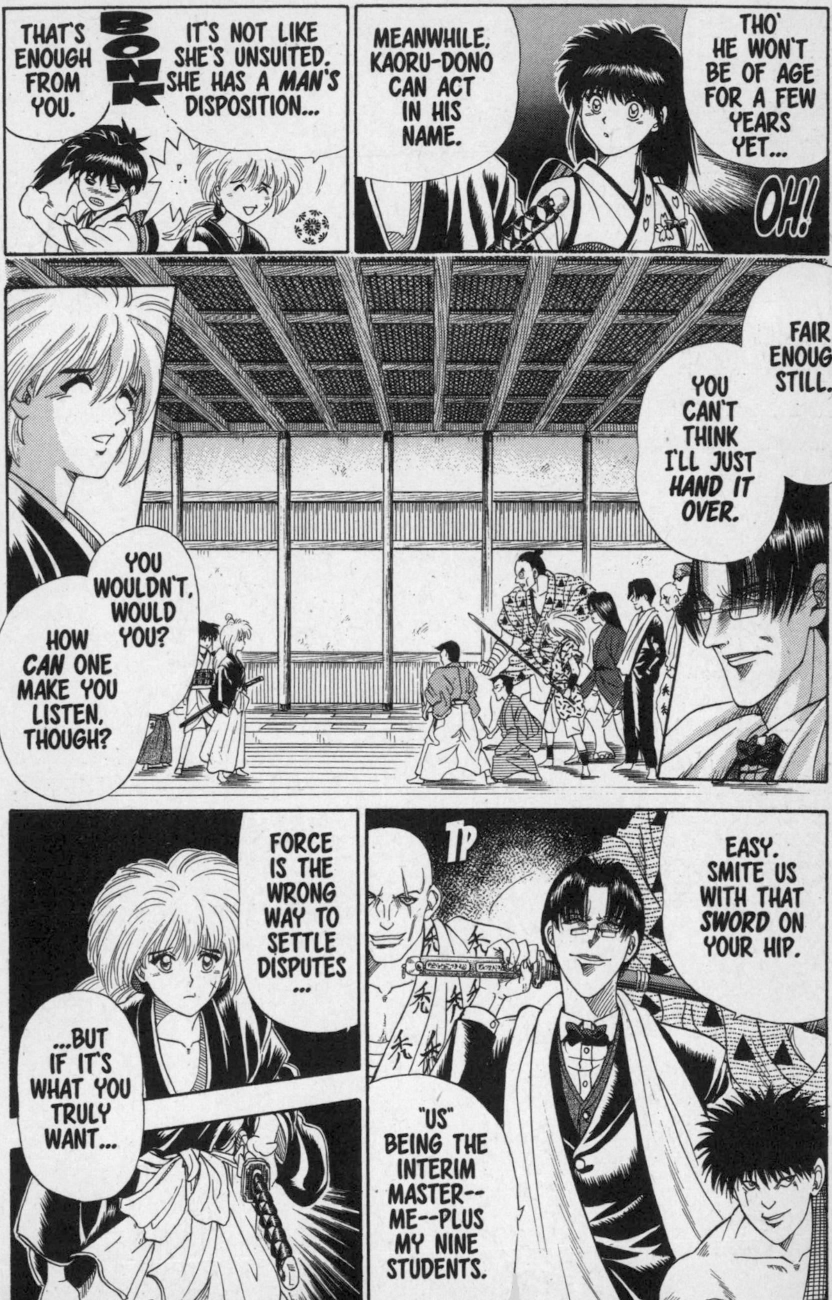
THO' HE WON'T BE OF AGE FOR A FEW YEARS YET...
MEANWHILE, KAORU-DONO CAN ACT IN HIS NAME.
OH!
IT'S NOT LIKE SHE'S UNSUITED. SHE HAS A *MAN'S* DISPOSITION...
BONK
THAT'S ENOUGH FROM YOU.
FAIR ENOUGH. STILL...
YOU CAN'T THINK I'LL JUST *HAND IT OVER.*
YOU WOULDN'T, WOULD YOU?
HOW *CAN* ONE MAKE YOU LISTEN, THOUGH?
TP
EASY. SMITE US WITH THAT *SWORD* ON YOUR HIP.
"US" BEING THE INTERIM MASTER--ME--PLUS MY NINE STUDENTS.
FORCE IS THE WRONG WAY TO SETTLE DISPUTES...
...BUT IF IT'S WHAT YOU TRULY WANT...

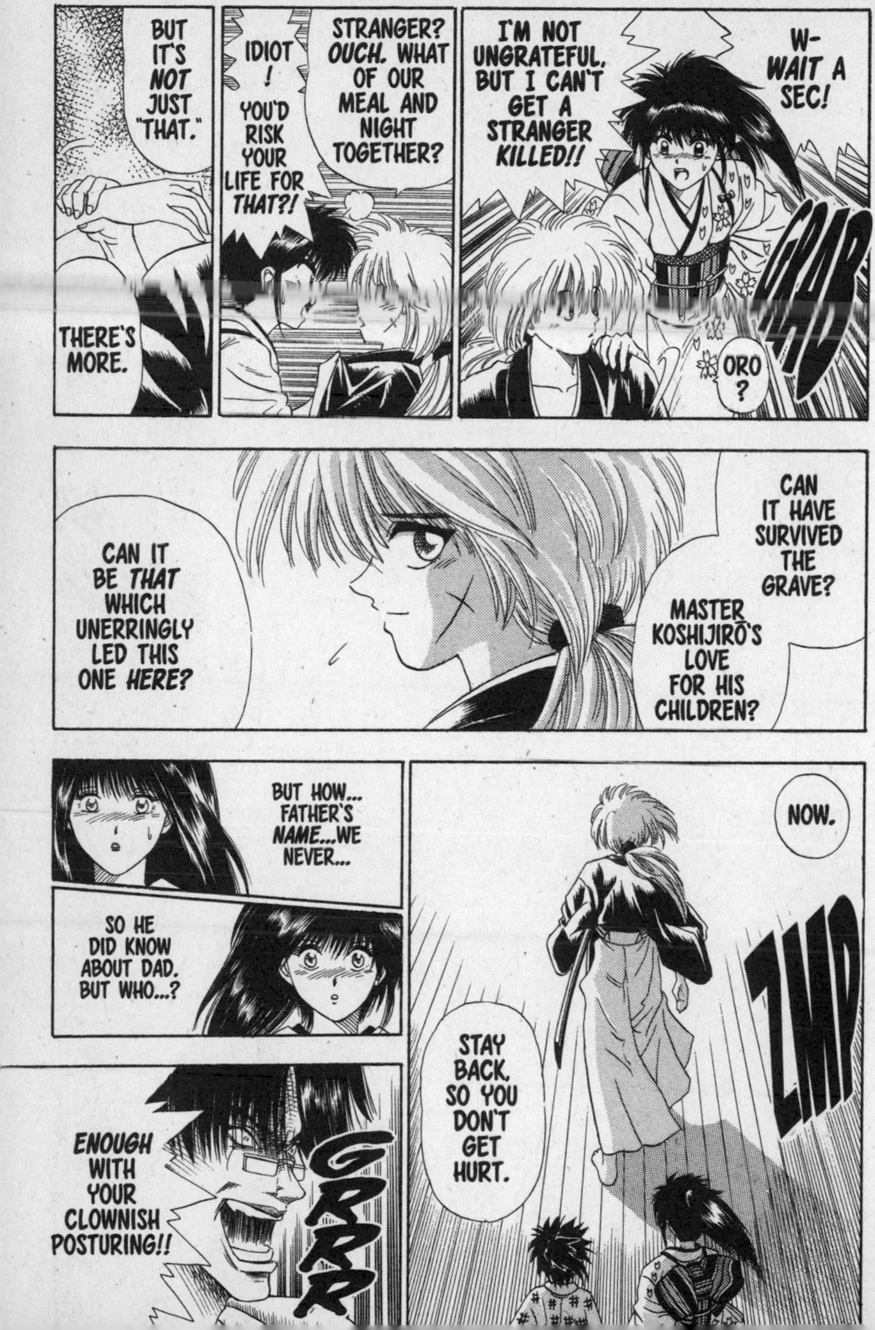
W-WAIT A SEC!
I'M NOT UNGRATEFUL, BUT I CAN'T GET A STRANGER KILLED!!
GRAB
ORO?
STRANGER? OUCH. WHAT OF OUR MEAL AND NIGHT TOGETHER?
IDIOT! YOU'D RISK YOUR LIFE FOR THAT?!
BUT IT'S NOT JUST "THAT."
THERE'S MORE.
CAN IT HAVE SURVIVED THE GRAVE?
MASTER KOSHIJIRŌ'S LOVE FOR HIS CHILDREN?
CAN IT BE THAT WHICH UNERRINGLY LED THIS ONE HERE?
NOW.
ZMP
STAY BACK, SO YOU DON'T GET HURT.
BUT HOW... FATHER'S NAME...WE NEVER...
SO HE DID KNOW ABOUT DAD. BUT WHO...?
ENOUGH WITH YOUR CLOWNISH POSTURING!!
GRRR

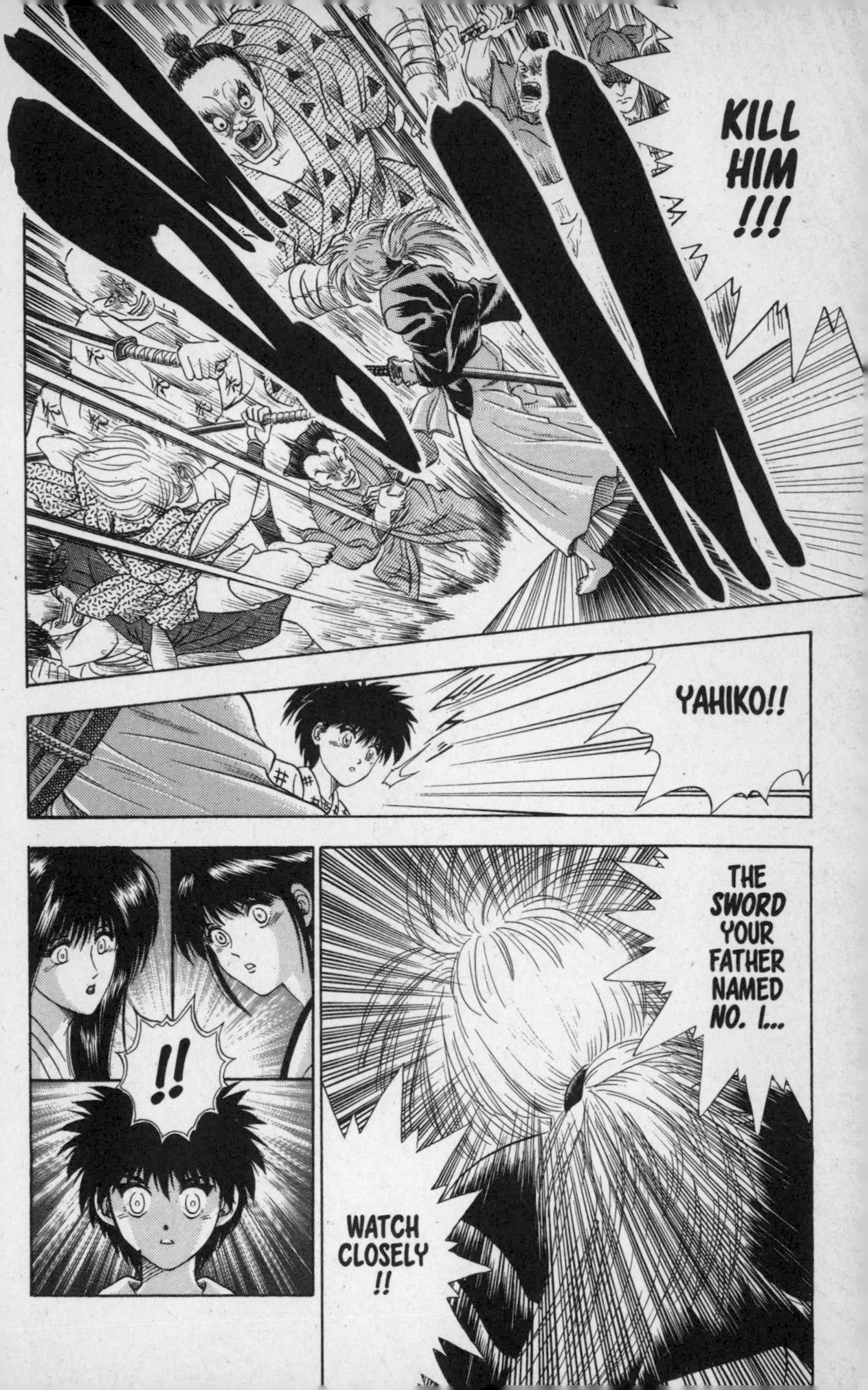
KILL HIM!!!
YAHIKO!!
THE SWORD YOUR FATHER NAMED NO. 1...
WATCH CLOSELY!!
!!

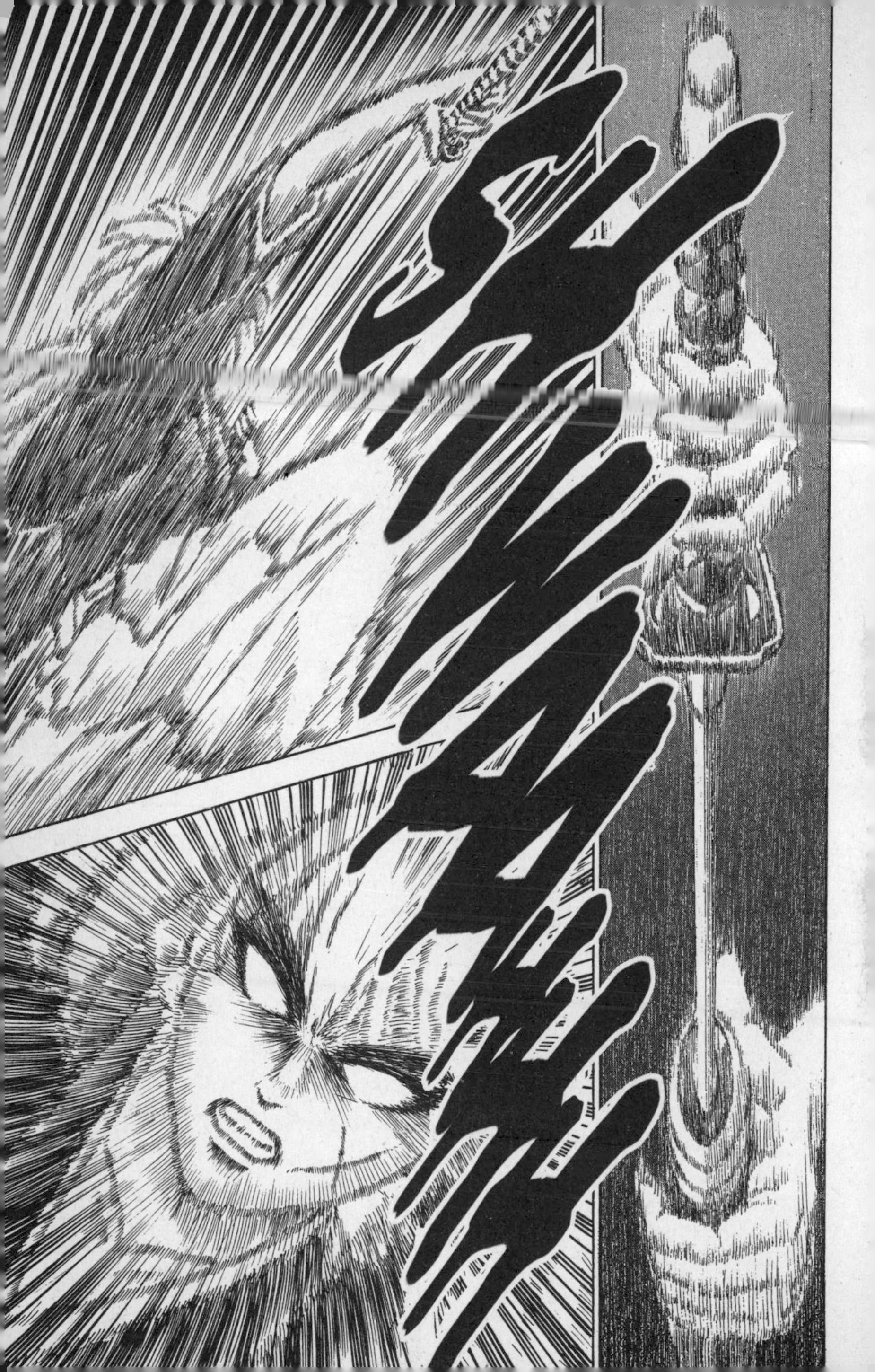

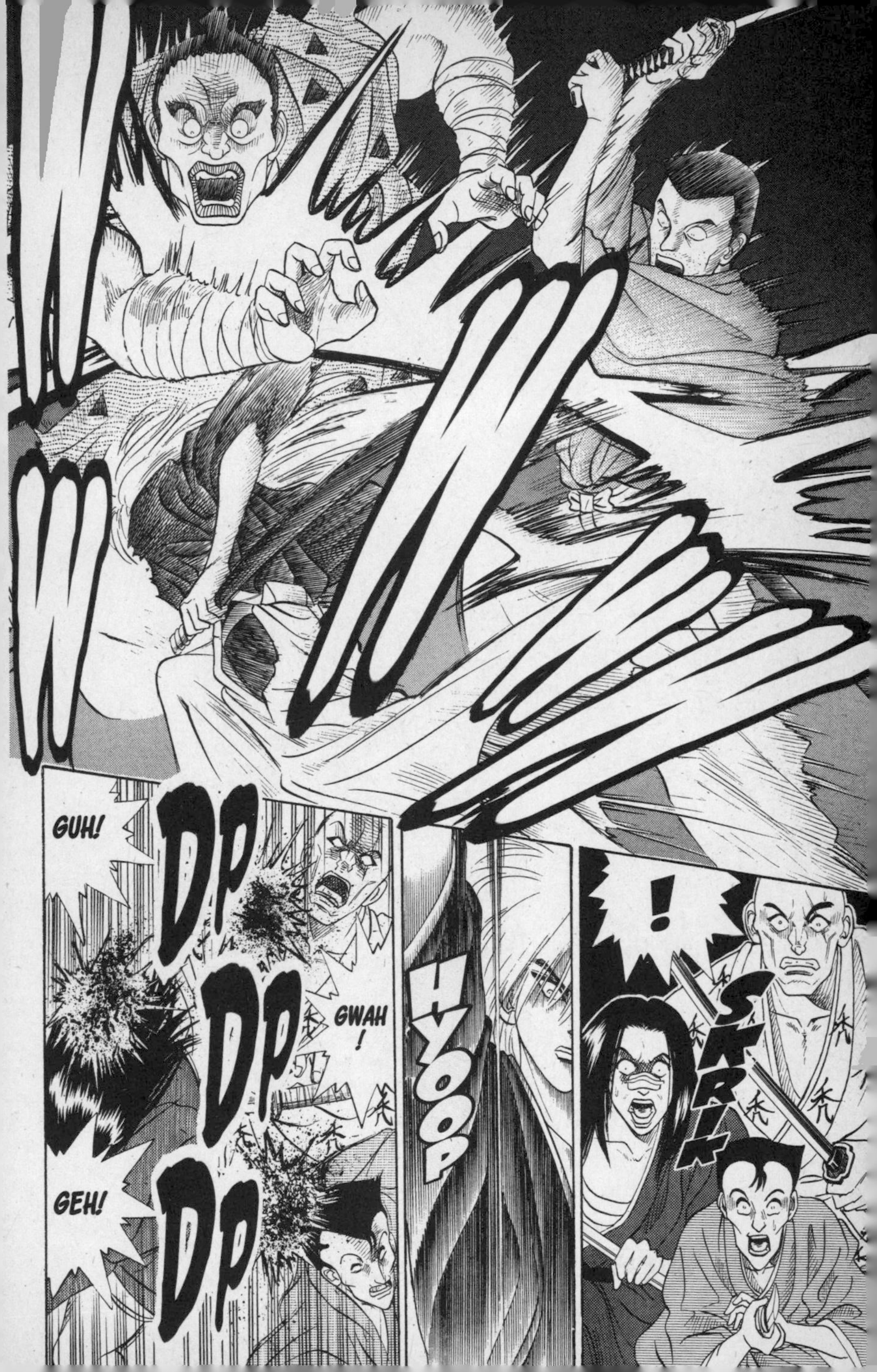
!
SKRIK
HYOOP
GUH!
DP DP DP
GWAH!
GEH!

READ THIS WAY

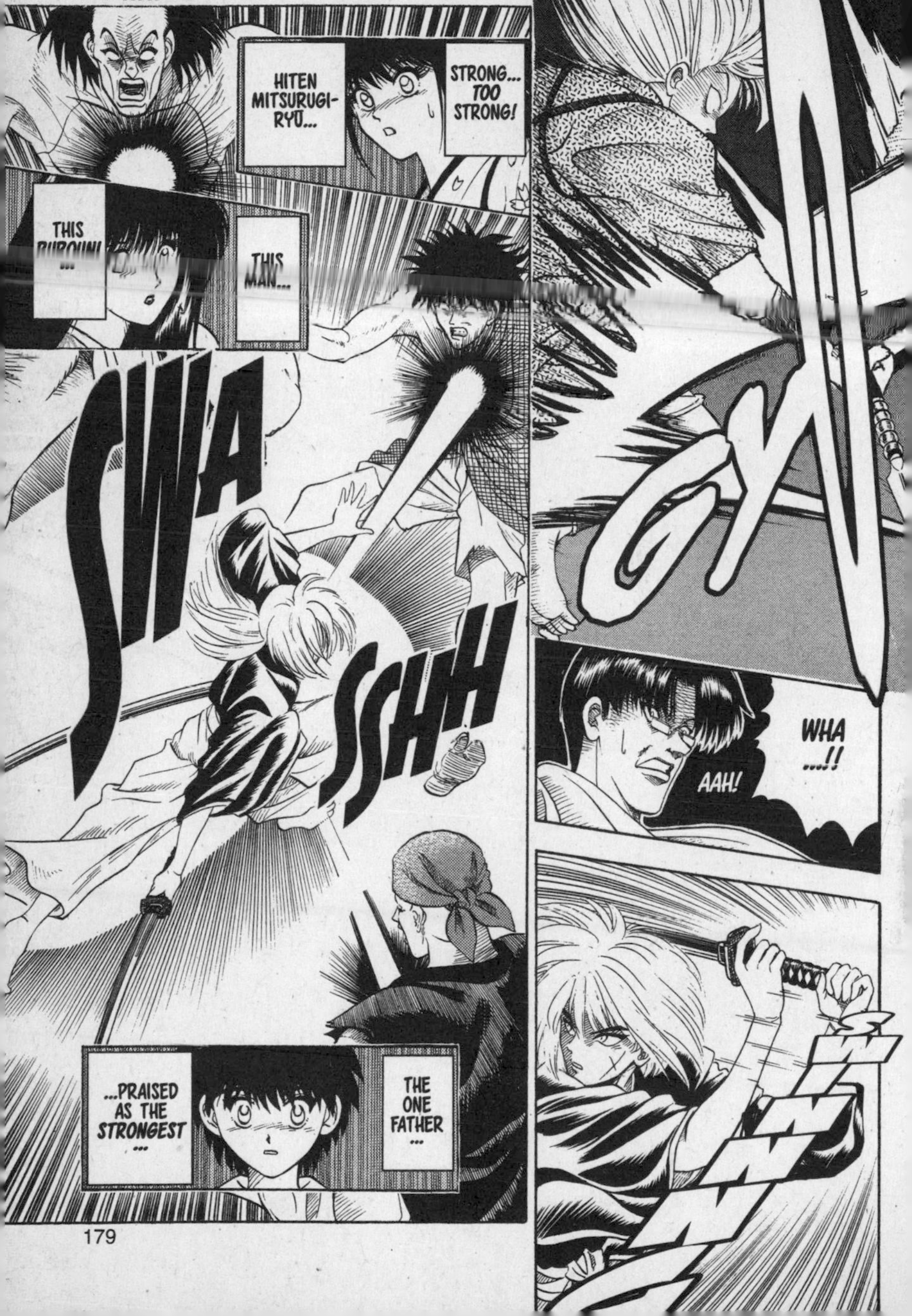

WHA ...!!
AAH!
STRONG... TOO STRONG!
HITEN MITSURUGI-RYŪ...
THIS MAN...
THIS ...
SWASSHH
THE ONE FATHER ...
...PRAISED AS THE STRONGEST ...

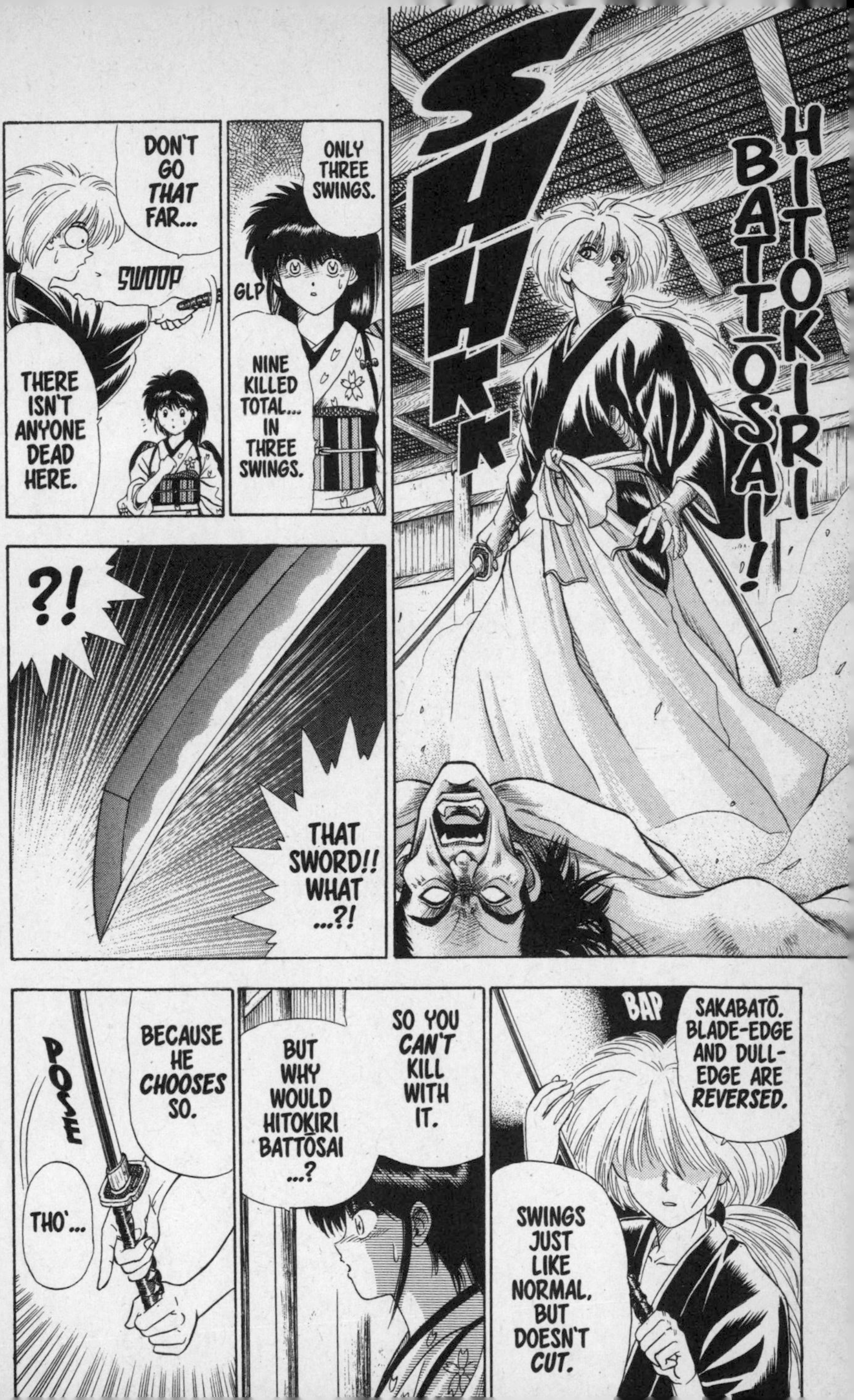
HITOKIRI BATTŌSAI!
SHHKK
ONLY THREE SWINGS.
GLP
NINE KILLED TOTAL... IN THREE SWINGS.
DON'T GO THAT FAR...
SWOOP
THERE ISN'T ANYONE DEAD HERE.
?!
THAT SWORD!! WHAT ...?!
BAP
SAKABATŌ. BLADE-EDGE AND DULL-EDGE ARE REVERSED.
SWINGS JUST LIKE NORMAL, BUT DOESN'T CUT.
SO YOU CAN'T KILL WITH IT.
BUT WHY WOULD HITOKIRI BATTŌSAI ...?
BECAUSE HE CHOOSES SO.
POSE
THO'...

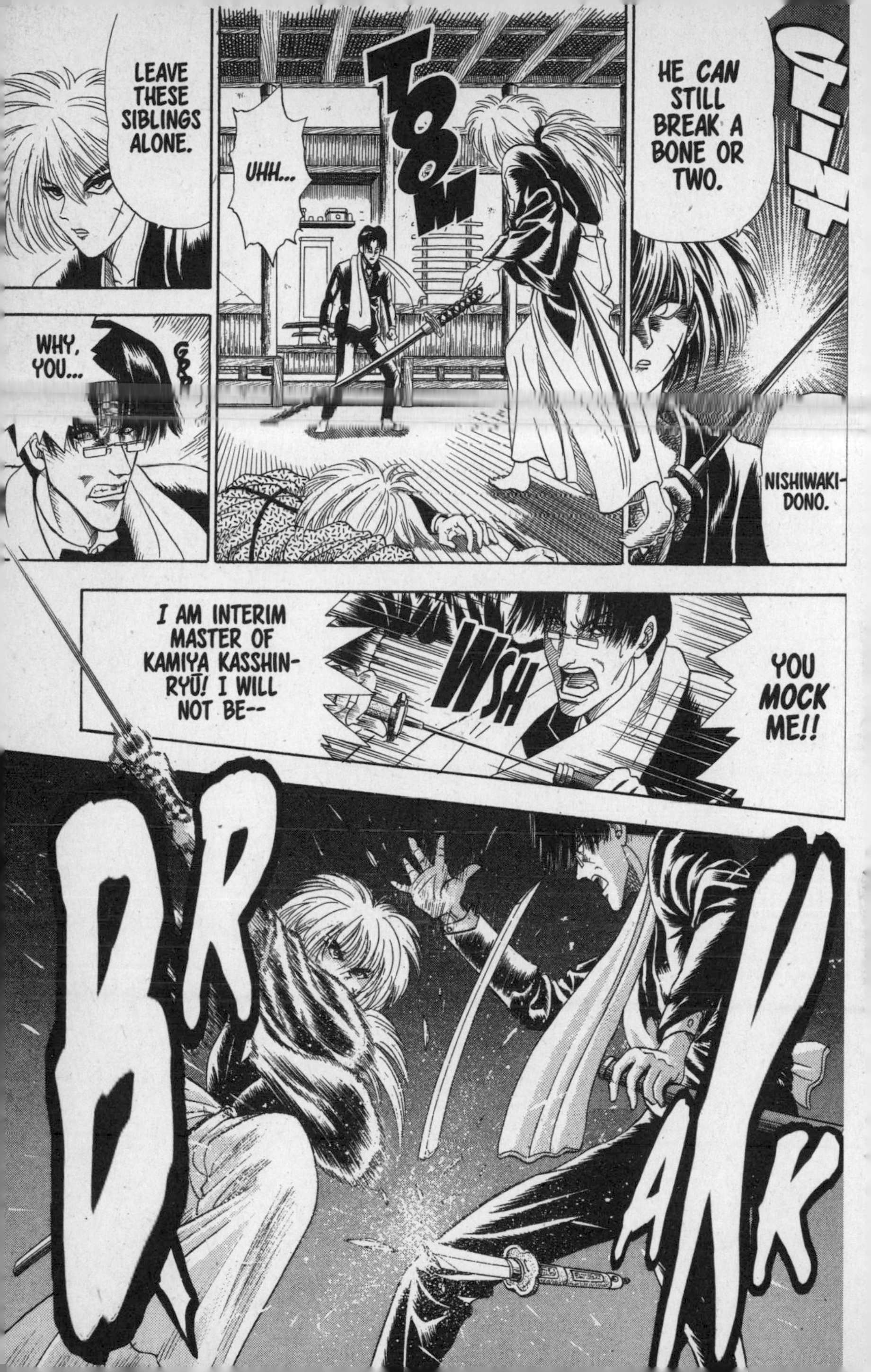
GLINT
HE CAN STILL BREAK A BONE OR TWO.
NISHIWAKI-DONO.
TOOM
UHH...
LEAVE THESE SIBLINGS ALONE.
WHY, YOU...
GRR
YOU MOCK ME!!
WSH
I AM INTERIM MASTER OF KAMIYA KASSHIN-RYŪ! I WILL NOT BE--
BRANK

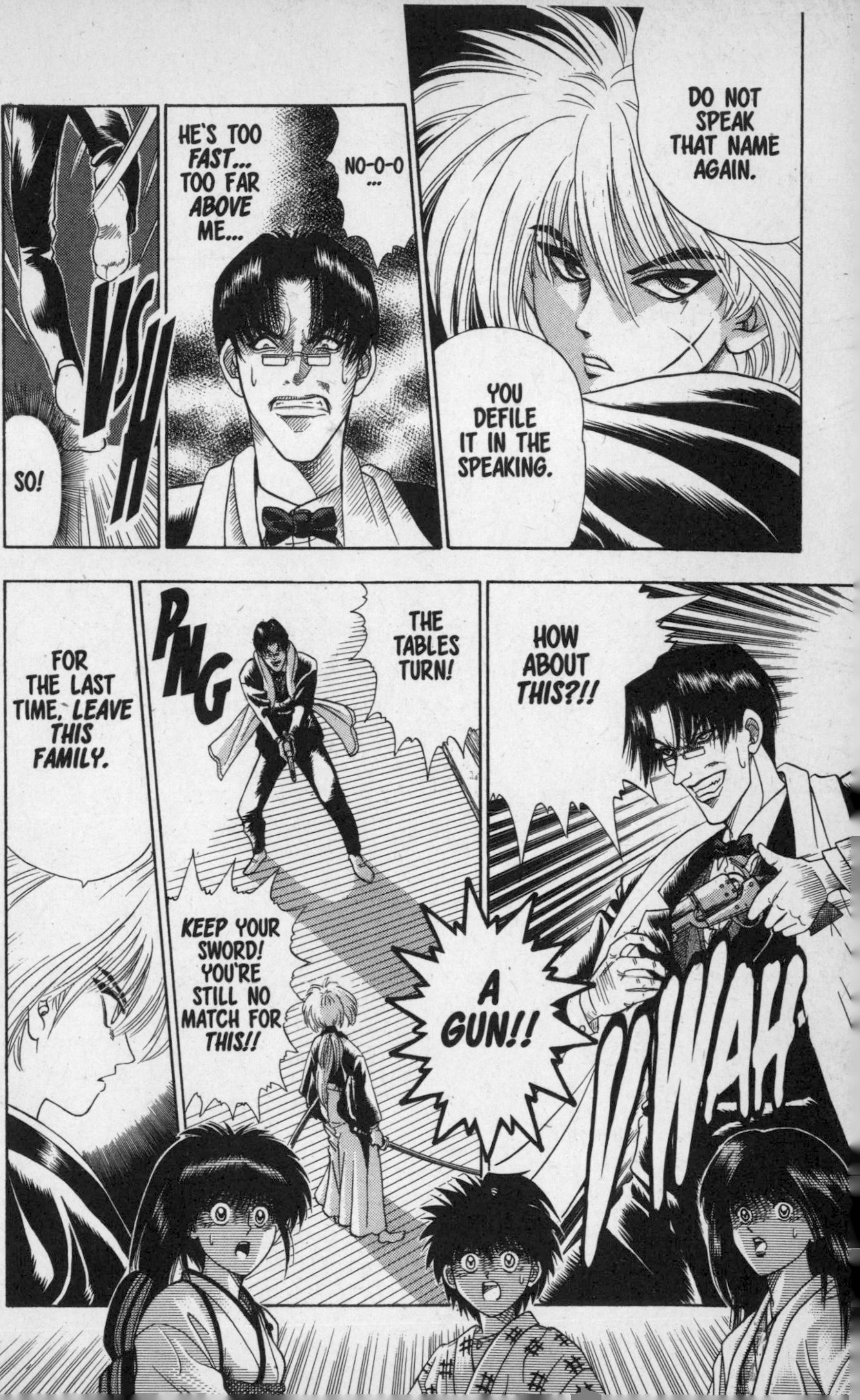
DO NOT SPEAK THAT NAME AGAIN.
YOU DEFILE IT IN THE SPEAKING.
HE'S TOO FAST... TOO FAR ABOVE ME...
NO-O-O ...
VSH
SO!
HOW ABOUT THIS?!!
WAH
THE TABLES TURN!
PNG
KEEP YOUR SWORD! YOU'RE STILL NO MATCH FOR THIS!!
A GUN!!
FOR THE LAST TIME, LEAVE THIS FAMILY.

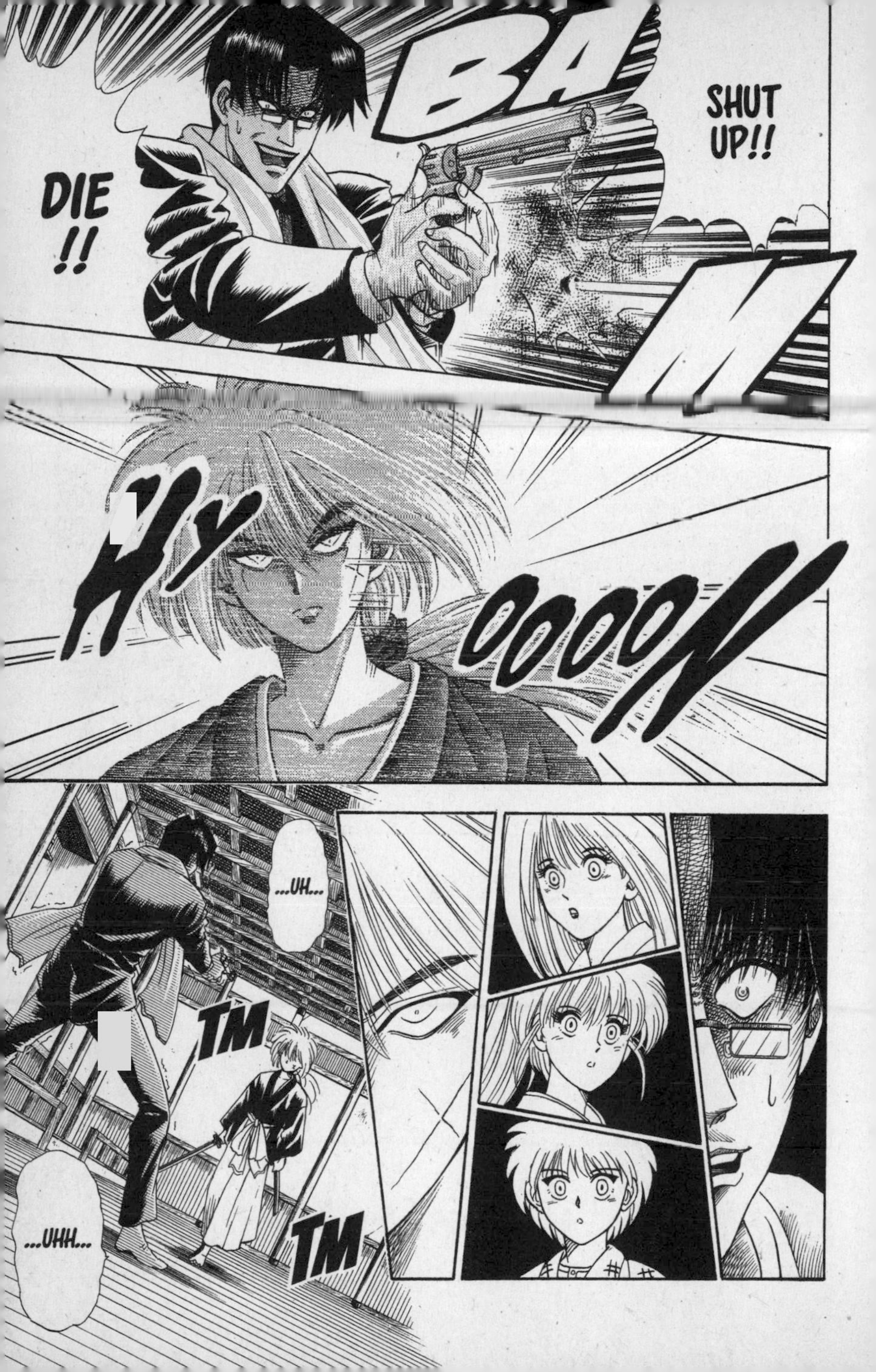
SHUT UP!!
BA
N
DIE !!
Hy
OOOO
...UH...
TM
TM
...UHH...

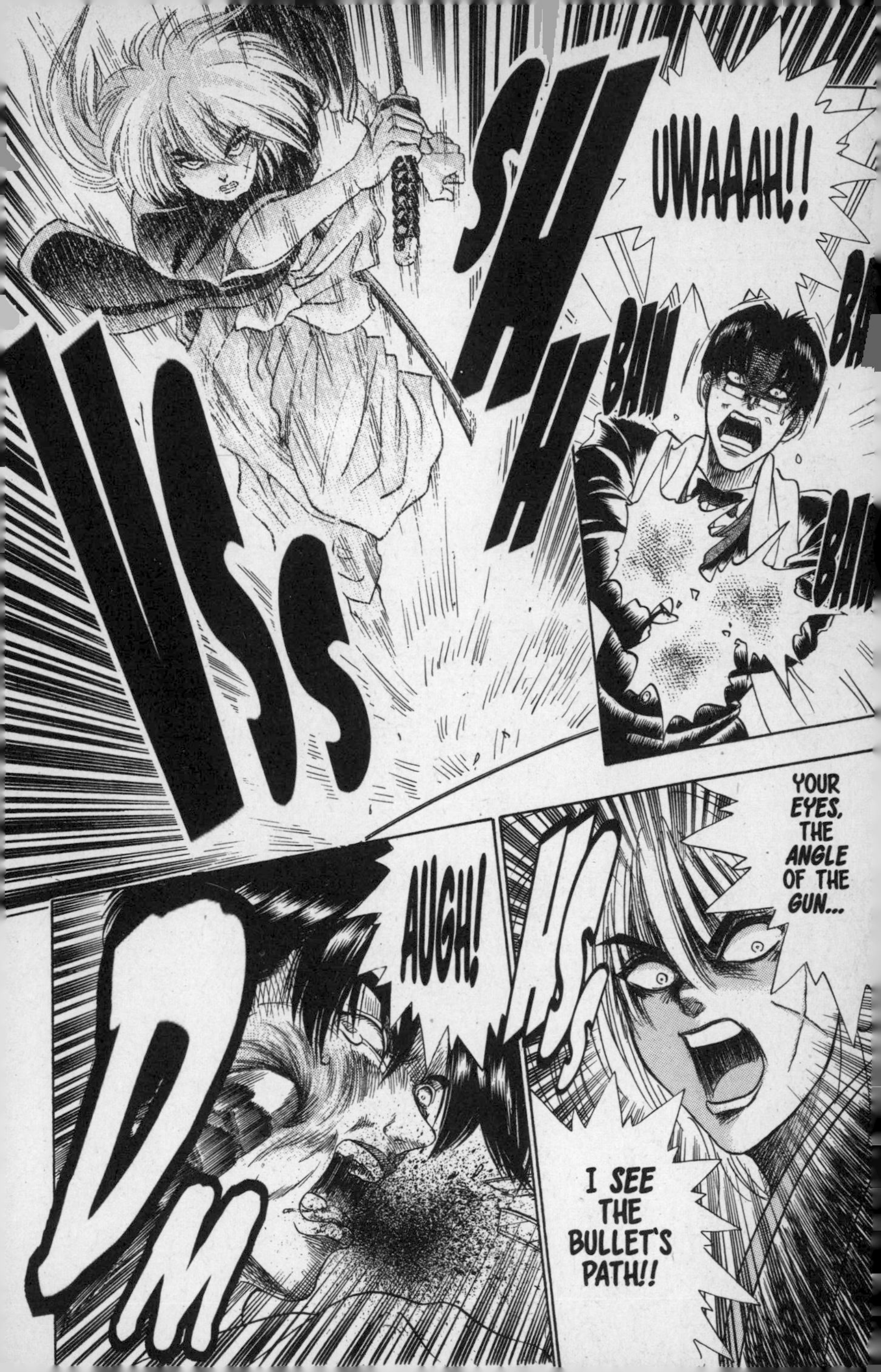
UWAAAH!!
BAM
BAM
BAM
BAM
YOUR EYES, THE ANGLE OF THE GUN...
I SEE THE BULLET'S PATH!!
AUGH!

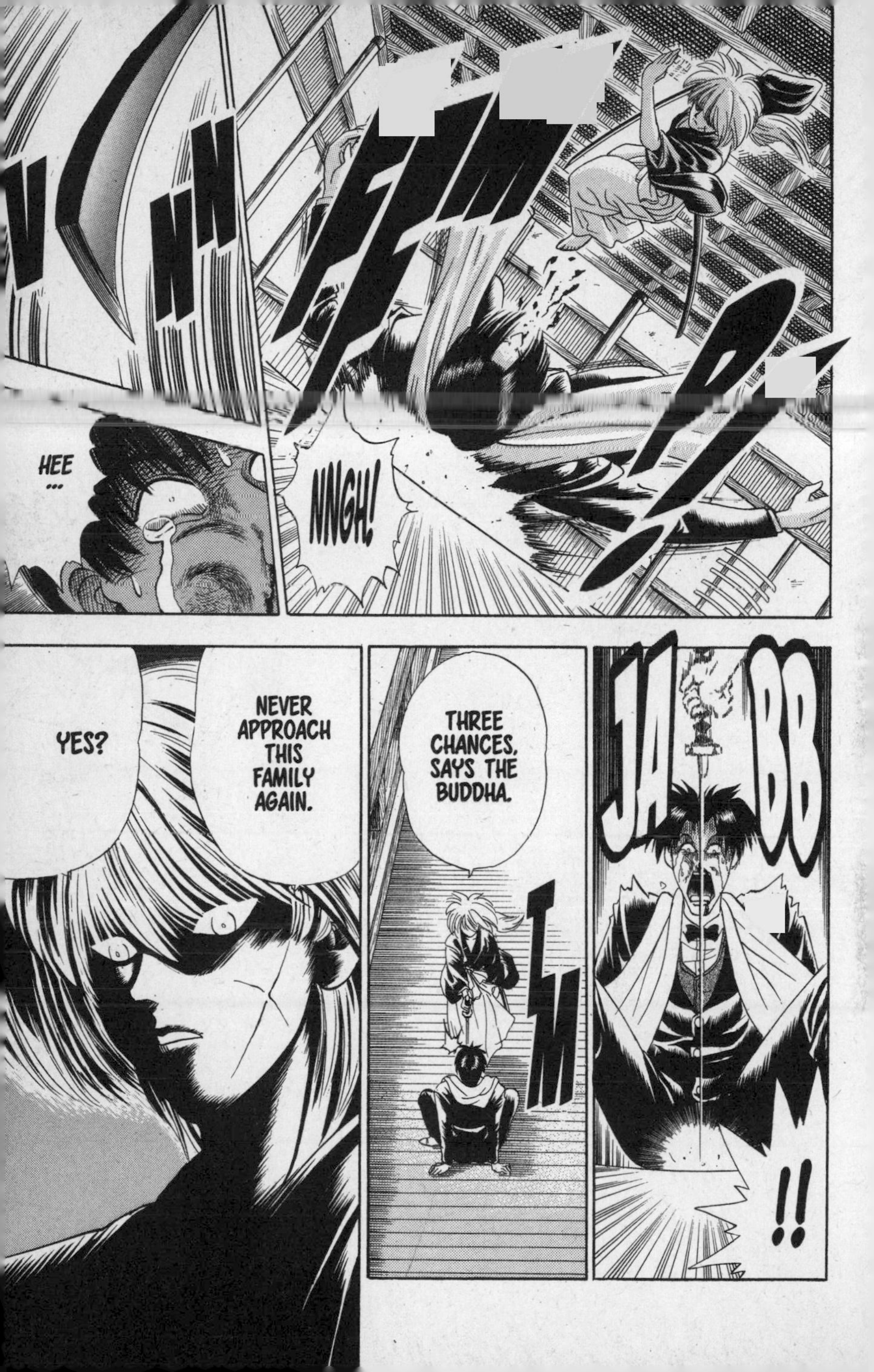
NNGH!
HEE ...
JA BB
!!
THREE CHANCES, SAYS THE BUDDHA.
NEVER APPROACH THIS FAMILY AGAIN.
YES?

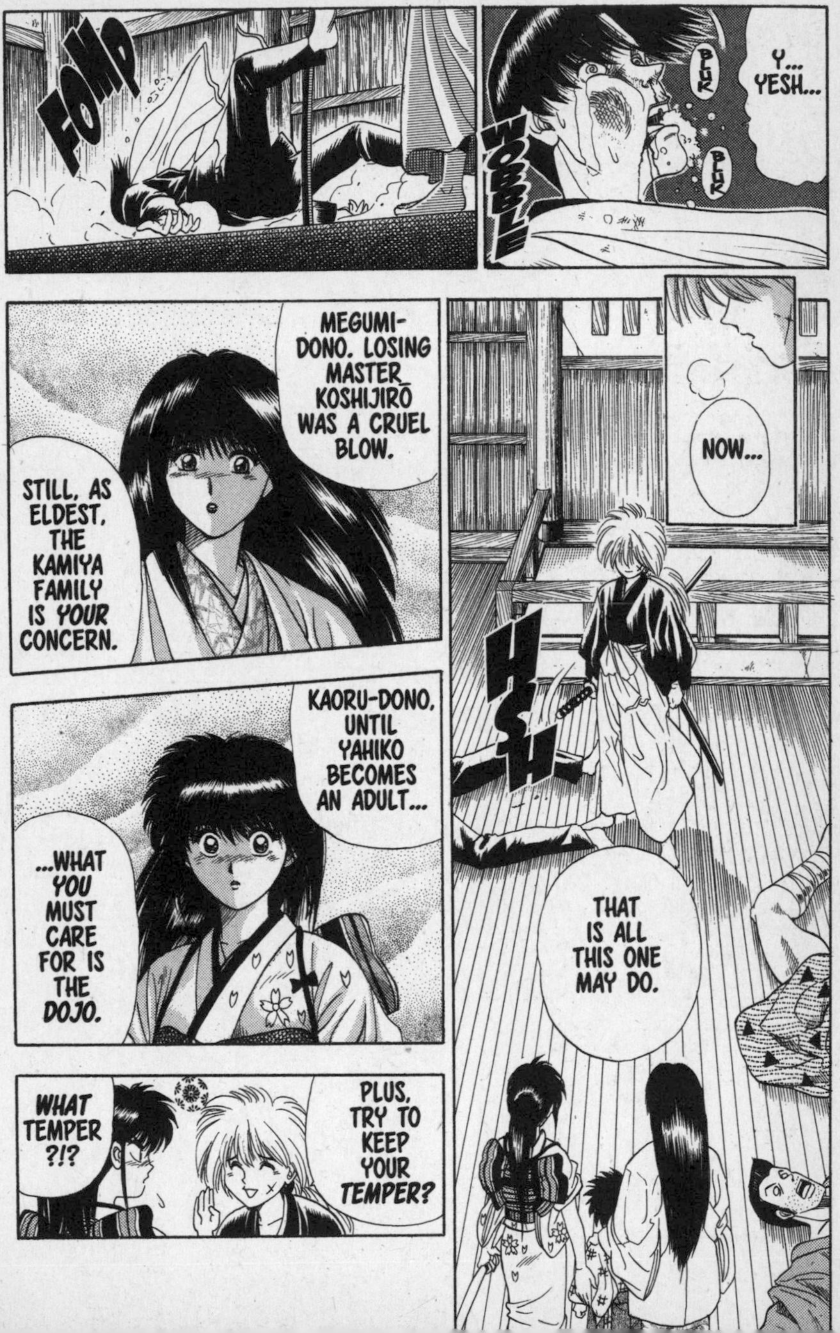

Y... YESH...
BLUK
BLUK
WOBBLE
FOMP
NOW...
HSH
THAT IS ALL THIS ONE MAY DO.
MEGUMI-DONO. LOSING MASTER KOSHIJIRŌ WAS A CRUEL BLOW.
STILL, AS ELDEST, THE KAMIYA FAMILY IS *YOUR* CONCERN.
KAORU-DONO, UNTIL YAHIKO BECOMES AN ADULT...
...WHAT *YOU* MUST CARE FOR IS THE *DOJO.*
PLUS, TRY TO KEEP YOUR *TEMPER?*
WHAT TEMPER ?!?

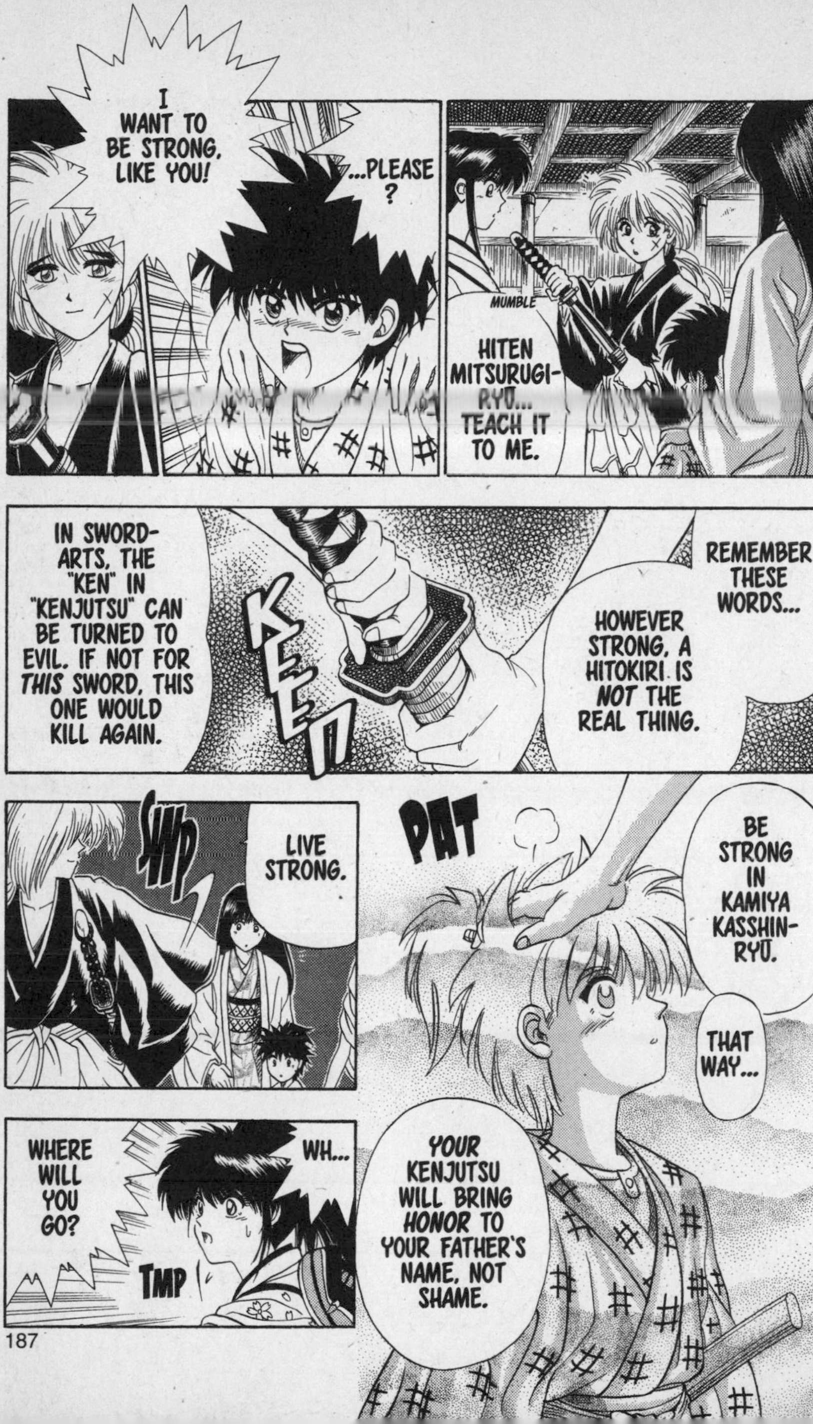
MUMBLE
HITEN MITSURUGI-RYŪ... TEACH IT TO ME.
I WANT TO BE STRONG, LIKE YOU!
...PLEASE?
REMEMBER THESE WORDS...
HOWEVER STRONG, A HITOKIRI IS *NOT* THE REAL THING.
KEN
IN SWORD-ARTS, THE "KEN" IN "KENJUTSU" CAN BE TURNED TO EVIL. IF NOT FOR *THIS* SWORD, THIS ONE WOULD KILL AGAIN.
BE STRONG IN KAMIYA KASSHIN-RYŪ.
PAT
THAT WAY...
YOUR KENJUTSU WILL BRING *HONOR* TO YOUR FATHER'S NAME, NOT SHAME.
LIVE STRONG.
SWP
WH...
WHERE WILL YOU GO?
TMP

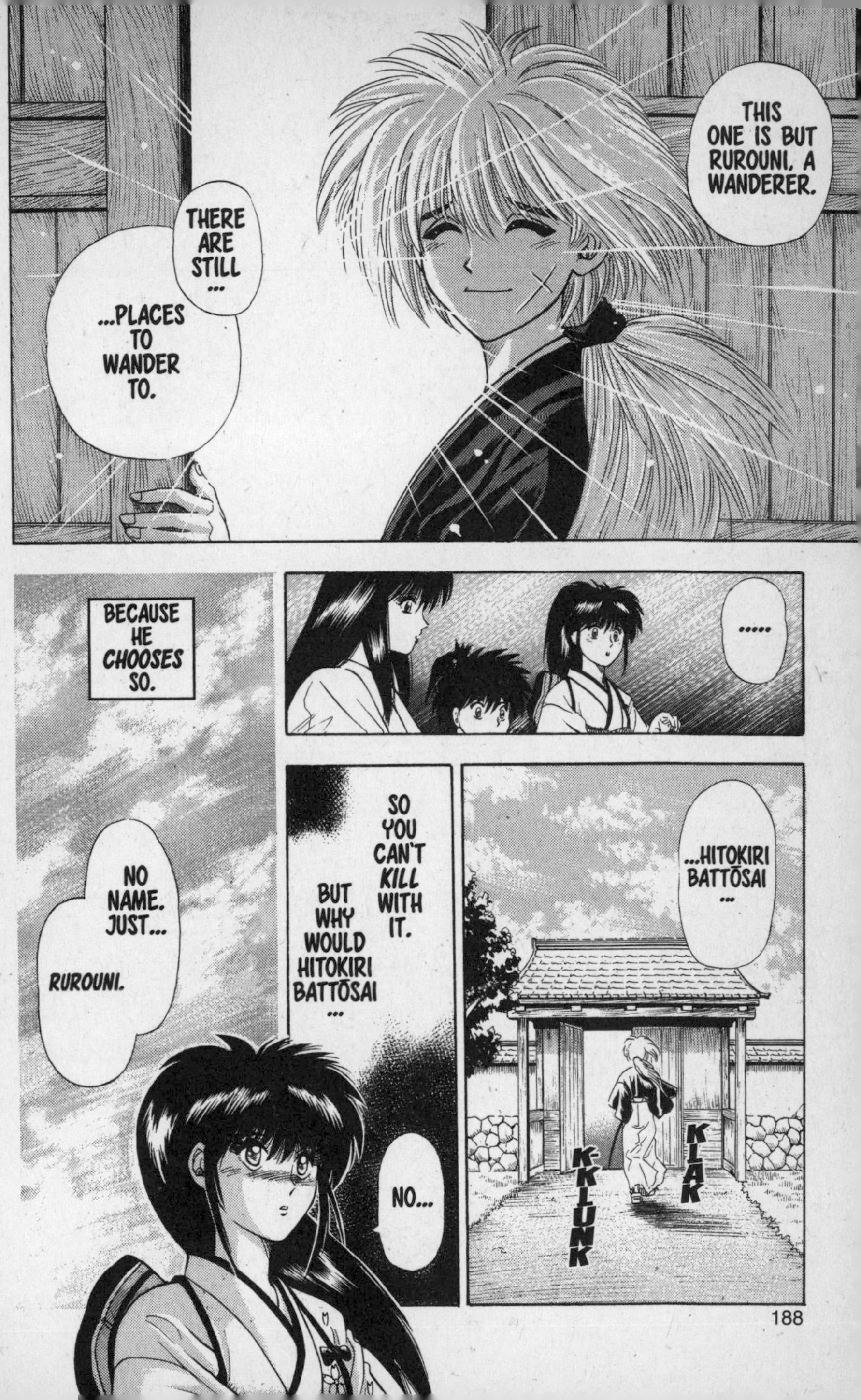
THIS ONE IS BUT RUROUNI, A WANDERER.
THERE ARE STILL ...
...PLACES TO WANDER TO.
.....
...HITOKIRI BATTŌSAI ...
KLAK
K-KLUNK
SO YOU CAN'T KILL WITH IT.
BUT WHY WOULD HITOKIRI BATTŌSAI ...
NO...
BECAUSE HE CHOOSES SO.
NO NAME. JUST...
RUROUNI.

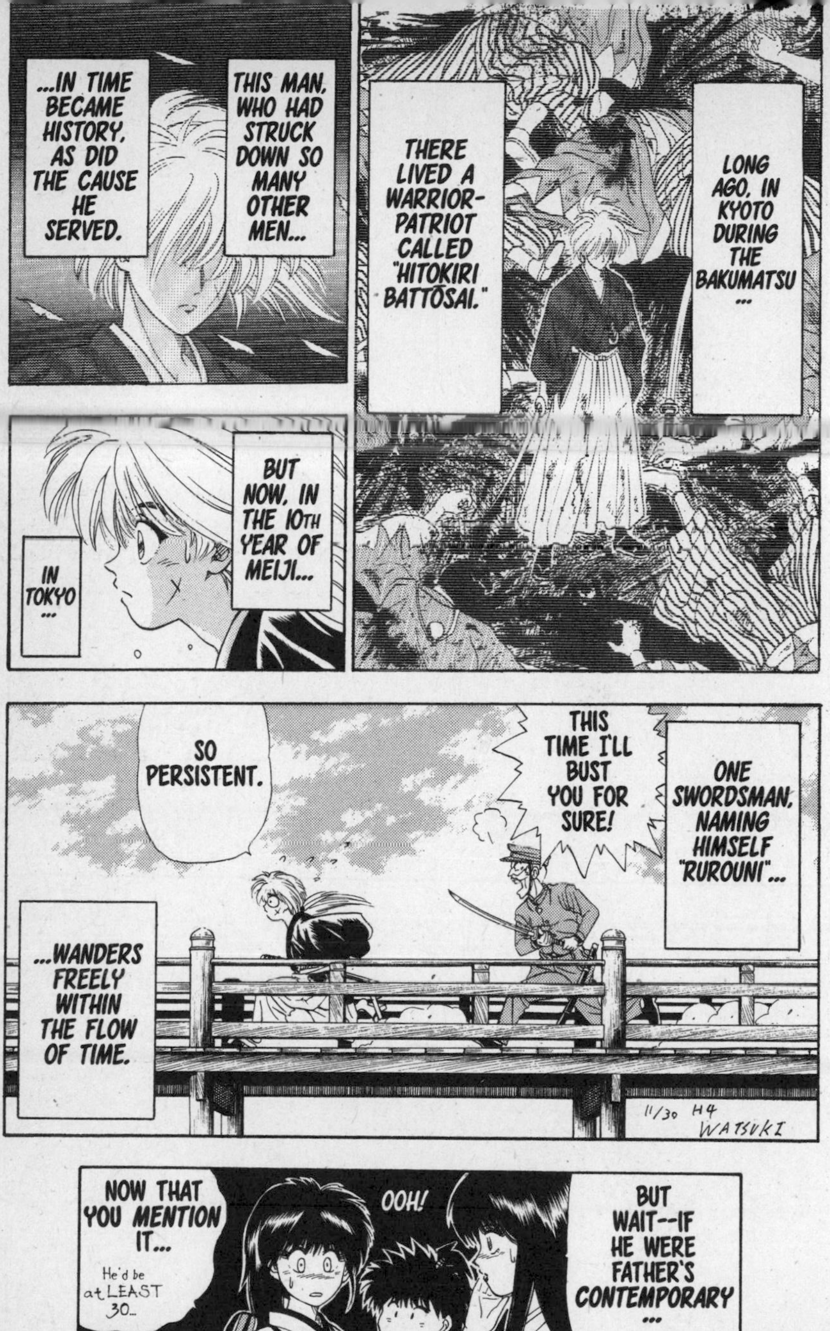
LONG AGO, IN KYOTO DURING THE BAKUMATSU...
THERE LIVED A WARRIOR-PATRIOT CALLED "HITOKIRI BATTŌSAI."
THIS MAN, WHO HAD STRUCK DOWN SO MANY OTHER MEN...
...IN TIME BECAME HISTORY, AS DID THE CAUSE HE SERVED.
BUT NOW, IN THE 10TH YEAR OF MEIJI...
IN TOKYO...
ONE SWORDSMAN, NAMING HIMSELF "RUROUNI"...
THIS TIME I'LL BUST YOU FOR SURE!
SO PERSISTENT.
...WANDERS FREELY WITHIN THE FLOW OF TIME.
11/30 H4
WATSUKI
BUT WAIT--IF HE WERE FATHER'S CONTEMPORARY...
OOH!
NOW THAT YOU MENTION IT...
He'd be at LEAST 30...

RUROUNI • END

GLOSSARY of the RESTORATION

*A brief guide to select Japanese terms used in **Rurouni Kenshin**. Note that, both here and within the story itself, all names are Japanese style—i.e., last or "family" name first, with personal or "given" name following. This is both because **Kenshin** is a "period" story, as well as to decrease confusion—were we to take the example of Kenshin's sakabatô and "reverse" the format of the historically established assassin-name "Hitokiri Battôsai," for example, it would make little sense to then call him "Battôsai Himura."*

hitokiri
An assassin. Famous swordsmen of the period were sometimes thus known to adopt "professional" names—**Kawakami Gensai**, for example, was also known as "Hitokiri Gensai"

Ishin Shishi
Loyalist or pro-Imperialist **patriots** who fought to restore the Emperor to his ancient seat of power

Jigen-ryû
Aggressive swordsmanship style, characterized by one-handed draws/cuts, and the use of turning. Used in this story by Ujiki, a corrupt officer of the Police Sword Corps

Kamiya Kasshin-ryû
Sword-arts or **kenjutsu** school established by Kaoru's father, who rejected the ethics of **Satsujin-ken** for **Katsujin-ken**

kanji
Japanese system of writing, based on Chinese characters

Katsujin-ken
"Swords that give life"; the sword-arts style developed over ten years by Kaoru's father and founding principle of **Kamiya Kasshin-ryû**

Kawakami Gensai
Real-life, historical inspiration for the character of **Himura Kenshin**

kenjutsu
The art of fencing; sword arts; **kendô**

Kenshin-gumi
Literally, "group of Kenshin"—translated (rather playfully) for our purposes as "Team Kenshin"

Kiheitai
Fighting force which included men of both the merchant and peasant classes

Aizu
Tokugawa-affiliated domain; fourth battle of the **Boshin War**

Bakumatsu
Final, chaotic days of the Tokugawa regime

Boshin War
Civil war of 1868-69 between the new government and the **Tokugawa Bakufu**. The anti-*Bakufu*, pro-Imperial side (the Imperial Army) won, easily defeating the Tokugawa supporters

-chan
Honorific. Can be used either as a diminutive (e.g., with a small child—"Little Hanako or Kentarô"), or with those who are grown, to indicate affection ("My dear...")

dojo
Martial arts training hall

-dono
Honorific. Even more respectful than **–san**; the effect in modern-day Japanese conversation would be along the lines of "Milord So-and-So." As used by Kenshin, it indicates both respect and humility

Edo
Capital city of the **Tokugawa Bakufu**, renamed **Tokyo** ("Eastern Capital") after the Meiji Restoration

Hijikata Toshizô
Vice-commander of the **Shinsengumi**

Himura Battôsai
Swordsman of legendary skills and former assassin (*hitokiri*) of the **Ishin Shishi**

Himura Kenshin
Kenshin's "real" name, revealed to Kaoru only at her urging

Hiten Mitsurugi-ryû
Kenshin's sword technique, used more for defense than offense. An "ancient style that pits one against many," it requires exceptional speed and agility to master

Seinan War
  1877 uprising of the samurai classes against the new Meiji government, ending in defeat by the government army. Also known as the "Satsuma Rebellion"

Seishû, Hanaoka
  Real-world Japanese physician (1760-1835) whose use of "tsusensan" in 1805 during an operation for breast cancer pioneered the use of surgical anesthesia

sensei
  Teacher; master

Shinsengumi
  Elite, notorious, government-sanctioned and exceptionally ~~[illegible]~~
  government (**Bakufu**) which had ruled Japan for nearly 250 years, the Shinsengumi ("newly selected corps") were established in 1863 to suppress the **loyalists** and restore law and order to the blood-soaked streets of the imperial capital (see **Kyoto**)

shôgun
  Feudal military ruler of Japan

shôgunate
  See **Tokugawa Bakufu**

suntetsu
  Small, handheld blade, designed for palming and concealment

Tokugawa Bakufu
  Military feudal government which dominated Japan from 1603 to 1867

Tokugawa Yoshinobu
  15th and last **shôgun** of Japan. His peaceful abdication in 1867 marked the end of the **Bakufu** and beginning of **Meiji**

Tokyo
  The renaming of "**Edo**" to "**Tokyo**" is a marker of the start of the **Meiji Restoration**

Toba Fushimi, Battle at
  Battle near **Kyoto** between the forces of the new, imperial government and the fallen **shôgunate**. Ending with an imperial victory, it was the first battle of the **Boshin War**

yakuza
  Japanese underworld; "the mob." Known (as in other times, and other countries) both by their colorful garb, and equally colorful speech

Yamagata Aritomo
  (1838-1922) Soldier and statesman, chief founder of the modern Japanese army. A samurai of Chôshû, he studied military science in Europe and returned to Japan in 1870 to head the war ministry

-kun
  Honorific. Used in the modern day among male students, or those who grew up together, but another usage—the one you're more likely to find in *Rurouni Kenshin*—is the "superior-to-inferior" form, intended as a way to emphasize a difference in status or rank, as well as to indicate familiarity or affection

Kyoto
  Home of the Emperor and imperial court from A.D. 794 until shortly after the Meiji Restoration in 1868

loyalists
  Those who supported the return of the Emperor to power; **Ishin Shishi**

Meiji Restoration
  1853-1868; culminated in the collapse of the **Tokugawa Bakufu** and the restoration of imperial rule. So called after Emperor Meiji, whose chosen name was written with the characters for "culture and enlightenment"

ohagi
  Traditional Japanese autumnal treat. Named after "hagi," bush clover, which flowers in the fall. Said to be especially delicious with *matcha* or green tea

okashira
  Literally, "the head"; i.e., leader, boss

oniwabanshû
  Elite group of *onmitsu* or "spies" of the **Edo** period, now known as "ninja" or "shinobi"

patriots
  Another term for **Ishin Shishi**...and when used by Sano, not a flattering one

rurouni
  Wanderer, vagabond

sakabatô
  Reversed-edge sword (the dull edge on the side the sharp should be, and vice-versa); carried by Kenshin as a symbol of his resolution never to kill again

-san
  Honorific. Carries the meaning of "Mr.," "Ms.," "Miss," etc., but used more extensively in Japanese than its English equivalent (note that even an enemy may be addressed as "-san")

Satsujin-ken
  "Swords that give death"; a style of swordsmanship rejected by Kaoru's father

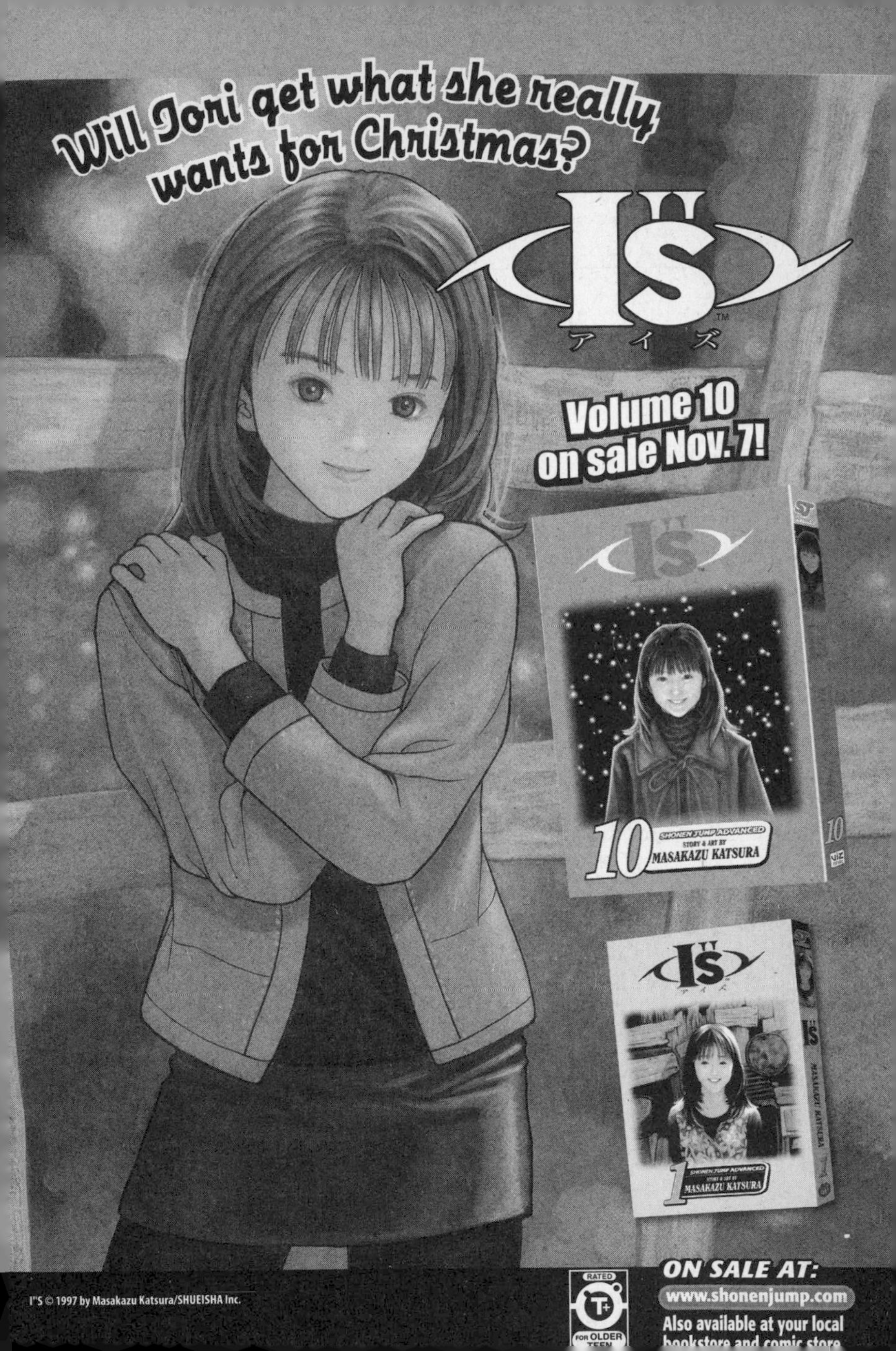
Will Iori get what she really wants for Christmas?
I"s
アイズ
Volume 10 on sale Nov. 7!
SHONEN JUMP ADVANCED
STORY & ART BY
MASAKAZU KATSURA
10
I"s © 1997 by Masakazu Katsura/SHUEISHA Inc.
RATED T+ FOR OLDER TEEN
ON SALE AT:
www.shonenjump.com
Also available at your local bookstore and comic store

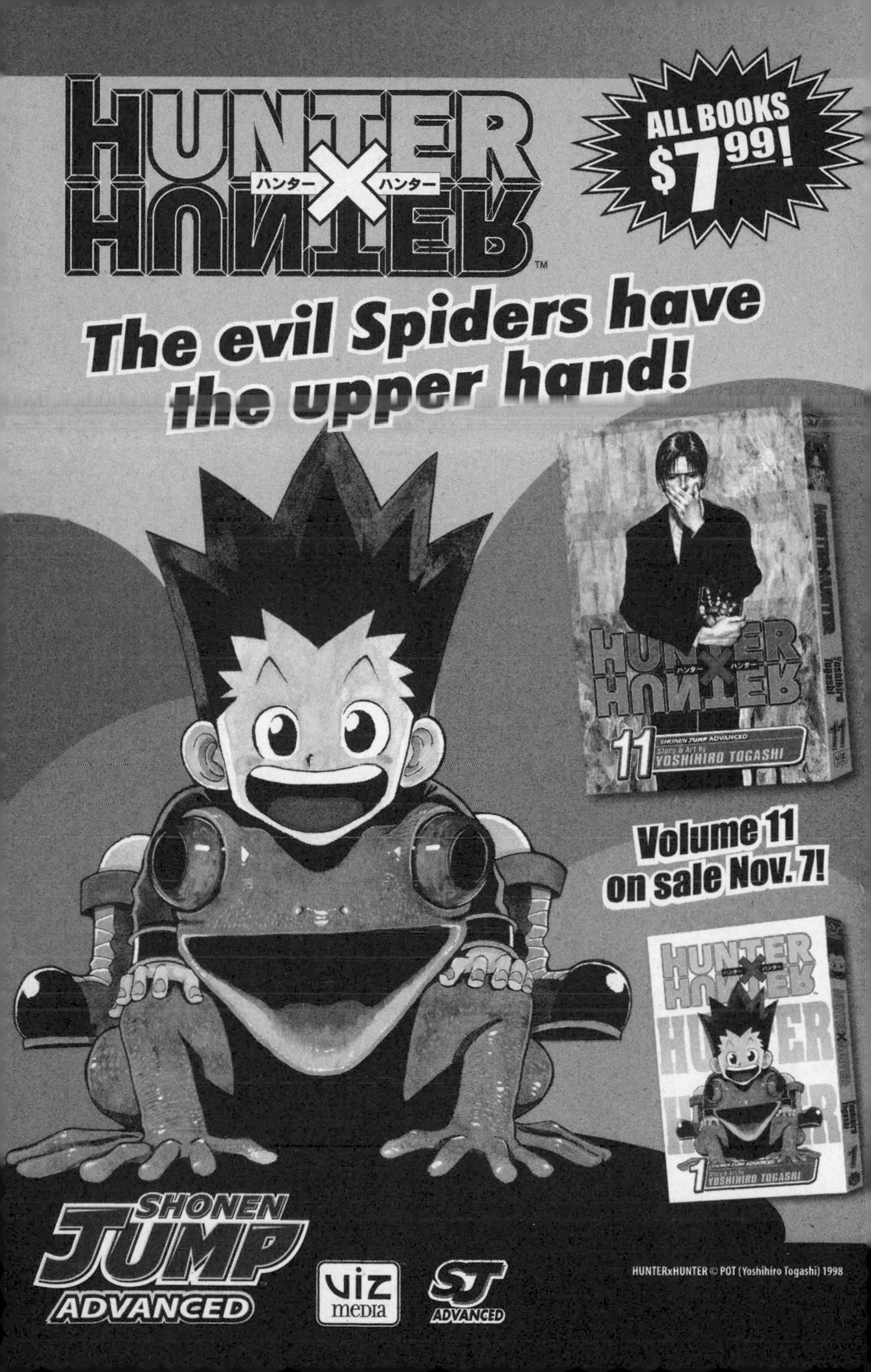
HUNTER × HUNTER™
ハンター ハンター
ALL BOOKS $7.99!
The evil Spiders have the upper hand!
HUNTER × HUNTER
SHONEN JUMP ADVANCED
11
Story & Art by YOSHIHIRO TOGASHI
Volume 11 on sale Nov. 7!
HUNTER × HUNTER
1
SHONEN JUMP ADVANCED
YOSHIHIRO TOGASHI
SHONEN JUMP ADVANCED
viz media
SJ ADVANCED
HUNTERxHUNTER © POT (Yoshihiro Togashi) 1998

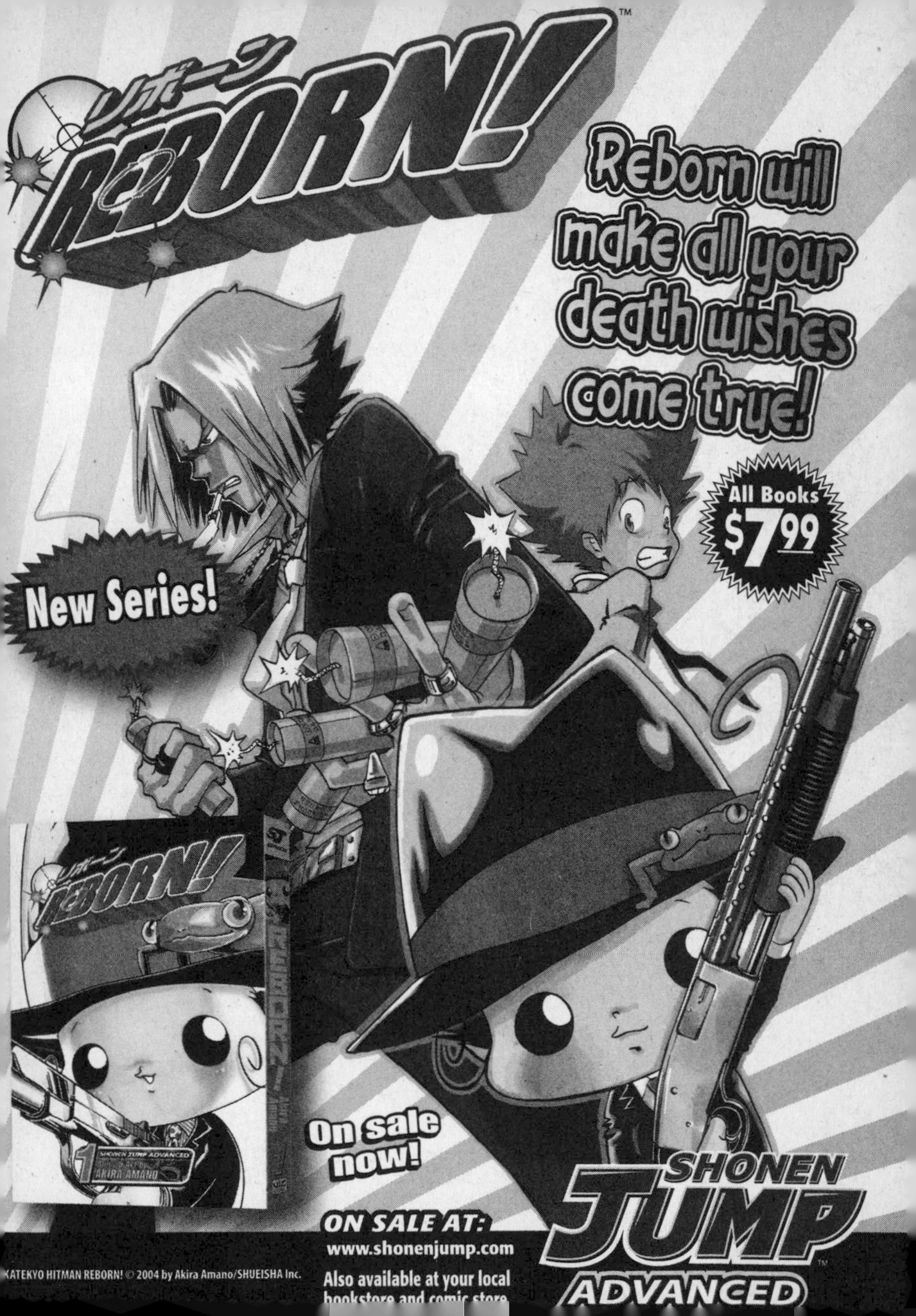

REBORN!
Reborn will make all your death wishes come true!
All Books $7.99
New Series!
REBORN!
SHONEN JUMP ADVANCED
AKIRA AMANO
On sale now!
ON SALE AT:
www.shonenjump.com
Also available at your local bookstore and comic store.
SHONEN JUMP ADVANCED
KATEKYO HITMAN REBORN! © 2004 by Akira Amano/SHUEISHA Inc.

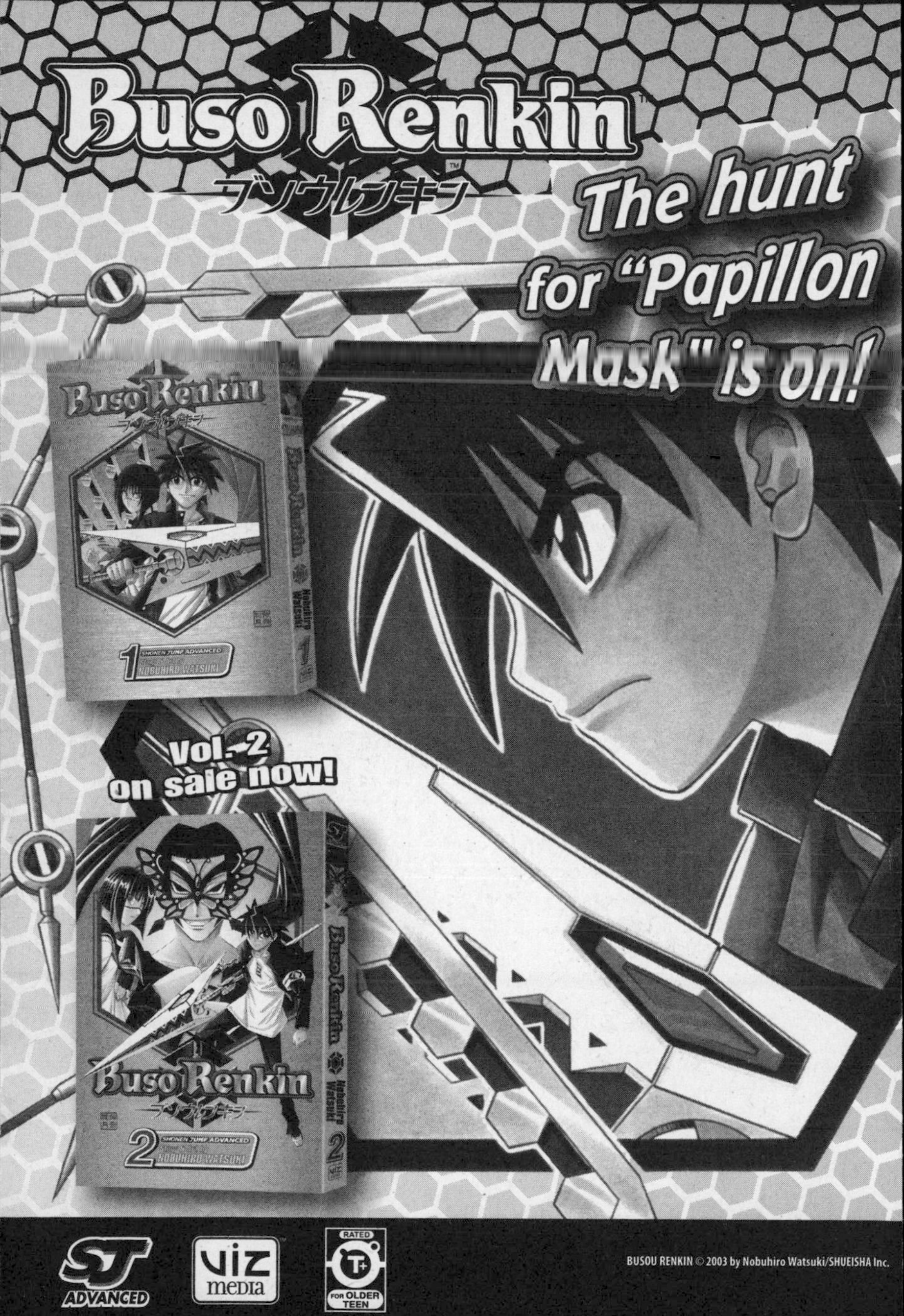
Buso Renkin™
ブソウレンキン
The hunt for "Papillon Mask" is on!
Vol. 2 on sale now!
SJ ADVANCED
viz media
RATED T+ FOR OLDER TEEN
BUSOU RENKIN © 2003 by Nobuhiro Watsuki/SHUEISHA Inc.

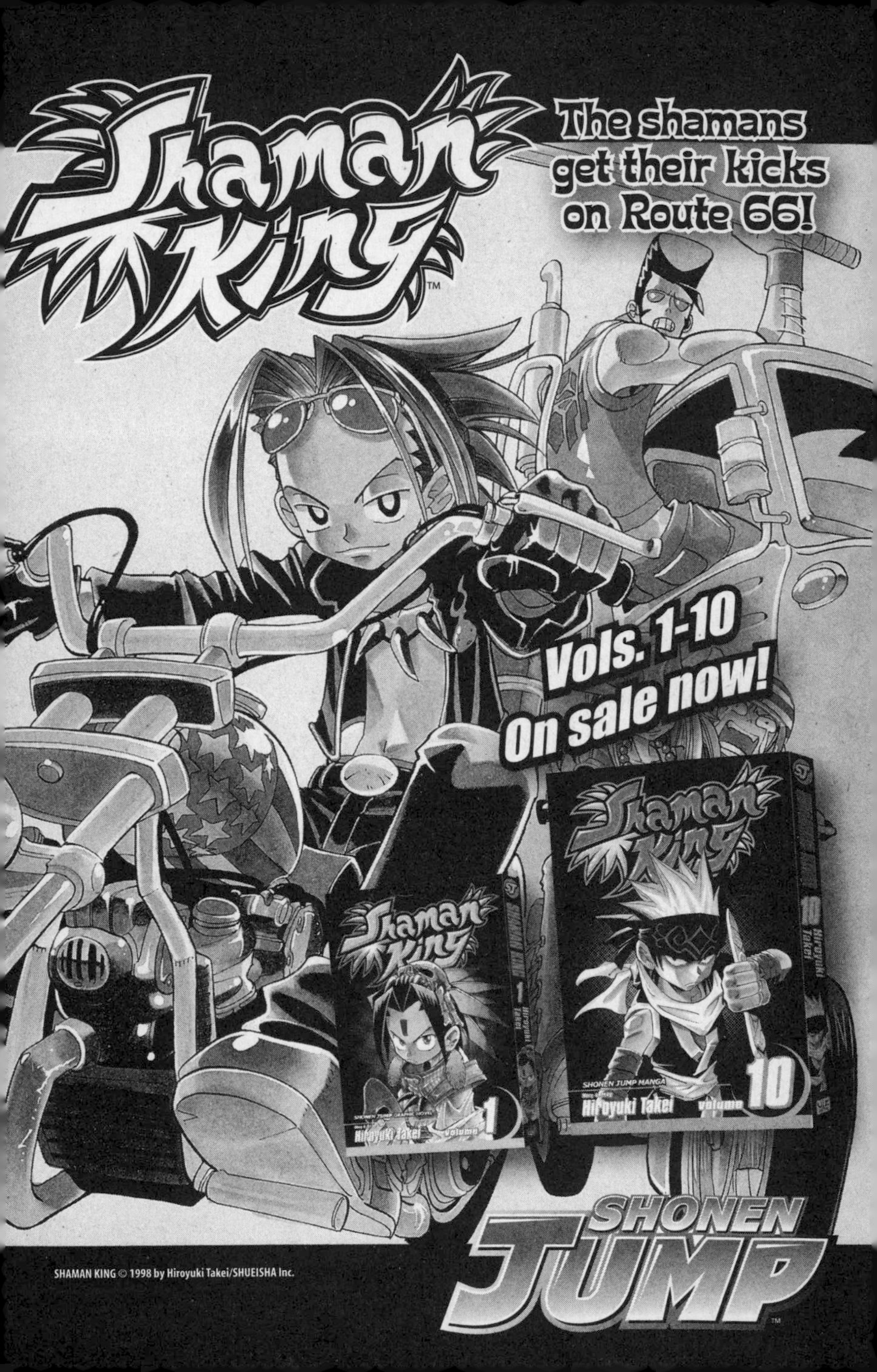
Shaman King™
The shamans get their kicks on Route 66!
Vols. 1-10 On sale now!
Shaman King
Hiroyuki Takei
volume 1
Shaman King
SHONEN JUMP MANGA
Hiroyuki Takei
volume 10
SHONEN JUMP™
SHAMAN KING © 1998 by Hiroyuki Takei/SHUEISHA Inc.

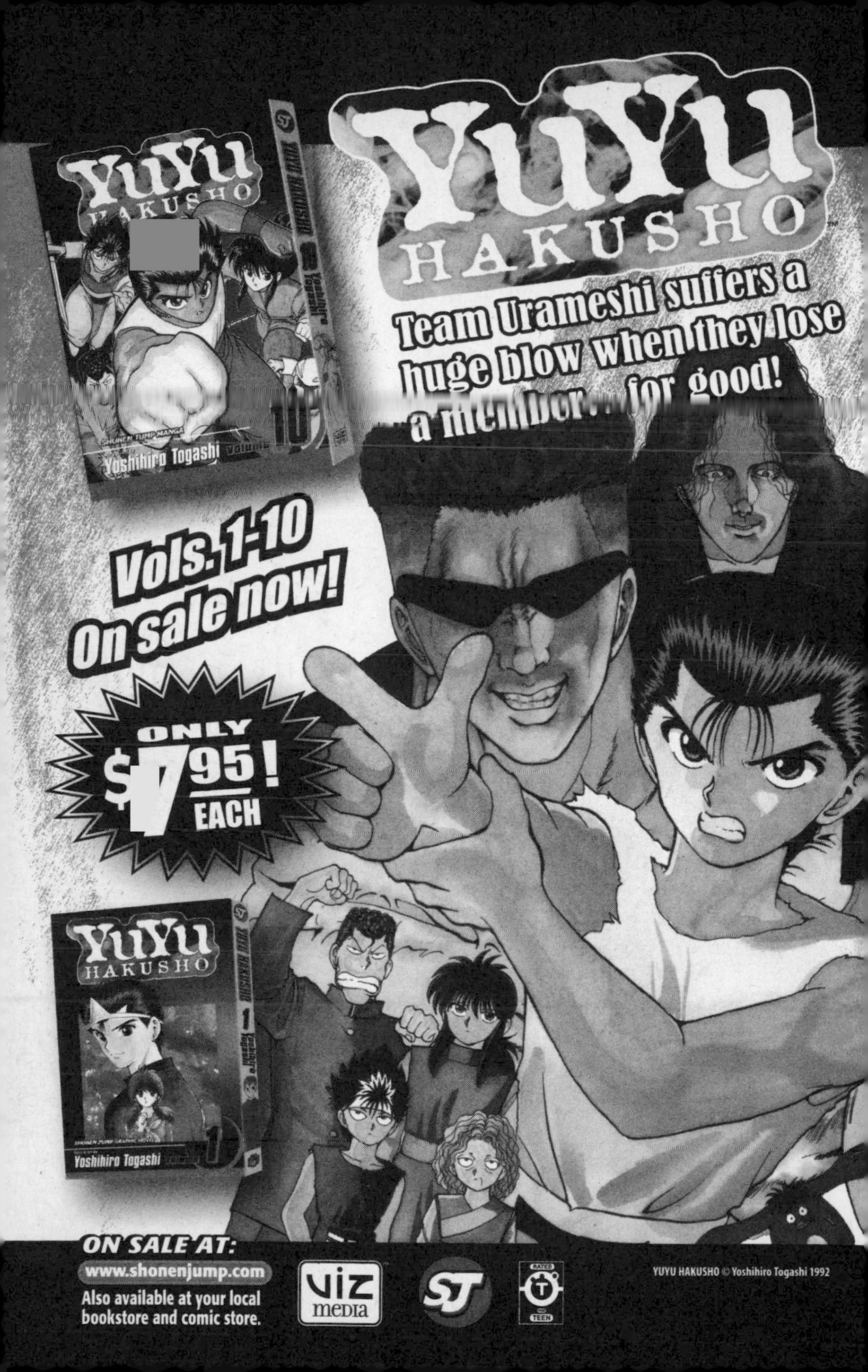
YuYu Hakusho
Yoshihiro Togashi
YuYu Hakusho
Team Urameshi suffers a huge blow when they lose a member... for good!
Vols. 1-10 On sale now!
ONLY $7.95! EACH
YuYu Hakusho
Yoshihiro Togashi
ON SALE AT:
www.shonenjump.com
Also available at your local bookstore and comic store.
viz media
SJ
RATED T TEEN
YUYU HAKUSHO © Yoshihiro Togashi 1992

Tell us what you think about SHONEN JUMP manga!

Our survey is now available online.
Go to: www.SHONENJUMP.com/mangasurvey

Help us make our product offering better!